Handbook
of Global
Social
Policy

PUBLIC ADMINISTRATION AND PUBLIC POLICY

A Comprehensive Publication Program

Executive Editor

JACK RABIN
Professor of Public Administration and Public Policy
School of Public Affairs
The Capital College
The Pennsylvania State University—Harrisburg
Middletown, Pennsylvania

Additional Volumes in Preparation

ANNALS OF PUBLIC ADMINISTRATION

Handbook
of Global
Social
Policy

edited by
Stuart S. Nagel
Amy Robb

**University of Illinois
Urbana, Illinois**

MARCEL DEKKER, INC.   NEW YORK · BASEL

ISBN: 0-8247-0357-X

This book is printed on acid-free paper.

Headquarters
Marcel Dekker, Inc.
270 Madison Avenue, New York, NY 10016
tel: 212-696-9000; fax: 212-685-4540

Eastern Hemisphere Distribution
Marcel Dekker AG
Hutgasse 4, Postfach 812, CH-4001 Basel, Switzerland
tel: 41-61-261-8482; fax: 41-61-261-8896

World Wide Web
http://www.dekker.com

The publisher offers discounts on this book when ordered in bulk quantities. For more information, write to Special Sales/Professional Marketing at the headquarters address above.

PRINTED IN THE UNITED STATES OF AMERICA

To the people who especially stimulated
my awareness of social policy, including:
Emory Bogardus, Helen Clarke, John Cuber,
Ruth Gavian, Clair Wilcox, and Kimball Young.

Preface

This handbook on global social policy is one in a set of six global policy handbooks. The other five deal with economic, technology, political, international, and legal policy.

Public policy studies in the past have tended to emphasize domestic policy rather than cross-national policy. This has been especially true of American policy studies, which tend to be especially nation-bound. This is also true, to some extent, of policy studies in France, Russia, China, Brazil, and elsewhere.

When American policy studies show an interest in other countries, those other countries tend to be exclusively Western European. This six-volume set, however, will include all the regions of the world—Africa, Asia, Eastern and Western Europe, Latin America, and North America.

Public policy studies also tend to place a great deal of emphasis on methods of analysis and the policy process. They do not get much into substance, especially at the professional or scholarly level, as contrasted to undergraduate textbooks. That is so because scholars have traditionally considered substance to be not as philosophical or theoretical as methods or process.

In this six-volume set, however, each volume is devoted to a different substantive field, including economic, technology, social, political, international, and legal policy. The discussions are more theoretical than most substantive discussions because they emphasize comparisons across places, across times, and across substantive fields. Furthermore, the discussions are practical in terms of applicability to real-world problems.

Scholars and others who study comparative government unfortunately tend to overemphasize such structures as federalism, separation of powers, legislatures, chief executives, and supreme courts while neglecting public policy, which this series emphasizes.

Comparative government scholars also tend to emphasize area studies, which involve specialization in a single country or subregion, as contrasted to this set of volumes, which cuts across six regions and six policy fields.

Thus, the key objective of these volumes is to encourage more cross-national and cross-policy research and applications. The set not only advocates more of this kind of research but practices what it advocates by providing almost 200 studies in six volumes, averaging about 30 studies each. This set of hand-books should be a landmark in the disciplines of both public policy studies and cross-national studies.

Stuart S. Nagel

Contents

Contributors

Victor Azarya Professor, Department of Sociology and Anthropology, Harry S Truman Research Institute for the Advancement of Peace, The Hebrew University of Jerusalem, Jerusalem, Israel

Susanne M. Birgerson Independent Scholar, Slavic and East European Library, University of Illinois, Urbana, Illinois

William W. Bostock Senior Lecturer, School of Government, University of Tasmania, Hobart, Tasmania, Australia

Marlies Galenkamp Associate Professor, Department of Law (Jurisprudence and Legal Philosophy), Erasmus University, Rotterdam, The Netherlands

Vlasta Jalušič Assistant Professor of Political Science, The Peace Institute, Ljubljana, Slovenia

Roger E. Kanet Professor and Dean, School of International Studies, University of Miami, Coral Gables, Florida

Amany A. Khodair Senior Lecturer, Political Science Department, Suez Canal University, Ismailia, Egypt

Hae S. Kim   Professor, Department of International Relations, Troy State University, Fort Walton Beach, Florida

Miran Komac   Associate Professor, Institute for Ethnic Studies, Ljubljana, Slovenia

Mira Marody   Professor, Institute for Social Studies, and Institute of Sociology, University of Warsaw, Warsaw, Poland

Stuart S. Nagel   Professor, Department of Political Science, University of Illinois, Urbana, Illinois

Réjean Pelletier   Professor, Department of Political Science, Laval University, Ste-Foy, Quebec, Canada

Linda K. Richter   Professor, Department of Political Science, Kansas State University, Manhattan, Kansas

William L. Richter   Associate Provost, Office of International Programs, Kansas State University, Manhattan, Kansas

Andrea K. Riemer   Senior Analyst, ARIS Research and Consultancy Office for Security Studies, Vienna, Austria

Wilma Rule   Adjunct Professor, Department of Political Science, University of Nevada, Reno, Nevada

Birgit Sauer   Assistant Professor, Institute for Political Science, University of Vienna, Vienna, Austria

Shyam Nand Singh   Associate Professor, Department of Political Science, M. D. S. University, Ajmer, Rajasthan, India

Deborah Stienstra   Associate Professor, Department of Political Science, University of Winnipeg, Winnipeg, Manitoba, Canada

Scott Turner   Associate Professor, Department of Behavioral and Social Sciences, University of Montevallo, Montevallo, Alabama

Tatu Vanhanen   Professor Emeritus, Department of Political Science, University of Helsinki, Klaukkala, Finland

Pelgy Vaz Associate Professor, Department of Sociology and Social Work, Fort Hays State University, Hays, Kansas

Steven K. Wisensale Associate Professor, School of Family Studies, University of Connecticut, Storrs, Connecticut

Bang-Soon Yoon Associate Professor, Department of Political Science, and Director, Women Studies Program, Central Washington University, Ellensburg, Washington

Tingwei Zhang Assistant Professor, Urban Planning and Policy Program, College of Urban Planning and Public Affairs, University of Illinois, Chicago, Illinois

Handbook
of Global
Social
Policy

1

Social Policy

An Introduction

Stuart S. Nagel
University of Illinois, Urbana, Illinois

I. INTRODUCTION

Win-win or super-optimizing analysis of public policy problems tries to find feasible solutions which can enable conservatives, liberals, and other major viewpoints to all come out ahead of their best initial expectations simultaneously.[1] The elements in the analysis include (1) conservative goals and alternatives, (2) liberal goals and alternatives, (3) relations between the major alternatives and goals, (4) the development of win-win solutions, and (5) feasibility hurdles to overcome. The feasibility hurdles to be overcome include economic, administrative, political, psychological, legal, international, and technological hurdles, and the disruption of displaced firms and individuals. As applied to social policy, we are especially talking about improving the quality of life of people at the bottom of the social hierarchy, but to the benefit of all. This means public policy that relates to (1) employment and job facilitators, (2) education, financing, and integration, (3) merit treatment, (4) voting and political participation, and (5) crime reduction.

 The computer revolution and contemporary globalization have the potential for generating great productivity and prosperity. They also have the potential for generating among so many people more unemployment and anger than the industrial revolution. This is because so many poverty-generating displacement factors are operating simultaneously throughout the world. These include productivity downsizing, free trade, defense conversion, and immigration. It also includes the employment of many groups of people who were not formerly competing as much for the available jobs, such as women, minorities, the disabled, and the elderly. Key objects of an antipoverty program should be to smooth the transition of displaced workers to other possibly better jobs as well as to provide for the transition of the poor toward middle-class status.

Being poor in this context relates partly to individual income. It is, however, not possible to say that being poor means having less than a certain income or being below a certain income percentile in one's nation. One can live better at a low income in some places in the world than others. Being in the bottom tenth percentile in a wealthy nation may be better than being in the top tenth percentile in an impoverished nation. Poverty should be measured in terms of food, shelter, clothing, and medical care. A person or family is impoverished if they cannot afford (1) enough food to avoid all forms of malnutrition, (2) enough housing not to freeze in the winter time, (3) enough clothing to satisfy minimal cultural standards of dignity, and (4) enough medical care so that all members of the family have better than a 50% probability of living to age 60. The fourth point illustrates how our standards keep moving up, since living to age 40 would have been considered good in medieval times, even by royalty.

Sometimes employment and education are included in the definition of poverty. Both employment and education are important for preventing poverty and for rising out of poverty, but they are not part of the definition. They are causes and to some extent effects of poverty. More important, they are policy variables subject to deliberate improvements through government decision making.

II. EMPLOYMENT

A. Conservative and Liberal Alternatives or Approaches

Constrained public aid refers to restrictions on eligibility, benefit levels, income retention, and due process, partly designed to deter applications for public aid. Generous public aid refers to broadness on those matters, partly designed to provide more dignity to the poor.

The key issues on those four matters have been (1) allowing an impoverished family that has a father and mother present to receive aid, (2) providing for minimal benefit levels on a nationwide basis, (3) allowing recipients to keep a certain number of earned dollars per month, and (4) providing hearings in welfare disputes, including right to counsel.

B. Win-Win Alternatives

The super-optimum solutions (SOS) emphasis is moving away from arguing over those legal matters and toward upgrading skills and providing job opportunities. Doing so may do more for decreasing poverty than a punitive deterrence ap-

Table 1 Win-Win Analysis of Public Aid and Jobs

	Goals	
Alternatives	*Conservative*: Deterrence of poverty and decreased taxes	*Liberal*: Dignity of the poor
Conservative: Constrained public aid	+	−
Liberal: Generous public aid	−	+
Neutral: Reformed public aid	0	0
SOS, or win-win: Job facilitation: 1. Contracting out job-finding 2. Wage vouchers 3. Training vouchers 4. GNP growth	+ +	+ +

proach and more for the dignity of the poor than a generous welfare approach (Table 1).

Deterring poverty means making the status of being poor even more unpleasant so people will have more of an incentive to avoid being poor. Decreasing poverty means removing people from poverty by providing them with jobs or other income.

Providing job opportunities may involve wage supplements to subsidize both potential employers into hiring welfare recipients and to subsidize recipients into accepting the jobs. The subsidy might also require employers to provide on-the-job training and recipients to pass the training course. On a higher level, it may be necessary for public policy to stimulate an expanding economy in order to create new jobs. Such stimulation might emphasize a payroll tax that is refundable if the money is used for increasing productivity by way of new technologies, upgrading skills, or developing day-care centers.

As for employment of displaced workers or people in the culture of poverty, there are a number of job facilitators that have been shown to be reasonably effective, provided that the nation or community is willing to make a substantive investment.[2] These job facilitators include:

1. Contracting out to employment services to find jobs for the unemployed on a commission basis. This means the job finder gets a substan-

tial amount of money from the government after the worker has been on the job for six months. Such a commission arrangement provides the job finder with an incentive to determine the worker's aptitudes and interests so the worker will not quit or be fired before the commission is paid.

2. Wage vouchers that are given by the government to the unemployed to supplement what an employer can afford to pay. In return for being able to cash in the wage voucher, the employer must agree to hire unemployed people and provide them with on-the-job training. The worker must agree to perform the work and pass the training within six months when the vouchers end.

3. Vouchers can also be given for training that involves going to school, obtaining day-care services, and moving to a new city. These voucher systems cost money. They may, however, soon more than pay for themselves if the workers get off some forms of public aid, pay taxes, and buy more goods and services with the multiplier effects that such buying has. Those employed workers may also refrain from anti-social activities and become better role models for their children and grand-children.

4. The most important job facilitators are probably under the list of productivity causes such as national training, new technologies, competition, and free trade. They provide an expanding economy with more jobs widely available to displaced workers and the chronically unemployed, regardless of the reasons for being displaced or unemployed.

III. EDUCATION

A. Financing

The second item under poverty reduction and prevention is education.[3] In this context, we are talking about elementary and secondary education, since adult training was already discussed. There are two big problems in providing better education for low-income children or children in families whose real incomes are falling, contrary to general trends. The first problem is lack of money for the local schools. Low-income communities throughout the world are generally not able to raise sufficient local funds to provide adequate school buildings and teachers. There is a great need for more allocation of national or federal tax money to local education. It is not politically feasible to expect rich communities in a region to provide much support for the low-income communities. It is more politically feasible for the national government to do so.

The funding as of 1998 could come from channeling defense expenditures into local education expenditures. Defense expenditures are still at near Cold War levels in most countries, but there is no longer an actual or potential warlike conflict between capitalism and communism. The height of the Cold War may have been when Russia was sending missiles to Cuba in the early 1960s. The U.S. defense budget was, however, twice as high in the peacetime of the later 1990s. Another advantage of federal funding is that the money could be used to provide differential salary incentives to teach in impoverished schools. That is something local school boards have been unable to do because of the power over the local school boards by local unions and seniority teachers.

B. Integration

The second big problem in providing better education for low-income children is the need to bring those children into more contact with middle-class children, who are above the poverty line as defined in terms of food, shelter, clothing, medical care, or income. The Coleman Report of the 1960s found great variation across school districts in the probability of an average student going on to college or high school. Of the total variation, about 20% can be explained by differences in school facilities, 30% in terms of differences in salaries and experience of teachers, and 50% in terms of interaction with middle-class students. Having low-income students interact more with middle-income students means they are indirectly interacting with the middle-class parents of those students, who encourage their children to think in terms of getting more education and qualifying for middle-class occupations (Table 2).

One of the best ways of promoting that kind of interaction is through housing vouchers, rather than school vouchers. The housing voucher enables the low-income family to move up one concentric circle in the city in which they live, or to move from an impoverished rural area to a livable urban area. Doing so increases the interclass interaction to the benefit of the low-income children without pulling down the middle-class children, so long as they are not overwhelmed. Middle-class families can also be encouraged to move into low-income areas that are close to urban employment by being sold condominium housing in sheltered communities. The developers of such communities (who receive free government land) are required to set aside about 25% of the condominiums for low-income families, and all children attend the same community public school.

When it comes to elementary and high school integration, conservatives want a minimum of government-imposed integration. This can be justified on the grounds that it saves money and it minimizes disruption.

Liberals advocate government-imposed racial integration, especially by busing black students to white schools, although it may be too politically unpopular to bus white students to black schools. Some black schools can be converted to experimental magnet schools or to nonschools. The remaining black schools can be upgraded through programs of special funding for better facilities and

Table 2 School Integration

Alternatives	Goals	
	Conservative: Save taxes and minimize disruption	*Liberal*: Improve education
Conservative: No government-imposed racial integration (forced busing)	+	−
Liberal: Government-imposed integration, especially busing	−	+
Neutral: Some busing for racial integration (upgrade low-income schools)	0	0
SOS: 1. Economic integration 2. Line drawing 3. Housing 4. Community development	+ +	+ +

teachers. This can be justified on the grounds that it improves inner-city education for the benefit of the total society. The neutral position would be some busing and some upgrading, but not as much as is advocated by liberals.

An SOS alternative might involve emphasizing socioeconomic integration, rather than racial integration. This may be especially important in cities where a high percentage of the public school students are black or other minorities, but vary in terms of family income and economic class background. This may also be important because the ambition level of poor kids is raised by contact with middle-class kids, whereas neither black nor white kids benefit from contact with each other if they are all from the same economic class.

Economic integration can partly occur by redrawing the lines of the neighborhood schools so as to provide a better economic mix for each school. Housing vouchers enabling poor families to move to more middle-class schools are also relevant. Some busing can also be used, but with more reliance on line-drawing.

The results would be to save more tax money and have less disruption than a program that relies more on racial integration and busing. The SOS alternative might do more for improving education in terms of changing peer groups across class lines than busing for racial integration.

IV. MERIT TREATMENT

The third item under poverty reduction and prevention is merit treatment.[4] It addresses the fact that poverty is frequently based on discrimination that relates to race, religion, or national origin. Merit treatment does not refer to giving preferences to redress past discrimination. It refers here to treating people on the basis of their individual merit with an outreach training program for those who are potentially well qualified, but who cannot meet high reasonable standards of employment or college admission. More specifically, this kind of outreach training means that applicants with low-income backgrounds who almost pass qualifying tests are invited to participate in a semester-long training program to better prepare them for the test, the job, or the education. Low-income in this context means that their elementary and secondary schools had per capita expenditures substantially below the national average. If they fail to qualify after the training program, then they are channeled elsewhere. Such an outreach training program increases the actual merit of those with high potential that has probably not been adequately nurtured, as indicated by the objective criterion of the per capita education expenditures (Table 3).

A. Conservative and Liberal Positions

With regard to race relations, the key conservative goal seems to be to judge people in accordance with merit. In the past, conservatives offered a variety of

Table 3 Equal Employment Opportunity

Alternatives	Goals	
	Conservative: Productivity of workforce	*Liberal*: Equity or fairness in distributing benefits
Conservative: Merit hiring	+	−
Liberal: Preferential hiring	−	+
Neutral: Seek qualified minorities	0	0
SOS: Upgrade skills	+ +	+ +

justifications for racism. That's no longer the case. Merit treatment is now the rule, and in that context they talk about colorblind hiring and colorblind admissions, in which no preferences are given for being black, female, or any kind of minority.

Liberals, on the other hand, talk about the need for diversity, equity, and better distribution, and feel quota systems should be abolished. A quota system implies, for example, accepting a certain number of black applicants for a job, or for a law school, regardless of qualifications. What liberals feel is that there should be preferences given, but only in cases where a white person and a black person are equally well qualified. More extreme liberals might even admit the black person when the white person is slightly better qualified. That's how the preference system can be used in order to achieve diversity.

B.   A Win-Win Alternative

A win-win alternative would be capable of achieving high merit, high diversity, fairness, and equity simultaneously. How might that be brought about? One alternative that makes a lot of sense is outreach training.

Outreach training does not involve giving any preferences to people who apply, for instance, to law school. Instead, if they have potential, they will be admitted into the program. In many cases they will have gone to an elementary school or high school in an area where the amount of money spent per student is below the amount spent across the country. In other words, they meet three criteria: (1) they cannot qualify on the basis of their present scores, (2) they have a lot of potential, and (3) they had an economically disadvantaged elementary or high school education. If they meet those criteria, then before entering law school they would be tutored on what's involved in doing well on the law school admission test, similar to a Kaplan or Princeton Review prep course for people who don't have the money available. They would not only be tutored for the law school admission test, but also trained for what is involved in being a good law student. They get college credit for passing these courses. If they fail the course, they are dropped from the program. This is not a gift, it has to be earned. After taking the prep course, if they still do not get a high enough grade on the LSAT, then they're disqualified. They get no preferences or points, but get the credits and grades for the summer course which can help bring their grade point average up to a minimal threshold for admission. A similar outreach training program has been used for years by West Point, Annapolis, and the Air Force Academy to work with various minorities to bring them to a level where they could be admitted without any kind of preferences at all. It does cost money, but it is worthwhile, because if the military provides diversity among officers, it may be very helpful in improving morale among the troops, many of whom come from various minorities.

Unfortunately, the current Congress has voted to almost completely wipe out the outreach training programs of the military academies. It's rather short-sighted, but if something involves spending money for human resources training, the payoff is not immediate, and Congress may be reluctant to put forth the money. Congress is very sensitive about producing results to show the American public before the next election, which is never far away. One might say, "What can be done to provide for more foresight on the part of American politicians?" One plan that might be tried is the establishment of something similar to the Japanese Ministry of International Trade and Industry, which consists of three representatives from industry, three from labor, and three from government. The government officials are not even directly elected. The president, or prime minister, appoints the government officials, and they are given money to invest in various kinds of programs, such as outreach training programs, the training of displaced workers, or promoting new technologies. They can do this with more long-range planning than members of Congress, who are only serving for two year terms. The member of Congress would have supervision over the new ministry. Such an organization, being nongovernmental, could be associated with the Department of Education.

The feasibility problem of outreach training is an economic one. It costs money. It costs money for the training, and the payoff may not be seen for a while. For instance, the training of minorities in a special summer program for law school may not pay off until after they graduate and become better role models for and provide better legal service to people in the minority community. Unfortunately, economic feasibility may require, as we've mentioned, institutions such as Congress having a longer time horizon than they presently do.

V. VOTING

As for the voting item, this refers to the fact that low-income people need to be empowered and be less dependent on public-aid systems.[5] Both conservatives and liberals use concepts like empowerment and "power to the people." Conservatives sometimes use such concepts in an overly paternalistic way. Liberals sometimes use such concepts in an unnecessarily frightening revolutionary way. Both sides are likely to agree that enfranchising poor people (at least in theory) is a good thing for society and especially democracy. In the context of voting, that means making it easier for qualified low-income people to vote as a minimal form of political participation. They are frequently disenfranchised, in effect, because they find it more difficult to register at the time of voting, as is done in some countries and states. Low-income people also find it difficult to lose time from work in order to vote. A simple solution is to make election day a holiday as some countries do, or at least to hold major elections on Sunday or on multiple

Table 4 Voting Registration and Turnout

	Goals	
	Conservative: Noneligible registration and voting concerns	*Liberal*: Increase registration and voting
Alternatives		
Conservative: Leave as is	+	−
Liberal: Facilitate registration	−	+
Neutral: Precinct registration, permanent registration	0	0
SOS: 1. On-site or same-day registration 2. Vote anywhere 3. Extended polling times 4. Invisible ink	+ +	+ +

days. One should also be allowed to vote at one's home precinct, workplace precinct, or any precinct. If more low-income people participate in politics and voting, then more public policies would be adopted that relate to the kind of job facilitators, education, and merit treatment discussed above (Table 4).

A. Conservative and Liberal Positions

The United States does not look good relative to the rest of the world when it comes to voter turnout. There are, in very round numbers, 200 million adults, of which approximately half are registered to vote. But only about half of those registered to vote actually do, about 50 million. That means just 26 million people can decide even a presidential election. This can be a landslide if each state is hotly contested, even though it's only 26 million out of 200 million possible voters. It's not so good when, in effect, 13% of the population can decide who will sit in the Oval Office. We're not undemocratic in the sense of prohibiting voting, but less democratic than we should be in the sense of facilitating voter turnout.

The true conservative goal might be to promote the election of conservative candidates, but they are not going to say that. What they actually say is that they want to avoid multiple voting. They do not want any schemes that will allow cheating at the polls. Liberals, on the other hand, are very concerned about people who do not vote, so they want to decrease nonvoting by adults who could be eligible. The conservative position promotes a decrease in multiple voting in a number of ways. One of the most extreme positions is to purge the voter rolls every ten years and make people register over again. This would guard against individuals still being present on the voter rolls who have moved or died. It greatly decreases the number of people who register as you have to do it over and over again. Having advanced registration may make a difference with regard to decreasing multiple voting, but it also decreases voting in general. Liberals also want advanced registration, but they want to make the process easier. They support ideas like postcard registration or registration at the time you get your driver's license, so-called motor-vehicle registration. They also support keeping the polls open a few hours later to make it easier to vote on election day. Unfortunately, the liberal solutions in total wouldn't make much of a difference, as more fundamental change is necessary.

B.   A Win-Win Alternative

What really needs to be adopted is the kind of system presently being used in many countries of the world, including Canada, South Africa, Mexico, and Mozambique, as well as states such as Wisconsin and Minnesota. It involves a few innovations. First of all, there is no requirement of advanced registration. You can register in advance if you want to, but you can also register on-site the day of the election. For many people who don't vote on election day due to the fact that there isn't on-site registration, that would no longer be a problem. Also, if elections were to be moved to a nonworking day, instead of a Tuesday, more people would be able to participate. In Catholic countries like Italy, France, and Mexico, election day is on a Sunday, when people don't work. Other nations string their elections over a couple of days. Another improvement would allow people to vote in either their home precinct or their work precinct, or to even allow them to vote in any precinct, provided there is some way of checking to make sure they haven't voted in another. Multiple-precinct voting can make a large difference in voter turnout.

With all these facilitators, however, the conservative problem of multiple voting rises again. The way that problem is solved in South Africa, Mexico, Mozambique, and other countries is by having voters dip their hand into a bowl of invisible ink. If you show up at a polling place any time after that, including your original polling place, your hand is viewed under an ultraviolet lamp. If it shows that you have already voted, you are denied the chance to vote again and can possibly be arrested. The invisible ink method works much better than asking people to sign their names, because names can be forged. It is a good example of a win-win solution because it would substantially decrease multiple voting and substantially decrease nonvoting. It helps to achieve both goals simultaneously, like the previously mentioned outreach training, or the more profitable, cleaner processes that relate to environmental protection and economic growth. All four ideas we have discussed so far are capable of achieving the conservative and liberal goals more successfully than either the conservative or liberal alternative.

On-site registration, the nonworking election day, multiple precincts, and the invisible ink method all have a political feasibility problem. This problem is political in the sense that it is very difficult to get such measures through Congress or through a state legislature. This is because one political party is likely to have enough strength to block it, namely the party that thinks it will suffer as a result of expanded voter turnout. As long as one party has enough power to stop these measures, they will never be adopted. If, however, they ever were adopted, they are not likely to be repealed. There is a kind of ratchet effect on new facilitators once they are adopted, because the party in power will look bad if it decreases the ability of people to register and vote. These measures are likely to be adopted when the Democrats have enough influence in the Congress or in the various state legislatures. The traditional thinking is that the Democratic party benefits more from expanded voter registration and turnout than the Republican party due to the fact that a higher percentage of nonvoters consist of people who are poorer and less educated than average and are more likely to vote Democratic. The problem is political, but it may only be a temporary problem, as one hopes, all the other feasibility problems may be temporary.

VI. CRIME

The fifth item under poverty reduction and prevention relates to crime.[6] Being poor may be a key factor in engaging in street crimes, like mugging and burglary, as contrasted to middle-class crimes, like embezzlement and swindling. Here we are concerned not with how poverty causes crime, but rather with how crime causes poverty, especially drug-related criminal activity. As with the other four antipoverty policy variables, we are talking about how anticrime improvements can be made that will result in poverty reduction and prevention. A big factor in inner-city poverty in cities throughout the world (especially the United States) is the highly negative influence on productivity that drugs such as the derivatives of opium and cocaine have. The availability of such drugs can turn a potentially productive person into a drug addict or, worse, into a drug dealer who creates other drug addicts.

One solution might be to medicalize the drug problem. That means drug addicts are considered sick people, rather than criminals guilty of the possession or sale of drugs. That further means such addicts would be treated under whatever national health-care exists, perhaps by being given a phase-out prescription that gets lower in dosage each month. If they stay on prescription opium or cocaine forever, like diabetics stay on insulin, this is still an improvement over the criminal drug market in multiple ways:

1. Drug dealers would have no incentive to give free samples, because they would just be creating patients for the health-care service, not new paying customers.
2. Almost 70% of all the muggings and burglaries would end, since that is the amount that are committed by drug addicts seeking money to buy drugs.
3. Likewise, almost 70% of the murders in the United States and some other countries are drug-related, meaning they are often committed by drug dealers fighting for territorial control or committed by addicts in a bungled mugging or burglary.
4. There would be a lessening of the corruption of police and government officials by wealthy drug dealers, especially in some developing countries.
5. There would be a tremendous saving in prison costs, court costs, police costs, and other costs that are part of the criminalizing of drug addiction, as contrasted to the relatively lower costs involved in medicalizing drug addiction. See Table 5.

Table 5 Dealing with the Drug Problem

	Goals	
Alternatives	*Conservative*: Decrease crime and reduce drug dealing	*Liberal goals*: Societal productivity
Conservative: Law enforcement crackdown	+	−
Liberal: Legalization	−	+
Neutral: 1. Treatment and education 2. Prohibit coke and heroin but not marijuana	0	0
SOS: Medicalization to de-profitize drug dealing	+ +	+ +

A. Conservative and Liberal Positions

The last policy problem regards drug-related crime, which has become an increasingly serious issue. It currently consumes a great deal of money in the United States, and is causing enormous losses in productivity. It is causing governments to engage in corruption and police officers to use abusive behavior due to the tremendous frustration brought on by the drug war.

The key conservative goal in this context is to eliminate or greatly reduce drug dealing. This means reducing the buying and selling of illegal drugs, most commonly heroin, cocaine, and marijuana. Cocaine and crack represent the largest problem, as it is involved in a large percentage that occurs. Sixty to seventy percent of all people arrested for crimes in low-income areas or crimes against persons are arrested under circumstances that indicate they are stealing in order to get money for drugs. Often, they are under the influence of drugs while committing the crimes. The crimes against persons usually involve power plays for staking out drug territory. They frequently lead to murder, because under the influence of drugs, people behave in a more aggressive way than they would otherwise.

Liberals are especially concerned about reducing the side effects of the war on drugs. These side effects include the police engaging in more illegal arrests, searches, and interrogations than before crack cocaine became widespread in the mid-1980s. They also include the tremendous amount of money necessary for the imprisonment of over 1,000,000 people in our prisons and 500,000 people in our jails. That money could be much better spent on health care, education, or other more useful purposes.

The conservative solution has been to try to repress the sale and possession of drugs. This law enforcement type of approach is an approach of repression, of prohibition. One of the more extreme liberal approaches, although becoming somewhat more popular, is legalization. The policy of drug prohibition and repression is analogous to the policy of liquor prohibition. Back then, the United States realized that liquor prohibition didn't work, and that the policy's abolishment was better, even if it meant more alcohol related crime. Legalization is the more liberal alternative to conservative police enforcement and repression.

B. A Win-Win Alternative

The object of the win-win solution is to come up with some kind of idea that wipes out the drug dealers, but will not increase the use of drugs. Another way to phrase it is to de-profitize drug dealing. If you de-profitize drug dealing, then you would also eliminate the side effects. The organized crime would decrease accordingly. Another side effect that would be eliminated is the corruption of government officials due to the availability of "mutually profitable arrangements" with large dealers. An ounce of pure cocaine has a street value higher than that of an ounce of gold. This causes a lot of frustration for the police, because as soon as one drug dealer gets arrested and imprisoned or killed, there's another set up to immediately take their place. The money is just too good for some people to turn down.

The way to de-profitizing drug dealing is to treat drug addicts like sick people, and to consider them criminals only if they engage in crimes other than the possession and use of drugs. But a key part of the treatment is to treat drug addicts as being in need of medical treatment under our current health care programs. As care plans move in the direction of becoming universal, the need to cover drug addiction is important. If drug addicts are considered to be sick people and eligible for prescription drugs, which could include a cocaine substitute or even actual cocaine under a cocaine maintenance program. The profits of drug dealing would be wiped out because addicts would be able to get what they need through their subsidized HMO. These maintenance prescriptions would usually be given on a long-term, phase-out basis until the person is clean. If they cannot kick their drug habit, their doctors will be able to prescribe additional doses. No more would drug dealers be interested in hooking ten-year-old kids with free samples; all they'd be doing is creating new patients for the HMOs. The dealers would eventually be forced to look for some alternative occupation as did the bootleg liquor dealers of the past. At the present time, there's nothing that wouldn't be better for society than the drug dealing they were engaged in.

The win-win solution is plagued by psychological feasibility problems. Many don't believe that such availability will have any effect other than to increase the use of drugs. The idea that people who are not drug addicts are going to go to their HMO and say "I'm a drug addict; I'm on cocaine," when they want to experiment is farfetched. Such a declaration would likely cause them to sacrifice many opportunities that they might otherwise have had. Employers are not too enthusiastic about hiring drug addicts. The real drug addicts, though, do have an incentive to go to the HMOs. There they can get a maintenance prescription without having to rob or kill for it and without having to run the risk of getting arrested or killed themselves.

This kind of approach appeals to some libertarian conservatives who think that a repression program involves more problematic government interference than interference in the economy. It should also appeal to liberals. It's better than legalization because legalization means that controls would be much less strict, and that anybody could have access to drugs, including children. Those children would likely grow up to be much less productive members of society. Legalization, in fact, would have a very bad effect on national productivity, whereas this kind of program, which is only for confirmed drug addicts, would have few new effects. There would not be a whole lot of new drug addicts created because there won't be a set of drug dealers encouraging the younger generation to become drug addicts.

As said before, the feasibility problem here is psychological. People are resistant to the idea of giving drugs to anyone, let alone those who are already addicts. That sounds somehow evil, but it's less evil than the present system might be perceived. Because this plan is psychologically hard to accept, it's very difficult politically to adopt. Economically, this solution would cost far less than what is currently being done. Cocaine, for instance, is very cheap to produce. Its high price largely has to do with police repression, which causes the costs of drug dealing to rise, and therefore the street price to rise also. There might also be some feasibility problems with regard to administering such a program. The drugs possessed by HMOs and hospitals must be carefully monitored so that they don't fall into the wrong hands. This can be taken care of by authorizing only one doctor in the HMO to prescribe drug maintenance programs or drugs. This would greatly decrease the amount of people with access, and would thereby decrease the risk. Also, in order to be eligible to receive a drug maintenance prescription, a person must be a confirmed addict. This would require testing, over time, of the levels of drugs in a person's system to see if they qualify. The administrative part of the program should not necessarily require people to accept a phase-out arrangement. Such restrictions would cause people to avoid the program and would cause the formation of a black market, which defeats the entire purpose. That's why a similar program didn't succeed in England. As long as these people are treated as sick people, not criminals, this kind of administration is likely to succeed.

NOTES

1. On win-win analysis, see Baumol, W. *Superfairness: Applications and Theory*. (Cambridge, MA: MIT Press, 1986); Nagel, S. *Super-Optimum Solutions and Basic Concepts and Principles*. (Westport, CT: Quorum Books, 1997); and Susskind L. and Cruikshank, J. *Breaking the Impasse: Consensual Approaches to Resolving Public Disputes*. (New York, NY: Basic Books, 1987).
2. On job facilitators, see Gueron, J. and Pualy, E. *From Welfare to Work*. (New York, NY: Russell Sage, 1991); Nightingale, D. and Haveman, R. *The Work Alternative: Welfare Reform and the Realities of the Job Market*. (Washington, DC: The Urban Institute, 1995); and World Development Indicators, *World Development Report 1995: Workers in an Integrating World*. (New York, NY: Oxford, 1995).
3. On education, see Anyon, J. *Ghetto Schooling: A Political Economy of Urban Educational Reform*. (New York, NY: Columbia University, 1997); Centre for Educational Research and Innovation. *Adult Illiteracy and Economic Performance*, (Paris: OECD,

1992); and Stromquist, N. *Education in Urban Areas: Cross-National Dimensions.* (Westport, CT: Praeger, 1994).

4. On merit treatment, see Danziger, S. and Gottschalk, P. *America Unequal.* (Cambridge, MA: Harvard, 1995); Gurr, T. *Minorities at Risk: A Global View of Ethnopolitical Conflicts,* (Washington, DC: Institute of Peace, 1993); and Nelson, B. and Chowdhury, N. *Women and Politics Worldwide.* (New Haven, CT: Yale, 1994).

5. On voting, see Atal, Y. and Oyen, E. *Poverty and Participation in Civil Society,* (New York, NY: UNESCO, 1997); Friedmann, J. *Empowerment: Politics of Alternative Development.* (London: Blackwell, 1992); and Piven, F. and Cloward, R. *Why Americas Don't Vote.* (New York, NY: Pantheon, 1988).

6. On crime, see Dorn, N. Jepsen, J. and Savona, E. *European Drug Policies and Enforcement.* (New York, NY: St. Martins, 1996); Walker, S. *Sense and Nonsense about Crime: A Policy Guide.* (Belmont, CA: Brooks/Cole, 1989); and Zimring, F. and Hawkins, G. *The Search for Rational Drug Control.* (Boston, MA: Cambridge, 1992).

2

Ethnic Nepotism as an Explanation for Ethnic Conflicts

Tatu Vanhanen
University of Helsinki, Klaukkala, Finland

I. INTRODUCTION

Ethnic conflicts seem to be common in all ethnically plural societies across all cultural boundaries. Experience shows that political and economic interest conflicts become easily organized along ethnic lines in such societies. In extreme cases, ethnic conflicts paralyze societies and culminate in violent confrontations and even civil wars. Social scientists have sought theoretical explanations for ethnic conflicts. Why are ethnic conflicts so common? Why has it been so difficult for ethnic groups to live in harmony with one another and to agree on the sharing of scarce resources? Further, how can we accommodate ethnic conflicts? Social scientists have not yet found satisfactory theoretical explanations for ethnic conflicts.[1] Many researchers argue that ethnic conflicts are cultural conflicts that need a separate explanation in each case. Consequently, there cannot be any general theoretical explanation for them. Some other researchers have attempted to formulate more general explanations for ethnic conflicts, but there does not seem to be any generally accepted theoretical explanation for them. My intention is to derive a theoretical explanation for the persistence of ethnic conflicts from the principles of the Darwinian theory of evolution by natural selection and to test it by empirical evidence. In this respect, I continue the line of argumentation started by Pierre L. van den Berghe.

II. ETHNIC NEPOTISM

I have argued in my books *Politics of Ethnic Nepotism: India as an Example* and *On the Evolutionary Roots of Politics*[2] that it is possible to deduce a cross-culturally valid evolutionary explanation for ethnic conflicts from a Darwinian interpretation of politics and from a sociobiological theory of kin selection. According to my Darwinian interpretation of politics, the struggle for scarce resources is the central theme of politics everywhere. This central and universal theme of politics can be derived from the Darwinian theory of evolution by natural selection. According to this theory, all organisms have to struggle for survival because we live in a world of scarcity in which all species are able to produce much more progeny than can be supported by the available resources. The permanent discrepancy between the number of individuals and the means of existence makes the struggle for survival inevitable and omnipresent.[3] Politics is one of the forums of this struggle. The evolutionary roots of politics lie in the necessity to solve conflicts for scarce resources by some means. We should understand that universal competition and struggle in human societies is an inevitable consequence of the fact that we live in the world of scarcity and that we are programmed to further our own survival by all available means. The Darwinian theory explains why it must be so. Thus it provides an ultimate evolutionary explanation for the necessity and universality of conflicts in all human societies.[4]

But why are so many conflicts taking place along ethnic lines? I think that we can deduce an answer to this question from the assumption that different kinds of behavioral predispositions evolved in the struggle for scarce resources. Different behavior patterns have competed for survival, and more appropriate patterns have gradually displaced less appropriate ones. One of those politically relevant behavior strategies, which evolved to help their users in the struggle for scarce resources, seems to be our universal tendency to nepotism. The term nepotism refers to favoritism toward kin, and it can be explained by a sociobiological theory of kin selection, or inclusive fitness, which was originally formulated by W. D. Hamilton.[5] He looked at evolution from the gene's point of view and realized that natural selection tends to maximize inclusive fitness; the survival of one's genes through one's own offspring and through relatives who have the same genes. It means that the logic of evolution presupposes individual selfishness together with favoritism toward relatives. Animals behaving in such a way have the best chances to reproduce their genes.[6] Pierre L. van den Berghe states, ''whenever cooperation increases individual fitness, organisms are genetically selected to be nepotistic, in the sense of favoring kin over non-kin, and close kin over distant kin.''[7]

Ethnic groups can be perceived as extended kin groups. The members of an ethnic group tend to favor their group members over nonmembers because they are more related to their group members than to the remainder of the population. The members of the same ethnic group tend to support each other in conflict situations. Van den Berghe uses the term "ethnic nepotism" in the connection of such mutual aid networks. He extends kin selection to ethnic groups: "My basic argument is quite simple: ethnic and racial sentiments are extension of kinship sentiments. Ethnocentrism and racism are thus extended forms of nepotism—the propensity to favor kin over nonkin."[8] This is an important insight on ethnic nepotism. Our tendency to favor kin over nonkin has extended to include large linguistic, national, racial, religious, and other ethnic groups. The term ethnic nepotism covers this kind of nepotism at the level of extended kin groups.[9]

From the perspective of ethnic nepotism, it does not matter what kinds of kin groups are in question. The crucial characteristic of an ethnic group is that its members are genetically more closely related to each other than to the members of other groups. Therefore, in my study "ethnic group" refers, not only to racial, tribal, and national groups, but also to linguistic groups, castes, and old religious communities.[10] A problem with this definition is that people are related to each other at many levels. We are related from the level of nuclear family to the level of Homo sapiens. Consequently, ethnic groups are never absolutely distinct and exclusive. As Horowitz says, "Groups that were once one may have split centuries before, with each of the resulting groups remaining largely endogamous, thus producing opposed but physically similar populations."[11] Any level can provide a basis for ethnic nepotism. What level of ethnic groups becomes politically relevant depends on the situation.

I assume that our behavioral predisposition to ethnic nepotism, because of its evolutionary roots, is shared by all human populations. This assumption makes it reasonable to present universal hypotheses on political consequences of ethnic nepotism. I hypothesize that

1. Significant ethnic cleavages tend to lead to ethnic interest conflicts in all societies.
2. The more a society is ethnically divided, the more political and other interest conflicts tend to become canalized along ethnic lines.

In principle, these hypotheses are testable, which means that it is possible to falsify them by empirical evidence. The first hypothesis claims that because ethnic nepotism is shared by all human populations, ethnic tensions and conflicts can be expected in all ethnically divided societies. It would be possible to falsify this hypothesis by empirical evidence that shows that there is no systematic relationship between the extent of ethnic cleavages and the emergence of ethnic conflicts. The second hypothesis complements the first one by claiming that the degree of ethnic conflicts depends on the degree of ethnic cleavages. In other words, the more ethnic groups differ from each other genetically, the higher the probability and intensity of conflicts between them. It would be possible to falsify this hypothesis by empirical evidence that shows that there is no clear relationship between the degree of ethnic cleavages and the degree of ethnic conflicts.

However, I have to complement my hypotheses by a reservation. The relationship between ethnic cleavages and ethnic conflicts does not need to be automatic and uniform. There are intervening factors that may increase or decrease the intensity of conflicts. I assume that political and social institutions constitute important intervening factors. Depending on their nature, they can help to accommodate ethnic interest conflicts, or they can deepen them. I further assume that political institutions based on equality and reciprocity are better adapted to accommodate ethnic interest conflicts than institutions based on hegemonic and unequal relations between ethnic groups. This is because we may have an evolved tendency to reciprocity.[12] It evolved in the struggle for existence in the same way as nepotism and other politically relevant behavioral predispositions. Our behavioral tendency to reciprocity provides a natural basis for different kinds of win-win policies.[13]

In politics, reciprocity appears in numerous forms, from the level of individual relationships to the relations between social groups, nations, and international alliances. The basic rules remain the same in all variations: we are ready to provide services and to help others if we can expect that the receiver will reciprocate. We are disposed to accept balanced reciprocal relationships, but we resist unequal reciprocity. I assume that these basic rules of reciprocity are cross-culturally similar in all human societies. This assumed behavioral predisposition to reciprocity explains many reciprocal relationships in politics.

I assume that the same rules of reciprocity apply to the relationships between ethnic groups, too. Consequently, we can assume that political institutions based on balanced reciprocity and equality between ethnic groups provide a better institutional framework for harmonious relations between ethnic groups than institutions biased to favor some groups and discriminate some others. This assumption leads me to hypothesize that

3. At the same level of ethnic cleavages, the degree of ethnic conflicts tends to be higher in societies in which political institutions are biased to favor some ethnic groups and discriminate some others than in societies in which political institutions are based on balanced reciprocity and equality between ethnic groups.

In principle, this hypothesis is testable, but it presupposes detailed information on the nature of institutional arrangements. Such information is not easily available.[14]

The evolutionary theory of ethnic conflicts outlined above differs from most other theories of ethnicity and ethnic conflicts in some important respects. First, according to this theory, ethnic groups are basically kinship groups, although the level of kinship and, consequently, the size of kinship group can vary greatly depending on the situation. In this respect, I agree more with the scholars who emphasize the primordial origins of ethnic groups than with scholars who regard ethnic groups as easily changeable and malleable cultural groups. However, the assumption on the primordial origins of ethnic groups does not mean that they should be unchangeable and eternal. It depends on political and social situation, what type of ethnic groups become politically relevant. I emphasize the crucial importance of genetic distance between ethnic groups. From this perspective, there are great differences in the degree of ethnic cleavages. The cleavage between blacks and whites, for example, is much deeper than the cleavage between white Catholics and Protestants, although the latter groups may also be regarded as ethnic groups if people have belonged to these different religious communities for several centuries and if intermarriages between Catholics and Protestants have remained relatively rare. Blacks and whites constitute clearly different ethnic groups, whereas it is not self-evident whether we should regard Catholics and Protestants as different ethnic groups, although they certainly can be regarded as different cultural groups.

Second, my theoretical explanation of ethnic conflicts differs from many other theoretical explanations because it is derived from the principles of evolutionary theory and from a Darwinian interpretation of politics. According to my theory, interest conflicts between ethnic groups are inevitable because ethnic groups are genetic kinship groups and because the struggle for existence concerns the survival of our genes through our own and our relatives' descendents. Therefore it has been rational for relatives to ally with each other in political and other struggles for scarce resources and survival. Our behavioral predisposition to ethnic nepotism evolved in the struggle for existence because it was rational and useful. It is reasonable to assume that ethnic nepotism is equally shared by all human populations. Consequently, all human populations and ethnic groups have approximately equal potential to resort to ethnic nepotism in interest conflicts. It explains the otherwise strange fact that ethnic interest conflicts seem to appear in all countries where people belong to clearly different ethnic groups and that ethnic interest conflicts have appeared within all cultural regions and at all levels of socioeconomic development. It is difficult to imagine any cultural explanation of ethnic conflicts that could explain the appearance of these conflicts across all civilizations and cultural boundaries.

Finally, I would like to emphasize that the same evolutionary argumentation provides a theoretical basis for the accommodation of ethnic conflicts and for the formulation of various types of win-win policies. Because we have a behavioral predisposition to accept balanced reciprocity in our relations with others, it is reasonable to assume that institutional arrangements based on balanced reciprocity and equality between ethnic groups make it easier to mitigate ethnic interest conflicts than institutions based on inequality of ethnic groups and on unequal reciprocity. It can be argued that attempts to accommodate ethnic conflicts on the basis of reciprocity represent a variant type of win-win policy because all parties have chances to benefit from reciprocal arrangements. The problem is, however, that reciprocity is not usually the first choice for conflicting ethnic groups. They do not resort to reciprocity as long as they can hope to win more by attempting to subjugate ethnic adversaries. Many strategies, from genocide to milder forms of suppression and discrimination, are used in ethnic struggles for hegemony. For that reason it is difficult to solve ethnic conflicts on the basis of equality and to establish institutions based on reciprocity.

III. A RESEARCH PROJECT ON ETHNIC CONFLICTS

My intention is to make a comparative study of ethnic conflicts in which I test the three hypotheses by empirical evidence covering 183 contemporary states.[15] A difficult problem is how to measure the degree of ethnic cleavages and the degree of ethnic conflicts, and how to find reliable and comparable empirical data for these purposes.

A. Indicators of Ethnic Cleavages

I have preliminarily measured major ethnic cleavages by taking into account three aspects of ethnic cleavages: (1) cleavages based on race, (2) cleavages based on nationality, language, or tribe, and (3) cleavages based on differences between old religious communities. All of these cleavages divide the population into separate ethnic groups, although the deepness of cleavages varies. I assume that cleavages based on race or color are genetically the deepest ones because they may be tens of thousands of years old, whereas most religious cleavages are usually not older than one or two thousand years, and often only a few hundred years or even less. Thus we have three dimensions of ethnic cleavages. I have used the percentage of the largest group as the principal criterion to determine the degree of ethnic cleavages in each dimension. It is calculated by subtracting the percentage of the largest racial, national (linguistic or tribal), or religious group from 100 percent. For example, if the percentage of the largest racial group is 80, the degree of racial cleavages is 20. The three percentages of ethnic cleavages are combined into an index of ethnic heterogeneity (EH) by adding them. Its value may vary from 0 to approximately 200.

B. Measures of Ethnic Conflicts

It is easier to get information of the existence of ethnic interest conflicts than to measure their relative significance by reliable empirical data. My intention is to measure the relative degree of ethnic conflicts (1) by taking into account the extent to which political competition and interest conflicts have become organized along ethnic lines, and (2) by estimating the relative significance of violent ethnic conflicts. Unfortunately there are no direct indicators for these purposes. I have had to use estimations based on empirical evidence on ethnic interest conflicts and violence.

An index of ethnic organizations and interest conflicts (IEO) is intended to measure the organized or institutional dimension of ethnic conflicts. Its values may vary from 0 to 100. The following criteria are used in estimations:

   0 = no significant ethnic organizations or ethnic conflicts
   5 = the share of the votes cast in parliamentary or presidential elections for ethnic parties is less than 10%; some ethnic organizations; occasional ethnic interest conflicts
  10 = the share of votes for ethnic parties 10–14%; some prominent ethnic organizations; sporadic ethnic interest conflicts
  20 = the share of votes for ethnic parties 15–29%; significant ethnic organizations; ethnic interest conflicts common
  40 = the share of votes for ethnic parties 30–49%; ethnic organizations cover a significant part of the population; extensive ethnic interest conflicts
  60 = the share of votes for ethnic parties 50–69%; most interest organizations are ethnic ones; ethnic interest conflicts more important than other types of interest conflicts
  80 = the share of votes for ethnic parties 70–89%; nearly all interest organizations are ethnically based; ethnic interest conflicts dominate national politics
 100 = the share of votes for ethnic parties 90–100%; all significant interest organizations are ethnic by nature; practically all interest conflicts take place along ethnic lines

An index of ethnic violence (IEV) is used to measure the extent and relative significance of violent ethnic conflicts. Its values vary from 0 to 100. Estimations on the extent and significance of ethnic violences are based on the following criteria:

   0 = no ethnic violence, although there may be tension between ethnic groups
   5 = occasional local ethnic violence involving single persons
  10 = sporadic violent ethnic conflicts in some parts of the country involving single persons or local ethnic groups
  20 = serious but not continuous ethnic violence involving significant number of people; local ethnic guerrilla movements; occasional ethnic terrorist acts
  40 = repeated violent conflicts between ethnic groups; suppression of

particular ethnic groups; ethnic guerrilla or separatist movements; significant ethnic terrorism

60 = violent ethnic conflicts dominate politics; separatist ethnic wars in some parts of the country

80 = prolonged violent ethnic conflicts involving significant parts of the country or of the population; ethnic civil wars or separatist wars

100 = violent ethnic conflicts or wars dominate politics completely

The two indices measuring two dimensions of ethnic conflicts are combined into an index of ethnic conflicts (EC) by adding the two index values of the sectional indices. The value of EC may vary from 0 to 200. This index will be used as the measure the degree of ethnic conflicts.

C. Research Hypotheses

The original hypotheses on the relationship between ethnic nepotism and ethnic conflicts can now be reformulated into research hypotheses using operationally defined variables in the place of original hypothetical concepts. It is possible to test the first hypothesis by separating the countries with significant ethnic cleavages from countries without significant ethnic cleavages, and, second, the countries with ethnic interest conflicts from countries without ethnic interest conflicts. For that purpose I have to define the minimal criteria of significant ethnic cleavages. The index of ethnic heterogeneity is a continuous variable without any natural threshold of significant ethnic cleavages. It is not self-evident at what level of ethnic heterogeneity ethnic cleavages become significant. Let us use an arbitrarily selected criterion of 10 EH index points to separate significant ethnic cleavages from insignificant ones. In the case of the index of ethnic conflicts, it is easier to define the threshold between ethnic interest conflicts and no ethnic interest conflicts. It is reasonable to regard that significant ethnic interest conflicts exist in all countries for which the value of EC is higher than 10. The first hypothesis can now be given in the following form:

1. Significant ethnic cleavages (EH higher than 10) tend to lead to ethnic interest conflicts (EC higher than 10) in all societies.

The first hypothesis can be tested by the simple method of cross-tabulation. The countries should cluster to the same diagonal. Deviating cases will be in the opposing diagonal. The strength of hypothesized relationship can be measured by Yule's Q. The hypothesis allows some deviating cases because my empirical variables are rough and errors of measurement and judgment are possible. However, if the number of deviating cases is large and the strength of the hypothesized relationship is not at least moderate, the hypothesis should be regarded as falsified.

The second hypothesis presupposes a clear positive correlation between the composite index of ethnic heterogeneity (independent variable) and the index of ethnic conflicts (dependent variable). The second hypothesis can now be given in the following form:

2. The more a society is ethnically divided (the higher the value of EH), the more political and other interest conflicts tend to become canalized along ethnic lines (the higher the value of EC).

The second hypothesis can be tested by correlation and regression analyses. Correlation coefficients measure the strength of the relationship. Because the hypothesized relationship between the level of ethnic cleavages and the level of ethnic conflicts is positive, correlations should be clearly positive. Weak positive or negative correlations would falsify the second research hypothesis. Regression analysis can be used to disclose how well single countries are adapted to the average relationship between the two variables and which countries deviate most from the regression line. Detailed analysis could then be focused on deviating cases.

Unfortunately the space does not allow a discussion of the variables in detail nor to present and document the empirical data used in this study.[16]

IV. SUMMARY OF PRELIMINARY RESULTS

The first research hypothesis was tested by cross-tabulating the 183 contemporary countries (1990–1996) of this study by the significant level of ethnic heterogeneity (EH higher than 10) and by the occurrence of significant ethnic conflicts (EC higher than 10).[17] The results are given in Table 1. The hypothesis claims that significant ethnic cleavages tend to lead ethnic conflicts in all societies. It does not exclude the possibility of ethnic conflicts at lower levels of ethnic heterogeneity, but it presupposes that ethnic conflicts emerge in all countries with EH higher than 10. Therefore, only the 12 countries with EH higher than 10 and EC 10 or

Table 1 183 Countries Cross-Tabulated According to the Significance Levels of Ethnic Cleavages (EH) and of Ethnic Conflicts (EC) in 1990–1996.

	EH 10 or less	EH higher than 10	Total
EC 10 or less	(a) 38	(b) 12	50
EC higher than 10	(c) 3	(d) 130	133
Total	41	142	183

Source: Ref. 17.

less contradict the first research hypothesis. However, nearly all of these deviations are very slight ones. The strength of the hypothesized relationship can be measured by Yule's Q. It varies from $+1.0$ for perfect positive association to -1.0 for perfect negative association. A perfect positive association occures if there are no cases at all in the b cell, or none in either b or c cells.[18] In this case, Yule's Q is 0.986, which indicates a very strong hypothesized relationship.

The second research hypothesis tries to explain cross-cultural regularities in the intensity and extent of ethnic conflicts by ethnic nepotism. The more a society is ethnically divided (EH), the more ethnic nepotism is assumed to canalize political and other interest conflicts along ethnic lines. The hypothesis is tested by correlation and regression analyses. The correlation between EH and EC is 0.74 in this comparison group of 183 countries, which means that the index of ethnic heterogeneity statistically explains 55% of the variation in the index of ethnic conflicts. The unexplained part of variation is 45%. It is due to measurement errors and to all other possible explanatory variables, including the significance of institutional factors. When the two most extremely deviating countries (Burundi and Rwanda) are excluded, the correlation rises to 0.801 and the explained part of variation to 64%. Empirical evidence supports the second research hypothesis strongly, although there are many countries that deviate from the average relationship between EH and EC.

Regression analysis was used to disclose how well the average relationship between EH and EC applies to single countries. The results of regression analysis are summarized in Figure 1. Negative residuals (countries below the regression line) indicate that the level of ethnic conflicts is lower than expected on the basis of the regression equation of EC on EH. The most extreme negative residuals (-40.0 or higher) are for Madagascar (-48.4), Mauritius (-44.2), Belize (-49.5), Suriname (-62.8), Brunei (-60.0) and Qatar (-42.2). Positive residuals (countries above the regression line) indicate that the level of ethnic conflicts is higher than expected. The most extreme positive residuals (40.0 or higher) are for Bosnia-Herzegovina (94.0), Croatia (92.6), Yugoslavia (42.1), Guatemala (48.9), Afghanistan (53.3), Burma (43.9), Iraq (49.9), Israel (77.0), Sri Lanka (62.1), Tajikistan (51.8), Angola (55.1), Burundi (134.5), Mauritania (46.4), Rwanda (141.5), Somalia (82.0) and Sudan (63.6).

My evolutionary explanation for the university of ethnic conflicts in ethnically divided societies is based on the assumption that ethnic nepotism belongs to human nature. We have evolved to favor our relatives in the struggle for existence because it has been an adaptive behavior pattern. Of course, there are good proximate explanations for every ethnic conflict, but the fact that ethnic cleavages seem to lead to some kind of ethnic conflict in all societies implies the existence of a common causal factor. According to my interpretation, our shared disposition to ethnic nepotism is the common factor behind all ethnic conflicts. It does not seem possible to avoid the emergence of ethnic conflicts in ethnically divided

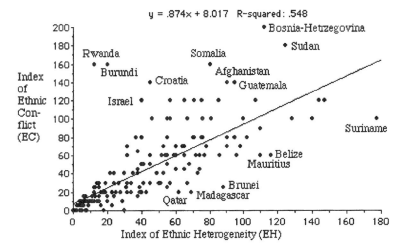

Figure 1 Results of regression analysis in which the index of ethnic heterogeneity (EH) is the independent variable and the index of ethnic conflicts (EC) is the dependent variable in a comparison group of 183 contemporary countries (1990–1996). (From Ref. 17.)

societies, but it is possible to mitigate them by inventing social and political institutions that help to accommodate the interests of different ethnic groups. It is a challenge for social scientists to invent institutions that could make it easier for different ethnic groups to coexist in our increasingly crowded world.

It would be interesting to examine the most extremely deviating countries in particular from this perspective. Could we explain much higher and much lower than expected degrees of ethnic conflicts by institutional factors? Are the institutions regulating ethnic relations exceptionally suitable in countries in which the degree of ethnic conflicts is much lower than expected? In other words, have they succeeded in mitigating ethnic interest conflicts by win-win policies? This assumption may apply to Mauritius and some other countries below the regression line but hardly to countries like Brunei and Qatar. Large negative residuals of Brunei, Qatar, and several other Arabian oil states are probably due to the fact that migrant workers of these countries are without any political rights. Until now the authoritarian governments have been able to control their large migrant populations belonging to other ethnic groups, but we cannot be sure about the future. In several African states, tribal cleavages have not yet generated violent ethnic conflicts and national movements, but it may happen in the future.

Extremely large positive residuals indicate the failure of political institutions and the lack of suitable win-win policies. They can also be interpreted to predict that the degree of ethnic conflicts will decrease in the future. In fact, it is

characteristic for most of these countries that serious attempts have been made
to solve ethnic conflicts by institutional engineering and inventions of some kind
of win-win policies based on reciprocity. Ethnic wars in Bosnia-Herzegovina and
Croatia were ended by peace agreements, and peace negotiations have also been
carried out in several other countries with extremely high positive residuals.

NOTES/REFERENCES

1. See, for example, Rabushka, A. and Shepsle, K. (1972). *Politics in Plural Societies:
   A Theory of Democratic Instability*. Columbus, Ohio: Charles E. Merrill Publishing
   Company; Horowitz, D. L. (1985). *Ethnic Groups in Conflict*. Berkeley: University
   of California Press; Smith, A. D. (1987). *The Ethnic Origins of Nations*. New York:
   Basil Blackwell; Rupesinghe, K. (1988) (ed.), *Ethnic Conflict and Human Rights*.
   Oslo: Norwegian University Press; Gurr, T. R. (1993). *Minorities at Risk: A Global
   View of Ethnopolitical Conflicts*. Washington: United States Institute of Peace Press;
   Esman, M. J. (1994). *Ethnic Politics*. Ithaca: Cornell University Press; Flohr, A. K.
   (1994). *Fremdenfeindlichkeit: Biosoziale Grundlagen von Ethnozentrismus*. Opda-
   len: Westdeutscher Verlag; McGarry, J. and O'Leary, B. (1994). (eds.), *The Politics
   of Ethnic Conflict Regulation*. London and New York: Routledge; Stavenhagen, R.
   (1996). *Ethnic Conflicts and the Nation-State*, London: Macmillan Press.
2. Vanhanen, T. (1991). *Politics of Ethnic Nepotism: India as an Example*. New Delhi:
   Sterling Publishers; Vanhanen, T. (1992). *On the Evolutionary Roots of Politics*.
   New Delhi: Sterling Publishers.
3. See Darwin, C. ([1859] 1981). *The Origin of Species by Means of Natural Selection
   or the Preservation of Favoured Races in the Struggle for Life*, 114–172. Harmondsworth: Penguin Books: Dobzhansky, T., Ayala, F. J., Stebbins, G. L., Valentine,
   J. W. (1977). *Evolution*, 96–99. San Francisco: W. H. Freeman and Company; Mayr,
   E. (1982). *The Growth of Biological Thought: Diversity, Evolution, and Inheritance*,
   479–480. Cambridge, Massachusetts: Harvard University Press.
4. Vanhanen, T. (1992). *On the Evolutionary Roots of Politics*, 24–27. New Delhi:
   Sterling Publishers. 1992, pp. 24–27.
5. Hamilton, W. D. ([1964] 1978). The genetic evolution of social behavior. In A. L.
   Caplan (ed.), *The Sociobiology Debate*, 191–209. New York: Harper & Row.
6. See Wilson, E. O. (1975). *Sociobiology: A New Synthesis*, 117–118. Cambridge,
   Massachusetts: Harvard University Press; Dawkins, R. ([1976]1979). *The Selfish
   Gene*. London: Granada Publishing; Smith, J. M. (1979). *The Theory of Evolution.
   Third Edition*, 180–182. Harmondsworth: Penguin Books; Alexander, R. D. (1980).
   Darwinism and Human Affairs, 45–46. London: Pitman Publishing Limited; Barash,
   D. P. (1982). *Sociobiology and Behavior. Second Edition*, 67–74 London: Hodden
   and Stoughton; Daly, M. and Wilson, M. (1983), 45–50. *Sex, Evolution, and Behavior. Second Edition*. Boston: PWS Publishers.
7. van den Berghe, P. L. ([1981]1987). *The Ethnic Phenomenon*, 7. Westport: Praeger.
8. van den Berghe, P. L. ([1981]1987). *The Ethnic Phenomenon*, 18. Westport: Praeger;
   see also Rushton, J. P. (1986). Gene-culture coevolution and genetic similarity the-

ory: Implications for ideology, ethnic nepotism, and geopolitics. *Politics and the Life Sciences 4*, 144–148; Dunbar, R. I. M. (1987). Sociobiological explanations and the evolution of ethnocentrism. In V. Reynolds, V. S. E. Falger, and I. Vine (eds), *The Sociobiology of Ethnocentrism*. London & Sydney: Croom Helm; Meyer, P. (1987). Ethnocentrism in human social behavior: Some biosociological considerations. In V. Reynolds, V. S. E. Falger, and I. Vine (eds.), *The Sociobiology of Ethnocentrism*. London & Sydney: Croom Helm; Silverman, I. (1987). Inclusive fitness and ethnocentrism. In V. Reynolds, V. S. E. Falger, and I. Vine (eds.), *The Sociobiology of Ethnocentrism*. London & Sydney: Croom Helm.

9. Vanhanen, T. (1991). *Politics of Ethnic Nepotism: India as an Example*, 11–12. New Delhi: Sterling Publishers.

10. Cf. Horowitz, D. L. (1985). *Ethnic Groups in Conflict*, 41–54. Berkeley: University of California Press; Riggs, F. (1995). Ethnonational rebellions and viable constitutionalism. *International Political Science Review 16*, 375–404.

11. Horowitz, D. L. (1985). Ethnic Groups in Conflict, 52. Berkeley: University of California Press.

12. For reciprocity, see Trivers, R. L. (1978). The evolution of reciprocal altruism. In T. H. Clutton-Brock and P. H. Harvey (eds.), *Readings in Sociobiology* Reeding: W. H. Freeman and Company; Trivers, R. L. (1981). Sociobiology and politics. In E. White, (ed), *Sociobiology and Human Politics*. Lexington, Mass.: Lexington Books; Trivers, R. L. (1985). Social Evolution. Menlo Park, California: Benjamin/Cummings.

13. Cf. Nagel, S. (1996). Win-Win Policy. Circular letter of February 1, 1996.

14. Cf. Riggs, F. (1995). Ethnonational rebellions and viable constitutionalism. *International Political Science Review 16*: 375–404.

15. Cf. Vanhanen, T. Ethnic conflicts explained by ethnic nepotism. *Latvijas Zinátnu Akadémijas Véstis*, No. 10, 4–8, 1992.

16. Data on the variables are given and documented in Vanhanen, T. (1999). *Ethnic Conflicts Explained by Ethnic Nepotism*. Stamford, Connecticut: Jai Press. That book covers 148 countries whose population was over one million in 1990.

17. Vanhanen, T. (1999). Domestic ethnic conflict and ethnic nepotism; A comparative analysis. *Journal of Peace Research 36*, 55–73.

18. See Buchanan, W. *Understanding Political Variables. Third Edition.* (New York: Charles Scribner's Sons, 1980).

3

Differences in the Determinants of Internal Conflict Between the Cold War and Post–Cold War Periods

Hae S. Kim
Troy State University, Fort Walton Beach, Florida

I. INTRODUCTION

One of the major features in the post–Cold War era is the rising civil wars and political violence within states. Despite the peace as manifested with the inception of the post–Cold War era in the international community, internal conflict and political violence have never been abated. Civil wars and political violence, of course, existed during the Cold War period, which also featured the tension in the international community. Do the determinants of internal conflict in a time of tension remain the same as in a time of peace? This paper addresses the question by analyzing the determinants of internal conflict and ascertaining the difference between the Cold War and the post–Cold War period based on cross-national data.

Civil war and political violence stem from a variety of reasons: racial, religious, ideological, and economic factors, as well as political and social structures. Such terms as ethnic conflict, ethnocentrism, ethnonationalism, and ethnic cleansing have been more widely used in the post–Cold War era than in the Cold War era, all of which portray internal conflict based on ethnic-racial lines within a state (Garment 1993; Maynes 1993; Gottlieb 1994; Gurr 1994, 1995). The inherent ethnocentrism underlying ethnonationalism is based on the belief that one's nationality is special and superior while others are secondary and inferior. It is generally argued that the resurgence of nationalism, which has led to internal political fragmentation and polarization, has been one of the forces behind change in the post–Cold War period.

Proponents' views of the ethnic-racial determinism of internal conflict are primarily based on the objective factors of nationalism, such as ethnic, linguistic, religious, cultural, and racial ones. But some argue that ethnicity is based on subjective belief rather than a necessary physical reality (Horowitz 1985; Yinger 1994). Whether objective or subjective, ethnic-racial determinists argue that distinctiveness of each of the diverse groups within a state is the very source of internal conflict.

Religious difference is also considered as a source of internal conflict. Advocates of religion as a factor for conflict argue that religious conflict spills over to the ethnic-racial conflict (Juergensmeyer 1993). Religious determinists argue that a system of belief provides religious believers with their main source of identity. This identification with and devotion to their own religion make them perceive that the values of their respective religion are superior to other religions or belief systems. This sense of superiority leads them to think that their religion should be universal. Thus, they actively engage in proselytizing to convert nonbelievers to their faith. The process of their efforts to proselytize could be either by peaceful means through persuasion or violent means through an extreme militant religious movement. When combined with political factors, these religious-political movements tend to view the existing government authority as corrupt, unfair, and illegitimate, all of which justify their militant and violent behaviors (Shultz and Olson 1994).

What has been emphasized by the religious proponents is that religious, rather than ethnic-racial, difference is the key factor of the civil wars and political violence. The religious determinism of internal conflict is distinguished from the previous ethnic-racial one in that the former is universalistic while the latter is parochial and exclusionist along the lines of ethnic-racial groups within a nation.

While dichotomy between the racial-ethnic and the religious-political determinism exists, there is an integrated view of the causes of internal conflict, undifferentiating between ethnic-racial, religious, and cultural factors. Cultural determinists explain the cause of internal conflict based on a broad concept of civilization. In their definition of civilization, cultural determinists hold catchall concepts in the sense that they incorporate virtually everything such as ethnic, racial, cultural, as well as religious sources of conflict.

Samuel Huntington (1993, 1996) argues that the conflicts of the future will occur along the cultural fault lines separating civilization.[1] He claims that the civilization fault lines can be observed in the contemporary international community, ranging from Bosnia in the former Yugoslavia to the Arab–Israeli conflict, to Tajikistan in Central Asia, Timor in Indonesia, the Philippines, etc. Civilizations, according to Huntington, are differentiated from each other by history, language, culture, tradition, and, most importantly, religion. Clearly the cultural determinism of conflict is more comprehensive than either ethnic-racial or religious determinism in explaining the causes of conflict. No attempt to conceptually differentiate between ethnic-racial and religious lines is made in cultural determinism.

Relative deprivation theory, which attempts to explain the causes of internal conflict, is based on psychological dimensions of the people in societies transitioning from underdeveloped to advanced in much of the developing world. The aspiration gap between the rising expectation (hopes) and actual level of satisfaction (realities) is particularly eminent in these transitional societies. The wider the aspiration gap, the more people suffer, which is regarded as one of the sources of frustration eventually leading to conflict (Gurr 1970; Lupsha 1971).

The relative deprivation theory, however, has the following difficulties in empirically verifying the relationship between the relative deprivation itself and the degree of internal conflict. First, the concept of relative deprivation is based on a psychological dimension of the people. Therefore, it is difficult to empirically verify the relationship between the psychological components of relative deprivation and the extent of internal conflict. Both the rising expectation and the level of satisfaction are subjective as well as psychological, making it difficult to operationalize them. These psychological variables are also subject to cross-national differences in culture, society, and tradition, adding further difficulty to the operationalization of the variables.

Thus the correlation between the different stages of development and the level of curves representing both rising expectations and satisfaction cannot be easily subject to an empirical verification. As a corollary, the amount of aspiration gap based on the difference between the rising expectation and the level of satisfaction cannot be easily subject to the empirical verification either. One caveat in this relationship is the so-called ecological fallacy. That is, if the level of economic development is based on GNP or GDP of the nation-state, the unit of analysis applies to be collectivities rather than individuals. When the relationships are estimated at one level of analysis (collectivities) and then extrapolated to another level (individuals), distortions are likely to result, which reveals the ecological fallacy (Robinson 1950). The relative deprivation is psychological, based on individuals as the unit of analysis.

The gap theory is also advanced by Simon Kuznets. The so-called Kuznets curve aims to explain the gap in income distribution between the traditional rural and advanced industrialized sectors during the early stages of modernization. Kuznets argues there is a connection between economic growth and war, indicating that rapid economic growth invites significant shifts of relative military power and such shifts may serve as the reason for frequent conflicts (Kuznets 1955, 1966).

Some argue that the gap between economic growth and quality of life serves as a source of internal conflict. It is generally argued that economic growth is not necessarily and positively correlated with the quality of life, although the economic growth itself will upgrade other broader indicators of living standards, such as literacy, health and nutrition, life expectancy, and infant mortality. Discrepancy between the economic growth and quality of life is generally considered more conspicuous in developing nations than in developed nations (Parente and Prescott 1993). The wider the gap, the more frequently the countries will experience internal conflict. Ethnic-racial heterogeneity, population growth, and excessive defense spending were found to be the detrimental factors in determining the quality of life level over per capita GNP level in developing nations, while these same variables were found to be insignificant or weak factors in the developed nations (Kim 1998).

In connection with the quality of life analysis of internal conflict, some argue that the amount of land area available for economic use contributes to internal strife. Many of the Third World countries still rely on same farming technology and the use of traditional nonlabor inputs such as simple tools, animal power, and traditional seeds. Given the principle of diminishing returns, as more and more people are forced to work on a given piece of land, their marginal (and average) productivity will decline. The net result is a continuous deterioration in real living standards for rural peasants (Weitz 1971; Todaro 1996), thus leading to an internal struggle for increased land area for economic use. Prolonged fighting destroyed crops and devastated agricultural areas, thus turning countries into ecological wastelands (Sivard 1993). This clearly shrinks the land area available to rural peasants, thus generating a vicious cycle between internal conflict and living standards for the rural peasants, which again prolongs internal conflict.

Power transition theorists argue that most of the internal crises and conflicts erupted when states were themselves locked in internal power transitions, usually characterized by new state formation, political revolution, or efforts to democratize autocratic regimes (Organski 1968; Wallace 1973; Vayrynen 1983; Levy 1987; Cederman 1994). It is based on rapid internal development, whether as a result of rapid social mobilization or of sharp advances in national economic development.

Polity categories of authoritarian, totalitarian, democratic-competitive were argued to have a significant effect on the frequency of internal conflict. Zinnes and Wilkenfeld (1971), in seventy-four states studied from 1955 to 1960, discovered that authoritarian states tended to have more than their share of internal conflict but their fair share of external conflict. Rummel (1983) also argues that libertarian regimes, in which he includes Western democracies with free-enterprise economies, were found to have less external conflict than totalitarian and authoritarian regimes.

Since the collapse of the Soviet Union, the legitimacy of the authoritarian regimes has been undermined. The world community has witnessed a growing democratization with the inception of the post–Cold War era, moving from authoritarian to democratic political systems. Clearly trends in contemporary political culture include, among others, democratization where weakening traditional sources of legitimacy devalues many alternatives to democracy. Citizens make claim to equal participation in policymaking. Although Huntington (1991) argues that a ''third wave'' of democratization began since 1974 in Southern Europe, East Asia, Latin America, and Eastern Europe; the wave of democratization has been particularly noticeable since the final years of the Cold War period.

Proliferation of arms and weapons, particularly shipped into many Third World countries, is thought to be a culprit for a great deal of the killings and repression (Tyler 1992). Weapons are used by all armed forces, government troops as well as insurgents and bandits. There are many reasons for arming, including regional rivalry, prestige, and maintenance of authoritarian or dictatorial regimes. It is argued that sophisticated arms and weapons have increased the death toll as well as the number of refugees (Sivard 1993).

Communication is thought to play an important role in reducing hostility. Communication theorists argue that communications among people can produce either amity or enmity. Depending on the extent to which the memories of communications are associated with more-or-less favorable emotions, people can be friendly or hostile. Deutsch (1964, 1968) argues that the building of political units depends on the flow of communication within the unit as well as between the unit and the outside world. He defines peoples as groups of persons joined together by an ability to communicate on many kinds of topics. Diverse peoples become integrated as they become interdependent. Lack of communication among the people leads to disintegration of the political community, thus serving as a source of conflict.

II. THEORY AND HYPOTHESES

The earlier theories and approaches reviewed have the following in common. They attempted to explain the cause of internal conflict primarily based on a single variable rather than a multivariate approach, where many variables, theoretically relevant, are employed to analyze the causes of internal conflict. Ethnic-racial determinism, for example, is solely based on ethnic-racial composition of a nation state, while economic, political, or even religious factors are ignored. This single approach, however, has an inherent weakness in that it cannot provide a pure effect of the single variable selected by each theory of internal conflict, since there are so many other variables which might cause internal conflict. None of the theories reviewed suggests that other variables were controlled for to isolate a pure effect of the single variable on internal conflict. None of the ethnic-racial, religious, cultural, relative deprivation, gap, power transition, political system, proliferation of arms, communication, or land use theories suggests that control variables were employed in the context of a multivariate analysis. This chapter employs a multivariate analysis (logistic regression) aiming to isolate a pure effect of each of the variables theoretically relevant to the cause of internal conflict.

In the light of growing democratization and increasing importance of quality of life issues, as featured at the beginning of the post–Cold War period, these two groups of variables are added to the existing variables presumed to be the causes of internal conflict. During the final years of the Cold War and the years of the post–Cold War era, many Third World countries have experienced a growing sense of individual equality and desire for citizen participation in the political process, serving as an engine for democratization. It is argued that internal power transition as represented by political change (democratization) and economic growth have a significant effect on the frequency of internal conflict and political violence.

Quality of life, based on improved living standards, education, life expectancy, as well as food and health, has become an increasingly important determinant of new trends in contemporary political cultures in the world community. One of the major features of the post–Cold War period, characterized by a low politics (unlike that of the Cold War period featuring a high politics), is the growing importance of quality of life issues in the world community. Countries with a high quality of life are less likely to suffer internal conflict than countries with a low quality of life. In order to isolate a pure effect of the quality of life variables on internal conflict, the effect of other variables needs to be controlled. It is hypothesized that the likelihood of internal conflict is affected by ethnic-racial heterogeneity, religious diversity, military spending, internal power transition (democratization and economic growth), as well as quality of life.

III. METHODOLOGY

Cross-sectional analyses based on both conflict-stricken and nonconflict-stricken countries (192 countries in all) are utilized.[2] The time span covered in the analysis is the 1987–1995 period, aiming to cover both the final years of the Cold War era and initial years of the post–Cold War period; the period 1987–1991 represents the Cold War period and 1991–1995 represents the post–Cold War era.[3]

The following four criteria were served as the basis for dichotomizing countries between conflict-stricken and nonconflict-stricken countries. Countries experiencing any of the following criteria were classified as conflict-stricken countries and the remaining as nonconflict-stricken ones:[4]

1. Civil war or internal conflict, as used here, are defined as conflicts involving ethnic, religious, and political violence causing the deaths of 1000 or more people during the period.
2. Forceful overthrows of government, attempted and unsuccessful.

3. Ethnic conflicts, religious conflicts, political and ideological conflicts, as well as conflicts involving warlords or druglords.
4. Riots and/or demonstrations.

Countries with internal conflict are coded as 1 and the remaining countries as 0. The variable is dichotomous and treated as a dependent variable. (See note 5 for a list of countries considered to have internal conflict.)

The following are treated as independent (explanatory) as well as control variables: ethnic homogeneity, religious diversity, quality of life variables (education, circulation of newspaper and TV, employment, and land use), defense spending, as well as democratization and economic growth. Each of the variables is hypothesized to have a significant effect on the likelihood of internal conflict. They are operationalized as follows:

Ethnic homogeneity is measured by percentage of the dominant ethnic group within each nation.

Religious diversity is measured by percentage of the dominant religious group within each nation.

Education, mass media (newspapers and TV), unemployment, and amount of land use, all of which are treated as quality of life variables, are operationalized as follows:

Education is measured by the literacy rate.

The mass media is measured by the circulation per 1000 population of daily newspapers and television by the number of receivers per 1000 population, representing print and electronic mass media, respectively.

Unemployment rate is based on the number of people previously employed and those seeking work for the first time.

Land use is based on arable land cultivated for crops that are replanted after each harvest. It is measured as percentage of arable land of the total land use, including permanent crops, meadows and pastures, forest and woodland, and others.

Defense spending is measured by the military expenditures as percentage of GDP.

Economic growth is measured by the difference in GNP per capita between the years 1987–1991 and 1991–1995, respectively.

Democratization, which reflects a degree of political change, is measured by the transformation made during the 1987–1991 and 1991–1995 period, respectively, from a single-party, authoritarian (totalitarian or military) political regime to a multiparty, competitive political regime. Polity categories are based on the following three different types of political systems: authoritarian, democratic-competitive, and mixed. The authoritarian political system includes military and totalitarian systems where no competitive-multiparty system is allowed; they are coded as 1. The democratic-competitive political system is characterized by a multiparty system where free electoral competition is allowed; they are coded as 3. Many of the countries locating between these two types of political system have been categorized as a mixed political system and coded as 2. Thus the Democratization Index (DI) ranges from 2 to -2, where 2 means countries moving toward a competitive-democratic political system, while -2 means moving from a competitive-democratic to an authoritarian political system. And 0 means no change during the specified period.

Since the dependent variable is dichotomous internal conflict vs. noninternal conflict countries, logistic regression analysis is conducted. This analysis will regress the dichotomous dependent variable on a series of independent variables enumerated above. The logistic regression analysis will estimate the probability that internal conflict occurs or not. In order to identify subsets of independent variables that are good predictors of the dependent variables, backward selection was conducted. The backward selection starts with all independent variables in the equation and sequentially removes them until good predictors of the dependent variable are identified.[6]

Table 1 indicates the difference in the means between conflict and nonconflict countries of the socioeconomic, military, and quality of life variables. The most glaring differences shown are from democratization and economic growth as well as from the quality of life variables (unemployment, circulation of newspaper, TV, and literacy rate). Conflict countries were documented as undergoing a higher rate of political change (democratization) than nonconflict countries, from authoritarian to democratic political systems. They also experienced a low economic growth as well as poor quality of life, i.e., a higher rate of unemployment and lower extent of mass communication. Ethnic diversity data show conflict countries were more heterogeneous (62.09%) than nonconflict countries (76.97%). But the two groups of countries were found to have no significant difference in religious diversity, conflict countries being 74.45% and nonconflict countries 75.24%. The two groups also showed no significant difference in defense spending or in the amount of land use.

IV. RESULTS

Table 2 presents the logistic model analysis of the likelihood of internal conflict and political violence. Columns give coefficient estimates and the Waldo statistic

Table 1 Difference in the Means of Socioeconomic, Quality of Life, and Defense Spending Variables Between Conflict and Nonconflict-Stricken Countries (1994–1995)

	Conflict countries		Nonconflict countries	
		(N[f])		(N[f])
Ethnic homogeneity (%)	62.09	(82)	76.97	(105)**
Religious diversity (%)	74.45	(83)	75.24	(106)
Democratization (1991–1995)[a]	.69	(83)	.15	(93)*
Unemployment (%)	17.79	(73)	10.84	(100)*
Newspaper circulation[b]	54.08	(79)	182.72	(85)*
TV[c]	204.41	(77)	18.76	(60)**
Economic growth (1991–1995) ($)	84.84	(83)	443.73	(100)**
Literacy rate (%)	61.54	(82)	85.20	(88)*
Defense spending (%)[d]	3.97	(80)	3.18	(84)
Land use (%)[e]	14.72	(83)	15.87	(104)

* Significant at .001; **significant at .05, based on two-tailed test for independent samples. Levene's test is first used for equal or unequal population variance, requiring pooled variance test and separate variance test, respectively, which the significance level ascertained above followed.

[a] Based on Democratization Index (DI), which ranges from −2 to 2; 2 means countries becoming liberal-democratic, 0 no change; and −2 change from liberal-democratic to authoritarian regime during the 1991–1995 period.

[b] Circulation per 1000 population.

[c] Receivers per 1000 population.

[d] Military expenditures as percentage of GDP.

[e] Percent arable land of the total land.

[f] Total number of countries under each category.

Source: Sivard 1993, 1996; *The World Factbook* 1992, 1997; *Britannica Book of the Year* 1995, 1996, 1997.

(coefficient/standard error)[2] corresponding to the independent variables with their level of significance.[7]

Ethnic homogeneity, religious diversity, democratization, unemployment, and circulation of newspapers were found to have a significant effect on the likelihood of internal conflict with the beginning of the post–Cold War era, while these same variables had no significant effects on the likelihood of internal conflict during the Cold War era.

Military spending had a significant effect on the likelihood of internal conflict during the Cold War era, while it no longer exerted a significant effect with the beginning of the post–Cold War period. This finding suggests that the post–Cold War period featured peace, rather than the tension of the Cold War, dimin-

Table 2 Logistic Regression: Internal Conflict

	1991–1995[a]			1987–1991[b]		
	b	Waldo	Sig	b	Waldo	Sig
Explanatory variable						
Ethnic homogeneity	−.023	4.94	.026	−.024	5.36	.021
Religious diversity	.019	2.74	.097	—	—	—
Democratization	.756	6.32	.012	—	—	—
Unemployment	.042	3.89	.049	—	—	—
Newspaper circulation	−.005	7.46	.006	−.013	15.40	.000
Military spending	—	—	—	.109	2.96	.085
Constant	−.044	.00	.967	2.195	8.54	.004
	−2LL (model chi square, 5 df)			−2LL (model chi square, 2 df)		
	47.875 (Sig .000)			51.863 (Sig .000)		
N	133			121		
Percent correctly classified	77.44			74.38		

Variables not in the equation

	(residual chi square 3.782 with 5 df, Sig = .5813)		(residual chi square 7.313 with 7 df, Sig = .3970)	
Variable	Score	Sig	Score	Sig
Democratization	—	—	1.351	.245
Religious diversity	—	—	1.242	.265
Economic growth	.000	.993	1.158	.282
Unemployment	—	—	1.384	.240
Mass media/TV	1.000	.317	.320	.572
Land use	.310	.578	.505	.478
Military spending	1.416	.234	—	—
Education	1.926	.165	.227	.132

[a] Both democratization and economic growth cover the 1991–1995 period, while the other variables are based on the years 1994–1995.
[b] Both democratization and economic growth cover the 1987–1991 period, while the other variables are based on the years 1990–1991.
Source: Sivard 1993, 1996; *The World Factbook* 1992, 1997; *Britannica Book of the Year* 1995, 1996, 1997.

ishing the importance of a defense priority in the international community. Previous levels of military spending, measured by the amount of military expenditures as a percentage of GDP, may have been justified by the internal conflict for security or defense-related reasons.

Democratization, notably experienced in many of the Third World countries with the beginning of the post–Cold War era, was found to have a significant effect on internal conflict regardless of economic growth, ethnic and religious diversity, quality of life (mass media, employment, education, and land use), or military spending. The finding suggests that countries experiencing a political change toward democracy document a higher frequency of internal conflict and political violence than countries that are not. Democratization, however, was found to have no significant effect on the likelihood of internal conflict during the Cold War period.

In contrast with democratization, economic growth was found to have no significant effect on internal conflict in either of the Cold War or post–Cold War period. Under any condition of political change, quality of life, or military spending, no significant and independent effect of economic growth was found to correlate with the likelihood of internal conflict, indicating that economic growth itself high or low, cannot be blamed for internal conflict and political violence. It is a political rather than an economic change that triggers internal instability and conflict.

The amount of land use based on arable land had no significant effect on the likelihood of internal conflict. Availability of the land for economic use, which was assumed to affect the living standards for rural peasants, was found to have no significant effect on internal conflict and political violence. Under any condition of ethnic or religious diversity, political change, or even under any condition of economic growth, no significant effect of the amount of land area available for economic use, whether large or small, was found to correlate with internal conflict and political violence. It is assumed that prolonged internal fighting destroyed land area for economic use, leading to a shrinkage of land area available to rural peasants. This generates a vicious cycle between internal conflict and living standards for rural peasants, which again prolongs internal conflict. But the vicious cycle between internal conflict and land area for economic uses is not supported by the findings, indicating that there is no such significant effect of the amount of land use on the likelihood of internal conflict.

The level of education, high or low, was found to have no significant independent effect on the likelihood of internal conflict under any circumstances of political and economic change, ethnic and religious diversity, mass media, or military spending.

Ethnic homogeneity, regardless of religious diversity, was found to have a significant effect on the likelihood of internal conflict, indicating that ethnically homogeneous countries are less vulnerable to internal conflict than ethnically heterogeneous ones. It is generally argued that an increase in internal conflict as notably manifested with the beginning of the post–Cold War era is primarily due to an ethnic-racial reason as contrasted with the Cold War era, during which period ethnic conflict was generally unprofiled in the world community. The finding, however, indicates that there is no such difference between these two periods in terms of the significant effect of ethnic-racial diversity on the likelihood of internal conflict. Regardless of the Cold War or post–Cold War period, ethnic-racial factors were found to have a significant and persistent effect on internal conflict.

Religious diversity was found to have a significant and independent effect on the odds of internal conflict regardless of ethnic heterogeneity or homogeneity. Countries with a high degree of religious majority by one dominant religious group were found to experience a higher, rather than a lower, frequency of internal conflict than countries with a more diverse make-up of minority denominational and/or religious groups. Unlike ethnic homogeneity, whose effect is to lessen the odds of internal conflict, countries with religious homogeneity, based on a dominant religious group, are more likely to experience a higher frequency of internal conflict than countries with diverse and heterogeneous religious groups, under any circumstances of ethnic-racial composition. Countries with a religious dominance by one religious group were found to be more vulnerable to internal conflict than countries with religious diversity. The Cold War era, however, had no such independent and significant effect on the degree religious majority or minority had on the likelihood of internal conflict. The religious variable emerges as a significant determinant of the likelihood of internal conflict with the beginning of the post–Cold War period along with democratization and unemployment.

Two components of the quality of life, circulation of newspaper (mass media) and employment, were found to have significant effects on internal conflict. The wider the circulation of newspapers, the less conflict the countries were likely to experience. But the findings on the effect on mass media were rather mixed. The visual quality of television, thought to be capable of conveying the emotional impact by pictures, was found to exert no significant effect on the likelihood of internal conflict. The finding holds regardless of political change, economic growth, quality of life, as well as ethnic and religious diversity. The print, not the electronic, mass media turns out to have a significant and persistent effect on the odds of internal conflict regardless of Cold War or post–Cold War period.

Unemployment was found to have a significant effect on internal conflict, indicating that countries suffering a high unemployment rate were more likely to experience internal conflict than not, regardless of economic growth and political change, ethnic and religious diversity, availability of mass media, and level of education. Unemployment, however, emerges as a significant determinant of the likelihood of internal conflict with the beginning of the post–Cold War era, while it remained an insignificant determinant during the Cold War era.

The findings suggest that in the post–Cold War period, unlike the Cold War period, the effects of political change as manifested by democratization, religion, as well as quality of life variables (circulation of newspaper and employment) play a significant and independent role on the likelihood of internal conflict and political violence.

Another significant difference between these two periods involves the effect of military spending, as briefly indicated previously. Regardless of economic growth, quality of life, and even regardless of political change during the Cold War era, countries spending a high percentage of GDP for military expenditures, indicating a high degree of defense priority, were found to experience more frequent internal conflict than other countries. As far as the Cold War period is concerned, the finding supports a long-held assumption that sophisticated arms and weapons, as purchased or developed by military expenditures, increased the death toll as well as the number of refugees. But the results suggest that this is no longer as tenable with the beginning of the post–Cold War period.

Under any conditions of quality of life and economic growth, each of which is generally assumed to have trade-offs with defense spending, no significant and independent effect was found for defense spending on the likelihood of internal conflict with the beginning of the post–Cold War era.

V. CONCLUSION

One of the major features in this analysis is that democratization shown during the post–Cold War period had a very significant independent effect on the likelihood of internal conflict, regardless of ethnic homogeneity, religious diversity, economic growth, or quality of life, and even regardless of defense spending. Politics clearly plays a very important role in determining the likelihood of internal instability leading to political violence and internal conflict.

Economic growth, particularly in the Third World, was generally considered to be a potential for internal conflict and social instability since it generates a gap between economic growth itself and quality of life, as well as a gap between the rich and poor. These two gaps were assumed to trigger internal conflict. Under any conditions of ethnic and religious diversity, political change (democratization), or quality of life, however, no such significant effect of economic growth was found to affect the likelihood of internal conflict. Political change, rather than economic growth, was found to be a significant determinant of the likelihood of internal conflict.

The insignificant effect of economic growth, rapid or slow, calls into question the idea of relative deprivation, argued to be experienced by the transitional societies of the developing nations when they are exposed to rapid economic growth in the process of modernization, leading ultimately to internal conflict. A wider exposure to the outside world through an ever-increasing role of mass media, particularly TV, in many parts of the developing (transitional) societies was assumed to reinforce the concept of relative deprivation generated among the have-nots, resulting in a source of social unrest and internal conflict.

Both economic growth and TV (mass media), however, were found to have no such significant effects on the odds of internal conflict under any conditions of ethnic heterogeneity, religious diversity, or political change, regardless of whether during the Cold War or post–Cold War period. Economic growth is not a culprit for internal conflict, suggesting that no significant effect of the gap between economic growth and quality of life, or the gap between haves and have-nots, was found on the likelihood of internal conflict.

Regardless of ethnic homogeneity or heterogeneity, religious diversity was found to have significant independent effect on the odds of internal conflict, suggesting that a conceptual distinction between the ethnic and the religious components of internal conflict need to be made in the conflict analysis. That is, ethnic-racial components of the internal conflict are different from religious ones. It is suggested that phrases such as ethnic-religious or ethnic and religious conflict, so widely used in the conflict literature, which make no conceptual differentiation between the ethnic and the religious components of internal conflict, need to be revised into either a singular ethnic or a singular religious conflict in the conflict analysis.

The effect of mass media, such as the circulation of newspapers, remains a persistent and significant determinant of the likelihood of internal conflict across the Cold War and the post–Cold War periods. Both economic security based on employment and opportunity to access information in print mass media were found to have positive effects on reducing instability and conflict within nations. Ethnically heterogeneous or not, countries capable of solving unemployment problems are less likely to experience internal conflict than countries not under any conditions of political or economic change.

The major difference in the determinants of internal conflict between the Cold War and post–Cold War periods comes from effects of democratization, religion, and quality of life variables, all of which emerge as significant determinants of the likelihood of internal conflict with the beginning of the post–Cold War period, while they were not significant during the Cold War era. Defense priority, significant at the end of the Cold War era, no longer emerges as a significant determinant with the inception of the post–Cold War period. The insignificant effect of economic growth during both the Cold War and post–Cold War periods calls into question the validity of the gap between haves and have-nots or relative deprivation (each argued to be generated from the process of a rapid economic growth) being determinant of internal conflict.

Internal conflict is either ethnic or religious rather than ethnic-religious, political rather than economic, and psychological as caused by economic insecurity and social alienation arising from unemployment and lack of mass media, respectively. Regardless of ethnic or religious diversity, countries with a rapid political change toward democracy but still with a low quality of life were found to be vulnerable to internal conflict at the beginning of the post–Cold War period. Particularly vulnerable are those countries undergoing a rapid political change toward democracy that are yet incapable of solving problems of unemployment, which causes economic insecurity and starvation, and that are incapable of penetrating society with effective political communication based on mass media.

NOTES

1. The major contemporary civilizations as classified by Samuel Huntington are as follows: Sinic, Japanese. Hindu, Islamic, Western, Latin American, and African (possibly).
2. The selection of 192 countries was based on the following criteria:

   a. All of the countries in the world community are included except the following: All of the dependent areas belonging to Australia (6), Denmark (2), France (16), Netherlands (2), New Zealand (3), Norway (3), Portugal (1), and the United Kingdom (15), except Hong Kong—still classified as one of the dependent areas of United Kingdom during the period covered under study, the United States (14), and 6 miscellaneous regions: Antarctica, the Gaza Strip, Paracel Islands, Spratly Islands, the West Bank, and the Western Sahara.
   b. Taiwan was included.
   c. Yemen covers the 1993–1995 period.
   d. (Former) Yugoslavia, the Soviet Union, and Czechoslovakia were all excluded from the entire 1987–1995 period under study in order to keep the consistency of data: Bosnia, Herzegovina, and Slovenia, once belonging to Yugoslavia, cover only the 1993–1995 period; countries such as Armenia, Azerbaijan, Kazakhstan, Russia, Tajikistan, and Ukraine, once belonging to the Soviet Union, cover only the 1992–1995 period.

3. Although the year dividing between the Cold War and the post–Cold War periods is somewhat controversial, 1991 was selected. The former Soviet Union was not yet officially dissolved as of December 1991, when the Minsk Agreement and the subsequent Alma-Ata Declaration enabled them to create the Commonwealth of Independent States (CIS).
4. Countries classified as conflict-stricken ones during the 1990–1995 period are based on information from *World Military and Social Expenditures* (Washington, DC:

World Priorities, 1993 and 1996, respectively) and *Political Development* by Monte Palmer (Itasca, IL: F. E. Peacock Publishers, Inc., 1997), 106–107.

Each of those countries listed as conflict-stricken is based on the 1990–1995 period. Throughout the period, the countries were experiencing any or all of the four types of conflict as specified.

5. Afghanistan, Algeria, Angola, Azerbaijan, Bangladesh, Bosnia and Herzegovina, Burkina Faso, Burundi, Cambodia, Cameroon, Chad, Colombia, Comoro, Congo, Cote d'Ivoire, Croatia, Djibouti, Egypt, El Salvador, Eritrea, Ethiopia, Gambia, Georgia, Ghana, Guatemala, Guinea-Bissau, Haiti, India, Indonesia, Iran, Iraq, Israel, Kenya, Laos, Latvia, Lebanon, Lesotho, Liberia, Libya, Lithuania, Madagascar, Malawi, Mali, Mauritania, Mexico, Moldova, Morocco, Mozambique, Myanmar (Burma), Nicaragua, Niger, Nigeria, Pakistan, Panama, Papua, Peru, Philippines, Qatar, Russia, Rwanda, São Tomé and Príncipe, Senegal, Sierra Leone, Slovania, Somalia, South Africa, Spain, Sri Lanka, Sudan, Suriname, Tajikistan, Thailand, Togo, Trinidad and Tobago, Tunisia, Turkey, Uganda, Venezuela, Vietnam, Yemen, Zaire, Zambia, Zimbabwe

6. I have tried both backward- and forward-selection procedures, and the outcome was same. Since many independent variables were hypothesized to be the determinants of the likelihood of internal conflict in the analysis, I prefer to utilize the backward-selection method, which starts all variables in the equation first and sequentially removes them until good predictors are selected.

7. The Waldo statistic (coefficient/standard error)^2 and the significance level for the Waldo statistic are presented in Table 2. When the absolute value of the regression coefficient becomes large, the estimated standard error is also large, producing a Waldo statistic too small, which leads to a failure to reject the null hypothesis that the coefficient is 0. Whenever there is a large coefficient, the Waldo statistic should not be utilized for hypothesis testing. The table, however, shows no such problem.

REFERENCES

Brecher, M., Wilenfeld, J., and Moser, S. (1988). *Crises in the Twentieth Century: Handbook of International Crises*, 171–201. Oxford: Pergamon Press.

Britannica Book of the Year: 1990. Chicago: Encyclopedia Britannica.

Britannica Book of the Year: 1992. Chicago: Encyclopedia Birtannica.

Britannica Book of the Year: 1995. Chicago: Encyclopedia Britannica.

Britannica Book of the Year: 1996. Chicago: Encyclopedia Britannica.

Britannica Book of the Year: 1997. Chicago: Encyclopedia Britannica.

Cederman, L.-E. (1994). Emergent polarity: Analyzing state-formation and power politics. *International Studies Quarterly*, December, 501–533.

Deutsch, K. W. (1964). *The Nerves of Government*, 77. New York: Free Press.

Deutsch, K. W. The impact of communications upon international relations theory. In A. Said (ed.), *Theory of International Relations: The Crisis of Relevance*, 75–90. Englewood Cliff: Prentice-Hall.

Garment, D. (1993). The international dimensions of ethnic conflict. *Journal of Peace Research 30*, May, 137–150.

Gottlieb, G. (1994). Nations without states. *Foreign Affairs*, May–June, 100–112.

Gurr, T. R. (1970). *Why Men Rebel*. Princeton: Princeton University Press.

Gurr, T. R. (1994). People against states: Ethnopolitical conflict and the changing world system. *International Studies Quarterly*, September, 347–377.

Gurr, T. R. (1995). Communal conflicts and global security. *Current History 94*, May, 212–217.

Horowitz, D. (1985). *Ethnic Groups in Conflict*, 52–53. Berkeley: University of California Press.

Huntington, S. P. (1993). The clash of civilizations? *Foreign Affairs*, *72*, Summer, 22–49.

Huntington, S. P. (1996). *The Clash of Civilizations and The Remaking of World Order*, 19–39, New York: Simon and Schuster.

Jones, W. S. (1997). *The Logic of International Relations*, 244–251. New York: Longman.

Juergensmeyer, M. (1993). *The Cold War: Religious Nationalism Confronts the Secular State*. Berkeley: University of California.

Kegley, C. W., Jr., and Wittkopf, E. R. (1997). *World Politics: Trend and Transformation*, 181–186. New York: St. Martin Press.

Kim, H. S. (1998). An analysis of the gap between growth and quality of life in the third world. *National Social Science Journal 10*, No. 2, 84–90.

Kuznets, S. (1955). Economic growth and income equality. *American Economic Review 45*, 1–28.

Kuznets, S. (1966). *Modern Economic Growth: Rate, Structure, and Spread*. New Haven: Yale University Press.

Levy, J. S. (1987). Declining power and the preventive motivation for war. *World Politics*, October, 82–107.

Lupsha, P. A. (1971). Explanation of political violence: Some psychological theories versus indignation. *Politics and Society*, *2*, Fall.

Maynes, C. W. (1993). Containing ethnic conflict. *Foreign Policy*, Spring, 3–21.

Norusis, M. J. (1990). *SPSS*, B39–61. Chicago: SPSS Inc.

Palmer, M. (1997). *Political Development: Dilemmas and Challenges*, 106–107, Itasca, IL: F. E. Peacock Publishers, Inc.

Parente, S. L. and Prescott, E. C. (1993). Changes in the wealth of nations. *Quarterly Review*. Federal Reserve Bank of Minneapolis, Spring, 3–16.

Robinson, W. S. (1950). Ecological correlations and the behavior of individuals. *American Sociological Review 15*, 351–357.

Rummel, R. (1983). Libertarianism and international violence. *Journal of Conflict Resolution 27*, March, 27–71.

Shultz, R. H., Jr., and Olson, W. J. (1994). *Ethnic and Religious Conflict: Emerging Threat to U.S. Security*. Washington, D.C.: National Strategy Information Center.

Sivard, R. L. (1993). *World Military and Social Expenditures*, 22. Washington, DC: World Priorities.

Sivard, R. L. (1996). *World Military and Social Expenditures*. Washington, DC: World Priorities.

Todaro, M. P. (1996). *Economic Development*, 303. New York: Longman.

Tyler, P. E. (1992). ''Pentagon imagines new enemies to fight in post–Cold War era.'' *The Washington Post*, February 17.

Vayrynen, R. (1983). Economic Cycle. Power transitions, political management and wars between major nations. *International Studies Quarterly*, December, 389–418.

Wallace, M. D. (1973). *War and Rank Among Nations*. Lexington, Mass.: D.C. Heath.

Weitz, R. (1971). *From Peasant to Farmer: A Revolutionary Strategy for Development*, 6–9. New York: Columbia University Press.

The World Factbook 1992. Washington: Brassey's.

The World Factbook 1996–97. Washington: Brassey's.

The World Factbook 1997–98. Washington: Brassey's.

Yinger, J. M. (1994). *Ethnicity*. Albany, NY: State University Press.

Zinnes, D. A. and Wilkenfeld, J. (1971). An analysis of foreign conflict behavior of nations. In W. F. Handieder (ed.), *Comparative Foreign Policy*, 167–213. New York: McKay.

4

Religion

For or Against Democracy?

Mira Marody
University of Warsaw, Warsaw, Poland

The question whether religion is for or against democracy might seem ridiculous and the answer self-evident. Since religion and democracy are focussed on such different domains of human life, there are no reasons for religion to define its standpoint toward democracy. From this perspective religion is neither for nor against democracy, it simply deals with issues completely different from those that are crucial for the latter. On the other hand, if we compare basic principles underlying these two concepts, the question becomes relevant since for religion such a principle is conformity, whereas democracy implies diversity. In this sense every religion is, almost by definition, undemocratic.

Yet, every religion is not only a set of dogmas and norms, but has its institutional and personal aspect, too. There are churches, some of them very powerful, whose institutional activities—irrespective of whether they have a strictly religious or more mundane character—can influence political processes or be a part of them. And there are people whose religion is an important element of their social identities, and thus their beliefs influence, either directly or indirectly, their political options and actions. These two aspects—institutional and personal—will be taken into consideration when discussing relations between religion and democracy.

Being concerned with the institutional aspect, one cannot omit the diagnosis formulated by Samuel P. Huntington in his well-known book *The Third Wave* (1991). Analyzing the processes of democratization that took place in the 1970s and 1980s around the world, he points to the crucial role played by the Catholic Church. ''[T]he striking changes in the doctrine and activities of the Catholic Church manifested in the Second Vatican Council in 1963-1965 and the transformation of the national churches from defenders of the status quo to opponents of authoritarianism and proponents of social, economic, and political reform" (1991:45) are mentioned as one of the five possible independent variables that explain the phenomenon of the third wave of democratization.

The general hypothesis formulated by Huntington is even more categorical since it asserts an equation between the proliferation of Christianity and the development of democracy (1991:72). The crucial argument supporting the hypothesis is the case of South Korea, where the transition to democracy occurred in 1987 and was preceded by the "transition to Christianity" of one-quarter of its population, mainly young people who were newcomers to the emerging urban middle class. Contrary to the passive Buddhism and authoritarian Confucianism, Christianity offered them a better emotional and institutional base for their adjustment to the changing economic and social conditions. On the one hand, it was focussed on individual vocation and stressed the idea of equality, and, on the other, many of the leading personalities of the opposition movement in South Korea were Christians. The churches and cathedrals were the public place where both faith and opposition against the authoritarian state could be expressed.

However, the case of Poland is more significant since it illustrates very well Huntington's statement that although there is a correlation between Christianity and democracy, the crucial factor for the third wave of democratization was not Christianity itself, but a fundamental change in the activities of the Catholic Church. Poland was always a country with a huge majority of Catholics. And yet, the mass opposition against the communist regime did not exist there until the end of seventies. It cannot be said that under the communist system the Catholic Church supported the status quo in Poland. Nevertheless, it would also be false to describe it as an opponent of authoritarianism. Rather, during most of the post-war period its activity was limited to strictly religious issues as it aimed at preserving the relative independence from the communist state, which tried to eliminate or at least seriously restrict the influence of the Church in order to gain total control over the minds of its citizens.

All this has changed with the development of the "Solidarity" movement. Before its emergence in 1980, Polish Cardinal Karol Wojtyła was elected Pope in 1978 and made his first pilgrimage to Poland in June 1979. The political importance of this visit, as many authors stress, was connected with two facts. First, during the numerous meetings with the Pope, people could not only confess their religious faith in public, but also experience the feeling of unity based on values different from those officially propagated, thereby destroying the ideological monopoly of the communist ideology. Second, public religious meetings gave people an opportunity to "count" one another and learn what a huge power they were and that they were able to organize themselves outside of institutions totally controlled by political authorities.

After the Pope's first visit, the Polish Catholic Church became actively involved in opposition against the communist regime. During the 1980 strikes,

Catholic priests blessed Solidarity banners and said masses before Solidarity debates. After December 1981, when martial law was imposed in Poland, the Church provided opposition activists with institutional infrastructure, interested more in their safety and continuity of their fight rather than in their Catholic orthodoxy. At the end of the 1980s, the Church participated in the "Round Table" talks as a moderator and guarantor of the negotiations between the communist authorities and opposition leaders.

In other Catholic countries, the process of "transformation" of national churches into institutions actively engaged in the fight for democracy started even earlier, in the 1970s. I will not repeat here Huntington's arguments that support the thesis. Rather, I would like to briefly discuss the question he deliberately omits in his work, commenting in a footnote that it goes beyond the scope of the book. The question is *why* and *in what way* did all these significant changes occur in the Catholic Church. I find this question particularly important. Without analyzing the mechanisms of the change, we are unable to say anything about the conditions on which this newly established relation between Catholicism and democracy depends, and, therefore, we cannot be sure of its stability and scope.

Such knowledge is also important because, according to some catholic writers (Gowin 1995), there is an irremediable tension between the Catholic Church and democracy. The tension is based not only on the structural difference between the authoritarian order of the Church and democratic order of many contemporary societies, but is also rooted in a deep discrepancy between the very principle of democracy and the Catholic understanding of the state. As Gowin writes: "The Church has accepted the state to a degree to which the latter has modeled its policies after the natural law order of values derived from Revelation" (1995: 66). Hence, according to him, the basic dilemma for a Catholic living in a democratic state becomes a tension between the truth and freedom.

I will return in a moment to the last statement, which is strictly connected with the personal aspect of religion. On the institutional level, as Gowin admits, the Catholic Church long declared itself for truth rather than for freedom. This was the view until the Second Vatican Council, which accepted democracy not only because of the political realism, but also—or even above all—as the type of political order that respects human dignity to the highest degree. This re-evaluation of democracy was based on a change of attitude toward the mentioned dilemma: truth or freedom. The Encyclical *Dignitatis Humanae* solved the dilemma assuming that "although the value of truth cannot be compared with the value of error, the dignity of a man basing himself on error is the same as dignity of a man living in truth" (Gowin 1995:69).

One can say, therefore, that the transformation of the Catholic Church from a defender of the status quo to an opponent of authoritarianism was based on a significant shift in the hierarchy of its fundamental values: the place of the metaphysical God's truth was taken over by the worldly interest of the individual.

Although this formulation may be shocking to a Catholic, it is aimed at highlighting the more general change in value systems, which occurred around the Western world in the 1960s. It drew on economic, technological, and sociopolitical changes that had been transforming the cultures of advanced industrial societies and brought, inter alia, a shift toward individual autonomy after a century of movement toward increasing central authority. According to Ronald Inglehart, "Whereas previous generations were relatively willing to make trade-offs that sacrificed individual autonomy for the sake of economic and physical security, the publics of advanced industrial society are increasingly likely to take this kind of security for granted—and to accord a high priority to self-expression both in their work and in political life" (1990:11).

This change did not omit religion in its personal aspect, too. The most prominent sociologists of religion agree that the religiosity of contemporary Western societies was shaped by two basic processes involved in the more general process of modernization (Wilson 1987, Berger 1967, Luckmann 1967). The first of them was the process of secularization with its sources in the functional differentiation of public life accompanied by the liberation of its particular domains from the institutional and axiological domination of religion. It has not only reduced the position of religion, but has also changed fundamentally the rules underlying social behavior, promoting the transition from a value-oriented rationality to a task-oriented one. The second was the process of individualization taking place in all spheres of people's lives. Its consequence for the individual religiosity was a retreat from institutionalized orthodoxy toward more selective and more "privatized" religious belief systems.

In other words, the analyzed change of relation between the Catholic Church and democracy reflects, and is based on, deeper changes in Western culture, changes that have their roots in modernization processes. By modernization, I mean (following Berger et al. 1977) a historical process "by which the entity 'modern society' was originally created and by which it continues to be diffused" (1977:15). Important parts of modernization processes were secularization and individualization of religion. Secularization has driven religion out of the public sphere and placed it in the private one, whereas individualization of religious beliefs has "undermined the taken-for-granted status of religious meanings in individual consciousness. In the absence of consistent and general social confirmation, religious definitions of reality have lost their quality of certainty, and instead, have become matters of choice" (1977:77).

I said earlier on, quoting Jarosław Gowin, that for a Catholic living under a democratic regime the basic dilemma is a tension between truth and freedom. For many Catholics, however, this tension simply does not exist, because the truth became the matter of choice, too. Or, more precisely, in the modernized and therefore pluralized society, every life-world has its own truth that is worked out in democratic negotiations between individual and institutionalized actors.

Under such circumstances, the role of the Church is seen as being reduced to the assistance in solving spiritual and moral dilemmas of the individual. The public sphere "has come more and more dominated by civic creeds and ideologies with only vague religious content or sometimes no such content at all" (Berger et al. 1977:76).

Even in Poland, where about 95% of the population declare themselves Catholic, only 19.4% of the respondents accept the involvement of the Church into politics.* Most Poles regard the authority of the Catholic Church as unquestionable, but only in the private sphere and mainly in connection with nonbehavioral problems. The political union of the Catholic Church and the society, which we witnessed in the 1980s during the fight against communism, ceased to exist after the introduction of democratic order. The Catholic Church more and more often has become an object of criticisms, triggered by its visible attempts to influence the shape of public life in Poland.

However, there are also groups of Catholics who do not want to reduce the influence of the Church to the private sphere and who ascribe to it certain public duties and responsibilities. Actually, taking into account these groups, one can now speak about two completely opposite visions of the Catholic Church in Poland and its potential role in public life. The first is maintained by the group of so-called open Catholics and is closest to the standpoint formulated by the Second Vatican Council. "Theologically, it is based on the conception of open and dynamic orthodoxy which is approximating the truth of God's Revelation through its continuous re-interpretation and deeper understanding in the perspective of the 'signs of time' " (Gowin 1995:241). Its supporters are convinced about the value of cultural plurality and recognize an ecumenism and dialogue with nonbelievers as the fundamental duty of the Church. Socially, they represent an intellectual elite of Polish Catholicism and were deeply involved in the democratic opposition against communism in the 1980s.

The introduction of democratic and market-oriented order was not, however, for all the Catholics in Poland, the end of the Church's ordeal experienced under communism. In the opinion of some of them, the new developments have only opened a subsequent stage of the fight against the Catholic identity of the Polish nation. According to this vision, a democratic-liberal order is simply another form of totalitarianism aimed at the destruction of Christianity. Therefore, the fundamental duty of the Catholic Church in Poland should be to condemn modern civilization and build an alternative one based on truly Christian values. One can find elements of this vision both in public announcements of clergymen

---

* Data from the European Value System Study, 1990. For France, the most secularized European country, the percentage is 14.9, whereas for Ireland it is 34.5 (Marody 1996).

from various rungs of the Church's hierarchy and in the opinions of ordinary Catholics.

The influence of this fraction on the identity of the Polish Church is significant, much more significant than the influence of the open Catholics. It is noteworthy that the vision of "Church militants" finds its support in some formulations being used in the Pope's encyclicals. As Gowin points out, the most important social encyclical of John Paul II, *Centesimus Annus*, which positively accepts democracy and condemns any temptation of using authoritarian means on behalf of truth, also contains important reservations about the former. It warns against the possible degeneration of democracy that stems from forgetting about values and leads to the "explicit or implicit totalitarism." According to it, "the true democracy is possible only . . . if based on the proper conception of the human person" (quoted in Gowin 1995:70. The clash between natural law and the majority law defines the limits of acceptance of democratic principle.

From the sociological perspective, the kind of fundamentalism present in the Polish vision of the Church militant is not anything specific. Actually, what we can now observe around the world is a revival of religious fundamentalisms, with the Islamic version as the most powerful and influential. According to Samuel Huntington's more recent paper (1993), they are one of the most important factors hidden behind the development of civilizational identities and increasing the probability of future clashes between religiously defined civilizations. Although he does not refer in that paper to his earlier book (1991), the thesis implicitly leads to the conclusion that in the future we should expect a decline in the present wave of democratization.

The political aspect of religious fundamentalisms is also stressed by Bassam Tibi (1995), according to whom fundamentalism reflects political ideology rather than any revival of religiosity. It does not mean that fundamentalists cynically use the religion for achieving political goals. Rather, they are faithful fighters on God's behalf who want to erase a border between religion and politics, between *sacrum* and *profanum*, between religious and political institutions. Politicization of religion goes hand in hand with sacralization of politics for them, and their goal is not simply a religious renewal but a foundation of a new, better political order based on principles opposed to democratic ones.

Whereas Huntington stresses the significance of globalization processes in the development of religiously defined civilizations, Tibi ascribes the basic importance to the fact that fundamentalists draw a distinct border between their imagined communities of *us* and other groups of people who do not believe or believe in a wrong way in God. Both authors, however, agree that the contemporary fundamentalism represents a revolt against modern Western civilization, which is based on democratic order and a cultural plurality that leads to uprooting the individuals from their local identities.

Let us dwell for a moment on this latter issue. As a consequence of secularization processes transforming contemporary religiosity, the "privatization" of religion has had an important effect on its social and psychological functions. As Peter Berger states: "Through most of empirically available human history, religion has played a vital role in providing the overarching canopy of symbols for the meaningful integration of society. The various meanings, values and beliefs operative in a society were ultimately 'held together' in a comprehensive interpretation of reality that related human life to the cosmos as a whole" (Berger et al. 1977:75). Due to the secularization processes, this age-old function of religion has been severely limited in the modern world, leaving individuals "homeless" not only in the society in which they are incessantly changing their social milieus, but also in the universe, since "[m]odern society has threatened the plausibility of religious theodicies, but it has not removed the experiences that call for them" (1977:166), the experiences of suffering and evil.

From a sociopsychological perspective, religious fundamentalism can, therefore, be interpreted as one of the responses to the homelessness of the modern mind. It provides individuals with a clear answer to the old question about whom to blame for all the suffering and evil in the world: *them*. Defining "them" as agents of Western civilization is only a logical consequence of the historical processes of modernization, which started in the Western countries and brought about both democracy and the homelessness. In the political dimension fundamentalists are fighting against democracy based on an individual freedom which deprives many people of certainty regarding social norms and meanings. And in the sociopsychological one, they want to build a new home, a community of believers who share the same life-world.

The blueprint for this new home is not a return to the past. Although oriented against modernity and referring very often to tradition, fundamentalists are not traditionalists (Tibi 1995). They do not fight against the technical and scientific achievements of modern civilization; on the contrary, they want to utilize them for the development of a new or renewed civilization shaped in accordance with religious principles, be it the Christian natural law or Muslim *szari'at*. In this sense fundamentalism resembles communism, another form of the "escape from freedom" that promised modernity and community, development and security. The experience of communism teaches that it is feasible to establish a political regime on such promises, but that it is impossible to keep those promises.

Analyzed from a sociopsychological perspective, the clash between religiously defined civilizations is, hence, a clash inside broadly defined modern civilization or, in other words, a clash between the need for security (not only economic and physical) and the need for freedom (which is also a freedom for "them"). Contemporary man cannot avoid it, since the homelessness of the modern mind is not produced only by cultural plurality, but by the very process of pluralization of individual life-worlds, intrinsic to modernity, not to mention post-modernity. But the individual can believe that religion offers not only a psychological but also a political solution to that problem. The future relation between religion and democracy may depend, therefore, on the number of people who will hold to such a belief.

REFERENCES

Berger, P. (1967). *The Sacred Canopy*. Garden City, NY: Doubleday.
Berger, P., Berger, B., and Kellner, H. (1977). *The Homeless Mind: Modernization and Consciousness*. Harmondsworth: Penguin Books.
Gowin, J. (1995). *Kościół po komuniźmie* [The Catholic Church after Communism]. Kraków: Społeczny Instytut Wydawniczy Znak and Warszawa: Fundacja im.Stefana Batorego.
Huntington, S. P. (1991). *The Third Wave: Democratization in the Late Twentieth Century*. Norman and London: University of Oklahoma Press.
Huntington, S. P. (1993). The clash of civilizations? *Foreign Affairs 72*, No. 3, 22–49.
Inglehart, R. (1990). *Cultural Shift in Advanced Industrial Society*. Princeton, NJ: Princeton University Press.
Luckmann, T. (1967). *The Invisible Religion*. New York: Macmillan.
Marody, M. (1996). Selektywnie religijni. In: M. Marody (ed.). *Oswajanie rzeczywistooeci. Miêdzy realnym socjalizmem a realn demokracj* [Taming the Emerging Reality. Between Real Socialism and Real Democracy]. Warszawa: ISS UW.
Tibi, B. (1995). *Der Religiose Fundamentalismus im Übergang zum 21: Jahrhundert*. Mannheim: Bibliographisches Institut & F. A. Brockhaus AG [quotations after Polish edition: Tibi, B. (1997). *Fundamentalizm Religijny*. Warszawa: PIW].
Wilson, B. (1987). *Religion in Sociological Perspective*. Oxford and New York: Oxford University Press.

5

Recasting Foreign Policy Analysis Using a Gender Analysis

Where to Begin?

Deborah Stienstra
University of Winnipeg, Winnipeg, Manitoba, Canada

Feminist analysis is beginning to find a toehold in the discipline of international relations. After many struggles to find voice and create cogent interventions into international relations, there is a legitimacy to undertaking gender analysis in research, teaching, and scholarship that has not been present in the past. While there is an increasingly substantial body of literature in the area of feminist theory and gender studies in international relations, one major indication of the growing prominence is the recent article on gender analysis published in *International Organization* (Murphy 1996). Yet feminist theory and gender analyses remain a ''poor cousin'' to the key approaches within international relations, and in some areas they remain invisible. Nowhere is this more true than in the area of foreign policy analysis. This paper is one attempt to come to grips with these silences. My comments are framed around a series of questions that reflect some of the key concerns: Why is foreign policy analysis so resistant to the incorporation of gender? What would it take to incorporate gender in the analysis of foreign policy? To what extent can or should gender analysis attempt to be policy-relevant? I argue that the primary approaches to foreign policy analysis stem from problem-solving theory, and that prevents them from addressing gender in any significant way. To incorporate gender in foreign policy analysis, critical or interpretative theory is needed.

I. WHY IS FOREIGN POLICY ANALYSIS SO RESISTANT TO THE INCORPORATION OF GENDER?

As Stanley Hoffman noted twenty years ago, over the past century foreign policy has become more "democratic" with the shift from foreign policy as "the calculations of the few to the passions of the many, both because more states joined in the game that had been the preserve of a small number of (mainly European) actors and (mainly extra-European) stakes, and above all because within many states parties and interest established links or pushed claims across national borders" (Hoffman 1977:43). This "democratization" reflected a shift in the class of those who practiced foreign policy as well as a shift in which powers dominate the world system. Yet "democracy" in foreign policy does not yet reach into the domain of gender. Both the practice of foreign policy and its analysis remain dominated by masculine approaches and remain resistant to the inclusion of gendered policies and analysis. To explore why foreign policy analysis is so resistant, we need to consider the purpose of foreign policy analysis, its tools, and its parameters.

While realism provided the foundation for much of international relations, many of the founding fathers, including Morgenthau, failed to focus on the study of foreign policy. Rather, they saw their work as bringing a realist framework for foreign policy action. This question of whether the work of scholars is to prescribe foreign policy action, advise foreign policy–makers, or critically reflect on the context, processes, and results of foreign policy remains an important one.

In part, the question is one posed by Robert W. Cox (1986) when he argues that there are two different, and equally valid, purposes for theory. Problem-solving theory "takes the world as it finds it, with the prevailing social and power relationships and the institutions into which they are organized, as the given framework for action. The general aim of problem-solving theory is to make these relationships and institutions work smoothly by dealing effectively with particular sources of trouble" (Cox 1986:208). Those who use problem-solving theory as their framework are more likely to focus on particular areas or issues of concern and may be able to determine a number of discrete variables to examine in detail. From this they may wish to or try to develop theories which seem to be generally valid within the parameters. By accepting the parameters of the existing system, problem-solving theory has a stake in the maintenance of the system and is a status quo or, in Cox's words, conservative theoretical approach. In many ways, problem-solving theory is like a frozen frame of a movie film. By examining the one frame in detail, analysts hope to be able to generalize about the entire film. Critical theory, on the other hand, attempts to reflect upon the existing world order and its institutions, and asks how they came to be, for what purposes, and in what ways are they changing. Critical theory seeks to understand the whole array of relationships and institutions at work. While it may begin at a particular juncture, it does not limit itself to that juncture. Analysts see the system in the continual process of change and try to explore what directs or influences the changes. By remaining apart from the existing system, critical theorists have the opportunity to reflect on how to address substantial change within the system itself. Critical theory is like exploring the entire film and its genre, trying to examine how they fit together and can be changed.

Most foreign policy analysts use the problem-solving approach. They take the existing system of foreign policy–making for granted. The role of analyst is to explain how policies have been made and how the organization or decision-making processes could be strengthened. Pre-eminent journals in the field, like *Foreign Policy*, have used their forum to provide commentary on foreign policy decisions and directions and give advice on where to proceed. There is also a fluidity between those who make foreign policy and those who analyze it. A number of significant foreign policy analysts, like Joseph Nye in the United States and former Prime Minister Joe Clark in Canada, have moved from the side of decision-maker to analyst or vice versa.

Within the foreign policy analysis framework, however, there is some criticism that analysts fail to provide sufficiently strong advice to governments, yet the solutions proposed continue to rely upon a problem-solving approach. Zelikow (1994) argues that academics fail to understand the language and frameworks within which policymakers work. They ask different questions from those required by policymakers. The analysts seek to "identify a problem, specify alternatives, evaluate them according to some explicit criteria, select the best one and implement the decision." (Zelikow 1994:155). Yet policymaking, he argues, is more than the recognition of the problem or the political processes that determine how the choices are made. It is also about what he calls policy engineering or "the application of knowledge, principles and methods (including both policy analysis and institutional analysis) to the solution of specific public policy problems" (Zelikow 1994:144). While this critique provides a useful reflection on some of the problems related to policy-related analysis, it fails to identify the inherent acceptance of the status quo in most foreign policy analysis.

Foreign policy analysis has also been dominated over the past 50 years by the direction of thought taken in the United States and by analyses of US foreign policy. Hoffman (1977) makes this argument in relation to the general field of international relations (IR) in the 1970s; Cox (1986) reiterates it in the 1980s. Cox suggests that there are two commonalities which lend IR to being an "American" field: "(1) the perspective of the United States as the preponderant of the two major powers in the system and consequently the sharing of certain measure of responsibility for U.S. policy, and (2) the organization of argument around certain obligatory debates, notably those of power versus morality and of science versus tradition" (Cox 1986:240). I would argue, even further than Cox, that approaches to foreign policy have been dominated by US thought primarily because foreign policy analysts who use problem-solving approaches fail to examine the parameters of the foreign policy system. (By lumping all foreign policy analysts together in one camp, I can be accused of oversimplifying the differences between different people. I recognize that there are variations within the problem-solving approach to foreign policy, but these differences appear to be less significant to me than the differences between those who use a problem-solving approach and those who explore foreign policy from a critical theory perspective.) They accept that the United States has been and continues to be one of the or the primary super-powers, and thus its foreign policy is the most significant in the existing world order. But they also assume the ways we understand US policy, or in some cases industrialized countries, offer a model for exploring other countries' foreign policies. This ethnocentrism pervades the foreign policy literature. For example, in Macridis's (1989) standard compilation on comparative foreign policy, we see discussion of the foreign policies of major power states and some regions (Europe, the Middle East, Latin America, and Scandinavia). This text fails to justify why Scandinavia is more important for foreign policy study than the entire continent of Africa. It is even evident in the title of McGlen and Sarkees's (1993) book, *Women in Foreign Policy: The Insiders*, which suggests a broad review of foreign policy and women but really is about US foreign policy.

Gender has remained primarily invisible in current foreign policy analyses. (I am relying primarily on analyses of Canadian and US foreign policy for this point and can be rightly accused of ethnocentrism as a result of this. I cannot generalize beyond these two examples, but see little evidence in the theoretical approaches to foreign policy that gender has been incorporated in any other jurisdictions.) Given the implicit acceptance of the existing system by most foreign policy analysts, it is clear that either the states have to begin to address gender in their foreign policy or the tools of analysis need to be changed to incorporate gender. Across the globe, however, few states have addressed gender in any sustained way in their foreign policies. The only area where there has been significant work on incorporating women in foreign policy decisions is development assistance. Work has been done since the early 1970s to include women in development policies, although as Rathgerber (1990) notes, their initial inclusion was primarily based upon stereotypical assumptions of their role in societies, and more recent attempts have failed to recognize the gendered power relations that underpin societies. Human rights policies, including access by refugees on the grounds of their gender, are becoming more sensitive to gender, although the monitoring and implementation of these policies is still primarily done through the machinery for the advancement of women rather than the foreign policy establishment. Most other areas of foreign policy have said little if anything about gender.

In general, foreign policy analysis addresses how and under what conditions specific foreign policies are made. Yet this seemingly unified approach belies some very different tools of research. Some argue for using the state as rational actor approach, suggested in more traditional realist approaches (Krasner 1978). Others, reacting to the uncomplicated understanding of bureaucracy found in the early foreign policy literature, have argued for the use of bureaucratic politics (Allison 1971; Allison and Halperin 1972), focussing on the organizational structures and processes within bureaucracies. Others have dissected the decision-making processes, whether they be in crisis or normal (Janis and Mann 1971; Snyder and Diesing 1977; Stein and Tanter 1980). Some have used psychology to analyze rationality and cognitive abilities (Falkowski 1979). Still others have focussed on societal constraints, whether found at the domestic or international level (Katzenstein 1978; Gourevitch 1978). An increasing number of foreign policy analysts have sought to provide a multifactoral approach to explaining foreign policy (Hermann et al. 1987). Throughout these areas of foreign policy analysis is one common thread: the acceptance of the realm of foreign policy as it appears to be.

In each of these areas of foreign policy, we can ask the question (although very few have), ''Where are the women and men in practice of foreign policy?'' This approach, often called feminist empiricism, argues that we can correct the gender disparities in research by recognizing the failure to include women in much academic research. See Harding (1986) for a general discussion of the constraints of feminist empiricism. Sandra Whitworth (1994) includes a general analysis of the application of feminist empiricism, which she calls the ''feminine'' perspective, to international relations. This methodological error can be corrected by including women in already-existing research programs or projects. Thus, our task would be to examine where women are or are not present and provide some explanation for their absence or presence. Most of the work done from this approach has focussed on women's activities, arguing that what is standard history is an account of men's activities. This approach is most important when women's presence in decision-making processes has been ignored, or when their absences have failed to cause note. But this approach often assumes that the biological differences between women and men will necessarily lead to different policy practices or approaches. By linking biology to policy actions, some presume that biology can explain different approaches between male and female policymakers, and ignore or minimize differences among women or men on the basis of class, race, ethnicity, ability, or sexual orientation. However, this approach fails to provide an answer for why the policies of Margaret Thatcher or Indira Gandhi have differed so little from their predecessors. Without reference to the social construction of gender, rather than simply the biological differences of sex, we are unable to explore how gender affects foreign policy. The distinction between sex and gender is somewhat overstated, since it is not easy to separate what is biological from what is socially constructed. The point is that it is important to place our analysis in the context of that which is socially constructed.

I should be quick to note that not all feminist empiricists fall into the pitfall of analysis on the basis of biological difference, nor do they all assume that differences among women and men are insignificant. Rather, as Spike Peterson notes, " 'adding women' to existing frameworks exposes taken-for-granted assumptions embedded in those frameworks" (Peterson 1992:8). When we examine where women have been included or excluded, recognizing that this is the result of unequal power relations within societies that systematically value what is masculine and undervalue what is feminine, we are able to identify the gendered basis of foreign policy and the alternatives many women have created. When we "add women" into traditional foreign policy analyses, we raise questions that are not considered in the existing literature. For example, if we ask, "Where are the women?" in the context of decision-making analysis we are forced to note their historical under-representation in the bureaucracy and public office. In the Canadian Department of External Affairs, in 1994, only 14 ambassadors or high commissioners of a total of 104 are women, and recruitment of women into the foreign service continues to be well below their representation in the Canadian population, although recruitment of women surpassed 40% between 1991 and 1994. (Canada 1995:8). If we were to concentrate on these women, we could explore the lives and activities of a small number of elite women. In the US context, McGlen and Sarkees (1993) outline some of the obstacles women face when they enter the US foreign policy establishment, and argue that at present their gender may make a difference, but that an "androgynous" management style will diminish these obstacles over time. Cracpol (1992) has outlined how women both inside and outside the foreign policy elite have affected (or not) US foreign policy development and practice. Weiers chronicles the lives of 22 women who were part of the Canadian foreign service, asserting that these women have been "influencing, developing, shaping, and implementing Canadian foreign policy at home and abroad" (Weiers 1995:9). These explorations tell us something about the individuals involved and some of the obstacles they face, but little explicitly about the gender relations at work in foreign policy.

When we ask, "Where are the women and the men?" we also note that women most often participate in foreign policy as "outsiders," as representatives of nongovernmental organizations or the attentive public. Women's groups have been recognized in some foreign policy analyses as part of "society" that affects foreign policy. (In the Canadian context, see Nossal 1989:103 and Matthews and Pratt 1988.) Whitworth (1995) suggests that in at least one example in Canadian foreign policy development, this role is much more complex than it initially appears to be. She argues that when the Canadian government undertook a foreign policy review exercise, as a means of "democratizing" its foreign policy, the women's groups involved brought forward their ideas, but these were ignored in the final report. Whitworth explains that there were very different understandings of foreign policy at work:

women's organizations make explicit the gendered nature of particular foreign policies, while the Special Joint Committee Report opts for gender neu-
trality; women's groups see a clear relationship between trade agreements,
the promotion of manufactured exports and the working conditions of women
who are locked in to factories and risk death, while the Report acknowledges
no such connections; women's groups explain the relationship between gender equity in UN staffing and civil societies while the Report simply names
gender equity as something to be considered; and so on. (Whitworth 1995:
94.)

This example suggests that women's groups have little effect on the development
of foreign policy if we understand foreign policy in the ways suggested by problem-solving theory. Yet it also illustrates that if we explore from a critical theory
perspective, we may understand more about the forces at work in the determination and development of foreign policy.

II. CAN GENDER BE INCORPORATED IN FOREIGN POLICY ANALYSIS? IF SO, HOW?

Those who have used problem-solving approaches in foreign policy and incorporated women have illustrated that it is possible to explore where women have
participated in foreign policy–making and some of the ways in which their participation has been structured out of the process. Yet, as discussed above, these
approaches fail to deal in any sustained way with the construction of gender
relations and its relation to foreign policy. For that we need to turn to the even
smaller and more recent literature of critical foreign policy studies.

In general, those within this approach argue that the state and its foreign
policies are not fixed or static; they have been constructed within the context of
a broader world order. Neufeld (1995) suggests that one important way to understand Canadian support for international institutions and their role in peacekeeping is to see these as a means to support the hegemonic order maintained by the
United States in the existing world order. Cox (1989) makes a similar argument
about the role of middle powers supporting the rules and practices of a hegemonic
order more generally.

Critical foreign policy also rejects the dichotomies often suggested by problem-solving analysts between domestic and international levels and between the
state and society. Rather, critical theorists argue that all contribute to the development and change within foreign policy and need to be considered. Campbell
(1992) argues that scholars need to locate foreign policy and the role of the state
more historically, for in so doing we will be able to resolve these dichotomies.
He traces the roots of our current Westphalian system and the particular role of
the state as providing security to a much earlier time when the state replaced the

role of the church and provided a ''new theology of truth about who and what 'we' are by highlighting who and what ''we'' are not and what ''we'' have to fear'' (Campbell 1992:54). Peterson (1992) provides a gendered historicization of states using similar arguments highlighting the construction of the state as protector. Foreign policy for Campbell includes all the practices or ways of differentiating and excluding others and gives meaning to these differences. While Campbell suggests that identity, both of individuals and of states, is constituted through differences, not all critical theorists accept this argument. Krishna argues convincingly that while this approach provides a wonderful antidote to the ahistorical problem-solving theory, it fails to provide the basis for political action. ''It is precisely the greatest victims of the West's essentialist conceits (the excolonials and neocolonials, Blacks, women and so forth) that are articulating a need for new strategic essentialism'' (Krishna 1993:405).

To use critical theory as a means of addressing gender in foreign policy we must recognize that the tools are somewhat different than in problem-solving theory. Critical theory uses interpretive method. Rather than looking for the ''natural laws'' in the social world, critical theorists recognize that the world is not limited to regularities in the natural or social world around us; it is also the meanings we give the world around us. ''[H]uman beings live in a world of cultural meaning which has its source in their own interpretations of that world; human beings act in the context of a 'web of meaning'—a web that they themselves have spun. As a consequence, the social world—in contrast to the natural world—'is itself partly constituted by self-interpretation' '' (Neufeld 1993:43). Thus to examine the world we must look for the meanings or interpretations of the world and how they are evident in human practices. Interpretation or meaning is not simply individuals' meanings or the sum of individuals' meanings; it is also collective meanings or the meanings of communities, often called intersubjective meaning. The role of researchers is not simply to interpret knowledge, we must also study the differing interpretations of the world around us.

Charles Taylor suggests this interpretive method leads to a ''hermeneutic circle'' in which social scientists seek to make sense of the world

> ''by demonstrating that 'there is a coherence between the actions of an agent and the meaning of the situation for him [sic].' 'Making sense' of the social world, then involves a process of 'testing' the adequacy of a proffered 'reading', that is (1) of the 'web of meaning' in terms of the concrete social practices in which it is embedded, and (2) of the 'coherence' of observed social practices in terms of the 'web of meaning' which constitutes those practices. As a consequence, the interpretation of a given 'web of meaning'/social practice can never be tested against an objective standard. Rather, the testing and refinement of particular interpretations is always done in terms of other interpretations. It is never possible to escape the 'hermeneutic circle' '' (as quoted in Neufeld 1993:47–48).

Exploring gender in the context of critical foreign policy thus entails looking historically at the development of world orders and the place of particular
states within those world orders and asking to what extent states and world orders
have been or are perpetuating unequal gender relations within their own countries,
through their actions towards other countries or in their practices in international
institutions. We need to ask how gender has shaped our language of and about
foreign policy; our foreign policy practices and the institutions of foreign policy;
as well as how these institutions, practices, and ideas restrict or perpetuate certain
gender assumptions. We need to consider how gendered assumptions and practices have reinforced or challenged other unequal power relations, such as those
based on ''race,'' colonialism, sexual orientation, or disability. (See Stienstra
1994–1995:118–126 for some general analysis of how this analysis could be
undertaken in relation to Canadian foreign policy.)

Let me give one brief example in the Canadian context. It is unusual for
foreign policy to include the issue of foreign domestic workers within Canada—
they would be considered under employment or child care policies (domestic
policies). In 1992, the Canadian federal government introduced a Live-In Care-
giver Program, which provides entrance for foreign domestic workers who have
the equivalent of a Grade 12 education, at least six months full-time training in
a related field, and live in their employer's home. (For further discussion of this
program, see Stienstra and Roberts 1995. See also *Domestics' Cross-Cultural
News* December 1992, September 1992, and May 1992.) In 1993, 1789 workers
entered Canada under this program, with over 57% from the Philippines
(CACSW 1994:71). This policy created different regulations for the admission
of foreign domestic workers, almost exclusively women from the Philippines and
the Caribbean, than for other immigrants. Other immigrants enter as permanent
residents, but the domestic workers receive only temporary work permits, even
though this is a very high-demand occupation. When they apply for permanent
status (which they can do after two years), the Department of Immigration assesses only their child-care responsibilities, not their housework. As a result,
many are unable to accumulate sufficient points to qualify as permanent residents.
In addition to the differential treatment these women receive, they also fail to
receive protection from sexual harassment or abuse from their employers; are
often subject to extreme work demands because they live with their employers;
and in most parts of Canada are unable to unionize or receive compensation for
lost wages and their contracts with employers are not monitored. The foreign
policies related to domestic workers support and perpetuate the unequal relations
between women and men as well as among women. Women who can afford to
hire these workers in Canada are primarily elite, usually white, women with jobs
in government, law, business or universities, and they receive the convenience
of child care in their homes, during the times they want and at wages they can
set (Enloe 1989:151–194). Yet the women who provide the child care, primarily

women of color from economically poorer regions of the world or white working class women, remain unprotected as workers and receive low wages. The program that allows them entry into Canada prevents or precludes them from equal treatment with other immigrants and reinforces class and race differences between the women who are employers and those who are workers.

Campbell suggests that we also consider the ways in which our identities, as individuals, collectivities, states, and world orders, have been gendered as a result of our practices of exclusion and creation of difference or otherness. This question encourages us not only to look at the constitution of meaning, but at how our identities or subjectivities are constructed. Campbell suggests, as many postmodern authors do, that there can be no one transcendent truth or complex of identities. Our job as scholars in this approach is to illuminate the construction and maintenance of these. The example of foreign policy related to domestic workers is an excellent example of how the ''other'' is constructed around class and ''racial'' lines. It also illustrates how we use the term ''foreign'' to create and maintain a sense of fear about the ''other'' in our societies. The policies that have been put into place to address ''foreign'' domestic workers create and maintain disparities between and among women and reinforce gender disparities.

Yet as many critics have argued, the move to historicize subjectivities and step away from essentialism has led many postmodernists to an inability to act politically. As noted earlier, this is just the point Krishna raises with respect to postmodern international relations. Drawing on the work of Gayatri Spivak, Krishna (1993:403) calls for the ''strategic use of positivist essentialism in a scrupulously visible political interest.'' ''The point is not to choose, in some final sense, where one stands (what else is the vacuous and ahistorical question for an 'authentic' self-identity?) but rather, paraphrasing Said, to be an informed skeptic, a secular wet blanket, even as one actively participates in the efforts to change reality in desired directions.'' (Krishna 1993:406) This, then, raises the final question of this paper. To what extent, if any, should gender analysis be ''policy relevant''?

III. COMPLETING THE CIRCLE: SHOULD/CAN GENDER ANALYSIS BE "POLICY RELEVANT"?

I began this paper by considering some of the reasons why problem-solving foreign policy analysis was unable and unwilling to include gender analysis, arguing that it accepted the world as it found it and saw as one of its purposes to be policy relevant. Some may argue that the framework for incorporating gender that I have sketched here rejects this goal, and to some degree they would be accurate. When we accept the political system without recognizing how and why it was historically constituted, our engagement with the system must be as those within it dictate. Our interventions then are related to the state's foreign policy, how it can be improved or changed either from the standpoint of giving policy advice or lobbying for specific changes from the "outside." When we analyze the structure and functioning of foreign policy, we are left with the varieties of analysis that are suggested above—looking at the components on the inside and the external factors that also affect policymaking. In the case of domestic workers, we would not even be able to call for policy action in this area because it is not considered by those within the state as foreign policy. Working from a problem-solving approach tells us one version of the stories of foreign policy, but this version is incomplete.

Critical theory offers a different interpretation of interventions in the policy process. First, it recognizes that specific policies can be shaped by much broader contexts than most foreign policy analysts would accept. Thus any intervention in the policy process will have to engage with the whole context or as much of it as possible. Also, critical theory challenges the positivist notion accepted by most traditional international relations scholars that researchers can be objective, neutral observers. Rather, critical theorists argue that researchers are part of the existing order, and therefore their work affects that order, and they must be aware of these effects. This then has repercussions for the type of research that critical theorists undertake and the methods they use. It also calls on researchers to be engaged in political work for emancipation. The critical analysis that we provide of how and why foreign policies have developed can be used to identify where there are opportunities or constraints for addressing specific policies or bringing about change. Indeed, some have argued that critical theorists are responsible for providing "a guide for strategic action" (Hoffman 1987:238) and identifying the potential for alternative world orders. In addressing how and why gender shapes foreign policies, we are also addressing the actions of states and nonstate actors. We are highlighting areas where further action can be taken and exploring why some actions have been ineffective. The example of "foreign" domestic workers illustrates how researchers can help to put issues like this on the policy table and support those who are working against these restrictions in their fight. Researchers can illustrate the forces at work based in class, race, colonialism, and gender. Interventions related to foreign policy can take place in many ways and do not have to be limited to the formal policy process, including providing support to the organizing efforts of domestic workers. This type of political activism and its basis in critical theory in relation to foreign policy is essential to the work of feminists and feminist theorists, and it is in this way that we can work together to bring about changes in our existing order.

REFERENCES

Allison, G. T. (1971). *Essence of Decision: Explaining the Cuban Missile Crisis*. Boston: Little, Brown.

Allison, G. T. and Halperin, M. H. (1972). Bureaucratic politics: A paradigm and some policy implications. *World Politics 24*, supp. (Spring), 40–79.

Campbell, D. (1992). *Writing Security: United States Foreign Policy and the Politics of Identity*. Minneapolis: University of Minnesota Press.

Canada. (1995). *Canada's National Report to the United Nations for the Fourth World Conference on Women*. Ottawa: Government of Canada.

Canadian Advisory Committee on the Status of Women (CACSW). (1994). *Work in Progress: Tracking Women's Equality in Canada*. Ottawa: CACSW.

Cox, R. W. (1986). Social forces, states and world orders: Beyond international relations theory. In R. O. Keohane (ed.), *Neorealism and Its Critics*. New York: Columbia University Press.

Cox, R. W. (1989). Middlepowermanship, Japan and future world order. *International Journal 44* (Autumn), 823–862.

Cracpol, E. P. (1992). *Women and American Foreign Policy: Lobbyists, Critics and Insiders, Second Edition*. Wilmington, DE: SR Books.

Enloe, C. (1989). *Bananas, Beaches and Bases: Making Feminist Sense of International Politics*. London: Pandora.

Falkowski, L. (1979). *Psychological Models in International Politics*, Boulder, CO: Westview Press.

Gourevitch, P. (1978). The second image reversed: The international sources of domestic politics. *International Organization 32* (Autumn), 881–912.

Harding, S. (1986). *The Science Question in Feminism*. Ithaca, NY: Cornell University Press.

Hermann, C. F., Kegley, C. W. and Rosenau, J. N. (1987). *New Directions in the Study of Foreign Policy*. Boston: Allen and Unwin.

Hoffman, S. (1977). An American social science: International relations. *Daedalus* (Summer), 41–60.

Hoffman, M. (1987). Critical theory and the inter-paradigm debate. *Millennium 16*(2), 231–249.

Janis, I. L. and Mann, L. (1971). *Decision-Making: A Psychological Analysis of Conflict, Choice and Commitment*. New York: Free Press.

Katzenstein, P. (1978). *Between Power and Plenty*. Madison: University of Wisconsin Press.

Krasner, S. D. (1978). *Defending the National Interest*. Princeton: Princeton University Press.

Krishna, S. (1993). The importance of being ironic: A postcolonial view on critical international relations theory. *Alternatives 18* (Spring), 385–417.

Macridis, R. C. (1989). (ed.), *Foreign Policy in World Politics: States and Regions*. Englewood Cliffs, NJ:Prentice Hall.

Matthews, R. O. and Pratt, C. (1998). (eds.), *Human Rights in Canadian Foreign Policy*. Kingston: McGill-Queen's University Press.

McGlen, N. E. and Sarkees, M. R. (1993). *Women in Foreign Policy: The Insiders*. New York: Routledge.

Murphy, C. N. (1996). Seeing women, recognizing gender, recasting international relations. *International Organization 50*(3) (Summer 1996), 513–538.

Neufeld, M. (1993). Interpretation and the "science" of international relations. *Review of International Studies 19* (Jan.), 39–61.

Neufeld, M. (1995). Hegemony and foreign policy analysis: The case of canada as middle power. *Studies in Political Economy 48* (Autumn), 7–29.

Neufeld, M. and Whitworth, S. (1997). Imag(in)ing Canadian foreign policy. In W. Clement (ed.), *Understanding Canada: Building on the New Canadian Political Economy*. Montreal and Kingston: McGill-Queen's University Press.

Nossal, K. R. (1989). *The Politics of Canadian Foreign Policy, Second Edition*. Scarborough, ON: Prentice-Hall.

Peterson, V. S. (1992). (ed.), *Gendered States: Feminist (Re)Visions of International Relations Theory*. Boulder, CO: Lynne Rienner.

Rathgerber, E. M. (1990). WID, WAD and GAD: Trends in research and practice. *Journal of Developing Areas 24*(4) (July), 489–502.

Snyder, G. H. and Diesing, P. (1977). *Conflict Among Nations*. Princeton: Princeton University Press.

Stein, J. and Tanter, R. (1980). *Rational Decision-Making: Israel's Security Choices*. Columbus: Ohio State University Press.

Stienstra, D. (1994–1995). Can the silence be broken? Gender and Canadian foreign policy. *International Journal 50* (Winter), 103–127.

Stienstra, D. and Roberts, B. (1995). *Strategies for the Year 2000: A Woman's Handbook*. Halifax: Fernwood Publishers.

Weiers, M. K. (1995). *Envoys Extraordinary: Women of the Canadian Foreign Service*. Toronto: Dundurn Press.

Whitworth, S. (1994). *Feminism and International Relations*. London: Macmillan.

Whitworth, S. (1995). Women, and gender, in the foreign policy review process. In M. A. Campbell and M. A. Molot (eds.), *Democracy and Foreign Policy: Canada Among Nations 1995*. Ottawa: Carleton University Press.

Zelikow, P. (1994). Foreign policy engineering: From theory to practice and back again. *International Security 18*(4) (Spring), 143–171.

6

Political Rights, Electoral Systems, and the Legislative Representation of Women in 73 Democracies

A Preliminary Analysis

Wilma Rule
University of Nevada, Reno, Nevada

> Achieving the goal of equal participation of women and men in decision-making will provide a balance that more accurately reflects the composition of society, and is needed in order to strengthen democracy and promote its proper functioning.
>
> [Governments pledge to] review the differential impact of electoral systems on the political representation of women in elected bodies and consider, where appropriate, the adjustment or reform of those systems. (From United Nations 1995.)

At the United Nations' Fourth World Conference on Women a commitment to achieve women's equal representation in parliament and other governmental bodies was made by unanimous vote on September 15, 1995. One-hundred eighty-eight nations and the Holy See participated in the conference held in Beijing, China. The delegates not only pledged to seek equality in governmental decision-making for women, but also specified in their *Plan of Action* how nations might achieve it. Methods included governmental review of electoral systems and adjustment or reform of them, and positive/affirmative action by political parties to nominate and elect women.

The delegates expressed rights of women which were previously largely unacknowledged: not only the right to participate in government by voting, but the significant rights to be represented and to be elected equally with men. Following up on the United Nations' "Universal Declaration of Human Rights," which specifies that every citizen has the right to participate in government, the Beijing conference adopted this statement: "Women's rights are human rights." Therefore, women are entitled—as a matter of simple justice and democracy— the delegates stated, to all the political rights now afforded men.

This paper examines the extent to which women's political rights approximate the equality goals expressed at the 1995 Beijing conference and the effect that electoral systems, governments, and political parties have in advancing or retarding efforts toward that ideal. Analysis of women's election to parliament as related to electoral systems follows. The relationship of electoral systems to positive/affirmative action and its utilization in long-standing democracies and partial and developing ones is the final subject of inquiry.

I. WOMEN'S PARLIAMENTARY REPRESENTATION

Worldwide the representation of women in single or lower national legislatures in 1997—including authoritarian, democratizing, and long-standing democratic countries—was 11.6% (Inter-Parliamentary Union 1997:83). The range was from 0% in Comoros, Djbouti, Kiribati, Micronesia, Palau, Papua New Guinea, and Tonga to 40.4% in Sweden. The range was scarcely different from six years earlier, although women's proportions in the democratic and democratizing parliaments are higher (Inter-Parliamentary Union 1991, 1997).

In order to analyze the factors that explain this range in women's representation, the author previously classified 114 parliamentary countries into three groups: long-standing democracies, recently developed democracies or partially developed democracies, and nondemocratic countries. Democratic criteria noted by Lijphart (1984:2–3) and civil liberties data from numerous sources, including *Electoral Studies* articles, were consulted (see Rule 1994a:29). Although future studies will no doubt result in refined classifications, the author's present one is useful here to compare with earlier research findings.

A. Proportional Representation and Women's Election in the Long-Standing Democracies

Proportional representation (PR) has been repeatedly documented as the most significant factor among contextual variables explaining women's election to parliament in the long-standing democratic countries (Rule 1981, 1987, 1994a; Norris 1985, 1997).

Tables 1 and 2 show the results of the author's three previous studies. The primary importance of the electoral system is shown in Table 1, while it is indirectly but positively related to the findings in Table 2. In the latter, electoral

Table 1 Most Powerful Predictors of Recruitment of Women Parliament Members, 1982: Multiple Stepwise Regression ($N = 23$)

Independent variables	Multiple correlation coefficient (R)	Cumulative percent of variance explained (R^2)	Percent variance explained by each variable
Party list/PR system of elections	.53	28	28
Percent women economically active	.73	34	26
Percent women college graduates	.82	67	13
Percent unemployed[a]	.87	76	9
Percent right M.P.s[a]	.89	80	4
Percent Catholic (logged)[a]	.91[b]	82	2

[a] The zero order correlation of this variable is negative.
[b] Significant at less than the .01 level when corrected for degrees of freedom.
Source: Almanac of Canada 1984; Banks and Overstreet 1983; Day and Degenhardt 1980; Europa Yearbook 1981; Flanz 1983; Lovenduski and Hills 1981; Kohn 1980; UNESCO 1982; I.L.O. 1982; and embassies of various countries and the Chicago Israeli and Japanese consulates. Reprinted by permission of the University of Utah, copyright holder.

Table 1A Most Powerful Predictors of Recruitment of Women Parliament Members, 1972: Multiple Stepwise Regression ($N = 19$)

Independent variables	Multiple correlation coefficient (R)	Cumulative percent of variance explained (R^2)	Percent variance explained by each variable
Proportional representation system of elections	.48	23	23
Percent women economically active	.62	39	16
Percent women college graduates	.71	50	11
Greater unemployment[a]	.95	90	40
Late women's suffrage[a]	.96[b]	92	2

* Titles have been changed slightly to conform to Table 1.
[a] The zero order correlation of this variable is negative.
[b] Significant at less than the .01 level when corrected for degrees of freedom.
Source: Rule 1981, 1987.

Table 2 Societal Factors for Women's Parliamentary Success in 23 Democratic Countries, 1987–1991; Multiple Stepwise Regression (Type of Electoral System Omitted)

Independent variables	Multiple correlation coefficient (R)	Cumulative percent of variance explained (R^2)	Percent variance, explained by each variable
Greater percent women in par-liament 1970–1973	.89	.79	79
Higher number of MPs per district (logged)	.91	.83	4
Percent women working out-side home	.94	.88	5
Percent women college gradu-ates	.96	.93	5

Note: The adjusted R^2 is .91. The significance of Ts in the regression is less than .001 for the first three variables; the fourth is significant at .006. The regression table is available upon request to the author. *Source*: Rule 1994a:21. Reprinted by permission of Greenwood Publishing Group, Inc., Westport, CT.

systems were omitted purposely from the table, and in so doing the highest corre-lation shown was with the percentage of women in parliament in 1970–1973. Almost all the leaders, laggers, and the middle range countries in women's re-cruitment were the same in 1991 as in 1970–73, with the party-list PR countries generally higher and the single member plurality/majority countries much lower.

Table 2 showed for the first time that district magnitude was a significant independent predictor of women's election (see also Rule 1987). It correlates very highly (.70) with proportional representation countries. High magnitude countries (seven or more representatives) also correlate highly with those nations that have a preference (personal) vote. It allows the electorate to choose candidates on an ''open'' party list. The preference vote has been used successfully by women in Finland and Denmark and others in Europe to elect more women to parliament (Haavio-Mannila et al. 1985:85; Shugart, 1994:37–39)

Further evidence that proportional representation facilitates women's elec-tion to parliament is shown by the results of PR and majority-plurality electoral systems in the same country and culture (Rule, 1994b). Women's representation in Australia in 1993 was 7% in the lower house as a result of the majoritarian system (the alternative vote) and 24% in the PR upper house. By 1997 the figures were 15% in the House, 30% in the Senate. On the same ballot, Germany had 12% women chosen by plurality and 28% by PR in 1990, and so on. These and subsequent elections in New Zealand and Italy, for example, as noted in this paper, continue to document the generalization that the PR electoral system results in twice to three times the proportion of women elected in single member contests in mixed systems.

Current socioeconomic conditions take second place to electoral systems, but are useful in further explaining about 80–90% of the variance in women's legislative recruitment within long-standing democracies. Higher proportions of women working outside the home and percent of women college graduates continued to be important in 1987–1991. No longer was left and center party strength an important predictor, nor unemployment and the dominance of the Roman Catholic Church. Neither year of suffrage nor gross domestic product was significantly related to women's proportions in parliament.

Anomalous cases among PR countries may be explained by low district magnitude, as in Greece, with an average of three members in a district, and Ireland, averaging four. In addition some PR countries, such as Portugal, have a smaller percentage of women in the workforce and a potent Catholic Church, factors which tend to mitigate the favorable aspects of the PR electoral system (Rule 1987).

B.   Changes in 1997

The updated percentages of women's parliamentary representation in long-standing democracies in roughly 1993 and 1997 are shown in Figures 1 and 2. In five or six years—depending on when elections were held—the average and the middle datum (median) has increased 4.3% and 4.4% respectively. Also most of the countries shown in Figure 2, including Japan at the bottom, had elected greater proportions of women parliamentarians. The Nordic countries and Netherlands are still leading. But two plurality countries in 1993 have shown large gains: New Zealand, now a PR country, has emerged as the sixth highest nation in women's representation, while the United Kingdom has jumped ranks and is now thirteenth instead of twentieth.

The three major explanations for general increases and some rather dramatic individual country increments in women's representation are: (1) Political party quotas or goals to nominate an increased percentage of women to parliament in PR countries, (2) Laws requiring that a proportion (quota) of women be placed on party lists in PR countries, and (3) Electoral system change from single member plurality to proportional representation.

1.   Political Party Quotas or Goals in Party-List PR Countries

Parties in PR countries have an incentive to place women on their lists to enhance their election chances, and they are also likely to agree to a goal of greater representation for them. Moreover, proportional representation facilitates quicker change than single member majority/plurality systems (Norris 1997:310). It is

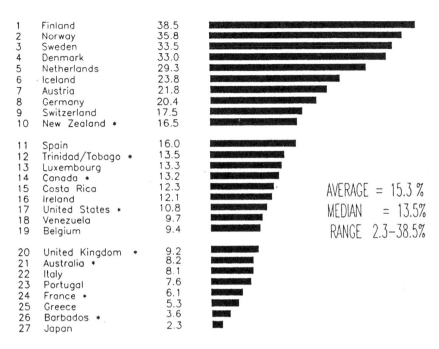

1	Finland	38.5
2	Norway	35.8
3	Sweden	33.5
4	Denmark	33.0
5	Netherlands	29.3
6	Iceland	23.8
7	Austria	21.8
8	Germany	20.4
9	Switzerland	17.5
10	New Zealand *	16.5
11	Spain	16.0
12	Trinidad/Tobago *	13.5
13	Luxembourg	13.3
14	Canada *	13.2
15	Costa Rica	12.3
16	Ireland	12.1
17	United States *	10.8
18	Venezuela	9.7
19	Belgium	9.4
20	United Kingdom *	9.2
21	Australia *	8.2
22	Italy	8.1
23	Portugal	7.6
24	France *	6.1
25	Greece	5.3
26	Barbados *	3.6
27	Japan	2.3

AVERAGE = 15.3%
MEDIAN = 13.5%
RANGE 2.3–38.5%

Figure 1 Percentage of women in single or lower houses of parliament in 27 long-established democracies, 1989–1993. (From Rule 1994a,b.) *Signifies the 8 countries which elect a single member in each district (single member district [SMD] countries) by a required majority or plurality of the vote. The remainder are 17 party-list/proportional representation (PL/PR) countries; and Ireland with the single transferable vote (STV), and Japan with the single nontransferable vote (SNTV) forms of proportional representation.

easier for a political party to add women to its lists for ten districts averaging ten representatives than it is to change 100 single member majority or plurality districts from male to female representatives.

Political party quotas or goals were first employed by the party-list PR countries of Denmark, Finland, Norway, and Sweden with great success, beginning in the 1980s. These countries have especially favorable election procedures: from 7–12 representatives in parliamentary election districts plus a preference (personal) vote. As a result of these positive/affirmative political party activities, women's proportions in the Nordic parliaments grew about 23% in the decade before the 1995 Beijing meeting. Northern European nations that also gained women MPs using this strategy were Germany, with a 30% increase, Netherlands with 51%, and Iceland with 66% (Inter-Parliamentary Union 1997).

Spanish parties introduced the quota for its 1996 elections, and women's representation rose 54% to 24.6% women members of parliament. The Labour and Liberal Parties in Great Britain did likewise for its 1997 election with a 100%

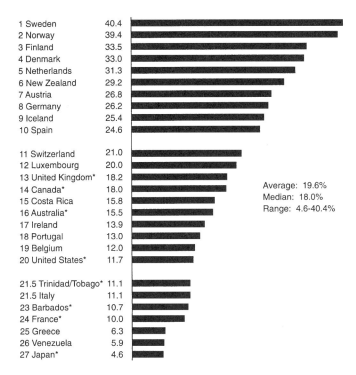

1 Sweden	40.4
2 Norway	39.4
3 Finland	33.5
4 Denmark	33.0
5 Netherlands	31.3
6 New Zealand	29.2
7 Austria	26.8
8 Germany	26.2
9 Iceland	25.4
10 Spain	24.6
11 Switzerland	21.0
12 Luxembourg	20.0
13 United Kingdom*	18.2
14 Canada*	18.0
15 Costa Rica	15.8
16 Australia*	15.5
17 Ireland	13.9
18 Portugal	13.0
19 Belgium	12.0
20 United States*	11.7
21.5 Trinidad/Tobago*	11.1
21.5 Italy	11.1
23 Barbados*	10.7
24 France*	10.0
25 Greece	6.3
26 Venezuela	5.9
27 Japan*	4.6

Average: 19.6%
Median: 18.0%
Range: 4.6-40.4%

Figure 2 Percentage of Women in single or lower houses of parliament in 27 long-established democracies, 1997. (Inter-Parliamentary Union 1997.) *Indicates the 8 nations that elect a single representative from each national district by a required majority or plurality vote. The remainder includes 18 nations with the party list form of proportional representation and Ireland, with the single transferable vote form of PR.

increase to 18.2% women members of parliament. The latter was an exceptional example of political affirmative action because Britain's Labour and Liberal parties appear to be the first, or among the first, in the long-standing democracies with the single member system to adopt a national quota for women's nomination. However, this affirmative action apparently ends with 1997. A British court has outlawed the practice, ruling that it contravenes the Sex Discrimination Act of 1975 by disadvantaging male candidates (Inter-Parliamentary Union 1997:68; for more on women's electoral quotas see Lovenduski and Norris 1993).

2. Laws Requiring a Quota of Women to be Nominated on Party Lists in PR Countries

Political parties fluctuate in strength, and come and go, to and from government, but laws that are enforced remain and bring continuity toward the goal of greater women's representation. This method usually requires that women's names be positioned so that they could be elected if their party won sufficient votes in the election. This strategy was adopted in Italy after the 1992 election in which only 8.1% women were elected (see Figure 1). A new election law provided that one-fourth of the Italian parliament was to be elected by party-list/PR and the remainder from single member districts. It required, in response to women's organizations, that the parties alternate the genders on their lists, which in theory would lead to equal representation in the PR election (Katz 1996:38).

However, this strategy was dependent on whether a man's or a woman's name was listed first. The result in 1994 was an Italian women's success rate on the party-list proportional representation ballot of 33%. But women won only 9% in the single member district elections, which comprised three-fourths of the parliament seats. This brought down their overall representation rate to 15% for Italian women parliamentarians in 1994. Still this was almost double the proportion of women elected to their Chamber of Deputies two years earlier. But Figure 2, with 1997 results, shows a decline to 11.1% in women MPs, which may be the effect of a Constitutional Court ruling that struck down the quota in 1995. (A similar ruling occurred in France in 1982, see Inter-Parliamentary Union 1997, 63)

Also in continental Europe, Belgium enacted in 1994 a law requiring that one-third of the candidates be women. But to date this has not been effective since apparently there is no requirement for women's favorable placement on the voting lists (Inter-Parliamentary Union. 1990, 63, 75). In contrast, Argentina's law, which is discussed in a subsequent section on developing democracies, has this requirement, and the law has proven to be an unqualified success.

3.   Electoral System Change from Single Member Plurality to Proportional Representation

In the previous example, Italy's electoral change was in mostly single member district elections, which are generally unfavorable to the goal of women's equal representation by 2005, the next U.N. World Conference on Women. In New Zealand we have the opposite change, from New Zealand's first past the post (FPTP) system to a mixed PR system. This approach resulted in New Zealand's rank as the sixth highest nation in women's parliamentary representation among the long-standing democracies by 1997.

Before the U.N. met in Beijing and recommended this strategy for increasing women's representation, a royal commission was established to examine New Zealand's electoral system and to recommend changes (Royal Commission on the Electoral System 1990). Like other former United Kingdom colonies, New Zealand had inherited the FPTP election system. Women's organizations were well aware of the adverse effects on women's candidacy in single member plurality elections. They worked with the Commission to obtain electoral changes that would facilitate women's nomination and elections.

The New Zealand Commission opted for a compromise, a combined party list–PR and a FPTP single member district arrangement (with adjustments in seats in proportion to the popular votes received by each party). About half the seats are selected by PR and the other half by single member district plurality. This mixed member proportional (MMP) satisfied those who preferred one district representative and those who wanted proportional representation (Nagel 1995). The New Zealand electoral reform was adopted in a national referendum by 54% of the voters in 1993. On the ballot paper, the party choice was first and the candidate choice was second, which may have abetted somewhat women's election. New Zealand's ballot order thus reversed that presently used in Germany (Lakeman 1991).

Women parliamentarians were elected to 29% of the lower house in the first reform New Zealand election on October 12, 1996. In the 1990 FPTP election they were but 16.5% percent, which was the highest representation of women achieved among single member plurality/majority systems, although just half as much as the leading PR countries (refer to Figure 1). As expected, more women were elected on the party-list PR side of the ballot than for the individual constituencies, the ratio being 3:1. New Zealand's electoral systems ratio was lower than Italy's in 1994 when 3.7 party-list women were elected for every woman selected from a single member constituency.

II. ELECTORAL SYSTEMS AND WOMEN'S REPRESENTATION IN 46 RECENTLY DEVELOPED OR PARTIALLY DEVELOPED DEMOCRACIES

In 1987–1991 the 46 countries displayed in Table 3 averaged 6.5% in women's representation, while male parliamentarians averaged 93.5%. However, at about the same time, this highly unbalanced representation was common also to single member plurality countries in the long-standing democracies of Australia, the United States, the United Kingdom, and France—and less so in only two of the nineteen PR countries in the same period (Rule 1994b:17).

By 1997 Greece and Japan (lower house) still had the very lopsided gender representation of developing democracies of the earlier period, while the other long-standing democracies moved considerably upward. The new democracies and the partially-developed ones by 1997 averaged a low 7.6% women parliamentarians. This represented a gain of about 1% over the earlier period, and it contrasts markedly with the increase of nearly 4% in the long-standing democracies in the same time.

A. Expectations for the Analysis

Expectations in analyzing the 46 recent and partially democratic countries were that those with proportional representation would have higher proportions of

Table 3 Percentage of Women in 46 National Legislatures of Recently Developed Democracies or Partially Developed Democracies, 1997

(A) Majority and plurality countries (N = 19)[a]	Percent	(B) Proportional and semiproportional representation countries (N = 27)[b]	Percent
Zimbabwe	14.7+	Argentina	25.3+
St. Christopher-Nevis	13.3+	Mexico	14.2
Jamaica	11.7	Taiwan	14.0+
Philippines	10.8+	Bulgaria	13.3
Zambia	9.7+	Poland	13.0
Bangladesh	9.1+	Senegal	11.7
Botswana	8.5	Hungary	11.4
Bahamas	8.2	Cape Verdi	11.1
Malaysai	7.8+	Peru	10.8
Mauritius	7.6+	Nicaragua	10.8
India	7.2	El Salvador	10.7
Maldives	6.3+	Russia	10.2

Thailand	5.6	Panama	9.7
Belize	3.4	Hondorus	7.8
Singapore	2.5+	Israel	7.5
Lebanon	2.3	Chile	7.5
Egypt	2.0+	Sao Tome and Principe	7.3
Papua New Guinea	0.0	Benin	7.2
St. Lucia	0.0	Uruguay	7.1
		Romania	7.0
		Bolivia	6.9
		Brazil	6.6+
		Malta	5.8
		Cyprus	5.4
		Sri Lanka	5.3
		South Korea	3.0
		Turkey	2.4
Mean = 6.9%		Mean: 9.4% (8.8 without Argentina)	
Median = 7.6%		Median: 7.8%	
Range = 0–14.7%		Range: 2.4–25.3%	

[a]Fourteen countries employ the First Past the Post (single member district) election system. Five use the block system (Maldives, Lebanon, Philippines, Singapore, and Thailand).

[b]Nineteen countries employ list PR systems, and one (Malta) uses the single transferable vote form. Three are mixed member proportional (Bolivia, Hungary, and Mexico). Four with the semi-PR parallel system are Taiwan, Senegal, Russia, and South Korea. South Africa, with 25% women MPs, is a list PR country that was omitted to match the author's 1994 original table.

Note: + signifies those countries that legally require a percentage of women nominated or elected to the parliament.

Source: Inter-Parliamentary Union 1997:64–77, 90–97; Reynolds and Reilly 1997:133–136.

women MPs than those with the single member majoritarian/plurality election system. The second major expectation was that if there were affirmative action laws, they would most likely result in the election of greater proportions of women.

The author also hypothesized that women's representation would be higher when there were multimember plurality or majority districts. This hypothesis was based on previous research at the state, province, and municipal levels that showed that generally women fared better in at-large or block elections than in single member plurality districts (see several studies in Rule and Zimmerman 1992, 1994). Also expected, as in the case of Germany, was that mixed systems would result in lower proportions of women's representation than PR-only systems.

Before investigating the first hypothesis, it was necessary to classify the 46 developing democracies by electoral system. Therefore the analysis began with determining whether the block system should be classified with the single member majority nations. Next to be decided was whether the mixed systems should be a separate category or grouped with the PR countries.

B. Block and Mixed Systems in Developing Democracies

When women's proportions were compared in the block nations, among the 14 single member majority or plurality countries, there was no appreciable difference in women's representation. The same can be said of three different systems using PR by itself or in conjunction with the plurality or majority system.

Block votes, it is now hypothesized, generally produce results the same as single member districts at the national level where the stakes are higher and the power greater. If a dominant political party or group votes as a block, the "threshold of exclusion" is 50%, just the same as for single member districts. The threshold of exclusion is the proportion of votes a particular group must have to elect one candidate, assuming that all other voters vote as a group or groups, i.e., strategically. The formula for the threshold exclusion proportion is as follows for both single member systems and the block (at large) vote:

$$\frac{V}{V + S}$$

where votes (V) and seats (S) have the same value (Still 1992:184,195 f.n. 4.)

The reason mixed PR and semi-PR systems in the developing countries do not show women's recruitment proportions between those of PR and majority countries may be a function of the small subsamples—three of one variation and four of another—compared with 19 PR countries (see Table 3B footnote). Majority and PR in Developing Democracies

As a result of the above empirical investigations, Table 3 was prepared with a bi-polar classification of proportional representation and majority/plurality countries. This division of electoral systems encompasses at least two different normative goals, the former oriented toward an accurate reflection in the legislature of the citizenry's vote, the other toward achieving a clear mandate to govern (Nohlen 1984).

A glance down the list of majority/plurality nations (Table 3, column A) shows that 17 of these new democracies were once a part of the British Empire or under her influence and adopted her electoral system. The exceptions were the Philippines and Thailand. On the other hand, the PR list of countries (Table 3, column B) includes several that had continental European influence, i.e., from France, Spain and Portugal, as well as other political and sociocultural impacts. Several, in turn, adopted the PR system used by the European countries, including France, immediately after World War II.

Table 3 (column A) displays the 19 majority and plurality countries, and Table 3 (column B) shows the 27 proportional representation countries. The mean percent of women in each electoral system, the middle figure in each set, and the ranges give a summary look at the similarities and differences in the two sets. The majority system countries average a bit lower in women's proportions than the PR countries do, but they converge around the midpoints. While two of the majority countries, Papua New Guinea and St. Lucia, have no women legislators, the PR countries are not quite as low. The two sets range as far as each other, if one discounts the large women's proportion in Argentina.

C. Affirmative Action Laws

The majority/plurality countries of the new and partial democracies lead in affirmative action laws, in contrast to the PR democracies. Some majority/plurality countries may have higher proportions of women in the workforce and professional women, who are the basis for their countries' women's movement, and who in turn have pressed their political parties and legislatures for greater proportions of women MPs.

Since the history and data on affirmative action by parties is sketchy in developing or partial democracies, attention here is upon laws designed to provide a presence of women in the national popular legislature. Nine (47%) of the nineteen majority/plurality countries have such laws (marked by a + in Table 3), seven do not, and three have missing data (Botswana, Lebanon, and Papua New Guinea).

These laws in majority/plurality countries do not appear to be correlated with the percentages of women MPs in Table 3, column B. But this may be related to whether the laws were in place for longer or shorter periods of time and whether the affirmative action law is enforced. Certainly the larger quotas of 13% (Zimbabwe), 18% (Philippines), and 20% (Maldives and St. Christopher-Nevis), if enforced, probably do have a favorable effect. Certainly the reserved seats law in Bangladesh is working, as has one in Taiwan, which is discussed in the next session. But the effect of the other laws in the partial and developing countries is subject to future inquiry. (For Cyprus, Lebanon, and Zimbabwe, see Lijphart 1986.)

In the 27 proportional representation countries shown in Table 3B only three have affirmative action laws—Argentina, Taiwan, and Brazil. In Brazil, a 20% quota law for women in parliament and municipalities was adopted in 1992. Since then their proportions have almost doubled to 11%, according to a recent news report (*Folha de S. Paulo*, June, 11, 1997.) One negative factor of importance in Brazil is the high monetary cost of parliamentary campaigns (Tabak 1994).

The differential experience of Argentina's and Taiwan's affirmative action for women parliamentarians is now described.

1. Argentina

Argentina adopted legislation in 1991 that required that at least 30% of candidates be women and that their names be placed in a favorable position to win on each party's list. Impassioned speakers declared that women—who were only 6% of the national legislature in 1991—not only had the right to vote, but also to be represented and elected to their national parliament (Archenti 1994). By 1997 women's representation in Argentina had more than quadrupled to 25% (Jones 1996).

2. Taiwan, Republic of China

A different procedure for the representation of women has been used by the Republic of China on the island of Taiwan since the 1950s. Taiwan was among the first noncommunist one-party countries to take steps to promote women legislators. In 1953 it chose the system of reserved seats. Whenever the quota of about 10% was fulfilled, then all the votes for women candidates were tabulated and the candidates with the highest votes would fill in the reserved seats. A unique feature of the election system provided that the seats reserved for women would be vacant if no women were elected. This system encouraged party nominations and election of women beyond the 10% quota to nearly 20% in some provincial and national parliaments in Taiwan by 1996.

Although women's nominations for the National Assembly, which previously elected the president, were originally limited to one women's organization allied with the dominant Nationalist Party, this is no longer the case. Taiwan is now a multiparty country, and the president is elected by popular vote. In 1996 women parliamentarians made up 14% of the Legislative Yuan and 18% of the National Assembly (*China Times*, March 26 and December 3, 1996.)

Candidates for the provincial legislatures and local councils run at large. More women are elected in areas that have a greater number of parliamentary seats (i.e., in greater magnitudes), as is the case among many of the long-standing democratic PR countries of Europe. However, unlike PR countries in Europe, where voters choose several representatives in a district, in Taiwan they could select only one in their multimember district. Their electoral system, called the single nontransferable vote, is an unfriendly one for women. Were it not for the reserved seats, it is likely that few women in the Republic of China would make it to parliament (Bih-er et al. 1990:194).

C. Election Patterns in Developing Democracies

In order to test the hypotheses that PR countries elect higher proportions of women MPs than majority countries in developing democracies, chi square tests were performed using the data from Table 3. While these analyses cannot have statistical inferences drawn from them, the findings are useful for further study.

Table 4 displays the first statistical test. It shows a tendency for countries with PR to be less frequent in the low percentages of women MPs and more frequent in the higher percentages of women parliamentarians than one would expect. Yet when the 7–11% category is examined, there are only minor differences between PR and majority/plurality countries in the frequencies of women elected in this category. This means that the systems are about equal in electing women at this rather low level in the developing countries. The chi square number is, therefore, statistically insignificant, and no relationship is shown. How-

Table 4 Electoral Systems and Women's Election to Parliament in 73 Developing and Developed Democracies, 1997

	Number of countries with women MPs			
	Under 7%	7–11%	Over 11%	Total
Proportional Representation Countries	7	12	8	27
	(8.8)	(11.7)	(6.5)	
Majority/plurality countries	8	8	3	19
	(6.2)	(8.3)	(4.5)	
Total	15	20	11	46

Note: Expected frequencies in parentheses. $X^2 = 1.156$. No significant relationship found.
Reprinted by permission of Greenwood Publishing Group, Westport, CT.

Table 5 Electoral Systems and Women's Election to Parliament in 73 Developing and Developed Democracies, 1997: Binomial Pattern of High-Low Percent of Women MPs

	Percentage of women MPs	
	Lowest third	Highest third
A. *Recently Developed and Partial Democracies (N = 46)*		
Proportional representation countries	26%	41%
Majority/plurality countries	42%	21%
B. *Long-Established Democracies (N = 27)*		
Proportional representation countries	21%	47%
Majority/plurality countries	62%	0%

Source: Inter-Parliamentary Union 1997.

ever, could it be that the high-low election pattern discerned in Table 4 is significant?

In Table 5 (row A), the relationship of PR countries to higher percentages of women in parliaments is shown clearly. PR countries have 41% of women MPs elected in the higher third of women's proportions in 46 developing democracies, while majority/plurality countries have 21%, a 2:1 ratio. In the lower third proportions of women MPs, 26% are in PR countries, while majority/plurality countries have 42%, a ratio of 1.6:1.

Four of the seven low PR countries—Cyprus, South Korea, Sri Lanka, and Turkey—are or have recently been in civil turmoil, when women, it appears, are unlikely to be nominated or elected to parliament. Lebanon and Egypt—of the eight single member countries—also have considerable civil disruption, which is not conducive to women's representation. If these unusual cases were removed from the table, the lowest third of women's parliamentary proportions would contain only 13% of PR countries and 35% of majority/plurality nations, a ratio of almost 3:1.

The favorable effect of PR is shown markedly in Table 5 (row B), which differentiates women's proportions among the long-standing democracies. There the PR countries have 47% of the highest third, as compared to 0% of the eight single member district countries. In turn, the latter make up 62% of the lowest third of the proportions of women MPs, while PR countries are only 21%, again a ratio of 3:1 (cf. Inter-Parliamentary Union 1997:134–136; Norris 1997:308–310.)

On reexamining Figure 2, one can see the pattern clearly—all the countries that are above the median, from Luxembourg to Sweden, are PR countries; all eight below the median are majority/minority single member countries with seven deviant PR cases, which reminds one that there are exceptions to the general pattern. The highest plurality country—the United Kingdom—has less than half the proportion of women MPs of the highest PR nation.

In conclusion, Table 4 is consistent with Table 3. The average percent of women in PR countries is higher (without Argentina), and is lower in majority/ plurality nations, but the middle range of 7–11 percent women MPs is evident in both types of electoral systems. Thus the hypothesis about the general level of women's representation and electoral systems is inconclusive with this nonrandom sample. However, a clear binomial pattern was discovered in the present sample. It agrees with a similar binomial pattern in the 27 long-established democracies, i.e., generally there are higher proportions of women MPs in PR countries and lower proportions in the majority/plurality ones.

Also expected was that affirmative action would be a booster to women's representation in developing countries. It perhaps accounts for the cluster of majority/plurality countries in the 7–11% range, but more data and time are needed to confirm this or discount it. Clearly the PR countries of Argentina, Taiwan, and Brazil have seen their women's representation rise with their affirmative action laws.

III. SUMMARY AND CONCLUSION

The United Nations' Fourth World Conference on Women in Beijing in 1995 set a goal of equal participation of men and women in national legislatures. It also called upon nations to review the impact of electoral systems on the political representation of women and, where appropriate, to adjust or reform those systems. Several democratic countries have done just that before or after Beijing. Most opted for adjustments through affirmative action within parties and less often through law. Legal action is more common in the majority/plurality democratizing countries than in the long-standing democratic nations included in this study.

The new and partial democracies and the long-standing democracies have a similar pattern: PR systems generally result in much higher proportions of women MPs, while majority/plurality systems result in much lower proportions. In the developing democracies, perhaps as a result of their quota laws, the frequencies of PR and majority/plurality countries are about the same at the 7–11% representation level. Also among these countries, there is little difference in women's parliamentary proportion between mixed PR-majority/plurality and semiproportional systems, and the list-PR systems. Also the block or at-large system did not advantage women any more than a single member majority or plurality one in the developing democracies.

Women's parliamentary representation in 1997 in the 73 democracies averaged a bit more than 12%. However, about 10% of developed and developing democracies are well on their way to achieving equal gender representation by the next United Nations Conference on Women in 2005.

REFERENCES

Almanac of Canada. (1984). Toronto: Corpus.

Archenti, N. (1994). Political representation and gender interests: The argentine example. Presented at the Sixteenth World Conference of the International Political Science Association, Berlin.

Banks, A. S. and Overstreet, W. (1983), (eds.), *Political Handbook of the World*. New York: McGraw Hill.

Bih-er, C., Clark, C. and Clark, J. (1990). *Women in Taiwan Politics*. Boulder, CO: Lynne Rienner.

Bystydzienski, J. (1992). (ed.), *Women Transforming Politics: Worldwide Strategies for Empowerment*. Bloomington: Indiana University Press.

Day, A. S. and Degenhardt, H. W. (1980), *Political Parties of the World*. Detroit: Research Co.

Europa. (1981). *Europa Yearbook*, Vols. I & II London: Europa.

Flanz, G. H. (1983). *Comparative Women's Rights and Political Participation in Europe*. Dobb's Ferry, NY: Transnational.

Haavio-Mannila, E. et al. (1985). *Unfinished Democracy: Women in Nordic Politics*. New York: Pergamon.

I.L.O. (1982). *Yearbook of Labour Statistics*. Geneva: I.L.O.

Inter-Parliamentary Union. (1995). *Women in Parliaments, 1945–1995*. Geneva: Inter-Parliamentary Union.

Inter-Parliamentary Union. (1997). *Democracy Still in the Making*. Geneva: Inter-Parliamentary Union.

Jones, M. P. (1996). Increasing women's representation via gender quotas: The Argentine Ley de Cupos. *Women and Politics 16*(4), 75–98.

Katz, R. S. (1996). Electoral reform and the transformation of party politics in Italy. *Party Politics 2*(1), 31–53.

Kohn, W. S. G. (1980). *Women in National Legislatures: A Comparative Study in Six Countries*. New York: Paeger.

Lakeman, E. (1991). *Twelve Democracies*. London: Arthur McDougall Fund.

Lijphart, A. (1984). *Democracies: Patterns of Majoritarian and Consensus Government in Twenty-One Countries*. New Haven: Yale University Press.

Lijphart, A. (1986). Proportionality by non-PR methods: Ethnic representation in Belgium, Cyprus, Lebanon, New Zealand, West Germany and Zimbabwe. In A. Lijphart and B. Grofman (eds.), *Electoral Laws and Their Political Consequences*. New York: Agathon.

Lovenduski, J. and Hills, J. (1981). (eds.), *The Politics of the Second Electorate*. London: Routledge & Kegan Paul.

Lovenduski, J. and Norris, P. (1993). (eds.), *Gender and Party Politics*. Thousand Oaks, Ca: Sage Publications.

Nagel, J. (1995). New Zealanders Choose MMP. In *Voting and Democracy Report*. Washington, D.C.: Center for Voting and Democracy.

Nohlen, D. (1984). Two Incompatible Principles of Representation. In A. Lijphart and B. Grofman (eds.), *Choosing an Electoral System*. New York: Praeger.

Norris, P. (1985). Women's legislative participation in Western Europe. *West European Politics 8*, 90–101.

Norris, P. (1997). Choosing electoral systems: Proportional, majoritarian and mixed systems. *International Political Science Review 18*, 280–297.

Reynolds, A. and Reilly, B. (1997). *The International IDEA Handbook of Electoral System Design*. Stockholm: International IDEA.

Royal Commission on the Electoral System. (1990). *Report*. Wellington: New Zealand Government Printer.

Rule, W. (1981). Why women don't run: The critical contextual factors in women's legislative recruitment. *Western Political Quarterly 34*, 60–77.

Rule, W. (1987). Electoral systems, contextual factors and women's opportunity for election in twenty-three democracies. *Western Political Quarterly 40*, 477–498.

Rule, W. (1994a). Parliaments of, by and for the people: Except for women? In W. Rule and J. F. Zimmerman (eds.), *Electoral Systems in Comparative Perspective: Their Impact on Women and Minorities*. Westport, CT: Greenwood.

Rule, W. (1994b). Women's underrepresentation and electoral systems. *PS: Political Science and Politics 27*, 689–692.

Rule, W. and Zimmerman, J. F. (eds.) (1992). *United States Electoral Systems: Their Impact on Women and Minorities*. New York: Praeger.

Rule, W. and Zimmerman, J. F. (eds.) (1994). *Electoral Systems in Comparative Perspective: Their Impact on Women and Minorities*. Westport, CT: Greenwood.

Shugart, M. S. (1994). Minorities represented and unrepresented. In W. Rule and J. F. Zimmerman (eds.), *Electoral Systems in Comparative Perspective: Their Impact on Women and Minorities*. Westport, CT: Greenwood.

Still, E. (1992). Cumulative and limited voting in Alabama. In W. Rule and J. F. Zimmerman (eds.), *United States Electoral Systems: Their impact on Women: and Minorities*. New York: Praeger.

Tabak, F. (1994). Women and politics in Brazil: Legislative elections. In W. Rule and J. Zimmerman (eds.), *Electoral Systems in Comparative Perspective: Their Impact on Women and Minorities*, Westport, CT: Greenwood.

UNESCO. (1982). *Statistical Yearbook*. Paris: UNESCO.

United Nations (1995). Report of the United Nations' Fourth World Conference on Women. Adopted September 15, 1995, Beijing, China.

7

Ethnicity, Democracy, and Conflict Management in Africa

Victor Azarya
The Hebrew University of Jerusalem, Jerusalem, Israel

I. INTRODUCTION

The relationship between democracy and conflict resolution has been a hotly debated issue among political scientists, especially among those interested in "democratic transition" in Asia, Africa, and Latin America.[1] Questions have been raised on whether democratization helps solve conflicts or, on the contrary, exacerbates and intensifies them, making them more difficult to solve. Turning the implied causality around, the question has been raised also as to whether there are some deeper, more intractable conflicts that are not only more difficult to solve by democratic means, but that hamper the very construction of democracy. Can we identify the types of conflicts that are more resistant to democratic devices and/or have more detrimental effects on democratization itself, and what role, if any, do the ethnic-based or ethnic-represented conflicts play in this regard? Such issues will be briefly discussed in this chapter, with specific reference to some African examples.

The relationship between democracy and conflict is discussed in academic circles at different levels of generality and scope. At the international level, some theories postulate that it is much less likely to find two democratic states engaged in violent conflict with each other than when at least one of the conflicting parties is autocratic. The relationship between democracy and conflict is also examined, quite naturally, at the level of domestic politics. Questions are raised on the kinds of institutional arrangements; the role and strength of the state vis-a-vis other societal actors; the expectations, fears, and outlooks of elites and their followers; and their impact on democratic instruments. The vitality and strength of civil society is commonly mentioned in this regard, though such discussion is usually bogged down by lack of clarity as to what exactly is meant by civil society, how different it is from political society and from democracy itself.

Narrowing the scope further, discussions have also focused on the specific role played by mass media, for example, or by nongovernmental organizations, in articulating public discourse and public dissent. This narrower focus aims, first of all, at giving more operational content to the concept of civil society and elucidating the specific role that it may play in the relationship between democracy and conflict resolution. I have previously touched upon the difficulties inherent in the concept of civil society and suggested some ways of attempting to operationalize it.[2] Hence, this topic will not be discussed here. I will, on the other hand, discuss more specifically the role that ethnicity may play in the articulation of conflicts and whether the involvement of ethnicity makes the conflict less, or more, amenable to management by democratic means. The crucial question is whether the very representation of a conflict as ethnic, and hence primordial, introduces an additional burden on it and makes a solution more difficult to achieve. Or is it, on the contrary, the unwillingness to recognize the ethnic bases of conflicts and the tendency to suppress them that prevents the provision of durable solutions? Finally, it is important to ask what specific role the state may play in the relationships between ethnicity, conflict, and democracy. How, for example, would the relative strength or weakness of the state vis-a-vis the society affect the ways conflicts develop and are handled and the extent to which ethnicity is interwoven in them? Can different patterns of conflict management and resolution be diagnosed, depending on the relative strength of the state or the type of its relations with its society?

These questions are, of course, as relevant to Asia and Latin America as they are to Africa, but because of my own greater familiarity with African examples, I will discuss these issues mainly in the context of Africa. Giving specific examples from Nigeria, Congo-Zaire, Uganda, and Ethiopia, I will discuss the specific relationships between ethnicity, democracy, and conflict and will assess the possible impact that ethnopolitical movements and the ethnorepresentation of cleavages may have on processes of transition to democracy.

II. CONFLICT RESOLUTION OR CONFLICT MANAGEMENT?

Before the above-mentioned issues are discussed in more detail, a more general doubt should be raised with regard to the very concept of conflict resolution, which is so popular in the social sciences literature. Conflict resolution has the connotation that conflict is some kind of deviation from the usual course of events, an irregularity that has to be fixed. It seems to imply that a harmony of sorts, a situation of nonconflict is the natural order of things. If a conflict emerges, mechanisms are quickly set in motion to try to resolve it, i.e., to restore harmony. This, of course, is a rather naive and utopian perspective. The starting point that I would suggest is closer to the opposite: as long as a scarcity of basic resources exists, conflict—not the lack of it—is the natural order of things. Conflict is endemic; it is the basic condition of existence. What we call conflict resolution is, in reality, a temporary cooling down of a specific flashpoint, not the elimination of the state of conflict. Conflict cannot be eliminated, it can only be contained. It can be managed in a way that may reduce the likelihood of its erupting out of control and leading to violence. What could be resolved are those specific flashpoints, but not the generic situation of conflict. Therefore, I would much prefer to use such terms as conflict containment or conflict management rather than conflict resolution. Rules, procedures, and norms can, indeed, be created, applied, and internalized so that conflict is checked, regulated, or kept under control, enabling order to be maintained and be considered legitimate by the parties involved.

This starting point is especially relevant to the concept of democracy. Democracy, after all, is not a situation of nonconflict. On the contrary, democracy assumes the endemic existence of conflict and dissent. It recognizes and legitimizes the existence of different opinions and interests. It recognizes the right to disagree. It provides mechanisms that accommodate those differences even if they cannot be completely resolved and eliminated. Democracy is the art of maintaining order despite disagreements. It does not suppress conflict, but accommodates it and manages it in a nonviolent way.

The question that should interest us, then, is not how democracy resolves conflicts, but what mechanisms it offers to maintain them within certain boundaries that would reduce the likelihood of opting for violence as a means of promoting one's views and interests. For such an objective to be reached, the conflicting parties should be offered an outcome they would consider acceptable because at least some of their needs and expectations are met, and because the outcome was reached by means they deem just, being achieved by the use of proper norms and procedures and having allowed the contestants some participation in making those decisions. I should add, however, that a sense of participation, in itself, would probably not be sufficient, in the long run, if not accompanied by some substantive satisfaction of demands made by the conflicting sides. Democracy, in other words, cannot be sustained in a winner take all situation. At the end of the contest, some rewards, albeit unequal, have to be offered to the different participating sides.

We could then ask what factors could facilitate the establishment of mechanisms that would accommodate conflict and contain it at a nonviolent participatory mode. Could such factors be found in the role and characteristics of the state or of social movements, in the value of civility or other norms, in the dissemination of information and opinion formation, in the sense of security (or insecurity) felt by various sectors of the population, in the type of order and balance established at the international level? We could also ask whether certain kinds of conflicts might be more amenable, or less, to management by democratic means. What would be the common characteristics of conflicts that are less manageable by democratic means? Would religious conflicts, for example, or ethnically represented ones, be such conflicts, and if so, why would democratic means be less likely to contain them?

From this vantage point, let us now look at the relationship between democracy, conflict, and ethnicity at various levels of analysis.

III. DEMOCRATIC PEACE THEORY

At the international level, our starting point is an interesting observation made by some scholars that democratic countries are less likely to go to war against each other than against authoritarian countries, or than authoritarian countries against each other.[3] This idea is contained within a body of literature generally called the democratic peace theory, which has attributed to democratic countries certain properties that facilitate the nonviolent management of conflicts and tensions between them.[4]

Even if such observation is empirically grounded and we assume that we do know what is meant by democratic countries, the question must still be raised whether this empirical fact has anything to do with democracy or derives from some other factors, such as a certain economic development, some particular commercial links, or constraints of the given international order that affect simultaneously both the development of democracies in certain countries and the peaceful relations between them, without the two being necessarily interrelated. However, it may also be suggested that there are, indeed, some inherent logical, as well as empirically grounded, connections between democracy and the avoidance of violent conflict between countries.

What could those connections be? Perhaps citizens in democratic countries internalize certain norms of conduct that restrain them, more than in other countries, from easily opting for violence as a means to settle differences. Other options are tried more assiduously before violence is chosen. Perhaps the political cost of violence, at the international as well as the domestic level, is deemed too high by the elite in a democratic country. Policymakers may fear losing the support of their constituencies, on whom they depend more in democratic countries than in authoritarian ones, if they opt for violent measures. Such restraining factors may be stronger when the counterpart is a democratic country than when it is an authoritarian one, perhaps because of the higher status and sympathy that a democratic rival country enjoys in the eyes of the citizens of a fellow democracy.

Citizens of the democratic country and their leaders may also have less confidence that their conflict could be solved by nonviolent means when the counterpart is not democratic and hence is not expected to play by the same rules. As Dixon noted,[5] autocracies may not generate the same respect or trust of policymakers and citizens in democracies as do other democracies.

The above propositions are based on political expediency, respect, and trust among policymakers and citizens in democratic countries. However, the argument may, perhaps, be pushed a bit further and address more directly the essential features of democracy that I have suggested earlier. If democracy recognizes and legitimizes the articulation of competing, and conflicting interests and preferences, it may also generate instruments that would try to manage them without resorting to violence. Autocracies, by contrast, may suppress or ignore conflicts, but when conflicts can no longer be concealed, while they continue to be considered illegitimate, there would be a greater tendency to stamp them out as thoroughly as possible, by violence if necessary. Under such circumstances, there might also be a greater tendency to sublimate the conflict as a heroic struggle in favor of one side, the virtuous one, against the other, the evil one. By contrast, democracy's recognition of conflict and the right to differ as a legitimate aspect of public life may also generate, or reflect, an ability to put oneself into the other's position, to acknowledge that the other may have legitimate, though different, views and interests. Processes may develop that would accommodate such differences and give some satisfaction to the views and interests held by the different sides to the conflict, thereby increasing the likelihood that a nonviolent settlement would be reached between the conflicting sides.

IV. INTERNAL CONFLICT MANAGEMENT

The arguments made so far were raised with regard to the international level, in the context of the democratic peace theory dealing with inter-state relations. There is little doubt, however, that they may be even more significant to the domestic scene. In his paper for the 1997 International Political Science Association (IPSA) conference in Seoul, John Harbeson raised the intriguing possibilities, and difficulties, of applying the democratic peace theory to the internal national scene.[6] If democracy is indeed a facilitator of nonviolent conflict management at the international scene, can it not be expected to fulfill a similar function at the domestic level? If citizens in democratic countries are reluctant to opt for violent methods to settle differences at the international level, may they not show a similar reluctance at the national level as well? And if citizens show such reluctance, would that not affect the elite, the policymakers, who, in a democratic system, would be especially dependent on their constituency's support no less in internal policy matters than in international ones? Furthermore, could there not be the same inherent link between the legitimacy to differ and the way conflicts are managed in the domestic arena as in the global one? If citizens have internalized norms that recognize the right of the other to have different opinions and interests, would that not lead them to a greater tendency to adopt ways of managing conflict based on compromise and negotiation and according to the other side some partial, though perhaps unequal, satisfaction of its needs, and hence a stake in a nonviolent settlement? Putting oneself in the other's place, acknowledging that it may have different and even contradictory views and interests, legitimizing public manifestations of dissent and contest, may lead to the establishment of certain rules and procedures by which dissent is handled and conflict is contained within nonviolent boundaries.

We should, however, beware of a tautological trap here. If we *define* democracy as the legitimization of public dissent and then claim that it therefore enables the nonviolent management of conflicts, the relationship may appear more definitional than empirical. If, however, the right to public dissent is considered a normative prerequisite, but is not included in the definition of democracy, whereas democracy refers to the procedures, the structural arrangements, the management tools that handle public dissent, then the danger of tautology is reduced and democracy may indeed be examined as a possible facilitator of nonviolent conflict management in the domestic as well as the international scene.

V. INSECURITY AND THE INTENSITY OF CONFLICTS

For the conflicting sides to give the democratic tools a chance, they should have some confidence that even if they do not win the contest, all will not be lost. Some of their most fundamental needs and interests would be recognized and accommodated (though obviously not all they strove for when they entered the contest). In other words, democratic tools have to include a provision that would negate a winner take all situation. The higher the level of anxiety of the conflicting sides about the possible results of failure in the contest, the less ready would they be to abide by the rules of the game, and the more would they try to achieve their goals by any means. This, in turn, would increase the likelihood that the conflict would erupt into violence. For this reason, I have stressed that for democratic rules to be set into motion it may not be sufficient to simply recognize the right to dissent. Provisions have to be made for the protection of some fundamental rights and interests of the dissenting side and the satisfaction of some of its most basic needs. This is not an absolute right, of course. Not every view, idea, or interest would be accommodated; some may be rejected outright and be suppressed if they contradict certain fundamental cultural values and human rights (the boundaries of which are, admittedly, difficult to determine). Still, while not every single view and interest would be accepted, attention should be paid not to create a situation that would leave the losing side no incentive to accept the existing rules of conflict management. This is especially important to remember in democratic transitional situations in which the respect for the other side's interests is not fully ingrained, and democracy is too often misinterpreted as winner take all. Under these circumstances the stakes of conflict rise considerably and so does its intensity. Insecurity sets in; the consequences of failure are perceived as catastrophic to the contestants, and the likelihood rises that they would attempt to prevent such failure at any cost, thus defeating the very premise upon which the democratic tools are being attempted. We shall return to this point when we look more specifically at democratic transitions in certain African countries and the role of ethnicity in them.

If conflict is inherent, what would be the best way to minimize the danger of its erupting into violence (1) under conditions prevailing in contemporary Africa, and (2) when ethnicity is part of the conflict, i.e., when the conflicting groups and their demands are defined or represented in ethnic terms? In his 1997 IPSA conference paper, Donald Rothchild examined two alternatives: (1) a maximalist majoritarian democracy option, with large scale popular participation in the political contest in the hope of promoting certain views and interests and overcoming those of rivals, and (2) a minimalist elite pact option, in which popular participation and contest is significantly reduced and elites representing different sectors come to an agreement between them on how to distribute the spoils of power so that each sector receives some share and attains some of its goals.[7] Under the best-case scenario of a strong state and a strong civil society, with widespread acceptance of intergroup political competition according to internalized rules of contest, the maximalist democratic option is preferred as it gives a larger group of people a sense of participation in the social order and thus strengthens their commitment to it. However, when these accompanying conditions do not exist, majoritarian democracy may quickly be transformed into an empty facade of unity and solidarity that the majority (or simply those in power) imposes on the entire population, thus implementing the complete opposite of what was intended by democracy. Under the conditions prevailing in Africa, when strong states and civil societies do not exist and there is no widespread recognition of legitimate contest under accepted rules of the game, Rothchild wonders whether it might not be more prudent to rely on elite pact arrangements as less risky means of conflict management and mediation.[8]

Rothchild, obviously, does not commit himself to any of these alternatives. He states, quite prudently, that the appropriate route would depend on a variety of factors that should be empirically examined in each case. We shall not discuss here those different factors, which may include the perception by the actors of the power relations between them, the responsiveness of the state to various sectoral demands, the collective memory of past conflicts and their outcome, and others. What transcends all these factors is the level of anxiety, or insecurity, felt by the conflicting sides as to the outcome of the contest. The crucial issue is the fear of the conflicting sides that they might find themselves on the losing side of a winner take all situation and suffer the consequences—that whoever does not prevail may lose everything: economic resources, freedom, identity, self-respect, even life. As mentioned, the higher such anxiety, the less likely that the rules of the game would be adhered to. Rivals would turn into enemies, overcoming them would be attempted at any cost, including violence, and conflicts would erupt out of control.

A high level of such anxiety may, indeed, hamper the majoritarian democratic option, as a large number of groups would not trust that their basic rights and interests would be protected within the rules of participation. The larger and more fragmented the participating groups and the more totalistic their demands (more on that later), the more difficult it would be to ensure the kind of reciprocative arrangements that would reduce the anxiety of all sides. A minimalist elite pact might be more efficient, under certain circumstances, in safeguarding at least some of the rights and interests of the conflicting sides and in preventing a winner take all situation. However, one cannot assume, a priori, that elite pacts will always have a built-in advantage in reducing such anxiety. All groups may not be represented in such pacts, and those left out would have their anxiety heightened even further. Elites could feel as fearful of total loss as could their followers. They may also, for their personal interests, exploit and exacerbate the feelings of anxiety and frustration among their followers to make conflicts more intractable, more difficult to contain. Elites are, indeed, notorious creators of anxiety, not only appeasers of it. They often exaggerate differences in their outbidding for influence and resources. Whether elite pacts would succeed in smoothing over differences, moderate conflicts, and implement mutual security arrangements between conflicting parties, or, on the contrary, would exacerbate and intensify the struggle is an open question that must be examined empirically in each specific case.

The relative strength or weakness of the state may also have an important bearing on how conflicts are represented and hence managed. If the state is too weak, it may not be able to perform the arbitration function that would be expected of it as the protector of the rules of the game by which the various conflicting sides are constrained. If the state is too strong, however, the balance between state and society may be broken: the state may become too assertive on behalf of one of the sides to the conflict at the expense of other actors in the political process. The state may also play an important role in how conflicts are portrayed, whether in more comprehensive or fragmented terms, for example, or whether or not related to ascriptive primordial features that may be collectivistic and more difficult to change, hence raising the level of anxiety they provoke. This last point leads directly to the role of ethnicity in conflicts.

VI. ETHNICITY AND CONFLICT MANAGEMENT

It should be stated at the outset that the question discussed here is not whether ethnicity is a real basis of conflict or is constructed and manipulated for political purposes. We take for granted that ethnicity is indeed constructed to a large extent, for political and other needs, and we have, therefore, stressed the ethnic *representation* of conflicts. The expansion or contraction of ethnic boundaries, the determination of which groups are included in a given category and which ones are not, and what entitlements this entails are obviously reformulated as conflicts unfold and political circumstances change. However, as the late Claude Ake used to say, the fact that ethnicity is constructed and politically manipulated does not make it any less real; there are still many people who are willing to kill for it or are being killed because of it. The question that should interest us, then, is not how constructed ethnicity is, but, however constructed, what effect does it have on the nature of conflicts and on the prospects of establishing democratic means to manage them.

It may be claimed that the representation of a conflict as ethnic raises its comprehensiveness, its totality. It spreads it to all the people ascribed to belong, primordially, to one of the conflicting sides in question. It reduces the possibility of removing oneself, individually, from the conflict or maintaining some middle position (sitting on the fence), as the outcome of the conflict is likely to affect the whole collectivity, irrespective of one's individual position in the conflict. The conflict is collectivized and encompasses larger groups allowing less possibility of disengaging oneself from them. The vulnerability of individual families or communities rises and is more broadly applied, hence raising the general insecurity and level of anxiety. This, in turn, raises the intensity of the conflict and may make it more prone to violence. If the conflict is total, and there is less protection from its consequences, one better make sure not to be on the losing side. As the stakes rise and insecurity sets in, so may fall the willingness to rely on democratic means to safeguard one's vital interests. Ethnic representation of conflicts may thus create an especially heavy burden on their democratic management.

The adverse effect that ethnicity may have on democratization processes has been strongly emphasized in Africa in both policymaking and academic circles. In Uganda, the current Museveni regime has wholeheartedly adopted the view that ethnicity exacerbates conflicts and makes them more difficult to manage by democratic means. Moreover, it has used this argument as the main reason (or should we say excuse?) for banning political parties and justifying a nonparty political system in which political contest is allowed on an individual basis without being organized in political parties. The stated rationale is that, in the postcolonial African context, political parties inevitably become tools of ethnic crystallization and politicization that are deemed detrimental to the democratic process.

Academic studies made of the role of ethnopolitical movements in Nigeria's quest for democracy have also generally concluded that they tend to exacerbate conflicts rather than curtail them, hence hampering the democratic process, or at least imposing an additional burden on it.[9] Ethnopolitical movements, as their name implies, *politicize* ethnicity, i.e., contribute to the ethnic representation of political conflicts and interest articulation. This raises the stakes of the conflict and the consequences of a possible loss, thus making the conflicts more difficult to moderate.

The predominance of ethnopolitical movements in Nigeria is attributed to certain historical circumstances and to the legacy of past military regimes and is considered an unfortunate burden on the present prospects of democracy.[10] Furthermore, the state itself appears to play an active role in the ethnic representation of conflicts, thus strengthening ethnopoliticization and endangering the transition to democracy. The Nigerian state is not portrayed as a neutral body trying to balance and regulate the antagonisms of different sectors. It is regarded as an active party to those conflicts, an active contestant itself, strongly identified with some groups against others.[11] As part of this involvement, state rulers tend to regard the citizens not as individuals but as agents of corporate ethnic groups and categories, sometimes concealed under the euphemism of regional representation. They respond to the activities of the citizens in that context, while publicly professing to be above such considerations. Despite public denials of rulers, there is little doubt that state action in Nigeria further strengthens the salience of ethnicity in political discourse.

It should be added that various sectors in the civil society are also willing participants in a discourse that highlights the ethnic dimension. Even when the objective is to reduce the dominance of a certain region or ethnic group and claims are made to that effect, the result could be a heightening of sensitivity to the ethnocultural dimension in political discourse. Laws passed on the obligation of political parties to have multiregional support (i.e., to gain a certain level of support in a number of regions in order to have their candidates elected to office) may have the paradoxical effect of making ethnoregional support a salient issue during election campaigns. A proposal floated during constitutional talks in Nigeria on the possibility of a regionally rotating presidency[12] is another good example of how much political discourse is permeated by issues of ethnoregional rights and representation and conflict lines are drawn along these terms. The fact that leading policymakers, including some quite close to government circles, were closely involved in those discussions also shows how strongly the state contributes to maintaining the salience of such discussions.

The salience of ethnicity and of ethnopoliticization reaches its peak in periods of political liberalization, during the alleged preparations for a transition to a democratically elected civilian government. The ethnopolitical movements become important tools of political participation. They help articulate collective interests, ask for a share of power, and demand an end to the marginalization that supposedly occurred in the previous ''less free'' period. However, by taking center stage, they also endanger the transition to democracy as they raise the anxiety level of the conflicting sides. The conflict becomes more comprehensive. Insecurity grows, as does fear of the consequences of the contest's outcome. A siege mentality sets in among those in power; they try to hold on to their positions at any cost, and the democratic process is derailed.

It is interesting to note a significant rise in ethnoregional references also in the events that led to the downfall of the Mobutu regime in Zaire and its replacement by that of Laurent Kabila. While there is no doubt that popular discontent with the Mobutu regime was very widespread and was certainly shared by a large number of regions and ethnic groups in the country, the events that led to the change of regime have been widely discussed in ethnoregional terms both within the country (now renamed Congo) and outside. After Kabila's advent to power, frequent references were made to an inevitable ''Swahilization'' of the country, to a gradual shift from the Atlantic Ocean to the Indian Ocean sphere of influence, and from Francophony to Anglophony. The growing influence of the Tutsi in the new armed forces was stressed, and its possible implications were pointed out on the new regional alliances of Congo-Zaire and on actions taken against Hutu refugees stationed in the country. Since then things have changed dramatically. Political alliances and power relations underwent a radical metamorphosis, but the ethnic representation of conflicts has remained salient. The erstwhile Tutsi allies of Kabila turned against him and were dominant in the attempts to overthrow him, with the help of Rwanda and Uganda. They have not succeeded (as of this writing). Kabila's regime appears to have turned the tide against the rebel forces, in large part due to the military help it received from some other neighboring states, mainly Angola and Zimbabwe. While the war was far from over, the threat on the capital city was lifted and the military struggle was pushed back to eastern provinces.

Whatever the outcome of these struggles, and however fragile alliances proved to be, the result was not only an internationalization of the conflict, with the active military involvement of neighboring states, but also a continuous heightening of the ethnocultural dimension of the conflict. Both factors contributed to the rise in the level of violence. The facts that such ethnocultural and regional representation of the conflict may be grossly inaccurate, exaggerated, or oversimplified and that it may hide many other points of grievance are beside the point. What is important is that, true or false, allegations of ethnic collusion and clashing are widely being heard, both in the country and outside, and this raises the intensity of the conflict. Public discourse is full of ethnic imagery that has already had a great impact on the direction in which the conflict has unfolded. It will be interesting to see to what extent such ethnoregional attribution of the conflict will continue in the future, how it will affect the management of conflicts in Congo-Zaire, and hence its political prospects in years to come.

So far our discussion has stressed the detrimental effects that ethnic representation of conflicts may have on their democratic management. There is, however, also a counterargument that maintains that ethnic identity is such a fundamental component of group formation, solidarity, and collective interest articulation that ignoring it would in itself lead to discontent and become a point of grievance. Suppression of ethnic claims and interests may be a futile exercise and may even be dangerous as it would put an artificial lid on conflicts that may later explode in more violent forms. While in Uganda, the regime has made great efforts not to legitimize ethnic-based interest articulation and political organization, in neighboring Ethiopia the current regime has followed the opposite policy. Ethnicity has been given full legitimacy as a basic bloc of society, even as the basis of representation and interest articulation. Rather than suppress its manifestation, it has been recognized as a fully legitimate tool of contest within a multicultural pluralistic framework. The adoption of this policy in Ethiopia could, possibly, be attributed to a latent objective, that of breaking the dominance of the central Amharic group to give better representation to other groups from whom the leaders of the present regime received stronger support during their armed struggle against the previous regime. One should note, however, that the Museveni regime in Uganda, too, has to contend with a dominant group in the country, the Baganda, but it chose to tackle the question of ethnic tension in the country in a very different way than its Ethiopian counterpart. Specific political contingencies may be at the root of state policies regarding ethnicity, but they can lead, at least at the declarative level, to significant variation regarding the legitimacy accorded to ethnicity in collective representation.

I shall not attempt to find out here why the Ethiopian and Ugandan regimes differ so widely in the role they attribute to ethnicity in their respective polity. It is important, for our purpose, just to note that such a difference exists and that ethnicity is not viewed uniformly as detrimental to democratic conflict management. This should sensitize us, again, to the crucial role states play in the way conflicts are allowed to be represented and in the rules that are set up to contain them. The larger question, to which no uniform answer is given, is what impact ethnicity has on the form of conflict management, and hence on the prospects of the establishment of democracy. Some favor suppressing and delegitimizing ethnic representation of conflict as it is perceived as a threat to the ability to manage conflicts within nonviolent boundaries. Others, by contrast, maintain that ethnicity should be recognized as just another basis of difference in the plurality of interest articulation, no less legitimate than professional, economic, gender, or class bases, hence an accepted component of the domestic conflict management process. Ethnicity then becomes an inevitable and legitimate component of pluralist democracy.

VII. CONCLUSION

I have tried to examine some major issues regarding the relationships between democracy, conflict, and ethnicity, a subject which is very popular in the current social science literature but does not always receive the conceptional clarity it deserves.

I started with a rather bold suggestion, that we drop altogether the concept of conflict resolution and focus instead on conflict containment, or conflict management. Not only does that choice indicate a better recognition of the endemic nature of conflict as part of human existence and social order, but it also brings us closer to the cultural-normative prerequisite at the root of any democratic structural arrangement: the legitimacy accorded to the public manifestation of dissent. Democracy derives from an underlying recognition that different groups may act to promote different, and even contradictory, views and interests. Moving on from that premise, the question becomes what mechanisms could best ensure that the conflicts, which inevitably develop between these groups, would be managed in a way that minimizes the risks of their erupting into violence.

Assessing the possible role of democracy as a facilitator of nonviolent conflict management, at both the international and the internal domestic level, I emphasized that winner take all situations could be a serious impediment to the implementation of that role. Special attention was paid to the level of insecurity and anxiety generated by the conflict among the different sides. It was suggested that the higher the anxiety, the more difficult it would be to contain the conflict within nonviolent boundaries. Hence, the art of nonviolent conflict management is reducing such anxieties while offering protection to losing sides, something that is sorely absent in current attempts at democratic transition, especially in Africa.

Finally, I examined the specific role that ethnicity can play in conflict management. On the one hand, the ethnic representation of conflict might make the conflict more comprehensive and hence might raise the level of anxiety of the parties involved and be detrimental to nonviolent democratic management. On the other hand, the argument was also made that artificially suppressing the ethnic dimension from interest articulation might heighten the anxiety it is supposed to reduce, and might lead to greater frustration that might intensify the conflict, perhaps as a delayed response at some future stage. This apparent contradiction cannot be settled here; the different views can only be presented with the hope that some future analysis might elucidate these points further. Attention has been drawn, however, to the important role that states play in the extent to which they prevent, allow, or encourage the ethnic representation of conflicts, thus affecting the way conflicts are handled. The issues raised here may also be applied to the religious representation of conflicts, a topic not discussed in this chapter, but which could be analyzed along the same lines, and whose implications for democracy and conflict management could not be more obvious in current times.

NOTES/REFERENCES

1. See, for example, O'Donnell, G. and Schmitter, P. (1986). (eds.), *Transitions from Authoritarian Rule: Tentative Conclusions About Uncertain Democracies*. Baltimore: Johns Hopkins University Press.
2. Azarya, V. (1994). Civil society and disengagement in Africa. In J. Harbeson, D. Rothchild, and N. Chazan (eds.), *State and Civil Society in Africa*. Boulder, CO: Lynne Rienner.
3. Harbeson, J. W. (1997). Democratization and conflict resolution in Sub-Saharan Africa: A research agenda. Paper presented at the 17th World Congress of the International Political Science Association, Seoul.
4. See Gleditsch, N. P. (1995). Geography, democracy and peace. *International Relations 20*(1), 297–320; Maoz, Z. and Abdolali, N. (1989). Regime types and international conflict, 1816–1976. *Journal of Conflict Resolution 33*(1), 3–35; Ray, J. L. (1995). *Democracy and International Conflict*. Columbia, SC: University of South Carolina Press.
5. Dixon, W. J. (1993). Democracy and the management of international conflict. *Journal of Conflict Resolution 37*(1), 42–68.
6. Harbeson, J. W. (1997). Democratization and conflict resolution in Sub-Saharan Africa: A research agenda. Paper presented at the 17th World Congress of the International Political Science Association, Seoul.
7. Rothchild, D. (1997). Ethnic insecurity, peace agreements and state building in Africa. Paper presented at the 17th World Congress of the International Political Science Association, Seoul.
8. Rothchild, D. (1997). Ethnic insecurity, peace agreements and state building in Africa, pp. 21, 34. Paper presented at the 17th World Congress of the International Political Science Association, Seoul.
9. Ibeanu, O. O. (1997). Ethno-political movements, ethnic conflict and transition to democracy in Nigeria, 1986–1996. Paper presented at the 17th World Congress of the International Political Science Association, Seoul.
10. Nnoli, O. (1995). *Ethnicity and Development in Nigeria*. Aldershot: Avebury; Ibeanu, O. O. (1997). Ethno-political movements, ethnic conflict and transition to

democracy in Nigeria, 1896–1996. Paper presented at the 17th World Congress of the International Political Science Association, Seoul.

11. Ibeanu, O. O. (1997). Ethno-political movements, ethnic conflict and transition to democracy in Nigeria, 1896–1996, p. 8. Paper presented at the 17th World Congress of the International Political Science Association, Seoul.

12. Ibeanu, O. O. (1997). Ethno-political movements, ethnic conflict and transition to democracy in Nigeria, 1896–1996, pp. 12–13. Paper presented at the 17th World Congress of the International Political Science Association, Seoul.

8

The Role of Mass Communication in Egyptian Family Planning Policy

Amany A. Khodair
Suez Canal University, Ismailia, Egypt

Steven K. Wisensale
University of Connecticut, Storrs, Connecticut

I. INTRODUCTION

At least three important facts have dominated Egyptian demographic studies over the last 50 years. First, there has been a consistently high birth rate, with the population doubling from 26 million thirty years ago to 57 million in 1994. Second, the population is maldistributed, both geographically and in age. Today, 99% of the people live on 3.8% of the land, and about half the population is under twenty years of age. And third, previous attempts at controlling the population have failed. However, that trend has changed significantly in recent years.

In 1994 President Hosni Mubarek of Egypt received the United Nations Population Award for both his national and international leadership on population issues. Despite decades of disappointments in addressing a rising birth rate and a maldistributed population, Egypt chose a strategy of collaboration over coercion and embarked on an aggressive educational program in the early 1980s that set as its goal a model "two-child family" by 2015.

One year later, in August, 1995, Egypt's National Population Council issued its report, *Perspectives on Fertility and Family Planning in Egypt* [1]. Consisting of eight separate studies that are based on the results of the 1992 Egypt Demographic and Health Survey, the 1995 report is the most recent and comprehensive study completed to date on Egyptian family planning policy. It reached at least three major conclusions.

First, Egypt's family planning program has made significant progress in supporting the efforts of Egyptian families to meet the nation's reproductive goal of two children per family. Second, future family planning services must be directed not only at public providers, but also at the private medical sector. And third, a primary reason for the success of Egypt's family planning policy thus far is its strong information, education, and communication program.

The purpose of this paper, therefore, is to examine Egypt's utilization of mass communication in an effort to achieve its national goal of a model two-child family by 2015. Discussed here is the vital role played by mass communication in family planning in Egypt, the structure of the Egyptian media, phases of media development in family planning and promotion strategies, and whether or not the selected strategies appear to be effective in achieving the national goal.

This presentation is divided into three major parts. The first is devoted to a historical overview of Egypt's family planning challenge, which has roots as far back at the 1930s. The role of mass communication in Egyptian family planning is then examined, with a particular focus on its structure and its use. And the third part will address the effectiveness of mass communication in achieving Egypt's family planning goal.

II. THE HISTORY OF FAMILY PLANNING IN EGYPT

Egypt's interest in population policy can be traced as far back as the 1930s when researchers began to identify a growing imbalance between available resources and people in need. Although the first book on Egyptian population policy (Professor Mohammed Awadh Mohammed's *The Population of this Planet* [2]) was published in 1936, official government intervention in family planning did not occur until the early 1950s. Since then, four distinct phases of Egyptian family planning have been identified. Each phase is discussed briefly below.

In phase one, "Discovery and Noninterference" (1953–1965), the National Committee on Population was formed. Initially, an increase in population was considered a major asset in both maintaining and enhancing Egypt's political position in the region. However, this policy changed in 1962 when the government concluded that a rapidly increasing population was in direct conflict with Egypt's desire to raise its people's standard of living. "Population increase is the most dangerous obstacle facing Egyptians in their attempts to raise the level of production in their homeland" [3].

In phase two, "The Period of Positive Interference" (1965–1972), the Supreme Council for Family Planning was formed. It immediately adopted a plan to reduce the birth rate to 30 per 1000 population by 1978. To accomplish this, two major goals were established: the reduction in childbearing rates and increased participation in family planning programs. Unfortunately, this phase was hampered by a number of weaknesses. It lacked a long-term strategy, was short on both funds and trained personnel, and failed to identify clear lines of responsibility for implementing the goals and objectives agreed upon.

By phase three, ''Setting Population Goals and Policies (1973–1984), the population problem in Egypt was being defined and addressed within a political framework that raised concerns about economic development on a national scale and the standard of living within the family. As a result, a ten-year national plan for population and family planning (1973–1982) was initiated. To help implement it, Egypt's Information, Education, and Communication Center (IEC) of the State Information Service (SIS) was established in 1979. It was given a threefold charge: first, to heighten public awareness of the economic need to limit family size; second, to encourage people to have smaller families; and third, to change people's behavior and raise the rate of contraceptive use among them [3: 5]. Thus began the use of mass communication as a major policy tool.

In phase four, ''Political Commitment'' (1985 to the present), President Mubarek expressed concern that earlier goals of population policy had not been achieved. Consequently, in 1984 he convened the National Conference on Population. As a result of this conference, the National Population Council was created in 1985, and it in turn produced Egypt's national population policy in 1986. Among its major principles are the goal to achieve a two-child family model by 2015 and a heavy emphasis placed on education and mass communication in achieving that goal [4]. How mass communication is structured in Egypt is now discussed in more detail.

III. THE STRUCTURE AND USE OF MASS COMMUNICATION IN EGYPT

The Ministry of Information, which is one of twenty-six ministries that constitute the Egyptian government, is the sole agency responsible for the mass communication task within the Egyptian political system. As presented in Figure 1, the Ministry of Information consists of three major divisions.

The Radio and Television Union was created in 1970 from a consortium of four separate divisions: Radio, Television, Drama Production, and Technical Engineering. Currently, there are seven radio networks, which include approximately twenty radio stations (Figure 2), two central or national television stations, six local television stations, and four cable stations, as well as the first satellite due to be launched by 1998 (Figure 3) [5].

The Press includes two important divisions: first, the National Press, which publishes materials produced by either The Press Foundation or the Middle East News Agency, and, second, the Party Press, which is affiliated with any of the thirteen political parties currently functioning within Egypt [6].

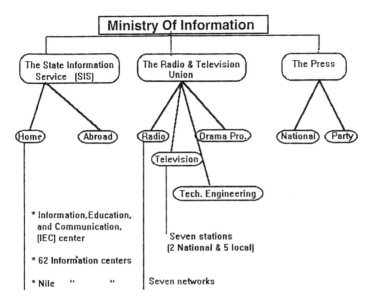

Figure 1   The three major divisions of Egypt's Ministry of Information.

The third component of the Ministry of Information, as presented in Figure 1, is the State Information Services, which consists of two major departments. There is the External Department, which provides information about Egypt to foreign countries, and the Internal Department, which seeks to inform the general populace of Egypt about various domestic matters, including family planning [3]. A key component of the Internal Department and a major player in Egypt's family planning policy is the Information, Education, and Communication Center.

As the heart and soul of Egypt's family planning policy, the IEC has employed five important techniques in reaching and educating the public about family planning. These techniques—which include the mass media, interpersonal communication, use of the enter-educate method, special training, and research—were created by the State Information Service. Each is now discussed.

A.   The Mass Media: Radio, TV, and the Press

Of the five techniques identified, perhaps the mass media is most relied upon to educate the public about family planning. For example, the Egyptian Radio and Television Union (ERTU) airs an average of 605 hours of family planning programs annually [5]. Radio (Figure 2) is an important component of Egypt's mass media structure. Its accessibility, affordability, and portability enable it to reach

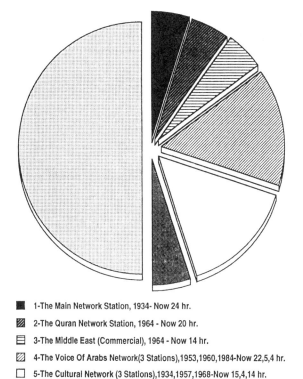

■   1-The Main Network Station, 1934- Now 24 hr.

▨   2-The Quran Network Station, 1964 - Now 20 hr.

☰   3-The Middle East (Commercial), 1964 - Now 14 hr.

▨   4-The Voice Of Arabs Network(3 Stations),1953,1960,1984-Now 22,5,4 hr.

☐   5-The Cultural Network (3 Stations),1934,1957,1968-Now 15,4,14 hr.

▦   6-The Directed Network (32 Languages).

☐   7-The Local Network (10 Stations) between 1975-1991,approx. 8 hr. each

Figure 2   Radio in Egypt.

out to even the most remote locations in the country. Equally important, the high rate of illiteracy among the population makes radio a convenient and effective information tool of the government.

Radio programs dealing with the population problem, produced by the IEC and broadcast by radio networks, averaged 140 programs monthly, totaling 1100 radio broadcasting hours annually [3]. In addition, there are radio talk shows, interviews, as well as short family planning messages integrated into ongoing topical radio programs at a weekly average of about 20 minutes of air time. Although these messages are carried out by all radio stations, special attention is given to regional and local radio stations, which have a special appeal to local populations [3].

With respect to television (Figure 3), Egypt's eight channels (national and local) offer full coverage to all corners of the nation. Using TV in promoting

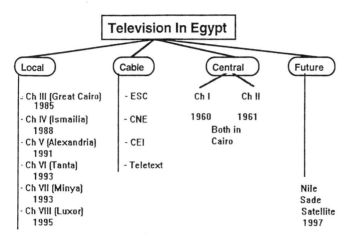

Figure 3 Television in Egypt.

family planning has undergone a process of gradual development, with all types of television formats having been employed, including evening dramas, mini-dramas, TV quiz shows, video songs, short inserts (in 55 TV programs) and innovative TV spots (10 per year, broadcast alternately four times daily) [3]

Recently, a TV series of 16 episodes of 45 minutes each, *And the Nile Flows On*, dealing with family planning issues was coproduced by the IEC and the ERTU. Mr. Nabil Osman, Head of the State Information Service, commented on the success of the series: ''This time we used a very strong and open approach with nothing to hide. This enabled us to win the 1994 Global Award for Media Excellence in media campaigns from the World Population Institute'' [7]. The IEC has also produced other short feature films (12–40 minutes each) that have family planning as their major themes. These include *Identity Card, A Day in the Life of a Happy Family*, and *Why Does the Canary Cry* [3]. These films are often used in small group settings through the 60 SIS centers scattered throughout the country.

Not to be overlooked is the role of the Egyptian press in addressing the issue of family planning. The IEC alone distributes nearly 800 press releases annually on family planning to newspapers and magazines. Cartoonists and photographers emphasize the dangers of overpopulation and two annual newspaper contests related to family planning draw an average of 9000 responses a year [3].

Also, each year the IEC center organizes a symposium on family planning in a different publishing house. Experts from related areas are invited to participate in the discussions. The proceedings are published in the press and in a booklet widely distributed to individuals, groups, and organizations concerned with family planning. Three symposia have been organized so far and, in turn, have produced three books: *Egypt's Time Bomb, War of the 90s*, and *The Economic Dimensions of the Population Problem* [8].

B. Interpersonal Communication

Interpersonal communication is another vital component of the Egyptians' use of mass communication as part of its family planning strategy. Although a 1990 survey showed that 95% of Egyptians gather information about population from TV and radio, knowledge represents only one segment of the KAP trilogy (knowledge, attitudes, and practice). To change attitudes and practices, the 62 local IECs conduct a total of 3200 group activities that reach an estimated 750,000 people annually. These include, but are not limited to, more than 800 meetings in health centers, hospitals, and factories; 950 discussion meetings in universities, youth camps, and community centers; over 900 meetings of religious and labor leaders, social workers, and members of agricultural cooperatives; 3 major conferences for mass media communicators; and 1 national school contest in drawing and research skills related to family planning [3].

As presented in Table 1, there are six different types of meetings that are held at the 62 local IECs. Clearly, the intended audiences range from opinion leaders to youth, and the approaches range from educational to religious to public health related. Although there is variation in the size of the audience (from 30 to 100) for the various types of meetings, there is more consistency in the number of meetings (300 to 900) held each year.

Table 1   Types of Interpersonal Communication Used by the IEC

Type of meeting	Directed to	Number of attendees	Number of meetings held annually
1. Educational	Opinion leaders	30	900
2. Discussion (after showing a film)	Small groups (homogenous)	40	950
3. Inter-agency	Other agencies	50	500
4. Public (health or economic approach)	The masses	100s	800
5. Youth	Students	100s	300
6. Ramadan (religious approach)	The masses	100s	500

Source: Ref. 6.

C. The Enter-Educate Method

The third strategy employed by the IEC is the use of the enter-educate method, a tool that has been used in Egypt for thousands of years. Directed toward those who would normally not attend lectures or other group activities, such programs with family planning themes include TV and radio mini-dramas, songs, local theatre, folkloric art forms, films, posters, brochures, puppet shows, informative booklets, zagal (local folk poetry), game competitions, and school festivals. The enter-educate method is especially useful in isolated rural areas where the illiteracy rate is high. A similar method has been employed in some U.S. communities to address the problem of teen pregnancy.

D. Training of Specialists

A fourth function of the IEC concerns the recruitment and training of specialists who are responsible for educating the public about family planning policy in general and contraceptive use in particular. Workshops are held for local media people, religious leaders, social workers, school teachers, health care personnel, youth leaders, and others. Most recently, training programs have focused on improving local meetings by stressing dialogue over lecture formats. Not to be overlooked is the fact that trainees are given special training in how to combat unfounded rumors and misinformation.

E. Research

Finally, the IEC is directly involved in research. Working closely with the National Population Council and other appropriate agencies, it has participated in at least 24 major research projects since 1984. Included in these studies are "Egypt's Contraceptive Prevalence Survey of 1984." "The Egyptian Demographic and Health Survey of 1988", and the 1990 "Survey of the Attitudes of Radio Listeners and TV Viewers of Programs Dealing with the Population Problem." Equally important, ongoing evaluations are designed to "detect the psychographic and geographic traits and concerns of different population strata, all of which would hopefully lead to more effective messages" [3:19]. The recent adoption of a sophisticated management information system will further assist the IEC in developing and maintaining a data base around population issues.

While citizens may listen to radio broadcasts and watch TV shows that include messages about contraception, there is no guarantee that such activities are directly responsible for a lower birth rate. What follows is a discussion of the impact Egypt's family planning policy has had on the population over the last decade or so.

IV. THE IMPACT OF A MASS COMMUNICATION STRATEGY

According to the National Population Council's 1995 study, *Perspectives on Fertility and Family Planning in Egypt*, mass communication—television and radio in particular—has played a significant role in Egypt's family planning policy. Data were collected on the access of women to both radio and television (Table 2) and their actual exposure to family planning broadcasts (Table 3).

As seen in Table 2, although access to television and radio is widespread throughout the nation (e.g., two-thirds of women watch TV daily), it is less extensive in Upper Egypt compared to Lower Egypt. And, not surprising perhaps, the coverage of broadcast media varies greatly according to governorate. For example, women in Aswan are 60% more likely to watch television daily than those in Fayoum. Similar differences emerge with respect to radio coverage. That is, 64% of the women in Aswan listen to the radio daily compared with 40% of the women in Menya.

While Table 2 illustrates the amount of access women have to broadcast media, it does not indicate the extent to which they are exposed to family planning messages. The results in Table 3, however, are more clear with respect to this matter. For example, in Lower Egypt about 80% of married women reported that they had seen or heard a family planning broadcast recently, compared to about

Table 2 Currently Married Women Who Watch Television or Listen to the Radio Daily, 1992

Region and governorate	Watch television daily (%)	Listen to radio daily (%)
Upper Egypt	71.8	52.0
Giza	85.2	62.2
Beni Suef	65.2	46.3
Fayoum	53.6	51.8
Menya	54.4	39.5
Assuit	65.3	44.8
Souhag	73.8	51.0
Qena	81.1	55.5
Aswan	91.5	64.2
Lower Egypt	86.7	71.1
All Egypt[a]	83.0	67.1

[a] Includes Upper and Lower Egypt and the Urban Governorates (not shown).
Source: Ref. 1.

Table 3 Percent Distribution of Currently Married Women by Exposure to Family Planning Broadcasts on the Radio or Television, 1992

Region and governorate	Neither	Radio only	Television only	Both	Missing	Total
Upper Egypt	37.6	0.9	49.1	12.3	0.2	100.0
Giza	19.9	1.7	52.8	25.4	0.2	100.0
Beni Suef	52.5	0.5	42.4	4.7	—	100.0
Fayoum	44.5	2.6	47.1	5.7	—	100.0
Menya	54.8	0.2	38.6	5.9	0.5	100.0
Assuit	50.0	0.6	39.6	9.8	—	100.0
Souhag	38.7	0.9	52.0	8.2	0.2	100.0
Qena	30.1	0.2	58.3	11.2	0.2	100.0
Aswan	18.6	0.0	67.9	13.5	—	100.0
Lower Egypt	20.5	1.2	53.0	25.3	0.0	100.0
All Egypt[a]	24.1	1.0	54.1	20.7	0.1	100.0

[a] Includes Upper and Lower Egypt and the Urban Governorates (not shown).
Source: Ref. 1.

two-thirds of married women in Upper Egypt. Again, differences vary considerably among governorates. While Giza and Aswan reported the highest percentage of married women exposed to family planning broadcasts, in Beni, Suef, Menya, and Assuit half or more married women said they had neither heard a radio message nor seen a television message about family planning during the previous month.

Clearly, designing and implementing a mass communication program is one thing; trying to isolate its impact and overall effectiveness, particularly within acceptable cost parameters, is quite another matter. Whether or not family planning is utilized is usually determined by four important variables: (1) the level of female education, (2) the availability of family planning services, (3) the infant mortality rate, and (4) the cost to the user of such a service. Because the government moved in a positive direction in all four areas, the use of family planning among Egyptian women increased from 24% of married women in childbearing age in 1980 to 49% in 1994—a more than doubling in use (Figure 4). As a result, Egypt's birth rate declined from 39.8 per 1000 in 1985 to 27.5 per 1000 in 1994 (Figure 5) [4].

With respect to families, total fertility rate fell from over five children per family in 1980 to under four children per family in 1994. If Egypt's fertility had remained at its 1980 level, its population by 1994 would have been about 62 million people, or 6 million more than the actual level of 56 million [4].

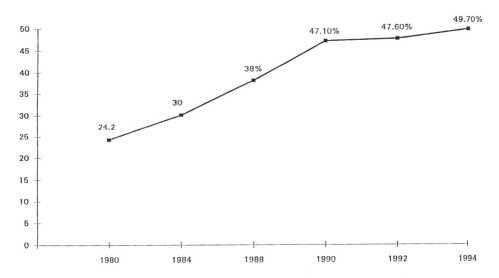

Figure 4 Prevalence rate of use of contraceptive methods.

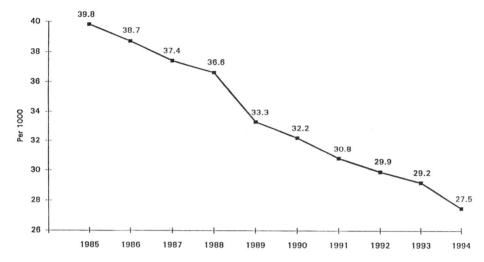

Figure 5   Birth rate in Egypt (1985–1994).

Despite these achievements over the past 12 years, however, there is much that remains to be accomplished. In 1990 the government set a national goal of an average of two children per couple by 2015. To achieve this, two more couples out of ten need to use family planning, to establish a total of seven users out of every ten couples. If successful, the Egyptian population would increase from 56 million in 1992 to 80 million by 2015, 12 million less than if fertility were to remain at its current rate [4].

Fortunately, perhaps, the 1992 "Egyptian Demographic and Health Survey" revealed that two out of ten of the women not using contraceptives would choose to either delay having more children now or have no children in the future. Thus, they are expressing an unmet need for family planning. More significantly, if this unmet need is addressed, Egypt should be able to accomplish its national goal of an average two-child family by the year 2015 [9]. The question remaining, however, is at what cost can this goal be met?

According to a recent report, "The Cost-Benefit Study of Family Planning in Egypt," [10] a successful family planning policy that controls a growing population will ultimately save the government significant expenditures on a variety of public services. The study projected the population under two different scenarios: one in which the use of family planning remained at its current level and one that saw an increase in the utilization of family planning to meet the national goal of two children per family by 2015. Savings under the latter scenario were calculated for education, health, food subsidies, housing, water, and sewage treatment.

At present, the annual public cost of providing family planning services to an Egyptian couple is £E 16. Without any change in the number of couples practicing family planning, the total national costs would nearly double between 1992 and 2015. However, if the national goal set for 2015 is to be met, the percentage of couples using family planning must also increase, and this too will create additional costs. According to the 1994 study, between 1992 and 2015 an additional investment of £E 635 million in family planning services will be required in order to achieve the national goal. Calculations and cost projections indicate that such a commitment would prove to be a sound financial investment for Egypt.

When applying a benefit-to-cost ratio for each of the six sectors identified, the 1994 study concluded that for every pound invested in family planning, the Egyptian government would save £E 9.34 in education costs, £E 2.05 in health care expenditures, £E 2.07 in food subsidies, £E 6.37 in housing costs, £E 5.82 in expenditures for water, and £E 4.44 in water and sewage treatment expenses. "Summing up all sectors, we can see that for each pound invested in family planning from 1993 to 2015, Egypt would save £E 30 in all sectors" [10:18].

Similar conclusions were reached on a macroeconomic scale. That is, with an increase in family planning, 1.5 million fewer jobs would be needed by 2010. This, in turn, would save about £E 85.3 in government supported job creation programs. And, because a smaller population would eventually mean a smaller work force, greater investment in machinery and technology is expected, thus increasing productivity overall. It is also projected that by increasing family planning by 2010 the gross domestic product will be 4.5% higher than under current family planning levels. Also, with respect to individual households, the average income is estimated to be 6.4% higher by 2010 [4]. Clearly, it appears that Egypt's family planning policy, particularly with its emphasis on mass communication, is a sound financial investment for the future.

REFERENCES

1. National Population Council. (1995). *Perspectives on Fertility and Family Planning in Egypt.* Cairo, Egypt.
2. M. Mohammed. (1936). *The Population of the Planet.* Alexandria, Egypt: Alexandria Press.
3. State Information Service. (1992). *The Challenging Task of Family Planning.* p. 5. Cairo, Egypt: Information, Education and Communication Center.
4. National Population Council. (1994). *Family Planning in Egypt: A Sound Investment.* Cairo, Egypt.
5. Ministry of Information. (1994). *Radio and Television Union Year Book, 1993–1994.* Cairo, Egypt.
6. Ministry of Information. (1987). *Encyclopedia of Politics, Volume 5, 1987.* Cairo, Egypt.

7. Osman, N. (1995). Interview with author, 11 January.
8. Information and Education Center. (1994). *Communication is the Key*. Cairo, Egypt: 15C.
9. National Population council. (1988). ''Egypt Demographic and Health Survey.'' Cairo, Egypt.
10. National Population Council. (1994). ''The Cost-Benefit Study of Family Planning in Egypt.'' Cairo, Egypt: The National Population Council and the Ministry of Population and Family Welfare.

9
Coexistence of Secularism and Fundamentalism in India

Pelgy Vaz
Fort Hays State University, Hays, Kansas

I. INTRODUCTION

In the past two decades, there has been religious strife and communal violence in India. In June 1984, the Indian Army attacked the Golden Temple in Amritsar, which is in the state of Punjab. This is a sacred shrine for the believers of Sikhism, an offshoot of Hinduism. The Golden Temple was occupied and fortified by militant Sikhs who demanded a separate Sikh state (Khalisthan) comprising the state of Punjab and other contiguous areas with a predominant Sikh population. The militant Sikhs described India as a Hindu India. Four months later in October 1984, Prime Minister Indira Gandhi was assassinated by two of her Sikh body guards. This led to an anti-Sikh riot where several thousand people (mostly Sikhs) were killed.

In Ayodhya, a city in the largest Indian state of Uttar Pradesh, is the nation's most explosive and sensitive religious site called the Babri Masjid. This site, disputed over the last five decades, had been claimed as sacred by both the Hindus and the Muslims. While Hindus claimed that it is the birthplace of Lord Rama, the Muslims insisted that the Moghul Emperor Babar built the mosque centuries ago. There were political and judicial actions that attempted to address the issue, but the Bharathiya Janata Party (BJP) and the Vishva Hindu Parishad (VHP), a religious organization led by Hindu religious leaders, were determined to demolish the Masjid. The demolition of the Babri Masjid on December 6, 1992, was the consequence of a huge rally organized and led by the BJP and the VHP. This led to violence in a number of states where thousands (mostly Muslims) were killed (Awasthi 1992b, 1994). More recently there has been violence against Christians, including the deaths of foreign missionaries, Indian priests, and nuns.

However, it is encouraging to note that in the last decade, two Indians, Baba Amte and Pandurang Shastri Athavale, were the recipients of the prestigious Templeton Prize for Progress in Religion. Amte, a Hindu lawyer, spent his life helping the Untouchables. He received the prize in 1990. Athavale is a leader of Swadhyaya, a self-study group based on the Bhagavad Gita (holy book of the Hindus), which promotes the recognition of God in every human being. This group is open to all faiths, and it discourages proselytizing. It has enhanced the self-esteem and self-respect of over 20 million people living in 100,000 villages (Swamy 1999).

But the reasons for these complex issues of religious hatred and communal violence are perplexing and challenging, as many times the violence is not driven by religious factors but by a wide array of political and socioeconomic realities. This chapter attempts to address these issues by providing (1) a brief historical overview of India and examination of the early development of religious diversity and ahimsa in India, (2) a discussion on the relation of secularism and Hinduism, and (3) an analysis of the political and socioeconomic realities as plausible explanations for the development of fundamental groups and communal violence.

II. HISTORICAL OVERVIEW

India is one of the oldest civilizations in the world. There are conflicting dates on its origin, but literature indicates a varied time frame of 10,000 B.C. to 3,000 B.C. Very little is known of this period as the texts and symbols inscribed on the clay tablets and palm leaves cannot be completely deciphered. Data are very fragmented and history, as it is written, has its own biases depending on who wrote it and how the data were collected, interpreted, and disseminated as public information. However, the review of literature on the history of India reveals that the period of the Indus Valley civilization was peaceful, as very few weapons or other indications of warfare have been found at the excavation sites. The reverence for life and the quest for nonviolent solutions seems to have emerged around this time (Murphey 1992:26).

Ahimsa (nonviolence) and reverence for all life is an ancient Indian concept. All creatures are part of the Divinity and, hence, considered sacred. This ancient concept of ahimsa was later widely used in modern India by the Father of the Nation, Mahatma Gandhi in India's struggle for freedom from British rule.

Hinduism is the oldest of all the major world religions. Hinduism is hard to define, and is often referred to as a way of life. The Vedic period is considered the origin of Hinduism and traditional Indian culture. ''Vedic India is thought in terms of Universal laws affecting all things—a supreme principle or indwelling essence, an order of nature'' (Murphy 1992:28). Vedas, the world's oldest religious text, is a compilation of the thoughts and experiences of several sages passed down over the centuries through the oral tradition. These have been gradually compiled as written text in Sanskrit. The Rig-Veda is the oldest and the longest of the religious scriptures. David Frawley, a scholar on the Rig-Veda, states that the Rig-Veda was compiled around 6,500 years ago. A quote from the Rig-Veda in Sanskrit, ''Ekam Sat, vipraha bahudha vadanti,'' when translated, reads as ''Truth is one, the wise call it by various names'' (Pandit 1996:8–10). This doctrine recognizes that the Ultimate Reality possesses infinite potential, power, and intelligence and, therefore, cannot be limited by a single name or form.

The Bhagavad Gita, a main text of classical Hinduism, states, ''ye yatha mam prapadyante, tan stathami bhajamyaham, mam bartmanubartante manushyah Partha, sarbashyah . . .'' This means ''that the way or the manner or the name in which people worship me, I am there for them as whatever way they worship, it is to me whom they worship'' (Prabhupada 1972:231).

Hence, Hinduism is based on the concept of advaitavada, which talks of the uniqueness of God. The various forms that are worshipped in the religion are different aspects of the same God as perceived by different people. Thus, it can be deduced that there is a universal law affecting all things, that God is one and that there are many paths to God. This means that Hinduism can coexist with any other religion. It has done so in the distant past and continued to do so— until now.

While the majority (around 80%) of India's population are Hindus, religious diversity continues to exist in India. Muslims comprise 12% of India's population. This makes India the second largest Muslim country of the world. It is said that Islam was brought to India by the Arab conquest in the eighth century and later by the Turks and the Afghans around the tenth century. This was followed by the Moghul rule in Delhi (Singh 1994b:66).

Christianity came to India with the missionary work of Apostle Thomas during the first century, long before it came to Europe (Fischer 1999). There were further missionary activities from the thirteenth century to present times, and now Christians comprise 3% of the population. Zoroastrians came from Persia to India to escape Muslim persecution around the eighth century. The world's largest Zoroastrian community lives in India. A small colony of Jews was set up on the west coast of southern India, probably around the first century A.D. which might be the result of the Jewish Diaspora (Murphey 1992:70–81).

Four of the major religions of the world, Hinduism, Buddhism, Sikhism, and Jainism, originated in India. Buddhism, Sikhism, and Jainism are considered to be offshoots of Hinduism but maintain their own identity. Buddhism and Jainism opposed the caste hierarchy and Hindu rituals. These two religions came around 600 B.C. (Sharma 1987:261–279).

Around the fifteenth century, Sikhism evolved, which worked on a compromise between Hinduism and Islam and tried to reform Hinduism. An important message of the founder Guru Nanak was that we are all children of God. There is no difference between Hindus and Muslims or among sects, tribes, and castes (Sharma 1981:271–279). Thus India has been a cradle of religions. Throughout its history, religious diversity existed in India. It was more prevalent in India than many neighboring countries or other countries in the world. The Hindu saying "God is one, but wise people know it by many names" could help explain the coexistence of many religious beliefs in India and a general tolerance of religious diversity. "Of all the world civilizations, India is the oldest still in continuous existence" (Murphy 1992:20).

Historically, India comprised several autonomous kingdoms, and a common thread that wove them together was Hinduism. While these Hindu kings fought among themselves, they also had to deal with foreign invasion. Some of the invaders included the Persians, Arabs, Turks, Afghans, Greeks, Mughals, Portuguese, French, Dutch, and British. The British ruled part of India in the late 1700s and gradually controlled a number of kingdoms to build their empire. In the mid-1800s, Indian intellectuals such as S. Banerje, M. G. Ranade, G. H. Gokhale, M. K. Gandhi, and B. G. Tilak, who were educated in England, began questioning foreign rule in their home country and the absence of the principles of democracy and justice. In 1885, the Indian National Congress party was founded. The Congress Party was the quintessence of India's liberation movement. It tried to be a secular organization, and the nationalist movement opposed fundamentalism and communal electorates. Given the complexity and diversity of India, along with its size and its long history of separate kingdoms and occasional communal strife, the founding fathers were determined to build a united nation. The two most important political figures of independent India, Mahatma Gandhi and Pandit Jawaharlal Nehru, envisioned a democratic and secular India. They realized that an independent India needed to be united despite the religious differences.

III. SECULARISM AND HINDUISM

The constitution of India provides for a democratic and secular state. According to the constitution, all citizens have equal religious freedom, and none will be discriminated by the state on the grounds of religion. Mahatma Gandhi, the Father of the Nation, believed that religion is a private matter and that all religions should be equally respected by the state. Pandit Jawaharlal Nehru, the first Prime Minister of India, had a modern-rational scientific outlook of the state and believed that the state and religion should be separated. The founding fathers took a firm position toward secularism and the issue of the separation of state and religion when they objected to any reference to God in the preamble of the constitution. They thought it would be contrary to the spirit of the constitution and would support a narrow sectarian spirit.

Critics of Indian secularism, such as T. N. Madan and A. Nandy, maintain that the separation of religion and politics as guaranteed by the secular Indian constitution is a Western product alien to the Indian tradition. They believe that since religion is so pervasive in the lives of the Indian people, this modernistic idea of separation of state and religion is an imposition on the Indian society by the elite nationalist leaders.

There have been two opposing views on the relation between religion and politics. The separatists, such as sociologist Louis Dumont and Indologist C. J. Heesterman, argue that religion and politics in ancient India were distinct. Madan and Nandy argue otherwise. While the debate continues, R. W. Perret states that ''both positions are authentically indigenous and both predate colonial influence. This means that there is no one traditional Indian perspective on this issue of the relation of religion and politics in ancient India'' (Perret 1997:12).

The distinctiveness to Indian secularism ''is the complementation or articulation between the democratic state and the politics of satya and ahimsa whereby the relative autonomy of religion and politics from each other can be used for the moral-political reconstruction of both traditions and the modern state'' (Pantham 1997:523). Gandhi integrated the traditional universal principles of satya and ahimsa, i.e., the principles of truth-force and nonviolence-tolerance, to the modern state—the democratic socialist republic of India. These moral universal principles were the means to the freedom of India and the functioning of a modern democratic secular state. Thus Gandhi made a connection with religion and the modern state.

Hence, Hinduism does not oppose secularism, but hindrances and obstacles on the path toward secularism can be and are being created by some, depending on how they choose to practice it. The spirit of catholicity and tolerance is the essence of Hinduism, for it supports the plurality of religions rather than a theocratic state. Thus, Hinduism and secularism complement and support each other in many ways. The following points demonstrate how this peculiar relation does exist.

1. Hinduism is not a simple, homogeneous, monolithic religion with a uniform set of practices and beliefs for the entire Hindu community. It incorporates diverse religious beliefs and lacks uniformity.
2. There are many paths to God, the Divine, and the Ultimate Reality.
3. There is no one form of God that the Hindus worship, though they believe in the uniqueness of one Almighty God.
4. There is no one founder of the Hindu religion, as is the case of other religions such as Buddhism, Islam, and Christianity.

5. Hinduism does not have one sacred book like the Bible or the Koran. It has several sacred books like the Vedas and Bhagavad Gita.
6. It has long been a nonproselytizing religion.
7. There is no regular structured group worship like the Sunday service in church. The worship is more individualized.
8. The concepts of dharma, satya, ahimsa (duty, truth, and nonviolence) seem to be some of the underlying Hindu concepts that connect and support secularism.
9. The traditional caste system had distinct social roles. The Brahmins were entitled to religious duties, while the Kashtriyas were the rulers and administrators.

IV. POLITICIZATION OF RELIGION

While communal strife and occasional violence did occur in earlier times, India in the last 15 years has experienced an increase in communal violence and an increase of power-hungry politicians who are politicizing religion. The politics of independent India until around the 1970s was almost secular. The Congress, which was the dominant party, played the secular card. The party tried to follow strictly the concept of unity in diversity envisioned by the founding fathers as the only way to strengthen an integrated and united India (Madan 1983:469–480).

Thus the Congress party gained much support from groups such as religious minority groups, the lower-caste people (Dalits), the nationalist-minded Indians, and the urban educated upper and middle classes. Since the late 1970s, a few fundamental groups among all the religious communities, including the Hindus, Muslims, Sikhs, and Christians, have been trying to grind their own axes for narrow sectarian causes. The then-ruling Congress party refused to oblige these groups. Some of the Hindu fundamental groups are the Rasyhtriya Swayamsevak Sangh (National Volunteer Corps, RSS), Vishva Hindu Parishad (World Hindu Council, VHP), Shiv Sena Party, and Vajranjdal. The RSS is a militant group which has been in the forefront of Hindu nationalism since 1925. The Vishva Hindu Parishad was founded in 1964 by Hindu religious leaders. The Shiv Sena, founded by Bal Thackery, is in the ruling coalition along with the Bharathiya Janata Party (BJP) in the western state of Maharashtra. It has become very prominent during the last decade in the state of Maharashtra. Vajranjdal is also a part of a group of organizations created nationwide by the BJP leaders for reinforcing Hindu values and ethics. The political and socioeconomic realities, such as the rigid caste system, unemployment, poverty, lack of a uniform civil code, religious conversion, and the Ayodhya issue, set the stage for these groups to gain popularity and power by playing the Hindu card.

Certain economic factors contributed to the Mumbai riots in 1992–1993; these factors created a context for the Shiv Sena party to gain popularity and power in the state of Maharashtra. One of the factors identified by Banerjee was deindustrialization of the city of Mumbai, which resulted in the decline of manufacturing jobs. While jobs were created in the service sector, they required training and skills not available to the urban poor. Another factor was the textile strike; these workers tried to save their jobs but failed. Unemployment was high, and in 1993 Jogeshwari, one of the poor urban slums, experienced the worst violence.

Banerjee argues that deindustrialization and the collapse of the textile strike are dramatic indicators of economic dislocation, and that these forces were integral to the economic context of violent confrontation between Hindus and Muslims in the Mumbai riots (Banerjee 1998:914). The Shiv Sena successfully mobilized a large number of supporters; they provided job training and small business loans to the unemployed. But this went along with anti-Muslim propaganda. Some of the messages conveyed were as follows:

1. Muslims are the cause of the economic problems.
2. Muslims are antinational; they support Pakistan.
3. Muslim conversion of the backward caste and the use of oil money from neighboring Middle Eastern countries for conversion is an imposition of Islam on Hindu India.
4. Muslim culture is alien and is widely spreading.
5. The Muslim criminal underworld is dangerous.

The Shiv Sena party successfully mobilized the urban poor, they organized Maha-artis (Hindu rituals) where they would gather on the street, distribute some prasad (food offered to God), and eventually create havoc in some Muslim neighborhoods. While the problems of unemployment, housing, and poverty were not solved, the economic hardships of the working class were further exploited by the politicization of religion. Thus deindustrialization, lack of jobs, lack of training for service jobs, increased unemployment, anti-Muslim propaganda, and the successful mobilization by the Shiv Sena party provide some explanation of the violent riots in Mumbai.

After the death of Prime Minister Indira Gandhi, the VHP and the BJP began a campaign to remove the sixteenth century mosque built in Ayodhya, the alleged birthplace of the Hindu God Rama. A number of factors prompted the Hindu nationalist groups to proceed with their rally. One argument was that the secular ideals of the Congress favored the fundamentalist Muslims, which irked the nationalist Hindus. This argument resulted from the infamous Shah Bano case in 1978, which sheds some light into the complexity of public policy. The 73-year-old Shah Bano, who divorced his wife after 43 years of marriage, was ordered by the Supreme Court to pay a monthly allowance to his ex-wife for her maintenance. While the allowance was considered by some as a meager amount, the Mullahs (Muslim clergy) still protested against it. The Indian government was then pressurized to revoke the order of the Supreme Court. This brought a lot of criticism from many quarters, including the BJP and its cohorts. They alleged that the government order went against the constitution. The BJP believes that this is pseudosecularism, not positive or real secularism. This case exemplifies how sometimes the lack of uniform law can perpetuate certain atrocities toward women and children. While the lack of uniformity in civil law and the existing public policy has created communal tension, it has helped certain Hindu nationalist groups like the RSS, VHP, and the BJP gain popularity and power.

Currently there is no uniform civil law in the country. There are personal laws protecting minority groups like Muslims and Christians. These laws, which existed during British rule, continued even after independence. The main objective of the nationalist leaders was to gain independence and to maintain a tolerance to a diverse India. Thus, the religious minorities have the privilege of living according to their personal laws even if these conflict with the constitution.

Some of the communal outbursts are due to public policies related to education and religious institutions. For instance, minority schools and places of worship have no public accountability. However, the same principle does not apply, in all instances, to Hindu schools or temples. These multiple standards of governance have alienated a section of Hindus and have added to the communal strife, as some see these as privileges enjoyed by minorities only.

The 1981 mass conversion of Untouchables to Islam in Meenakshipuram in southern India was considered by some Hindus as misuse of oil wealth from Middle East countries. It was another incident that gained and helped the BJP and other Hindu groups to gain popularity.

There are a wide range of factors that contribute to the understanding of some of the communal strife between Hindus and Christians. Among them are forced conversion of the poor lower-caste Hindus, imposition of foreign culture, and the increasing political and social activism from both sides. India is a diverse society with a rigid and complex hierarchy of castes and subcastes. The Indian Constitution officially abolished the lowest caste, Dalits, and described them as Schedule caste. Seats are reserved for them in schools, colleges, and government jobs at different levels. This kind of affirmative action policy was further extended to the remaining 3,743 backward castes in the country in 1980. Christians are not included in the government policy of quota and reservations because Christians are not supposed to uphold the caste system. But in reality the newly converted Christians are also affected by the caste system, experiencing discrimination in their community and even church. Now these ''Dalit Christians'' have appealed to the government for the benefits for the backward classes. This has raised several concerns among fundamentalist Hindus.

Others link missionary activities to the secessionist movement found in the northeastern states like Nagaland. Some of the missionaries encourage the tribal population who have been converted into Christianity to see themselves as a distinct nation. ''The American Baptist Churches/USA not only maintains close relations with the two million tribal population but it even encourages the converts there to battle with India for their cultural and religious survival'' (Vedantam 1999:416). The political leaders are equally guilty because they are blinded by the craze for power. Instead of trying to uplift the socioeconomic conditions of the masses, these leaders confine their vision to getting votes and trying to appease religious leaders in several ways. On the other hand the religious leaders, with their own sectarian views and interests, influence the general voters who are undereducated and poor. ''A quid pro quo is established by which political leaders gain votes while the religious leaders retain their hegemony in their houses of worship'' (Vedantam 1999:418).

On August 15, 1999, India celebrated 53 years of independence. While the country did make progress in reducing famine and treading along the path toward both agricultural and industrial self-sufficiency, India still has a myriad of social problems. Some of them are poverty, unemployment, illiteracy, population explosion, corruption at different levels, and the curse of the caste system.

V. CONCLUSION

The challenge to deal with social ills continues for the nation. While the leaders and social workers are seized with the problem of how to bring about communal and religious harmony, the need for the economic progress of India is pressing and urgent. Secularism, no doubt, is a very important tool to meet the challenges and achieve these goals. But secularism in and of itself would not erase intercommunal tension and conflict.

The society and religion are interconnected, and this dialectic process will continue. Thus there should be a national consensus where the statesmen and leaders from different fields—such as politics; education; and economic, religious, social, and other spheres—join together to formulate national policies in this regard. This will help maintain the continuity of the tradition of unity in diversity. The national policies should be discussed, debated, and approved by the populace, and the print and electronic media should play an important role in dissemination of information to the masses.

The policies should also be widely discussed by the National Integration Council, National Security Council, and the National Defense Council, and this should be implemented after getting approval from both the houses of parliament and at least a majority of the state legislators. Thus the general population should be assured that the national policies provide opportunity for all faiths to practice their religion freely. Also agencies should be set up to monitor the development and outcome of these policies and to assess the level of communal harmony or lack of it.

REFERENCES

Awasthi, D. (1992a). "Ayodhya crisis, battle of wits." *India Today*, December 15.
Awasthi, D. (1992b). "Ayodhya: Nations shame." *India Today*, December 31.
Awasthi, D. (1994). "Ayodhya, temple cauldron bubbles." *India Today*, August 31.
Baber, Z. (1998). Communal conflict and nostalgic imagination in India. *Journal of Contemporary Asia 28*, 27–45.
Banerjee, S. Political secularization and the future of secular democracy in India: The case of Magarashatra. *J Asian Survey 38*, 907–927.
Bowes, P. (1976). *The Hindu Religious Traditions*. London: Rutledge & Kegan Paul.
Fischer, M. (1999). The fiery rise of Hindu fundamentalism. *J Christianity Today 43*, 46–49.
Garewal, S. S. (1995). Why India needs to do more. *India Monitor 27*.
Ghandhi, an Autobiography. (1993). Boston: Beacon Press.
Ghurye, G. S. (1986). *Caste and Race in India*. Bombay: Popular Prakashan.
Gore, S. C. (1986). India in the next millennium. *News India-Times*.
Islam, S. S. (1997). The tragedy of the Babri Masjid: An expression of militant Hindu fundamentalism in India. *Journal of Muslim Minority Affairs 17*, 345–351.
Joshi, B. (1996). "Bomba blasts greet Abdullah's ultimatum." *India Abroad, New York*, November 28, vol. 27, no. 6.
Joshi, L. M. (1987). *Studies in Buddhistic Culture of India*. Delhi: Motilal Banarsi Das.
Kachroo, J. L. and Kachroo, V. (1985). *Society in India*. New Delhi: Bookhive Publication.
Madan, G. R. (1983). *Indian Social Problems*. New Delhi: Allied Publishers Pvt. Ltd.
Mandelbaum, D. G. (1970). *Society in India*. Berkeley: University of California Press.
Mascaro, J. (trans.) (1962). *The Bhagavad Gita*. New York: Penguin Books.
Mehta, V. (1993). The mosque and the temple: The rise of fundamentalism. *J Foreign Affairs 72*, 16–21.
Morgan, K. (1953). *The Religion of Hindus*. New York: The Ronald Press.
Murphey, R. (1992). *A History of Asia*. New York: Harper Collins.
Novak, P. (1994). *The World's Wisdom*. San Francisco: Harper.
Pandit, B. (1996). *Hindu Dharma*. Glen Ellyn, IL: B&V Enterprises, Inc.
Pantham, T. (1997). Indian secularism and its critics: Some reflections. *The Review of Politics 59*, 523–541.
Perrett, R. Religion and politics in India: Some philosophical perspectives. *Journal of Religious Studies 33*, 1–14.
Prabhupada, A. C. B. S. (1984). *Sri Isopanishad: Discovering the Original Person*. Los Angeles: The Bhaktivedanta Book Trust, ISKCON.
Prabhupada, A. C. B. S. (1972). *Bhagadabad-gita As It Is*. New York: Collier Books, Macmillan.

Sangha, B. S. and Yatiswarananda, S. (1990). *Reflections on Hinduism*. Calcutta.

Sharma, A. (1996). Religion and politics in India: The 1996 election. *Cross Currents 46*, 352–361.

Sharma, R. N. (1987). *Indian Society*. Bombay: Media Promoters and Publishers.

Sheean, V. (1941). *Lead Kindly Light: Gandhi and the Way to Peace*. New York: Random House.

Shukla, R. and Phadnis, A. (1994). "After the Judgement." *Sunday*. November 6.

Singh, I. J. (1994a). *Sikhs and Sikhism: A View With a Bias*. Columbia: South Asia Publications.

Singh, Y. (1994b). *Modernization of Indian Tradition*. New Delhi: Rawat Publications.

Subhani, O. (1997). "Pakistan's caretaker govt. saved country's economy: Burki." *The Asia Observer*, January 31, vol. 1, no. 50.

Sullivan, T. (1990). Promotion of secularism. J *International Souvenir*, 1–8.

Swami, P. (1997). "Kashmir, Blasts in the Valley." *Frontline*, January 24.

Swamy, P. (1999). "Conversions unwelcome, says Sir John Templeton." *News India-Times*, March 19.

Van der Veer, P. (1996). The ruined center: Religion and mass politics in India. *Journal of International Affairs 50*, 254–278.

Vedantam, V. (1999). Privilege and resentment: Religious conflict in India. *The Christian Century 116*, 414–418.

10
Caste and Class Relations in Bihar

Shyam Nand Singh
University of Ajmer, Ajmer, India

I. INTRODUCTION

In Bihar, India, the Kishan Sabha, Congress Socialist Party, Socialist Party, Communist Party, Naxalites, and trade union movements made vigorous attempts to organize the rural and urban masses in terms of class in the last fifty years. But they failed in their endeavor to inculcate class consciousness among them and to free them from the traditional loyalties. Bihar is traditionally a rural society where semifeudal relationships still exist. It checked the emergence of contradictory class interests of the seller and purchaser of labor or landless laborers and feudal lords. Even the emerging clash of interests between the landless laborers and rich peasants failed to generate substantial class consciousness among the rural dehumanized subordinate classes. In the industrial sector the trade union movement is devided, controlled by the different political parties, and confined to urban areas. In the last few years Central Bihar has gradually come under the influence of class organization, and class contradiction is evolving slowly. Caste and Class conflict is a permanent characteristic of polity and society in Bihar. This chapter examines the various aspects of caste and class relations in Bihar in the light of class formation.

The class formation in this "backward" society and economy is checkcd by the issue of job reservation, on the basis of birth in the backward castes. It has divided the society in terms of primordial loyalties depending on caste. The contradictory caste federation emerged, going against the emerging new dialectics of caste and class in Bihar. The ruling class in Bihar happens to be from the upper castes and those with a landlord background. Generally speaking, political leadership in Bihar has not been stable and has shifted from one upper caste and class to another. Exceptions were witnessed only in 1967–1970, 1977–1979, and currently, as political power is controlled by the backward castes and classes as well.

The policies and programs of the political parties have a secondary importance in the institutionally regulated caste-ridden society like Bihar. Therefore, in the present situation there is very little chance for a political party based on class ideology to combat politicized forces of numerous mutually hostile caste groups. Both communist parties, CPI and CPM, are supporting the most controversial Mandal Commission recommendations and advocating caste as the basis of a state affirmative action, or reservation, policy. Therefore, it will go against the class formation and strengthen casteism. In the different legislative assembly elections held in Bihar, CPI never won even 10% of the state legislature seats.

The upper castes—Brahman, Bhumihar, Rajput, and Kayastha—are approximately 13% of the total population of Bihar. They are, however, dominant in all walks of life. They are moving toward urban areas in search of better opportunities. In rural areas the place of the upper castes is being taken by some of the newly prosperous backward castes like Yadava, Kurmi, and Koiri. They were clean castes and earlier assigned a service relationship with the upper castes. Along with Banias, they constitute 19.3% of the population of Bihar. The Banias are forward in respect to all variables of social and political development though they claim themselves to be backward. Previously they were moneylenders, and even now they are in control of trade and commerce in Bihar. The more backward castes constitute 32% of the state population. They are mostly landless workers in the rural areas.

II. CASTE AND POLITICS IN BIHAR

Caste politics has deep roots in Bihar. It began with the movement for the partition of Bihar from Bengal in the early twentieth century. The English-educated Kayasthas became leaders of the freedom movement in the 1920s. They were challenged by the land-owning, numerically stronger Bhumihars in different spheres. Subsequently, the Brahmans and the Rajputs joined the race. Until 1967 these four castes dominated the political scene. In 1967 a number of backward castes of kulaks emerged, such as the Yadava, Kurmi, Koiri, and Bania. The emergence of the backward castes on the political scene in Bihar was due to

1. The leaders of the upper castes felt impelled to align themselves with the politicians of the backward castes because of the intense rivalry among them. For example, there was keen political rivalry between the land-owning dominant castes, the Rajputs and the Bhumihars. Both had played an active role in the freedom movement. In fact, until the

1950s they were both in the limelight of state politics. However, owing to their mutual rivalry, the Brahmans and the Kayasthas found it possible to wrest the leadership from them.

2. Whenever the leaders of the Brahmans and Kayasthas were weak, they sought to use the backward castes to counterbalance the dominance of the Rajputs and the Bhumihars.

3. The economic and educational development of certain backward castes, like the Yadava, Kurmi, Koiri, and Bania castes, made them conscious of their rights and of their numerical superiority in the democratic politics based upon universal participation. The antireservation agitation of 1977 and again of 1990 united them to gain preferential treatment from the state authority. They started proreservation agitation in favor of central government reservation of 27% for OBCs in central government services.

The backward castes first emerged as a political force in 1967. Their percentage in the Legislative Assembly increased in the coming elections. High party posts in the different political parties went to them. Political conflict in Bihar is now between the traditional forward castes (the Brahmans, the Rajputs, the Bhumihars, and the Kayasthas) and advanced backward castes Yadava and Kurmi. Among the backward castes the power and resources are not properly distributed. Yadava, Kurmi, and Koiri are emerging as the exploiters the Scheduled Caste (SC), Scheduled Tribes (ST), and Most Backward Castes (MBC). They are also fighting with upper castes on issues of land and social domination. Now the social situation has changed. They have learned the importance of their votes.[1] The caste consciousness became stronger among them. They prefer to vote for their caste candidates. Therefore, they will maintain newly acquired political power.

III. SOCIAL CLASS

The division of society into classes in a hierarchical order on the basis of wealth, prestige, and power is an almost universal feature of social structure and has attracted the attention of social theorists and philosophers everywhere. Different interpretations of this social feature have been advanced. Marx takes the economic determinist view.[2] Max Weber emphasises human behavior and values, attitudes, and beliefs in relation to class.[3]

The term class is a complex conceptual apparatus so far as it denotes various notations in the historical life of all human social oders. The Marxian theory of class is radically opposed to all possible variant notions of class that find their expression in a single invariant theory of liberalism.

The concept of class is to a large extent a contribution of Karl Marx. He speaks of the capitalist class and the working class not on the basis of any occupational division of the people in terms of income, occupation, or education, but on the basis of control of the means of production relations in a privately organized economic structure. He also mentions a number of other classes like landlords, petty bourgeoisie, etc. The basis of his whole stratification is ownership/nonownership of property.

This view has been seriously challenged by Althusser,[4] who presents an antiessentialist, antideterministic, and antireductionalist reading of Marx's works. For him the Marxist theory of class asserts that class conflict is prior to class, justifies the primacy of contradiction over the terms of contradiction, and provokes the logical primacy of contradiction over the process of social formation. It has three expressions: economic, political, and ideological. Thus the structuralists' interpretation of of class negates the role of human agency so far as man is supposed to be a *Trager* (bearer/support) of given relations of production.

An effective oppositional current has been attested by anti-Althusian Marxist philosophers like Lukas,[5] Gramschi, Sarter, E. P. Thomspon,[6] and others. They have considered class as a process that develops and expands through the objective expression of human consciousness and human objective-subjectivity. Thus this contradiction has not been resolved as to whether class is a structure or a process or a combination of both.

Liberal theorists define class in terms of income, occupation, economic interest, and education, and do not explain the relations between classes as the relations of contradiction. Even if contradiction/conflict appears between social classes at the level of empirical reality, it is ultimately sealed off or is resolved by various mediating agencies and forces. That is, the reason Weber does not find an acute conflict between classes either in the commodity market or in the labor market is because of the existence of a theoretical relative casual pluralism through economic forces, political force, and status force, which mediate one another and make a tacit holy alliance of mutual support against the forces of mutual negation of the elements of social order.

A class (the economically constituted class) in itself does not lead automatically to the class-for-itself (self-conscious class). Marx does not define class-in-itself and class-for-itself. He stresses that the formation of a class depends considerably on class struggle. A class-in-itself becomes a class-for-itself only when economic differentiation leads to the emergence of class consciousness on the realization of antagonistic interests among the subordinate classes. This is the motor of social revolution.

The bourgeoisie in India has made the transition from being a class-in-itself to being a class-for-itself. The working class has not made such a transition. For instance, several working class areas in the country vote for parties of the ruling class rather than for a working-class party.

Weber suggests a multidimensional model. He acknowledges the importance of economic factors in any system of stratification, but claims that political power is another, independent yet complementary, determinant that produces its own hierarchical order. A third determinant is social prestige, or honor, which consists in the ranking of man according to the amount of esteem in which he is held as a member of a traditional aristocracy, or in terms of occupation, education, or living standards.

Weber's notion of status refers to the way people are ranked in terms of the esteem in which society holds them. A status group refers to a group of people who have common esteem, prestige, social code, life style, and life chance, and the boundary of such a group is maintained and reinforced by primodial criteria such as membership based on religious belief, birth, marriage, locality, theory of descent, and so on. Achieved status may be acquired through improvements in education, occupation, and income, whereas ascribed status is achieved by religious forces and descent principles, as is the case with the Indian caste system, based on the notions of purity/impurity dislocations, religiously defined divisions of labor, and mutual repulsion or perial distance.

Interclass conflict, however, is often superimposed on the traditional social hierarchy so that castes with a high social status may be found in control of economic resources, and those with a low social status may be victims of economic deprivation.

IV.   CLASS STRUCTURE IN BIHAR

When one talks about the class structure in Bihar, one has to study it differently for rural and urban areas. One finds different types of classes with different characteristics in rural and urban areas. In rural Bihar, land is still the basic source of livelihood. Andre Bateille divides the rural population of India into four or five main socioeconomic groups according to their position in the system of production.[7] In Bengal these are the zamindars, the jotedars (most often big tenants), the bargadars (sharecroppers), and the Khetimajdurs. Then, of course, there are the merchants and artisans. In rural Bihar, Max Harcourt distinguishes ashraf (landlords), bakal (village shopkeepers), Pawania (artisans), jatiya (small peasants directly cultivating their land), and a class of low castes at the local level.[8]

The actual effect of social class varies from one culture to another. What constitutes a class in one place may not do so in another. Are Indian farmers, for example, a class distinct from businessmen and workers? Or are farmers and businessmen together members of a class distinct from workers? In this context many problems are judged not in terms of class, but in terms of interests.

Let us take for instance, the small and marginal farmers in Bihar. There are also agricultural laborers who possess little or no land. In addition, there are unskilled manual laborers. Most of these are economically poor and socially and educationally backward. And yet, they all have specific roles, functions, and positions within the system as casual, unskilled laborers, as tenants, as artisans, and so on. Any attempt to organize them on a class basis would affect not only the rural poor but also the rural rich, who are their landlords, their moneylenders, their employers, and so on. It would threaten the established patterns of privilege and exploitation.[9]

A.   Rural Areas

If one starts right from the bottom, one finds that there is a class of landless workers. They sell their labor to landlords and village headmen just to ensure their own survival. Some of them are bonded laborers. Most are from the Scheduled Castes, the Scheduled Tribes, and the backward castes. The number of those belonging to the upper castes is negligible. They are engaged in their respective skilled or unskilled occupations. They have not added to their landholdings. They are today where they have always been.

Above the class of landless laborers, there is the class of sharecroppers. They possess some land, some capital, and instruments of production, such as fertilizers, ploughs, cattle, and seeds. They sometimes work as laborers in fields belonging to others also.

There is a third category of people in rural Bihar, i.e., marginal farmers. They usually possess not more than five acres of land. They have sufficient surplus labor and tools of production, and also work as sharecroppers. They mainly employ what is called family labor on their own farms. They are essentially self-producers without hired labor. Occasionally they hire labor to work on their behalf. They have considerable control over labor power as occasional employers of hired labor. Because they have a little land, they are regarded as landowners; and because they cultivate others' land they are regarded as tenants. Economically they depend upon the assistance of the rich and middle farmers. They are self-sufficient at the bare subsistence level.

And then there are farmers who possess between five to ten acres of land and the instruments of production. As they cannot themselves cultivate all the land they possess, they employ laborers in their fields. Although they take part in agricultural activities, they do not cultivate land belonging to others. They secure income from agricultural activities. They cooperate with the rich peasants and do not perceive their interests and the interests of the rich peasants as antagonistic.

The rich peasants are an emerging prosperous class with substantial political and social influence. They get most of the necessary developmental resources from the government. They have about twenty acres of land. They carry on mechanized farming and are, therefore, able to produce a large surplus for the market.

They usually rent out some land. Although they depend heavily upon hired laborers, they do supervisory work on their farms. They are the neorich. The emergence of the rich peasants has been rather slow in Bihar owing to lack of a large urban market for rural produce.

The landlords are in a class by themselves in rural areas. They no longer have their old power and are fast losing ground to the rich peasants. They have more than twenty acres of land. They are getting great surplus production solely by hired labor. A large number of them are shifting to urban areas as bureaucrats, technocrats, and professional people. Middle-class tenants, who were cultivating their land on their behalf in the past, have bought their land.

The rural areas have other classes as well. The artisan class is one of them. The rural artisan class is identifiable in terms of skill. Members of this class pursue their occupations as village artisans and are governed by the jajmani relationship. Large numbers of them have shifted to urban areas as barbers, cobblers, goldsmiths, sweepers, and so on.

Another class is that of moneylenders. They are generally rich peasants or village shopkeepers. Women belonging to the families of the rich peasants also use their small savings to lend money. Village shopkeepers work as intermediaries between the village people and the big businessmen of the cities or of suburban areas at the time of the harvesting of crops. Some of them play a dual role. For example, the village goldsmith is an artisan by occupation, but he also works as a moneylender.

In rural areas a class conflict is developing between the rich peasants and the landless laborers over such issues as wages and land distribution.[10] It is held that the frequent atrocities on the Harijans are nothing but a manifestation of the class conflict between the rich peasants and the landless workers.

B.   Urban Areas

In the industrial sectors of society there has emerged a new class that may be termed as an urban working class. This class includes unskilled industrial workers, fourth-grade employees in government and semigovernment offices, and employees in private establishments. They participate in the production process and doing manual labor. They receive very low salaries and live in slums in misery.

The urban situation is much more complex than the rural. Urban workers have formed organizations. They are grouped into an organized and an unorganized, or informal, sector. The relationship between urban workers and their employers is impersonal and contractual. If and when a man gets employment, his activity is contractual and constant. One thing that is common to all urban workers is that they live by selling their labor. The chief difference is that those in the unorganized, or informal, sectors are unprotected unlike those in the organized sector.[11] Middle and upper classes in Bihar are working as supervisors and executive staff getting good salaries. The industrial bourgeoisie are not active in state politics. Their interests are protected by the various political parties.

The occupants of the highest position in bureaucracy, a few members of parliament and the State Legislative Assembly, are part of the ruling class and are also considered as the in Bihar. It is a class composed of government contractors and senior bureaucrats and technocrats. Some landlords and rich peasants may also be included in this class. They have given up their old feudal ways and have invested their income in small-scale industries, for example, buses and cinema houses. They enjoy economic and political dominance. They may be considered as part of ruling class of Bihar.

The bourgeoisie own and control the means of production. They are big landlords and entrepreneurs. They exploit the working class and influence their cultural and intellectual life in subtle ways. The word exploited has been used because the working class is paid less than the value of the commodities it produces for the market. However, this has gradually been changed by adopting the policy of paying bonuses of a share in production. It creates surplus value for the benefit of the capitalist class. Some workers are engaged in distribution or commerce. Their scales of remuneration are settled by haggling. Such workers too are petty bourgeoisie in Markist terminology.[12] They are the small merchants of urban areas and shopkeepers of the rural areas. Marxists consider even the middle classes as petty bourgeoisie. The bourgeoisie and kulak members of the various castes make use of their caste identity to line up members of their own castes behind them to break the solidarity of the farming class.

V. CASTE AND CLASS RELATIONS

Indian society is based on ascribed status regulated by the mutual opposition of pure and impure, which is purely religiously based. It has not, as in Western society, moved appreciably in the direction of acquired status for want of industrialization, education, and income. Along with the caste categories, there have emerged class categories that cut across the traditional caste stratification.

The working class in the cities is basically a product of the urban milieu and is made up of individuals who have migrated to citieies to better their economic status. Industrialization, urbanization, and the spread of education has led to the attraction of cities, as has the deterioration of rural life. The rural people have been pulled toward urban areas. The establishment of many other trades and businesses have provided new avenues. In this process people have changed their traditional occupations and become members of a new class. This is economic stratification, not class formation.[13] Economic stratification does influence the lifestyle and values of the individuals concerned. The lifestyle of highly paid industrial workers differs from that of the low-paid workers in the same factory. Such differences do not necessarily lead to the emergence of antagonistic class interests. Needless to say that economic differentiations have yet to go beyond caste boundaries to result in the formation of classes.

However, industrialization has given birth to new classes, weakening the traditional caste system. In industrial establishments one type of job is done by people of different castes at, for example, the Bata India Company. The same is the case of the textile industry, where not only julahas (weavers), but others also work. In the iron and steel industry, castes other than the lohar (ironsmith) work. In the ready-made garment industry, people of all castes are employed. The business and trade occupations have been adopted by other caste people. Thus, the present picture of society does not exist totally along the traditional lines.

The owner-cultivators and the rich tenants, who are mostly from castes traditionally engaged in farming, have emerged as exploiters of wage labor and different forms of other labor belonging to the lower castes. Now the sharpest conflict of interest is no longer between the middle and low-caste peasants on the one side and high-caste landlords on the other. It is between the rich farmers and the agricultural laborers and the poor peasants. This signifies that the caste structure of rural Bihar has changed, although one cannot say that a class-based society has emerged in a caste-ridden society. Rather caste and class co-exist, and they lay base for each other, as in the last instance.

The zamindars, the tenant landlords, and the rich peasants are mostly upper-caste Hindus. The poor-middle the middle castes. Their caste consciousness is a major obstacle to the growth of class consciousness. There are many rich people in backward castes like Yadava, Kurmis, Koiri, Baniya, Suri, Teli, and Goldsmith. They like to be labelled as backward castes in order to enjoy privileges, but they identify themselves with upper castes for all other purposes. They too exploit people of their own castes.

The changes that have occurred in independent India have generally increased the power and prestige of the backward castes, usually at the expense of such higher castes as the Rajputs and the Brahmans.[14] In the opinion of E. M. S. Namboodripad, caste associations were "the first forms in which the peasant masses rose in struggle against feudalism. At present these caste organizations are not the class organizations of the peasantry; they do, on the contrary, consolidate the caste separatism of the people in general and of the peasantry in particular, so that the grip of these organizations on the peasantry has to be broken if they are to be organized as a class."[15]

Owing to their rural connection, the working class in urban areas cannot even behave like a class at this level of essence. In industry they are members of a class according to their occupation, but in the villages they behave like members of their respective castes. Even in trade unionism, caste is a potent factor. So in India in general and in Bihar in particular, the emergence of an industrial culture is only a distant possibility as long as caste enters into the cognitive consciousness through backdoor agencies.

Thus caste and class go together. They cannot be separated from each other at the level of operation. Gail Omvedt also observes that caste and class continue to be heavily interlinked.[16] The educated elite are overwhelmingly drawn from the higher castes, who have a literacy tradition. Men from the peasant and artisan castes of Shudra constitute the large majority of factory workers. Members of the Scheduled Castes have been able to find openings in the factories and in the transport industry (including the railways).

The peasent social picture of Bihar is divided into two hostile forces: one toward strengthening existing ties and one working toward the dissolution of existing ties. Traditional caste and religious customs are giving way to modern thinking in a very obscure way. Relationships between castes and occupations have added a new dimension, breaking customary relationships. Changing economic opportunities, the spread of education, and a changing consciousness toward new ways of life have changed the rural and urban social picture.[17] The granting of democratic rights and the issue of job reservation have aroused political consciousness, which has changed social life. Thus, the fast-changing modern economic, social, and political environment and market economy on the one hand and universal participatory democratic politics on the other have helped in changing traditional relationships between castes, classes, occupations, and social and political status.

REFERENCES

1. Singh, S. N. (1990). "Caste, Caste and Politics in India", *Janata*, (Bombay) Independence Day, Number 1990, p. 52.
2. Dahrendorf, R. (1959). *Class and Class Conflict in Industrial Society*. p. 3. Berkeley, CA.
3. Weber, M. (1969). Class, status and party. In C. S. Helles (ed.), *Structural Social Inequality: Readers in Comparative Social Stratification*. New York.
4. Althusser, L. (1976). *Essays in Self-Criticism*. (trans.) p. 175. London.
5. Lukas, G. (1971). *History and Class Consciousness: Studies in Marxist Dialects* (trans.) p. 52. London: Merlin Press.
6. Thompson, E. P. (1978). *Making of English working Class* p. 10. London: Penguin.
7. Betellle, A. (1974). *Studies in Agrarian Social Structure* p. 126. Delhi.
8. Harcourt, M. (1977). Kisan populism and revolution in rural India. In D. A. Low (ed.), *Congress and the Raj*. Colombia, South Asia Books.
9. Joshi, P. C. (1978). "Organising rural poor: Some basic issues." *Mainstream* (New Delhi), August 12.

10. Sinha, A. (1978). "Class war in Bhojpur." *Economic and Political Weekly* (Bombay) January, 7. 1978, p. 10.

11. Desai, I. P. (1984). "Should 'caste' be the basis for recognising backwardness." *Economic and Political Weekly*, July, 14.

12. Cole, G. D. H. (1955). *Studies in Class Structure*, p. 12. London.

13. Shah, G. (1985). "Caste, class and reservation." *Economic and Political Weekly*, January, 19.

14. Srinivas, M. N. (1982). *Social Change in Modern India*, p. 21. New Delhi.

15. Namboodripad, E. M. S. (1952). *The National Question in Kerala*, pp. 102–106. Bombay.

16. Omyedt, G. (ed.) *Land, Caste and Politics in Indian States* p. 20. Delhi.

17. Singh, S. N. (1988). "Roots of caste war in Bihar." *Mainstream*, January, 16.

11
Identity Collapse and Ethnic Politics
A Sri Lankan Example

William W. Bostock
University of Tasmania, Hobart, Australia

I. INTRODUCTION

A twelve-point list of the preconditions for the successful accommodation of ethnic minorities with national integration has been proposed by Safran [1]. In the case of Sri Lanka, to some extent at least, none of the twelve preconditions appear, to a greater or lesser extent, to be present: the elite is not significantly transethnic, the institutions of interethnic collaboration are not present, the ethnic minority community is not permeable and nonexclusivist, the dominant community is not open and tolerant, members of ethnoracial category groups are excluded from membership in the political community, membership of an ethnic community does foreclose membership in nonethnic units, the offer of official legitimacy to a minority without sacrifice has not been made, the existence of separate ethnic schools has implied obligatory minority attendance, the basic values of the minority do conflict with transethnic political values and civic disobedience has occurred, extraterritorial influence has occurred, a "mother country" (in this case a provincial state) does exist, almost contiguously, and the state is overweening, or at least attempts to be.

One of the features of the scheme is that as well as being comprehensive it has no particular bias toward either a dominant power or a subordinate group, which is particularly important in the Sri Lankan case where there are clearly rights and wrongs on both sides.

The aim of this chapter is to propose a concept that might help to explain the breakdown of minority accommodation and integration in Sri Lanka and elsewhere, specifically as it relates to this "gravitational collapse" in national identity.

147

II. THE CONCEPT OF NATIONAL IDENTITY

State is defined as a legal, political, and coercive category, whereas *nation* is a psychological one requiring psychological tools for its analysis. Nation has been defined as "a body of people who possess some sense of a single communal identity" [2:331], as well as shared culture, traditions, and territory. In other words, without an identity there can be no nation, and without a sense of nationhood, little prospect of a single state. *Identity*, from the Latin *idem* (the same), means (1) of one thing, at different times, the same, and (2) of different things, agreeing in all details. Classical writers such as Rousseau, Montesquieu, and Herder all had something like national identity in mind when they wrote of national character and national spirit, but identity in its modern form came to political science from psychoanalysis. For Freud, identification was a fundamentally important mechanism of adjustment. "Identification is known to psycho-analysis as the earliest expression of an emotional tie with another person" [3:105]. In Freud's theoretical formulation, identification was the process by which a child would recognize his or her self through interaction with a parent. This theme was taken up by Erikson [4], who saw a strong sense of identity as necessary for both a successfully functioning individual and a society. Erikson discussed the dysfunctional states of confusion, crisis, and panic of identity; and saw a strong sense of identity as a generator of energy, and a weak or confused sense of identity as a source of decline [5]. Individual identity, in the psychoanalytic view, is organized and has continuity in time and space but is flexible. Where a sense of identity is not strong, stress can cause disintegration. At the group level, identity can be interpreted either as a collective phenomenon, or as an emergent one, metaphorically like an individual, and similar to those many other aspects of society that have been called emergent properties [6]. Thus one can say that just as a sense of individual identity is a necessary condition for the survival of an individual, national identity is a necessary condition of national survival. But it can be accepted that the subjective process of sense of self, often conceived in metaphor and experienced collectively, as Brewster Smith [7] has argued, is vital for collective survival of a nation, even though that process cannot be directly observed. When there is disruption, violence, civil strife, or even civil war, failure of adaptation, and generalized lack of collective will at the level of the state, I will argue that this is evidence of a weak sense of national identity.

Paraphrasing Brewster Smith's definition of individual selfhood, one could conceive the sense of national identity as a process of collective self-awareness; having boundaries; having continuity in space and time; being in communication and communion internally and externally; engaging in enterprises with the world with forethought and afterthought; appraising performance; feeling responsible for actions carried out collectively and individually and holding others responsible for theirs—with the end product being successful adaptation or survival. Not all of this process occurs within the medium of language: there is music, painting and plastic arts, physical sport and other nonverbal achievement. Here one could note a possibly unifying effect of Sri Lanka's recent World Cup cricket victory. Even so, national identity takes place in language, and language thus plays an essential role in its construction as both medium and message, a situation of particular importance to newly emerging states and about which there has been considerable academic debate [8]. The fundamental connection between language and human organization has been remarked upon by, for example, the historian Borkenau who wrote that language is

> a generalised form of expression for everything, a fluid, epitomising instinctively all attitudes and modes of behaviour to be found in a society. *Language, in one word, is the most direct reflection of the instinctive underlying attitudes of a civilisation* (emphasis in original) [9:138].

National identity requires agreement within the collectivity about the legitimacy of inclusion within a political boundary, though not necessarily ethnicity. Erikson calls this sense of agreement *ideology*, that is, a force which "unifies the striving for psychosocial identity" [4:63], and this term does in fact combine political, social, and economic organization, about which one could expect substantial consensus in a successfully integrated state. Where it is salient, religion can have a strong influence on the creation or destruction of a sense of collective identity, that which Erikson called a "striving for an omnipotent identity" [4].

In regard to the question of why national identity is so ubiquitous and so pervasive, A. D. Smith has proposed three specific functions that it serves: (1) to answer the problem of personal oblivion and so overcome the finality of death, (2) to offer personal reward and dignity by becoming part of a political "superfamily," and (3) to realize the ideal of fraternity [10:160–163]. I will argue that a sense of national identity that fulfills these three functions is essential to the survival of a state.

III. IDENTITY VACUUMS AND THE GRAVITATIONAL COLLAPSE

The concept of the political vacuum is well-known and refers to a situation of emptiness that must soon be filled, as in the aphorism that nature hates a vacuum. The concept of the identity vacuum was proposed by Erikson when he wrote of "the dread of an existential vacuum devoid of spiritual meaning" [4:65], which in fact is none other than the emptiness of the nonfulfillment of any or all of Smith's three functions of identity. The vacuum caused by a crisis in identity can release very powerful forces, which can, Erikson wrote, "arouse in man a murderous hatred of 'otherness'" [4:62].

Here it is appropriate to extend the metaphor from the vacuum to the hypothetical gravitational collapse, which in astrophysics is seen as the remnant of a burnt-out star possessing five characteristics: (1) its energy (thermonuclear fuel) is exhausted, (2) it is unstable, (3) it gravitationally collapses inward upon itself, (4) its escape velocity is so high that it is (almost) impossible to escape, and (5) it is invisible, its existence only being observable indirectly by its effect on other bodies [11:255].

The gravitational collapse is an appropriate metaphor for a human group that is or, more importantly, perceives itself to be near the end of its existence in a particular form, and which has become unstable, falling, collapsing inward upon itself, difficult to escape, and whose sense of identity can only be observed indirectly by violent actions and reactions, notably in the widespread occurrence of homicidal/suicidal behavior. As an example of this phenomenon, one could refer to the Third Reich in the final stages of its existence, which can be interpreted as a gravitational collapse of identity as well as, of course, a military, political, and moral collapse. As it drew nearer to its demise, which became recognised as inevitable in 1941, the sense of immortality, dignity, and fraternity (Smith's functions) were undermined in a gross way, with the result that a homicidal/suicidal behavior pattern came to prevail. At this stage, the regime became specifically genocidal. The timing here is significant in that the Wannsee conference in January 1942, where the Final Solution was decided upon, came soon after the failure of the attack on the Eastern front became apparent. Ultimately, the German people themselves were expected to be destroyed if not victorious. Hitler is reported to have said: "If the German nation is now defeated in this struggle, it has been too weak. That will mean that it has not withstood the test of history and was destined for nothing but doom" [12].

It is also possible to extend the metaphor from a community with its own gravitational pull over its own members to the relations between communities, which can be conceived as fields of gravitation between bodies and which in a stable situation hold the various communities within a nation in a certain complex pattern of countervailed attraction, not unlike objects in space.

In its astrophysical conceptualization, a gravitational collapse can exist in isolation, or it can form a system with another body as, it is believed, does one of the component stars of a binary X-ray system. Alternatively, as in Hawking's theorization, it can occur as a series of small gravitational collapses. Yet another theorization is that a proton and an antiproton can annihilate each other and the gravitational collapse can evaporate, a further extension of relevance to politics, where examples of communities that have "imploded" are abundant.

The generalized insecurity focussing as panic by a group facing mortality—another form of falling—has been discussed by historians. In his theorization of the cycles of cultures by which cultures cycle between phases of civilization and barbarism, Franz Borkenau wrote

> If the phenomenon we have called a "dark ages" arises from the collapse
> of a death-transcending culture into death-denying and paranoiac barbarism,
> it would seem logical that the reverse process gives rise to a different conclu-
> sion. Loss of faith in survival leaves a void which must be filled; on the
> contrary, where such a faith asserts itself, there is no void and no room seems
> left for a paranoiac retrogression [9:85–86].

Other writers have also suggested that there is a link between a sense of insecurity
and ethnic conflict that can arise even when the insecurity is not necessarily well-
founded. Horowitz noted that

> two or more incipient societies in a single state is an uncomfortable situation,
> and it often produces impulses to make the society homogeneous, by assimi-
> lation, expulsion or even extermination. This leads me to speculate that the
> fear of extermination is actually a projection [13:180].

It is also possible that the lack of confidence or faith in survival felt by some
communities can be related to the experience of colonialism. Erikson has referred
to Gandhi's conception of the "fourfold ruin" wrought be colonialism: cultural
and spiritual, as well as political and economic [14:296]. In this way, one could
say that spiritual ruin has connotations of the vacuum referred to by Erikson, the
void of Borkenau, or the lack of immortality, dignity, and fraternity of Smith.
Thus one can visualize a state with one or more gravitational collapses in its
national identity(ies), where a group (or groups) is perceiving its own annihilation
within that state and reacting in an accordingly unstable, violent, and unpredict-
able way through symptomatology reflecting the malaise of a lack of immortality,
dignity, and fraternity. This is also consistent with Safran's twelve-point scheme
of ethnopluralistic accommodation, where the criteria of nonexclusive religion
(immortality), legitimacy (dignity), and a nonoverweening state (fraternity) are
not being met.

IV. CIVIL WAR IN SRI LANKA

According to *Stern* magazine, there are currently 43 major civil wars in progress
[15], including that in Sri Lanka, which since 1983 has taken 110,000 lives [16:
1994] (although no official figures are available, this estimate seems more realistic than others) and has cost the country possibly as much as US$2 billion in
only its first five years [17]. This civil war can be interpreted as one caused by
incipient gravitational collapse of identity in not one, but two communities
(through a collapse in just one community is often a sufficient condition for a
civil war). This interpretation can be made on the basis of the evidence of expressions of insecurity by political actors and observers, though a precise instrument
for assessing insecurity of identity that would enable correlation with conflict is

not yet available. However, there are many studies of state stability and state longevity [18], and some, such as the CIA's State Failure Task Force [19], take into account a wide range of factors likely to correlate with regime change.

Sri Lanka, the island state separated from the southeastern tip of the Indian subcontinent by the 80-km-wide Palk Strait, has a population of 18 million. Its most ancient inhabitants are the Veddas, a people who were conquered in the sixth century B.C.E. by the Sinhalese, who came from northern India and whose few remaining descendants live today on the north central and eastern plains. Settling in the north of the island, the Sinhalese developed an elaborate infrastructure, including an irrigation system, and introduced Buddhism from India in the third century B.C.E. Sri Lanka became a major center of Buddhist activity; a cutting of the tree under which Buddha gained enlightenment was planted at Bodh Gaya (which in recent times became the scene of a massacre), and the temple of the Tooth at Kandy remains an extremely important Buddhist sacred site. When Buddhism was supplanted in southern India by the revival of Hinduism, it persisted in Sri Lanka in the Theravada form, in which the Sinhalese had a custodial role.

Proximity to the Indian subcontinent resulted in many invasions, mostly by Tamils. Although South Indians had come in B.C.E. times, in the twelfth century C.E. a Tamil kingdom was established in the north of the island, and the Sinhalese were driven southward. Arab traders made regular trading visits, and the Portuguese conquered parts of the coastal fringe in the early sixteenth century. These possessions were taken over by the Dutch in the next 100 years and then the British in 1795, who gained possession of the whole island in 1815 when the Kingdom of Kandy was conquered. There were rebellions against British rule in 1815 and 1845, but the British were able to establish plantation industries of tea, coffee, and other crops, and imported a large number of Tamils to provide the necessary labor.

During World War I an independence movement arose, and the island was finally granted independence in 1948. Since then, the road to nationhood has become extremely hard, which is hardly surprising given the diversity of ethnic, religious, and cultural raw material and military and imperial residues with which the nation-builders have been required to work. Although the picture today is not without some rays of light within a generally sombre atmosphere, there is obviously a very long way to go to achieve a minimal acceptable level of Safran's twelve-point scheme of successful ethnic accommodation.

The ethnolinguistic composition of Sri Lanka is dominated by the two major ethnic groups. The Sinhalese number 14 million and make up 74% of the state's population. They are located mainly in the south and west of the country, especially in the capital Colombo, where they constitute 79% of the city's population of 650,000. Buddhism is the religion of the majority of Sinhalese, and as a result 69% of Sri Lankans are Buddhist. The Sinhalese speak Sinhala, or Sinhalese, an Indo-European language descended from Sanskrit.

The Tamils, numbering 4 million or 18% of the population, are the other major group; they occupy three main areas of the country. The Ceylon Tamils of the northern and eastern provinces make up 10% of the national population, and the Indian Tamils in the plantation districts of the Kandyan Central Highlands constitute 8%. While the Tamils predominate in the Jaffna Peninsula and the surrounding area (which together they have named Tamil Eelam), some 47% of Tamils live in areas of Sinhalese numerical dominance—often in peace and harmony. The Tamils are mostly Hindu in religion and account for practically all of the nation's 18% Hindu population.

In addition, there are smaller but still significant minorities of Muslims, who have been on the island since the eighth and ninth centuries; the Burghers, people of Portuguese or Dutch extraction dating from the colonial periods; and Christians of various ethnic origins, who often play an important role as mediators. The main principle of social stratification in Sri Lankan society, both Sinhalese and Tamil, has from ancient times been caste, though it is not as important today as ethnicity. Class and English education are also important [20:19].

In addition to its ethnolinguistic composition, Sri Lanka has other important residues resulting from its long colonial history. While there is somewhat less of a remaining trace of the Portuguese and Dutch periods of settlement, the British influence still permeates all aspects of the country. In justice, no less than five legal systems still operate today: the Roman-Dutch, the English, the Tsewalamai, the Islamic, and the Kandyan.

Probably more than anything else, it is the English language that is Britain's lasting source of influence upon Sri Lanka and, through it, systems of education, administration, and political institutions; sport (especially cricket), and postcolonial statehood through membership of the Commonwealth.

From these diverse origins, the attempt to build a nation-state has been made with obvious difficulty, such that there is evidence of serious areas of weakness in national identity, indeed gravitational collapses in the metaphor of astrophysics that I am proposing as being relevant.

V. NATIONAL IDENTITY IN SRI LANKA

As already stated, national identity is a psychic entity that can only be observed indirectly. In a state with a strong sense of national identity, there will be evidence of a sense of direction, purpose, and achievement, or "unified striving" as Erikson called it [4:63]. Conversely, a weak or failing sense of national identity can be recognized by the presence of various symptoms such as the nonfulfillment of

Safran's twelve-point scheme or Smith's three-function conceptualization. Here a three-symptom scheme of language and culture conflict, political violence, and population displacement is proposed.

A. Language and Culture Conflict

During the period of British rule, English was the official and prestigious language, and prior to independence there was a Swabhasha movement for Sri Lanka's "own language," which embraced both Sinhala and Tamil [21:179]. After independence the communities separated. Sinhala is an Indo-European language descended from Sanskrit, as noted, but its rounded script more closely resembles that used for the Dravidian languages of southern India [22:201]. Long cut off from its distant relatives in northern India, Sinhala is spoken by 14 million Sinhalese in Sri Lanka but not in wide use outside of the country. The isolation of their language is relevant to understanding the political imperative of the Sinhalese to safeguard and strengthen its position. As a Sri Lankan writer of Tamil origin was to state, perhaps with hyperbole, "The Sinhala language . . . was in danger of extinction—and with it the Sinhala people. Where else in the world was Sinhala spoken but in Ceylon?" [23:217]. Horowitz also reports language insecurity among Sinhalese activists, who stated "if they didn't do something there would be no more Buddhism and no more Sinhalese—they'd all be Hindu priests, speaking in Tamil" [13:176]. To complicate matters language reinforced, and was reinforced by, religion. De Silva observed, "Buddhism and the destiny of the Sinhala language were so closely intertwined that it was virtually impossible to treat either in isolation from the other" [24:7].

Thus three witnesses have testified to the existence of the fundamental, quasireligious place of Sinhala in the fabric of Sinhalese society, but one that is at the same time deeply troubled by a sense of insecurity. It is thus possible to detect a fear of gravitational collapse in identity among Sri Lankan Sinhalese and in particular among the Sinhalese Buddhist elite, who also have the most to lose by any change in existing relative power positions in any domain, including that of language.

In contrast, Tamil is one of the major languages of southern India and one of India's fifteen Schedule Languages, or official languages. It is one of the oldest of the Dravidian languages and is spoken by about 60 million people in India, mainly in Tamil Nadu. It also has sizeable numbers of speakers in Malaysia, Singapore, Fiji, Mauritius, Trinidad, Guyana, and East Africa, as well as its 4 million speakers in Sri Lanka [22:199].

Unlike the Sinhalese case, where language and religion were inextricable bound, for the Tamils language was paramount and religion was not as central to ethnic identity [20:216].

The fact that Tamil nationalists in the Indian state of Tamil Nadu had actively resisted the efforts of their national government to introduce Hindi as India's national language [24:4], was not lost on Sri Lanka's communities of Tamils, who saw themselves as being engaged in a similar struggle, such that it is possible to see Sinhalese language insecurity reacting to Tamil language insecurity and then escalating in a chain reaction.

Although the language issue goes far back in Sri Lankan history, it has dominated the process of politics since independence. The enactment of the Official Language Act in 1956 provoked the first of many language riots, in which Tamils reacted against the installation of Sinhala as the sole official language. This act of language particularism, later described as the "triumph of the language extremists," of whom the Prime Minister of Sri Lanka was "prisoner" [24:14–16], set an unfortunate precedent severely prejudicing the possibility of interethnic collaboration. And, in denying legitimacy to the minority language, it created a vacuum in language identity among Tamil speakers who resented Sinhala. In the view of N. Islam, it was the "Sinhala only" policy that began the polarization process leading ultimately to Tamil demands for a separate state [25].

In 1972, in response to further protests from Tamils, the Sinhalese-dominated government changed the Constitution. However, not only did it reaffirm the dominant position of Sinhala, but it also gave state blessing to Buddhism [21:179]. The economic position of the various communities is complex and changing. To some extent Tamils had some overrepresentation in the administration under the "protective umbrella of British rule" [20:95], which had been changing since independence.

There is evidence that language policy was used as a blocking mechanism in relation to the aspirations of Tamil speakers in their quest for civil service positions [26:75]. In some recognition of the legitimacy of Tamil demands for recognition of their language rights, the Constitutional Amendment of 1978 made Tamil a national language (which was still less than an official language) [27:10]. Finally, Tamil was recognized as one of the three administrative languages in the Sixteenth Amendment to the Constitution in 1988 [28:7], but unfortunately this was still not enough in the eyes of many Tamils.

While at the time of independence the Jaffna Tamils were generally ahead of the Sinhalese in economic terms, and the Indian Tamils, or plantation workers, were behind; it is possible that the Jaffna Tamils are now behind the Sinhalese. On the other hand, the Indian Tamils are reported to have made some gains since the 1970s [29].

It is significant that an attempt to address the language issue was a feature of the Indo-Lankan Peace Accord signed between the governments of India and Sri Lanka in 1987, in that Tamil was at last given equal official status to Sinhala.

But this belated step has not been sufficient to remove the underlying causes of the civil war. Riots over language, culture and ethnicity have been a frequent occurrence until the outbreak of the civil war in 1983, when all issues became submerged by the question of independence (see Table 1).

The language issue has manifested itself not only in employment recruitment, but also in legal administration and education. In the 1960s, such Sinhalese-oriented policies as the Language of Courts Act and school standardization came into being. In 1971 standardization was introduced for university entrance examinations. It has been reported that all Tamil candidates had their scores marked down in relation to Sinhalese candidates, with the result that Tamils, who in 1969 had won 50% of medical school places, by 1977 had been reduced to 28% of places [31]. Moreover, in the view of Sivanandan [23:234], school texts have stressed Sinhalese superiority and depicted the Tamil minority as invaders and immigrants.

The issue of language conflict is inextricable from the issue of the conflict of cultures. Kapferer [32] has argued that there are also myths of Buddhist triumphalism propagated through the Sinhalese education system. Government attempts at creating ethnic quotas have further exacerbated the ethnolinguistic conflict.

Horowitz reports a study of cultural stereotypes—admittedly of several generations ago, but possibly still relevant today—in which Sinhalese saw themselves as kind, good, and religious, but twice as lazy as the Tamils, whom they saw as cruel and arrogant as well as diligent and thrifty [13:142]. Even the historical existence of stereotypes is a factor undermining the chances of successfully constructing a single inclusive national identity.

At a specific level, the establishment of a Ministry of Cultural Affairs was interpreted badly by many Tamil intellectuals. For example, one commentator saw it as being based on Sinhalese Buddhist culture and alleged that when Sri Lanka hosted the Non-Aligned Nations Conference in 1976, festivities celebrated

Table 1 Language and/or Ethnic Riots in Sri Lanka

Dates	Areas
June 1956	Colombo and the Eastern Province.
May 1958	Throughout the country. The worst areas were Colombo, Batticaloa, and Polonnaruwa.
August to September 1977	Colombo and Kandy.
July 1979	Jaffna and Colombo.
August 1981	Amparai, Negombo, and Jaffna.
July to August 1983	Kandy, Colombo, and Matale.

Source: Ref. 30.

Buddhist art, music, and dance and excluded Tamil culture. From the Sinhalese side, there is fear of the power of Hindu culture, in particular the Hindu form of caste system, and the nearby presence of the giant power of India; more specifically the influence of the powerful state of Tamil Nadu has been remarked upon [26:124]. Thus, at the level of language and culture, it is possible to visualize two major vacuums in national identity with resultant insecurities.

B.   Violence in the Political System

A pattern of political violence is an unmistakable manifestation of a national identity that is breaking down. In Sri Lanka, assassination has been a leit-motiv of the operation of the system, and many leaders have fallen, reflecting the intensity of the political process in the deadly theater of Sri Lankan identity politics (see Table 2).

Prophetically, an early Prime Minister, S. W. R. D. Bandaranaike stated, "I am prepared to sacrifice my life for the sake of my community, the Sinhalese" [32:91], as indeed he was to do, assassinated not by a Tamil but by a Sinhalese Buddhist priest for personal and political motives not associated with the ethnic situation.

The assassination of the Prime Minister of India, Rajiv Ghandi, has been linked to Tamil separatists, the rationale being excessive concessions to the Sinhalese-dominated Sri Lankan Government [33,34].

In an eight day period in April 1993, both the Sri Lankan President Ranasinge Premadasa and the opposition leader Lalith Athulathmudali were assassinated. President Premadasa had made some concessions on language, culture,

Table 2   Assassinations of Major Political Actors

Name	Position	Date
Solomon Bandaranaike[a]	Prime Minister	25/09/59
Harsha Abeywardene	UNP Chairman	21/01/88
Lionel Jayatillete	Government Minister	26/10/88
Appapillai Amirthalingman	TULF Secretary-General	13/07/89
Ranjan Wijeratne	Government Minister	02/03/91
Rajiv Gandhi[b]	Indian Prime Minister	21/05/91
Lalith Athulathmudali	Opposition Leader	23/04/93
Ranasinge Premadasa	President	01/05/93
Gamini Dissanayake	Presidential Candidate	23/10/94

[a] Not because of the ethnic issue.
[b] In India, but believed to have been by Tamil Tigers.
Source: Ref. 30.

and religion, and he had regularly visited Hindu temples and made public utterances in the Tamil language [35].

Political violence is spread throughout all levels of society. The 1983 ethnic violence against the Tamils of Colombo [32:29], in which hundreds were killed, was a particularly clear manifestation of the breakdown of civil society and thus, I would argue, of national identity. In the presidential election of 1988 another estimated 500 deaths occurred, while the parliamentary elections of February 1989 saw the deaths of an estimated 850, including 14 candidates [36:690].

The commencement of the civil war in 1983 between the Sri Lankan Government and the Liberation Tigers of Tamil Eelam (LTTE), who still control a considerable section of the northeast of the country despite the fall of the city Jaffna to Government troops in December 1995, is an incontrovertible indication of the breakdown of national identity.

The election to office of President Chandrika Kumaratunga in 1994 on a promise to end the civil war was followed by a truce that broke down on April 19, 1995. Her plan to create a federation of strong provinces was supported in Colombo but rejected by the Tamil Tigers, and the deadline of her promise to replace the present system of executive presidency with a return to a parliamentary system by July 15, 1995, has also passed with little sign of fulfilment [37].

The effect of the proximity of a nearby homeland state of some 60 million Tamils cannot be underestimated. The presence of this homeland, which also is a major source of supply and sustenance for the Tamils, is a cause of insecurity to the Sinhalese. The 1987 Indo-Lankan Peace Accord gained some language recognition for the Tamils, an agreement for the repatriation of some 130,000 Tamils who had fled Sri Lanka for southern India, and provided for the disarming of the Tamil militants in exchange for a general amnesty. To oversee the agreement, Indian troops numbering ultimately 70,000 were stationed in Sri Lanka, a number which was still to prove inadequate to the task entrusted to them [36:692].

But the Indian government, hard pressed with its own problems of ethnic separatism, was not in support of a separate Tamil state, as Rajiv Gandhi had stated in 1985 [38:183]. Despite various reassurances, the fear among Sinhalese Sri Lankans of an Indian invasion still persists [38:222]. With Tamil Eelam, one could say that a separate state has come to exist, and the Tamil Tigers have achieved such power that the Sri Lankan Government has not yet been able to overcome them [39:17].

C. Population Displacement

The movement of large numbers of people within a nation and from a nation can also be interpreted as symptom of the breakdown of national identity due to gravitational collapse. Endemic violence is a major causal factor, and it is possible to say that displaced people are ones whose psychic needs of security, dignity, and fraternity are not being met. Specifically, they fear death, the burning and looting of homes and places of business, and rape. In discussing systematic sexual violence against women, a United Nations report stated that a review of European asylum case law indicated that a deplorably high number of Tamil refugee women from Sri Lanka had been raped [40:70].

Since 1983 some 500,000 people have left Sri Lanka [35]. A major proportion of these are Tamils, with some 240,000 relocating to south India and 200,000 to the Western world. Fewer than 10,000 Tamils have been successfully repatriated to Sri Lanka [41].

The current status of the civil war in Sri Lanka is such that an end does not appear to be in sight. President Kumaratunga is reported to have expressed "unqualified acceptance of the fact that the Tamil people have genuine grievances for which solutions must be found" [42:23]. Her policy of devolution, a federalist solution offering some measure of autonomy, is being strongly resisted by the Buddhist clergy and also by supporters of the Jana Vimukti Permian, a xenophobic group committed to the "Sinhala only" policy [42:24]. For their part, the LTTE show no sign of wavering in its commitment to its cause [43].

VI. NATIONAL IDENTITY AND GRAVITATIONAL COLLAPSE IN SRI LANKA

We have noted Safran's twelve-point scheme for the successful accommodation of ethnic minorities into a state and seen that these preconditions are not currently being met in Sri Lanka. I have argued that the reason is to be found in the application of a concept of identity, a psychic force necessary for the survival of a state, specifically by—as in Smith's formulation—performing the functions of providing a sense of immortality, dignity, and fraternity. Erikson called the non-fulfillment of the identity function an existential vacuum, causing a crisis in which there is a murderous hatred of otherness.

This explanation can be encapsulated in the metaphor of the gravitational collapse of astrophysics, which when applied to human affairs visualizes a body collapsing inward after its psychic energy resources of security and confidence are spent and the bonding of its components has failed.

In Sri Lanka, the evidence presented of language and culture conflicts, political violence, and population displacement is strongly suggestive of two communities deeply lacking in security and confidence about their future in the island state of Sri Lanka. The Tamils are fearful for their position in Sri Lanka, and the Sinhalese are fearful of being overcome in their struggle to maintain a distinctly Sinhalese identity, which they have tried unsuccessfully to secure through an attempt to enshrine it as national identity. These two gravitational collapses in national identity are at the basis of the failure in the case of Sri Lanka to achieve Safran's model ethnic accommodation within one state. If they could somehow be filled, then a single national identity could, with the passage of time, develop and the "resplendent isle" could move toward unified statehood.

REFERENCES

1. Safran, W. (1994). Non-separatist policies regarding ethnic minorities: Positive approaches and ambiguous consequences. *International Political Science Review 15*, No. 1, 61–79.
2. Robertson, D. (1994). *The Penguin Dictionary of Politics*. London: Penguin.
3. Freud, S. (1955). Beyond the pleasure principle, group psychology and other works. *Standard Edition 18* (1920–1922). London: Hogarth.
4. Erikson, E. H. (1968). Identity, psychosocial. In D. R. Sills (ed.), *Encyclopedia of the Social Sciences*. New York: Macmillan and Free Press.
5. Mackenzie, W. J. M. (1978). *Political Identity*. Harmondsworth: Penguin.
6. Etzioni, A. (1971). Toward a macrosociology. In F. E. Katz (ed.), *Contemporary Sociological Theory*. New York: Random House.
7. Smith M. B. (1985). The metaphorical basis of selfhood. In A. J. Marcella, G. de Vos, and F. L. K. Hsu (eds.), *Culture and Self: Asian and Western Perspectives*. London and New York: Tavistock.
8. Ozolins, U. (1996). Language policy and political reality. *International Journal of the Sociology of Language 118*, 181–200.
9. Borkenau, F. (1981). *End and Beginning: On the Generations of Cultures and the Origins of the West*. New York: Colombia University Press.
10. Smith, A. D. (1991). *National Identity*. London: Penguin.
11. *The New Encyclopedia Britannica*, 15th ed., s. v. "black hole."
12. Speer, A. (1971). *Inside the Third Reich*. London: Sphere.
13. Horowitz, D. L. (1985). *Ethnic Groups in Conflict*. Berkeley, Los Angeles, London: University of California Press.
14. Erikson, E. H. (1968). *Identity Youth and Crisis*. New York: Norton.
15. "Vergeblicker Traum vom Frieden." (1994). *Stern*, No. 21, May 19.
16. *Quid*. (1996). Paris: Editions Laffont.
17. Richardson, J. M., Jr. and Samarasinghe, S. W. R. A. (1991). Measuring the economic dimensions of Sri Lanka's ethnic conflict. In S. W. R. A. Samarasinghe and R. Loughlan (eds.), *Economic Dimensions of Ethnic Conflict* London: Pinter; New York: St Martin's Press; and Colombo, Sri Lanka: International Centre for Ethnic Studies and Friedrich Ebert Stifting.
18. Lane, J. E. and Ersson, S. (1994). *Comparative Politics: An Introduction and New Approach*. Cambridge, UK: Polity Press.
19. "Pakistan, India at Risk: CIA." (1996). *Mercury* (Hobart, Tasmania), February 5.
20. de Silva, K. M. (1986). *Managing Ethnic Tensions in Multi-Ethnic Societies: Sri Lanka 1880–1985*. Lanham, New York, London: University Press of America.
21. Edwards, J. (1985). *Language, Society and Identity*. Oxford and New York: Basil Blackwell, in association with Andre Deutsch.
22. Katzner, K. (1977). *The Languages of the World*. London and Henly: Routledge and Kegan Paul.

23. Sivanandan, A. (1990). *Communities of Resistance Writings in Black Struggles for Socialism*. London and New York: Verso.
24. de Silva K. M. (1993). Ethnicity, language and politics: The making of Sri Lanka's Official Language Act No. 33 of 1956. *Ethnic Studies Report 11*, No. 1 (January).
25. Islam, N. (1990). Ethnic differentiation, relative deprivation and public policies in Sri Lanka. *Canadian Review of Studies in Nationalism 17*, Nos. 1–2, 15–30.
26. Tambiah, S. (1986). *Sri Lanka: Ethnic Fratricide and the Dismantling of Democracy*. Chicago: University of Chicago Press.
27. Manor, J. (1984). Introduction. In J. Manor (ed.), *Sri Lanka in Change and Crisis*. Sydney: Croome Helm.
28. Rajan, A. T. (1995). *Tamil as Official Language: Retrospect and Prospect*. Colombo: International Centre for Ethnic Studies. Reviewed in (1995). *New Language Planning Newsletter 10*, No. 1 (September), 7. Mysore: Central Institute of Indian Languages.
29. Peiris, G. H. (1991). Changing prospects of the plantation workers of Sri Lanka. In S. W. R. A. Samarasinghe and R. Loughlan (eds.), *Economic Dimensions of Ethnic Conflict*. London: Pinter; New York: St. Martin's Press; and Colombo, Sri Lanka: International Centre for Ethnic Studies and Friedrich Ebert Stifting.
30. *Keesing's Contemporary Archive*. London: Keesings.
31. Meares, P. (1991). "Tearing itself apart." *Asia-Pacific Defence Reporter*, February, 1991.
32. Kapferer, B. (1988). *Legends of People, Myths of State: Violence, Intolerance, and Political Culture in Sri Lanka and Australia*. Washington and London: Smithsonian.
33. *Keesings Contemporary Archive*. S. V. "Rajiv Gandhi," Vol. 37, art. 38175 A.
34. *Europa Yearbook: 1995*, p. 2834. London: Europa.
35. "A hole in Sri Lanka." (1993). *The Economist*, May, 8.
36. Derbyshire, J. D. and Derbyshire, I. (1989). *Political Systems of the World*. Edinburgh: Chambers.
37. "Sri Lankan leader mired in civil war and broken promises." (1995). *Weekend Australian*, August, 26–27.
38. Wilson, A. J. (1988). *The Breaking of Sri Lanka: The Sinhalese Tamil Conflict*. London: Hurst.
39. Rudrakumaran, V. (1994). Secession in Aland, Tamil separatism, and international law. *Canadian Review of Studies in Nationalism 21* Nos. 1–2, 17.
40. United Nations High Commissioner for Refugees. (1993). *The State of the World's Refugees, 1993: The Challenge of Protection*. New York: Penguin.
41. Central Intelligence Agency. (1995). *CIA World Factbook*. (Internet: http.www. research.ah.can/cgi/wald/abaccess/411 [sighted 7.17.95]).
42. Dixit, A. (1996). "Resolving the Sri Lankan ethnic crisis: Options for Chandrika Kumaratunga?" *Asia-Pacific Defence Reporter*, March.
43. McPhedran I. (1996). "A nation's long search for peace with justice." *Canberra Times*, July 6.

12

Politics of Agenda-Building in South Korea

Imperial Japan's Military Sexual Slavery Case

Bang-Soon Yoon
Central Washington University, Ellensburg, Washington

I. INTRODUCTION

During the China War, the Pacific War, and World War II, Korea (undivided) was under Japan's colonial control (1910–1945), and an unspecified number of young females from the Korean peninsula (historians' rough estimations range between 100,000–200,000) were abducted or conscripted by the Japanese military and sent to war zones for coerced sexual services to Japan's Imperial Army (JIA). Those females were better known in South Korea as *Jungshindae* (Women's Voluntary Labor Corps).[1] They were euphemistically called *Wianbu* in Korea and *Ianfu* in Japan (both translated into English as "comfort women"), and recent publications often refer to them as "military comfort women" (MCW) or "comfort women."[2]

The Japanese military sexual slavery (JMSS) was an important element of Japanese military imperialism. The systematic and full-scale draft of Korean young females for forced sexual services is believed by many researchers to have begun around 1937 when Japan started the military buildup in China. It was under direct and organized government involvement, although the Japanese government has still not fully accepted responsibility. The rationale as well as purpose of the draft of the JMSS were manifold.[3] First, there were public relations and diplomatic considerations. Initially the conscription of JMSS began to restore Japan's public image in world diplomatic circles after the Nanking Massacre of 1937. Instead of raping local women in China, Korean females were an ideal substitute

163

given their colonial status. Second, from a military strategy perspective, protection of local women was necessary to dilute rising anti-Japanese sentiments that might disturb Japan's military operations. Third, "comfort women" raised military morale, strengthened military imperialism, and, it was argued, made soldiers "fit to fight" physically and spiritually.

For nearly one-half decade, the JMSS case had not been raised as a political issue either within or outside the Korean peninsula. The *Jungshindae* was what every parent in the Korean peninsula wanted to avoid during the World War II era. They did not know about the systematic sexual enslavement, but rather were worried about hardships those young girls might encounter away from home. They did fear that the young girls might be sexually assaulted, but that was hypothetical. They knew nothing about gang rape in the military through the systematic, bureaucratization of sexual violence. Nonetheless, the *Jungshindae* has been widely known about in South Korea among the older generation, although hardly any graphic description of the sexual slavery situation under JIA were known to Koreans. Some Korean men who served in Japan's military (either as voluntary joiners or draftees) as well as those Koreans working for Japan's military establishment during wartime must have known about the JMSS. Given the size of JMSS and its relationships with JIA's military system, it seems likely that older generations in Japan also knew about this abusive system.

And yet, it was not until in December 1991 when the public in South Korea began to openly debate the JMSS issue. Hak-Soon Kim, then a 67-year-old JMSS survivor, came forward to reveal her past experience and followed with a lawsuit against the Japanese government for damages, the first legal case ever filed by a Korean JMSS survivor.[4] Kim's case has certainly illuminated the JIA's sexual slavery issue in Korea (both South and North), Japan, and in other victim's countries in Asia: the Philippines, Taiwan, China, and Indonesia. It began to receive attention from the mass media throughout the world. In south Korea alone, more than 157 women (as of June, 1997) have identified themselves as victims of this sexual holocaust. Many more survivors are believed to reside in China and elsewhere in Asia, as well as in the United States.

Various study groups and activist groups have formed both in and out of South Korea, of which the Korean Council for Women Drafted for Sexual Service by Japan (KCWDSSJ) of 1990 has been the central organization.[5] Much literature is now available on the nature of sexual slavery, the systematic involvement of the Japanese government in the slavery system, legal issues involving the Japanese government's reparation to victims, and feminist analyses of the JMSS.[6] Intellectual women-centered activism also pushed the sexual slavery issue into the public arena and pushed the South Korean government to provide some welfare measures for the surviving victims. Lobbying activities initiated by the KCWDSSJ and other women's organizations pressured the South Korean government, and the National Assembly in 1992 passed a Special Law to assist JMSS survivors.

Survivors who have registered in the Ministry of Health and Social Affairs in South Korea (MOHSA) received a lump sum payment of 5 million won (about $6,500) in 1992 (this applies to new registrants as well) and receive financial support of 500,000 won (about $570) per month, as of March 1997, in addition to various kinds of welfare support such as low-income housing facilities, medical care, and so on.

Women's activist organizations (e.g., KCWDSSJ) have also appealed to various international organizations such as the United Nations to conduct a thorough investigation of JMSS to help restore the victims' human rights and dignity. They have also appealed to the international community to pressure Japan to take responsibility for those women's lost human dignity and well-being (through such means as apology and reparation). Since the 1993 UN World Conference on Human Rights in Vienna, there has been increasing attention on the JMSS issue. At the 1995 NGO Forum held in conjunction with the Fourth UN World Conference on Women in China, the JMSS attracted great attention from the participants. The case has certainly contributed to the identification of rape and other forms of violence against women in war as one of the most significant findings of the NGO Forum.[7] The UN Human Rights Commission has also begun to investigate the JMSS issue, on its formal agenda in 1996.[8] Increasing pressure from the international community led Japan to create the Asian Women's Fund in July 1995 to raise funds in the private sector to support JMSS victims financially and to provide other welfare measures (e.g., medical service). The Asian Women's Fund's ''sympathy money'' has encountered strong opposition though from the victims themselves and women's advocacy groups as well.[9]

Why then has the JMSS case never been openly discussed in public, inside or outside the Korean peninsula, for a half century? Some of the most important contributing factors have been (1) Korea's traditional Confucianism-based culture suppresses debate regarding female sexuality; (2) the peculiar political-economic relationships between South Korea and Japan in recent decades; (3) the Cold War politics of East Asia; (4) the powerless social status of the victims in South Korea's power hierarchy; and (5) the androcentric orientation of South Korea's political culture. This chapter, however, focusses only on the internal political situations.

The central argument is that agenda-building for public debate requires a certain policy environment: conducive political contexts allow the public to make particular issues a matter of social concern; and a dedicated organizational structure would help place an issue on the political agenda. From a policy analysis perspective, this chapter analyzes how South Korea's political contexts and women's organizations affected the suppression or emergence of the JMSS issue. In South Korea's political context, nation-building, national security, and rapid industrialization were ''fundamental policy'' goals of society.[10] Related to these policy goals is the bureaucratic-authoritarian political system wherein autonomous interest-group activities are limited, while the national government's power is centered around the president. South Korea's so-called democratization, allowing more people's input in polity, has been a rather recent phenomenon, observed only since the late 1980s. The women's movement in South Korea, despite its long history, was not effective in raising the JMSS issue as an agenda for public debate until the late 1980s due partly to the peculiar sociopolitical situation of South Korea and partly to the orientation of the women's movement itself.

II. POLITICAL CONTEXT OF NATION-BUILDING AND NATIONAL SECURITY

The early history of Korea's postwar era situation reveals the significance of the sociopolitical situation in agenda-building. Liberation from Japan's colonialism (1945), the partition of the Korean peninsula into north and south (1945), the establishment of two separate political entities in the south and north (both in 1948), the Korean War (1950–1953) and the post–Korean War situation created a great deal of social unrest as well as political instability. The geopolitical situation and colonial history made the Korean peninsula a test case of the Cold War era superpower rivalry, as evidenced by the partition of the peninsula and the Korean War. In such a situation, nation-building and national defense captured immediate social attention in South Korea's polity, for reasons of political stability as well as economic survival. Such issues as the plight of both the men and women who were enslaved as forced laborers,[11] or sexual slaves, thus failed to attract social attention. Furthermore, political leadership had not shown any inclination to bring justice to the victims of colonialism.

Immediately after Korea's liberation, the United States played a key role in South Korean polity. Despite the fact that the United States had known of the JMSS as early as 1942, the U.S. Army Military Government in Korea (USAMGIK), which took over the southern part of Korea from 1945–1948, did not investigate it. The U.S. government had certainly been informed that a large number of young Korean females were systematically being sent to China and Manchuria during World War II.[12] Numerous U.S. military documents of 1944 and afterward also deal with "Japanese Army Brothel" and "Korean comfort girls" issues, some with detailed information about the process of recruitment by the Japanese, living/working conditions, and the "comfort girls" relationship with the Japanese military.[13] U.S. troops, which occupied Okinawa in the spring of 1945, captured pornographic photos of JIA soldiers and young oriental women who must have been "comfort girls" abandoned by the defeated Japanese forces stationed at the headquarters of the Japanese Army at Shuri Castle near Naha.[14] Yet during the International Military Tribunal for the Far East (the Tokyo war crimes trials,

1946–1948), the JMSS issue was not raised at all. The newly liberated Korea (as a non-Allied member country) was not even allowed to participate in the Tokyo war crimes trials, nor were any other Japanese war crimes against Koreans brought to the court for trial.[15]

The West-centered international politics focussed on the Military Tribunal of Nuremberg to punish Nazi leaders, and paid little attention to war criminals in the East. European affairs captured primary attention in world politics, whereas things in Asia were considered as unimportant, unrelated to Westerners, unfamiliar, not interesting in postwar power distribution, and so forth.[16] While Korean and other Asian ''comfort women'' victimization cases were buried, Japanese soldiers responsible for coerced sexual services against Dutch women in Indonesia were tried and punished (including execution) in 1948 by the Allies at the Batavia (Jakarta) Court, and the Dutch victims were materially compensated.[17] A Korean ''comfort girl'' was perceived as nothing more than a prostitute or a professional camp follower attached to the Japanese Army by the U.S. military interrogation team.[18]

The onset of the Cold War further shifted U.S. policy toward Japan, from political and economic sanction to rebuilding Japan for strategic balance in East Asia. Japan's emperor system, although stripped of political power, was maintained by the U.S. occupied forces in Japan, thus legitimately allowing him to escape from war crimes responsibilities. Cold War strategy outweighed the war trials.

In South Korea, colonial victims were not properly dealt with by either the USAMGIK or the Syngman Rhee regime (1948–1960). Collaborators not only escaped punishment, they were also recruited to fill important posts vacated by the colonial government. Communist insurgencies as well as political factionalism were threatening South Korea's political stability, thus anticommunist nation-building through institutionalization of political, social, and economic infrastructure was the immediate concern. In the process of nation-building, anticommunists who held conservative political views were recruited to fill the administrative vacuum (including in law enforcement agencies) left vacated by the colonial government. Maintaining the government structure of the colonial era, the USAMGIK recruited educated people, technocrats, and those who knew English to fill government offices for their functional merits. Such management was necessary to restore law and order. Many collaborators later resumed leading roles in every corner of South Korean society (e.g., in politics, economics, education, the military, the so-called women's community [*Yoseong gye*],[19] literature, and so forth), and many of them are still in power in their chosen fields.[20] South Korea had an opportunity to investigate the pro-Japan, anti-Korean activities by creating the National Assembly of the Special Committee to Punish Anti-National Acts During the Japanese Colonial Period. Despite popular support from the public, however, the Committee was short lived (1948–1949) challenged by strong counteractions by pro-Japan collaborators, especially police, who were central power elites. South Korea's power structure was then built upon those collaborators. Rhee, despite his long-lived overseas independence movement activism, strongly opposed the Committee and abolished it. In fact, Rhee himself during the early tenure of his regime very much owed his political and economic survival to those power elites.[21] Furthermore, given the transitional and chaotic nature of the social situation, the nation-building and national defense issues were given higher priority. In such a political context, it was highly unlikely that trials of collaborators who helped Japan mobilize millions of Koreans for Japan's military efforts (including JMSS) would have occurred. The Rhee government negotiated with Japan a few times over colonial compensation, but Rhee's strong anti-Japan posture and the somewhat "emotional" demand for compensation ($3.6 billion, representing $100 million a year for 36 years of colonial suffering) bore no fruit.[22] The fact is that even if South Korea under Rhee had received the compensation money from Japan, it is unlikely that it would ever have reached the JMSS victims.

Intellectual orientation too has inhibited discussion of the Korean JMSS issue. History books on East Asia and World War II written by Koreans, Japanese, and other nationals as well ignored the issue deliberately or, in some cases, out of genuine ignorance of the incidents. Given the particular postwar political situation, which partitioned the Korean peninsula along the two competing ideological camps (capitalist democracy vis-a-vis communism), the academic orientation of Korean history has until very recently focussed on the left–right wing clashes of Korea's nationalist movement, whereas colonial victims' issues including JMSS received little attention.[23] Local historians and political leaders were preoccupied with independence movement heros. They focussed on elites, not on underclass victims of the colonial era. Even books on past and present Korean women's issues published in South Korea did not mention of the Korean JMSS case.[24] Beginning in the 1970s, some literature became available in Japan and South Korea, but it was not geared to the political community for investigation or policy action.

III. INDUSTRIALIZATION AND AUTHORITARIAN POLITICAL SYSTEM

In May 1961, Chung-Hee Park led a military coup d'etat, and South Korea's political system under military rule was characterized by bureaucratic authoritarianism wherein interest group activities were limited. Political power was concentrated in the presidency. Military power occupied the top of the power pyramid, and technocrats ("task elites") were mobilized as junior partners of the power elites for their functional merit. The Park regime articulated economic development and national defense as primary goals of the nation. These were considered symbiotic: economic prosperity was a necessary condition to defend the south from the communists' aggression from the north; strong national defense was a necessary condition for economic growth. Beginning in 1962, Park launched a series of national economic development plans with well-defined target goals, which resulted in the so-called Korean miracle economy. For Park, successful economic accomplishments were vitally important to solve his regime's political legitimacy problem. In order to achieve economic growth goals, South Koreans under Park were forced to sacrifice (under martial law, emergency measures, national security laws, for example) key elements of democracy, such as civil rights and civil liberties (including freedom of association, freedom of speech, and so forth). Public input in policy processes was limited. Interest group politics involving issues of civil rights or civil liberties, such as labor or human rights issues, were severely suppressed with sanctions. The ambiguous "national security" laws and "anticommunism" laws were used as oppressive tools to control political opponents or block civil rights and civil liberties.

In order to fuel the ambitious economic development plans, the Park regime also aggressively looked for outside funding sources. The 1965 Republic of Korea (ROK)–Japan Basic Treaty (diplomatic normalization treaty) was an example of such efforts. Included in the treaty was a provision on claims ("Properties and Claims"), that is, Japan's compensation of colonialism in monetary terms. The treaty negotiations took over four years. The main controversy evolved over the claims issue: the governments of South Korea and Japan showed a huge difference in the amount of compensation[25] according to their perceptional differences toward benefits/losses of colonial rule. Japan offered minimal payment arguing that Japan too lost properties in Korea. Furthermore, many Japanese had a rosy view of its colonial legacy. They argued that Korea was saved and protected from Western imperialism and that colonization helped Korea to modernize. When the negotiations were halted, South Korea even indicated that it would give up the Syngman Rhee Peace Line in exchange for more colonial compensation, but Japan would not agree to the South Korean terms.[26] The basis of South Korea's claims were mostly on property rights (i.e., bond holdings, postal money orders, land holdings, stocks, unpaid wages, forced savings, and so on), rather than on compensation for individual victims. The JMSS was not even included in the negotiation agenda at all. Ei Whan Pai, who, at the ambassador rank, led the ROK negotiation team between 1961–1965 (just before the treaty was formally signed), recalls that he had never heard about the JMSS, nor was it an agenda item during the treaty negotiations with Japan.[27] His knowledge would not have made any difference anyway, for the claims had to be factually documented to be considered valid. Besides, the settlement of the claims amount between the two countries was more a political decision than a legal settlement.[28] In formal records, the JMSS didn't exist. The victims of JMSS were simply referred to as "military commodities" when they were shipped around to battle fields.[29] For the Park regime, normalization with Japan was urgent to implement industrialization projects with Japan's capital and technology.[30] Beyond his ambition for political power, Park (a Japanese military trainee in Manchukou) was knowledgeable of Meiji, Japan's success of modernization, and highly valued industrialization as a tool for national survival to protect South Korea from potential aggression from the North. Economic indicators in the 1950s and the early 1960s showed the North outperforming the South.

The ROK–Japan treaty of 1965 was counteracted by fierce opposition in South Korea. It set the fire of nationalism. Through student demonstrations, media columns, protests from civilians and anti-Japan groups, opposition was powerful enough to halt a speedy ending of the treaty negotiations, which the South Korean government had originally estimated would be done in two months time. Still, the JMSS issue was not linked to those protests, even those protests on women's college or university campuses or led by the women's organizations. The treaty gave the South Korean government a free hand over the disposal of the claims money. The compensation money was released to draftees who died while in service (300,000 won each) until 1972, but the JMSS victims were not included.[31] No one in the government raised the JMSS issue. No JMSS survivors came forward. It was as if the JMSS had never even existed. The JMSS issue was completely left out of the treaty and claims benefits.

After the 1965 treaty, however, there were two incidents that could have served as momentum to raise the JMSS issue, but the goal of the industrialization and the authoritarian political system of the Park regime aborted these opportunities. The first case is that of Kum-Joo Whang; the second is the *Kisaeng Kwankwang* (sex tourism) case of the 1970s.

A. The Case of Kum-Joo Whang

Whang is an educated woman who survived her five-year JMSS life.[32] When she heard about the compensation money to the colonial era war veterans and other draftees, she invited herself to meet Chung-Hee Park's wife, the First Lady Young-Soo Yook at her maiden family home in Okchun in May 1966. But the First Lady's response caused her to continue to keep silent. Whang argues:

> I came from a good family, a scholar family although my parents were poor. One of my mother-side uncles was a lawyer, another a National Assembly member who was later assassinated in the 1950s. Because of my family background, I dare could not come forward to reveal my wartime identity. When I heard about the compensation money to military draftees, I thought about myself over and over. Over one hundred times. I finally made a big decision to talk directly with Yook, Young-Soo *Yosa* [Mrs.]. I went to visit her at her countryside home. I thought meeting her in her official house [the Blue

House] was impossible. So I chose her country home. Since I brought with me [to sell?] good, precious dried mountain vegetables from the Kangwon province where I was then living, together with my leadership role as the president of a women's club involved in the rural housing modernization project, I thought I would not be stopped from seeing her. I waited for her in the outhouse area for a while and had a chance to talk with her. It was a very brief encounter. I talk less than in five dialogues. But I told her that I wanted to meet her personally to see whether I too am eligible for the money. I told her that I was drafted and served in the Japanese military. At that time, I did not know such terms as "military comfort woman." Nor did I explain to her what I did in the Japanese military. But Yook, Young-Soo *yosa* immediately understood what I had done. She said she did not know whether I can get the money. But she firmly told me that if I speak out about such things, I will be in big trouble. She said I should hide the story under my foot if I do not want to die, and never speak out about it at all. She also told me that I should keep the story under my foot until peaceful time arrives, a total peace. Then people will get to know about it. I dare could not talk back to her. My tears were running down like a rainfall. Afterwards, I have never spoken about it at all, to anybody. Not until Kim, Hak-Soon revealed her story in 1991.[33]

The Whang incident illustrates that the issue being raised was not only suppressed, but even manipulated by a power holder (the First Lady). In the absence of a pluralist political system, and without patronage or an advocate from the power circle, Whang's claim went nowhere.

B. The *Kisaeng Kwankwang* Case

In the 1970s, South Korea witnessed a flood of Japanese male tourists attracted to *Kisaeng Kwankwang* (*Kisaeng* is a female entertainer in traditional Korea often providing sexual services, an equivalent of the Japanese *geisha*). Japanese tourists accounted for 41% of total tourists visiting South Korea in 1971, 73.5% in 1972, and 80% in 1973; and 70% of the Japanese tourists were males who thought the "*Kisaeng* party" was the most impressive.[34] This new social phenomenon caught the attention of some women intellectuals and women leaders of the Christian church who saw a connection between the JMSS tragedy and the new "industrial model" of prostitution, both commonly serving Japanese males: "The Japanese tourists joined with the *Kisaeng Kwankwang* for sex are descendants of the colonial era militarists who hunted for *Jungshindae*."[35] The church-based women's group conducted factfinding field trips in local hotels and concluded that the sex tourism as well as the JMSS were violations of women's human rights. Through coalition-building with concerned Japanese women, the Korean church women's activism spread. Their efforts in public education and political agenda-building in the early 1970s, however, were forced to retreat by state power.[36] South Korea in the early 1970s experienced a huge setback from democracy: the *Yushin* (revitalization) system was instituted in 1972 through constitutional amendment allowing further consolidation of power in the hands of the president. Under the *Yushin* system, the separation of power principle further deteriorated, pressure group politics was further suppressed, and discussions on women's human rights were considered so radical as to challenge the stability of the nation. For the sake of economic growth, on the other hand, the promotion of tourism was an important tool for earning hard currency. As an observer notes:

> In 1972 when . . . Park, Chung-Hee declared martial law, . . . he simultaneously adopted a policy of intensively promoting tourism as a source of foreign exchange to replace that previously acquired through participation of Korean troops in the Vietnam War. Thus the "sale of men's blood was succeeded by that of women's flesh," as the number of Japanese tourists flocking to South Korea jumped from 96,531 in 1972 to 217,287 in 1973, in just one year of promoting sex tours in the "Land of the Morning Calm," to use the name for Korea popular in tourist brochures. The Japanese made up the majority of all tourists for the first time, and in 1973 income from tourism reached US$270 million. Foreign exchange earnings at the height of the Vietnam War in 1968 were only, by contrast, US$150 million.[37]

Oo-Chung Lee, a professor and former National Assembly member who was then a leading force in this anti–sex tourism campaign, recalls that she was under constant surveillance by government agents. She was later arrested by the Korean Central Intelligence Agency (KCIA) under the 1974 Presidential Emergency Measures (Number 4), which caused the arrest of a large number of students on college campuses and terrorized the whole nation. Lee was interrogated by the KCIA for a week, and it was torturous (no sleep was allowed). No matter what the official charges were, the latent reason for her arrest was her anti–sex tourism activism, which was regarded as an antigovernment movement—sabotage to prevent the successful accomplishment of the *Yushin* projects, and thus a challenge to industrialization and national security goals. Lee's arrest had a tremendous chilling effect, and under the continued oppressive *Yushin* system public discussion of the sex tourism issue disappeared. Clearly, latent in the government control of women's activism on anti–sex tourism was the fear that it may cause South Korea's economic relationship with Japan to deteriorate. Japan had by this time become a major source of technology, raw and semiprocessed industrial materials, and capital investment for South Korea's export processing zones. Significantly, South Korean politics were then handled at *Yojung*, a high-class restaurant with *Kisaeng*. *Yojung* has been a popular de facto informal office for politicians, businessmen, and other social elites where many important decisions would be made. *Yojung* (conceptually similar to the "smoke-filled rooms" of the United States) served as an important political tool in local politics where political bargaining, negotiation, and all sorts of business deals were made in the 1970s. Nothing seemed to be wrong with the *Kisaeng* tourism given South Korea's androcentric political culture. A 1973 speech by Kwan-Shik Min, the Minister of Education, in Japan allows us to read the state of mind of Korea's political culture, probably shared by many other male politicians in South Korea: "Korean women are sacrificing their bodies in order for economic construction and for obtaining foreign currencies. Particularly, a large number of Korean *kisaeng* and hostess who came to Japan and sell their bodies day and night are wonderful patriotic endeavors."[38]

The government's involvement in tourism was more than regulatory in nature: the tourism bureau in the City Government of Seoul even provided educational programs to women in the tourist industry, checked them for venereal disease, and issued licences as well as ID cards. The educational curriculum emphasized the importance the *Kisaeng* contribution to national economic growth by selling their bodies. Such ideas as selling one's body to foreigners is not prostitution but a patriotic endeavor were promulgated. Remarkably, those lectures were given by social leaders and college professors, and they much resembled the colonial era *Jungshindae* education (or indoctrination).[39] In the 1970s, the repressive political system for interest group activities, combined with the male-centered culture so pervasive in South Korea's political context, did not allow any room for public debate on issues such as sexual violence against women and the JMSS. With economic growth and national defense setting the parameters of the local polity, it was unlikely that the JMSS issue would get any real attention.

IV. DEMOCRATIZATION AND THE WOMEN'S MOVEMENT

Literature on JMSS became available in Japan beginning in the 1970s and in South Korea mostly in the 1980s. In 1982 a JMSS survivor, Su-Bok Noh, residing in Thailand came forward to the Korean public, the first case of its kind. The personal trauma experienced by Noh was a hot media topic widely read about in South Korea. Her revealing story revived many Koreans' anger toward the Japanese and evoked sympathy for her tragedy. But nothing happened in terms of an investigation of JMSS, nor was any kind of solution sought at either governmental or societal levels. Her case did not capture the attention of the women's movement in South Korea. It was not until late 1991 that the issue was openly raised, debated, and criticized in the media, eventually forcing the South Korean government to talk about the issue with the Japanese government and officially investigate these incidents.

The JMSS issue requires an understanding of women's human rights and the linkage between state power and sexual violence against women.[40] Lack of consciousness of the women's movement toward women's human rights and, furthermore, the conceptualization of sexual violence against women in only personal terms have both contributed to the half century of silence around the JMSS issue. The lack of women's consciousness toward women's human rights is deeply rooted in Korea's particular history of colonization and division. National independence and patriotism occupied the center stage during the early twentieth century. Korea lacked the experience of an evolved democratic civic society that values such concepts as individualism, equality, and political and economic rights.[41] Women's suffrage in South Korea was given as a gift by outsiders, in contrast to the United States where women had aggressively fought for it over half a century.

The women's movement in South Korea in the 1960s was, by and large, lead by few leaders without mass membership. Its weak organizational structure (and funding) allowed the leadership to be co-opted by the government.[42] Such an organizational situation not only created disunity between the leadership and the rank-and-file members, but also made it difficult to raise political rights, human rights, or other democratization issues as supreme agenda items, particularly given South Korea's authoritarian political system. The women's movement in the 1960s was "conservative, easy-going, and quite limited to certain issues" (including consumer protection, self-help, friendship, etc.), and often women's activities were government guided (i.e., sponsorship). On the other hand, women's organizations did almost nothing to raise social consciousness or political awareness regarding women's status or women's rights.[43]

The 1970s saw rapid changes occurring in the women's movement. Externally, the UN Women's Conference was held in Mexico, and the UN declared the Decade for Women; internally, the repressive political system of the *Yushin* era was challenged by a student protest movement demanding democratization and the guarantee of individuals' basic rights. Thus "radical" elements were added to traditional and conservative women's groups activism.[44] Women college students began to join with the broader democratization movements in the 1970s and began to work with female industrial workers in labor union activism. Women student activitists also helped industrial workers to raise their social consciousness and to reexamine their human rights situations. Some of them further joined with other established women's organizations, such as the Korean Church Women United, and challenged the government's sex tourism policies.[45]

As yet, both mainstream conservative women's organizations and the young "radical" women's organizations had failed to tackle the JMSS case. The former groups hadn't raised the issue because of its reformist, incremental orientation and lack of awareness of women's human rights. The "radical" groups were preoccupied with larger, broader social goals of democratization, Korea's reunification, labor issues, and so forth, which go beyond the assertion of basic individual or group needs for women. The connectedness of the JMSS forced rape and women's human rights was not recognized until the mid-1980s.

The political situation in the early 1980s under another military junta Doo Whan Chun, did not allow mass-based social activism and adversely affected the women's movement. In the late 1980s a new regime headed by Tae Woo Roh began to allow some increased freedom of speech and association. The wave of people power was too strong for political rulers to suppress the public demand for democratization of Korea. The latter part of the 1980s was characterized by a massive democratization movement in South Korea. Students, workers, intellectuals, and middle-class citizens all participated in this reform movement, often in violent protests. Both male and female students, in particular, exerted significant power.

As the JMSS was being exposed, a number of incidents contributed to reconceptualizing rape as a social and political issue wherein state power plays a large role. In-Sook Kwon's sex-torture (1986) is a case in point. Kwon, a college student activist who disguised herself to work in a factory in support of the labor movement, was sexually assaulted by police while she was being investigated for antigovernment activism. With the support of 166 human rights lawyers (the largest defense team ever formed in Korea's judicial history) and feminist groups, the victim was released from jail, and the police perpetrator was imprisoned. Kwon's case was monumental in challenging state power, which used sexual assault, or sex-torture (e.g., forced kissing, fondling, stripping, rape, and so on) as a suppressive tool used only against females during police investigations in the 1970s and 1980s. Such gender-specific control mechanisms surfaced in Kwon's case, raising public awareness about the relationship between state, sex, and gender. The second case is a landmark event in 1988 at an international seminar on "Women and Tourism" organized by the Korean Church Women United. In the seminar, suppressed, socially taboo, or intellectually neglected issues for academic research, such as prostitution and the JMSS, became public, resulting in limited but somewhat positive political rewards to the JMSS survivors. The 1988 tourism seminar articulated the connection between JMSS and sex tourism, calling the latter "neo-*Jungshindae*":

> For the sake of our national pride and the lives of persons directly involved, *Kisaeng* tourism, long promoted by the Korean government, must be stopped immediately. The government has focussed on tourism development in order to earn foreign exchange, but in fact such a policy has driven countless numbers of Korean women into prostitution. We Korean women, who experienced the humiliation of "*Jungshindae*," the forced mobilization of young women to fulfill the sexual demands of the Japanese Imperial Army in the 1930s–1940s, must reject *Kisaeng* tourism, which is a kind of "neo-*Jungshindae*."[46]

In addition, the seminar also conceptualized sex tourism as a structural problem of South Korean society: "*Kisaeng* tourism is not the moral problem of individual women but an issue which arises from the Korean economic structure due to its dependency on imperialistic countries such as Japan and the U.S.A."[47] A report based on field trips to the *Jungshindae* sites by Jung Ok Yoon and her research team further focussed South Korean feminist activism on the necessity of investigating the JMSS issue. Yoon's research further articulated the sociopolitical dimensions of rape in the military. She clarified its connections to the JMSS and other forms of contemporary sexual violence against women:

> The comfort girl for the Japanese Armed Forces was regarded as a gift from the Japanese Emperor made in an attempt to enhance the morale among the troops and as pay in return for their loyalty . . . The "*Jungshindae*" is the root of the present-day issue of *Kisaeng* tourism. Unless the root is eradicated, there is continuous danger of sexual invitation from Japan.[48]

V.   CONCLUSION

Despite the fact that a large number of young Korean females were victimized by a systematic, concerted state activity by wartime Japan, the JMSS case was not publicly debated as a political issue in South Korea until 1991. In the immediate postwar period, the national energy was focussed on nation-building and national security. Collaborators with Japan maintained their status and became centers of the power elite. This situation might have been necessary, given Korea's divided nation status and a direct confrontation with the communist North. Yet it clearly provided an environment antagonistic to the full public debate of the JMSS issue. During Chung-Hee Park's tenure of power, rapid industrialization and national security set the parameters for various policy actions. The ROK–Japan Basic Treaty completely omitted the JMSS issue. Kum-Joo Whang's incident as well as the anti-*Kisaeng* tourism movement could have provided a context for the JMSS exposure, but the repressive authoritarian system once again prevented public debate. Mainstream conservative women's organizations were not raising women's human rights issues or other sociopolitical rights issues. Due to their particular relationship with government, the conservative feminists never raised the JMSS issue. Feminist activism in the 1970s and 1980s also failed to capture the JMSS issue in their agenda. These "radical" women were focussed on democratization, labor unions, and other human rights issues. They failed to appreciate the importance of the connection between the JMSS and human rights. Kwon's sex-torture case and the sex tourism issues of the 1970s and 1980s clearly educated both feminist activists and the public, finally providing the social context for the JMSS to emerge as an agenda item.

The JMSS is a social problem, beyond the horizons of individual victims, a political issue that needs to be properly dealt with by government. The JMSS case also helps us to reconceptualize sexual violence against women as a gender-based, and often class-based, social crime which requires more interventionist government action and social support systems. Yet, South Korea's political situation, power maps, political system, androcentric political culture, and even the orientation of the women's movement all played key roles in suppressing debate for so long. The JMSS victims themselves are powerless. In bringing their issue to the public they rely heavily on institutions or political tools for interest articulation (that is, the Korean Women Church United, KCWDSSJ, and the media to a certain extent). Until 1991, no such tools were available.

ACKNOWLEDGMENTS

This paper was read at the International Political Science Association's XVII World Congress held in Seoul, Republic of Korea, During August 17–21, 1997. Minor editorial revisions have been added. The author is thankful to the Office of Graduate Studies and Research and the Office of International Studies and Programs at Central Washington University for financial support for this study. I also extend many thanks to Dr. Michael A. Launius of Central Washington University and Dr. Lloyd Jeff Dumas of the University of Texas at Dallas for their valuable editorial comments.

NOTES/REFERENCES

1. In general and in most cases, the *Jungshindae* were workers assigned to various defense industries during wartime by the Japanese colonial government. In some cases, the *Jungshindae* workers were transferred to positions of sexual slavery.
2. I myself often use the term MCW with quotation marks. I simply mean to use the term as a pronoun in compliance with historical naming in an attempt to familiarize a wider audience in society with the issue. However, the term devised by the JIA, "comfort women," needs to be replaced with a more accurate description, such as "Japanese military sexual slavery." Refer to Yoon, B.-S. (1996). Military sexual slavery: Political agenda for feminist scholarship and activism. *In God's Image* 15(2), Summer, 86–94; and Chin Sung Chung, (1997). The Origin and Development of the Military Sexual Slavery Problem in Imperial Japan. *Positions East Asia Cultures Critique* 5(1), Spring, 220–222.
3. Japanese military documents dated June 27, 1938; July 13, 1938; and June, 1939, for example, clearly indicate Japan's deep concern for these issues. Refer to Ministry of Foreign Affairs, ROK, Report #92–175, Section 4: Documents found by the Japanese government (Seoul, July 3, 1992). Japanese soldiers' brutal rape cases are well

described in Brownmiller, S. (1975). *Against Our Will*. New York: Simon and Schuster; and Chang, I. (1997) *The Rape of Nanking*. New York: Basic Books.

4. Hak-Soon Kim died in 1997 in Seoul.

5. The KCWDSSJ and the Korean Research Group of Women Drafted for Military Sex Slavery by Japan (KRGWDMSSJ) have published many reports on these issues. They also function in the Republic of Korea as a clearinghouse with up-to-date information about JMSS as well as house many historical documents found in Japan and the United States. The Asian Women's Solidarity Forum on Military Sexual Slavery was organized in 1994, and the Fourth Asian Women's Solidarity Conference was held in March, 1996, in Manila, Philippines. In October 1996, the People's Solidarity for Resolution of the Military Sexual Slavery Issue (The People's Solidarity in short) was formed in South Korea by 40 civil organizations and individuals in various social sectors, and have already launched a series of activities, including sponsorship of an international seminar, fund-raising, and so on.

6. For example, Hicks, G. (1994). *The Comfort Women*. New York: W. W. Norton & Co.; Yoon, B.-S. (1996). Military sexual slavery: Political agenda for feminist scholarship and activism. *In God's Image 15*(2), Summer, 86–94; Howard, K. (ed) (1995). (trans. by Y. J. Lee), *True Stories of the Korean Comfort Women: Testimonies Complied by the Korean Council for Women Drafted for Military Sexual Slavery by Japan and the Research Association on the Women Drafted for Military Sexual Slavery by Japan*. London: Cassell; Henson, M. R. (1996). *Comfort Woman: Slave of Destiny*. Manila: Philippine Center for Investigative Journalism; Chung, C. S. (1997). The origin and development of the military sexual slavery problem in Imperial Japan. *Positions East Asia Cultures Critique 5*(1), Spring; and various publications by KCWDSSJ and KRGWDMSSJ. English language films are: *Unfortunate Incidents*. (1992). Great Britain: British Broadcasting Corp.; and *Senso Daughters (Daughters of War)*. (1990). Australia: Tenchijin Productions & Siglo Co., Ltd. Internet information is rich, see, for example: http:witness.peacenet.or.kr/e_comfort/library.

7. *Forum '95* (The Independent Daily of the NGO Forum on Women, Beijing '95), September 3, 1995, and September 8, 1995.

8. The UN Commission on Human Rights, 52nd Session, April (1996). Also refer to Coomaraswamy, R. (1996) "Report of the Special Rapporteur on Violence Against Women." (E/CN.4/1996/53/Add.1).

9. The Asian Women's Fund involves a 20,000 yen ($18,000) lump-sum payment and medical costs. So far, seven from South Korea have accepted the money. Most survivors reject the funding for they view it allows the government of Japan to escape legal and public responsibilities from the abuse.

10. The fundamental policy refers to "a set of priorities and directions, themselves grounded in basic societal values, ideology and the basic elements of our economic and societal system . . . which play a significant role in shaping public policies." Dolbeare, K. M. (1974). The impact of public policy. In C. P. Cotter (ed.), *Political Science Annual 5*. Indianapolis and New York: Bobbs-Merrill.

11. During Japan's colonial period, a total of 7.5 million Koreans were estimated to be sent (as forced laborers or soldiers) to foreign countries (Japan, China, Russia, Pacific islands, and others), among whom one million are estimated to have died while

in forced service. The South Korean government did not begin to investigate the colonial era forced laborers or the military draft issue until 1994. In academic circles, a joint symposium on the Korean forced laborers by Japan attended by both Korean and Japanese scholars was held in 1992 for the first time. Refer to *The Hankuk Ilbo, 1994. 12.* 22nd edition and *The Hankuk Ilbo, 1992. 2.* 28th edition.

12. Pang, S.-J. (1992). Review of the Korean "military comfort women" appeared in the U.S. document. *Kuksakwan Nonchong* (Korean) (Review of National History) *37,* 218–219.

13. Inter-Ministerial Working Group on the Comfort Women Issue, Republic of Korea. (1992). "Military Comfort Women Under Japanese Colonial Rule, Interim Report." Seoul, July. For example, the United States Office of War Information Psychological Warfare Team Attached to U.S. Army Forces India-Burma Theater APO 689 reports (Report No. 49, October 1, 1944) the results of interrogation of "20 Korean Comfort Girls" who were "captured on August 10, 1944" as "Japanese Prisoner of War."

14. Schubert, G. (1992). "Concerning the Use, by the Japanese Army, of Females as Sexual Slaves." March 6, 1992. Schubert, Professor of Political Science at University of Hawaii at Manoa served as a First Lieutenant cryptanalyst, Tenth Army HQ, during the Okinawa campaign during early April and mid-December, 1945.

15. Park, W. S. (1994). The Tokyo War Crimes Trial: Humiliation and forgotten history. *The Yuksa Bipyung* (The Critics of History) *26,* Fall, 233–256.

16. Hosoya, C., Ando, N., Onuma, Y., and Minear, R. (eds.) *The Tokyo War Crimes Trial,* p. 7. Tokyo: Kodansha Ltd.

17. Hicks, G. (1994). The Comfort Women, pp. 168–169. New York: W. W. Norton & Co.

18. Refer to the United States Office of War Information Psychological Warfare Team Attached to U.S. Army Forces India-Burma Theater APO 689 report. Report No. 49, October 1, 1944.

19. The *Yoseong gye* refers to women's groups, organizations that advocate the rights and welfare of women. In local politics, the *Yoseong gye* functions as a distinctive social group in political representation. A few seats in the National Assembly or in the cabinet are reserved for *Yoseong gye* leaders, who are all women.

20. Kim, S.-W., Lee, H.-C., and Chung, W.-H. (eds.) (1993). *Chin-Il Pa.* Seoul: Hak-Min Sa; Internet websites in South Korea provide a list and activities of Korean collaborators who have been considered by locals as leading intellectuals who hold leadership roles in their chosen professional fields, which is quite shocking.

21. Kim, S.-W., Lee, H.-C., and Chung, W.-H. (eds.) (1993). *Chin-Il Pa,* p. 25. Seoul: Hak-Min Sa.

22. Pai, E. W. (1991). *Borit Kogae nun Numkyotjiman: Memoire* (Although We Crossed Over the Spring Hunger), p. 143. Seoul: The Korea Herald and The Naewoi Kyungje Shinmun.

23. Kang, M.-K. A Historical Approach to the Japanese Military 'Sexual Slavery' Issues (Korean), p. 2. mimeo.

24. Kim, Y.-C. (1976). *Women of Korea: A History from Ancient Times to 1945.* Seoul: Ewha Womans University Press; and Chung S.-W. (ed) (1986). *Challenges for Women: Women's Studies in Korea.* Seoul: Ewha Womans University Press.

25. The amount fluctuated over a period time. Nonetheless, ROK's demand under Park was at least $500 million, whereas Japan proposed between $50–70 million. See Pai, E. W. (1991). *Borit Kogae nun Numkyotjiman: Memoire*, pp. 143–146, 161, 168. Seoul: The Korea Herald and The Naewoi Kyungje Shinmun.

26. The Peace Line was drawn in 1952, which resulted in restricting Japan's fisheries and became a controversial issue thereafter between South Korea and Japan.

27. Pai, E. W. (1992). Interview with author August 3, in Honolulu, Hawaii.

28. Pai, E. W. (1991). *Borit Kogae nun Numkyotjiman: Memoire*, p. 141. Seoul: The Korea Herald and the Naewoi Kyungje Shinmun.

29. Noriko, S. (1990). *Senso Daughters* (film). Australia: Tenchijin Productions and Sigle Co., Ltd.

30. The Japanese government was also under pressure from its business community, which saw South Korea as a wonderful market for its economic activities. E. W. Pai, op. cit., p. 206.

31. B. W. Yu (1994). Interview with author. September 7. Yu was Director General, Asian Affairs Bureau, Ministry of Foreign Affairs, ROK.

32. For details of her life story, refer to KCWDSSJ and KRGWDMSSJ (1993). *Kangjero kulryugan Chosonin Kunwianbudul* (Military Comfort Women Dragged by Force), pp. 93–106. Seoul: Hanwool; or its English translation version: Howard K. (ed) (1995). *True Stories of the Korean Comfort Women: Testimonies Compiled by the Korean Council for Women Drafted for Military Sexual Slavery by Japan and the Research Association on the Women Drafted for Military Sexual Slavery by Japan*, Ch. 8. London: Cassell.

33. Whang, K.-J. (1994). Interview with author. September 14 at her residence in Seoul. I spent seven and a half hours with her, and she cooked two meals for me while being interviewed.

34. Lee, H. S. (1992). *The 25 Year History of the Korean Church Women United* (Korean), pp. 82–83. Seoul: The Korean Church Women United.

35. Lee, H. S. (1992). *The 25 Year History of the Korean Church Women United* (Korean), p. 84. Seoul: The Korean Church Women United.

36. Lee, H. S. (1992). *The 25 Year History of the Korean Church Women United* (Korean), pp. 92–93. Seoul: The Korean Church Women United.

37. Hicks, G. (1994). *The Comfort Women*, p. 174. New York: W. W. Norton & Co.

38. Lee, H. S. (1992). *The 25 Year History of the Korean Church Women United* (Korean), p. 89. Seoul: The Korean Church Women United.

39. Lee, H. S. (1992). *The 25 Year History of the Korean Church Women United* (Korean), pp. 88–89. Seoul: The Korean Church Women United.

40. Yoon, B.-S. (1993). Redefining the Role of State in Sexual Violence Against Women: The Korean 'Military Comfort Women' Case,'' mimeo.

41. Lee, H.-J. (1989). *Korean Women's Movement: Past and Present*. Seoul: Chung-Woo Sa.

42. Lee, H.-J. (1989). *Korean Women's Movement: Past and Present*, p. 246. Seoul: Chung-Woo Sa.

43. Lee, H.-J. (1989). *Korean Women's Movement: Past and Present*, pp. 246–247. Seoul: Chung-Woo Sa.

44. Palley, M. L. (1994). Feminism in a Confucian society: The women's movement in Korea. In J. Gelb and M. L. Palley (eds.), *Women of Japan and Korea*, pp. 279–280. Philadelphia: Temple University Press.

45. Lee, H. J. *Korean Women's Movement: Past and Present*, pp. 249–251. Seoul: Chung-Woo Sa.

46. Korea Church Women United. (1988). "Women and Tourism," p. 100. (Report of International Seminar, April 20–23, 1988, Seoul and Cheju Island). Seoul: Korea Church Women United.

47. Korea Church Women United. (1988). "Women and Tourism" (Report of International Seminar, April 20–23, 1988, Seoul and Cheju Island). Seoul: Korea Church Women United.

48. Yoon, J. O. et al. (1988). "Footsteps of the '*Jungshindae*,' Women's Volunteer Corps," pp. 111–112. (Report of International Seminar, "Women and Tourism," April 20–23, 1988, Seoul and Cheju Island). Seoul: Korea Church Women United.

13
Public Participation in China's Urban Development

Tingwei Zhang
University of Illinois, Chicago, Illinois

I. INTRODUCTION

China's economic reform and its effects have been discussed from many perspectives. But the reform's impact on decision-making in urban development has not attracted much attention. With China's rapid urbanization in the last two decades, the reform has brought significant changes to its urban residents, from better housing with higher housing expenditure to changes in urban life. This chapter intends to answer the question: what was the relationship between local government decision-making and citizen participation in urban development before and after the reform?

Public participation is viewed as the determining criteria for democratic decision-making (Arnstein 1969; Smith 1989). A huge body of literature on participation concens and is based on the experiences of developed Western countries (see, for instance, Dalton 1988; Price 1993). Participation in less developed countries, especially in Latin America, receives the attention of both practicing planners and academics (such as Turner 1967, 1968; Portes and Itzigsohn, 1994). Although the form of participation may vary in different contexts, the key factor remains the same: the distribution of decision-making power. Literature suggests that only when the public holds decision-making power through citizen's organizations can a meaningful participation be reached.

Figure 1 Distribution of the cases.

II. METHOD, DATA, AND STRUCTURE

This analysis is based on interviews conducted in five Chinese cities in the summer of 1997 and case studies submitted by Chinese planners in eight cities (Shanghai, Hangzhou, Ningbo, Xiamen, Shenzhen, Harbin, Beihai and Wuhan; see Figure 1) in the spring of 1997. A total of 47 interviewees and eight case studies have provided valuable information (see Table 1).

Table 1 Occupation of Interviewees

Occupation	Number	Percentage of total
Planner[a]	27	57.4
Government officer	6	12.8
Developer	3	6.4
Professional[b]	6	12.8
Urban resident	5	10.6

[a] Includes planners working in city planning institutions and teaching in planning programs of four universities. In China, "city planner" generally refers to a physical planner associated with a government planning institution.

[b] Includes bankers, journalists, and architects.

The interviewees were selected based on two considerations. The first is that they should be able to represent the current participation practice in China. More planners were selected for the research focussing on participation in urban development. However, since the profession of city planner in China refers to physical planning in most cases, and social development issues received much less attention, people other than planners were interviewed on social issues. They included senior government officers, developers, bankers, journalists, and ordinary urban residents. For the same consideration, cities not only at China's coastal area, where an advanced market system has been developed, but also cities inland (such as Wuhan and Harbin) were selected. The second criterion of sample selection was the availability of information. A random selection may result in a data availability problem in the Chinese context. A face-to-face interview with friends provided more reliable information than other methods.

This chapter begins with a comparison of decision-making processes under the old planned system and the new planned-market system, then focusses on the two different channels of decision-making practiced today, and draws some conclusions at the end. Since the term "urban development" in China generally means urban physical development, "decisions in urban development" in this study basically refers to two key issues: land acquisition and construction funding, although some urban social problems have also been analyzed.

III. DECISION-MAKING IN CHINA: BEFORE THE REFORM

China built a social structure featuring "a big government, a small society" with the founding of the People's Republic in 1949. Table 2A illustrates the power structure before the reform. The "big" government made decisions on all activi-

Table 2 Decision-Making Structure

A. Before the reform

Government		
Administrative (public affairs)	Enterprises (production activities)	Community (daily life)

B. After the reform (decentralization)

Government				
Administration (public affairs)	Enterprises (production)	Communities (daily life)	Enterprises (production)	Community (daily life)

ties in urban areas, from public affairs and factory production to residents' daily life.

The decision-making structure was characterized by a dual-role hierarchical organization (representing the Communist Party and *danwei*—the work unit one works for). According to the Constitution of China, there were four power groups (*si tao banzhi*) at the city level: the Communist Party's city committee, the municipal government, the People's Congress, and the People's Political Consultative Conference of the municipality. The secretary of the Communist Party's city committee, who represented the party, was the most powerful person, although he did not have an official position in the municipal government. The mayor, as the head of the city administrative bureaucracy, was the second figure of importance; he was usually the party committee's deputy secretary, so he had to follow the secretary's (read as the party's) decisions. The city's People's Congress was the official legislative body at the local level, usually headed by another deputy party secretary. With some 80% of congressional representatives being party members, the party's decision was ensured passage through the congress. The People's Political Consultative Conference (PPCC) played a role as "friend of the party" and advised the party on important policy issues. The chairperson of the PPCC was usually a party member, although he or she usually had several non–party member deputies. The whole system thus supported the party's decision and gave it legitimacy through the decision-making process: a decision was first initiated (and made) by the party, then introduced to and approved by the Congress in the form of a bill, advised by the Consultative Conference, and finally implemented by the city government. The nomination and election of representatives of both the Congress and the Consultative Conference were under the control of the party.

The decision system at the city level was a duplication of the system at the national level. The party's central committee generated policies and made final decision. The National People's Congress and the National People's Political Consultative Conference provided legitimacy to the decision, and the administrative body implemented these policies. This decision-making system had been in place since the birth of New China.

In urban development, land acquisition and construction funding are two key issues. Under the planned system before the reform, land use was controlled by the municipal planning committee and the city planning bureau, and funding was provided through ministries of various industries. For instance, if a factory located at the city limit were planning to construct an additional workshop and had found an adjacent site being used by farmers of a neighboring village, the factory had to first get support from the municipal industry bureau in charge of their particular industry. Then the industry bureau and the factory would make a joint application to the Municipal Planning Committee to get approval and to establish a registration record for the project (*li xian*). When the project was approved and registered, the Planning Committee would notify several government bodies: the City Planning Bureau for land selection and site planning, the Municipal Finance Bureau for construction financing, and the county government (the administrative body supervising the village) for land acquisition. With the Planning Committee's approval, the City Planning Bureau would issue a land use permit and a building permit as well as a license to the contractor. With those documents, the factory could start negotiating with the village that was using the land. Normally the factory had to pay the village for the land (the land was theoretically owned by all villagers, according to China's Constitution) and had to recruit surplus labor caused by land loss in the village. However, the land acquisition cost was just symbolic; the land was theoretically required by the *state*, the owner of the factory. From the 1960s through the early 1970s, the token cost was about RMB 300 Yuan (then US$90) per Mu (0.16 acre), together with the absorption of surplus agricultural labor into the factory's workforce. By 1988, regardless of location or intended use of land, one Mu of land cost RMB 10,000 Yuan (then US$2,700), plus the purchaser's requirement of hiring one worker for every Mu of land in Shanghai (from interview with Shanghai City Planning Institute, May 1988).

The whole decision-making process, from project planning to starting construction work, had provided little if any room for public input. For villagers, to do whatever was required to support the state was a citizen's responsibility. Workers of the factory had nothing to say since this was "not their business."

In a more general sense, urban development was totally a government activity. Over 80% of urban residents lived in public housing managed by the public sector (the Municipal Housing Bureau and work units), and the government owned all work units. Moreover, the government controlled the land and building materials; private construction activity in urban areas was almost nonexistent.

The government managed not only urban development, but also urban residents' lives. In order to understand to what extent the government was controlling things in urban areas before the reform, let us take as an example the life of a typical urban professional in Shanghai. She was born into a family of workers. Both parents worked in a state-owned manufacturing factory. Construction and operation of the factory were planned and controlled by the public sector. Her mother delivered her in a hospital with all expenses covered by the factory's healthcare plan, which was planned and provided by the public sector. Actually, the birth itself was planned—under the family plan of 1965. The government would, through its many branches, right down to neighborhood committees (NCs), suggest the best age for marriage, childbirth, and the optimal number of children, which in an urban family was one. She was sent to a day-care center managed by the factory, which provided the service as a benefit to its employees. Her parents paid token fees to the day-care center, about 5% of their wages. Then she went through her education, from kindergarten to high school, without paying any tuition.

After graduating from high school she passed the examination and became a college student. Higher education was also free, except for the expenses of books, food, and clothing. But these costs were not too bad under the planned economy; because of government price controls, inflation was almost nonexistent. During her college days, health-care was also provided by the public sector. But her major, Urban Planning, was not what she really liked—she was dreaming of becoming a writer. However, the government told her, and other students like her, that the nation needed to build more highways, factories, and houses, and therefore engineers and city planners, not writers, were in high demand. So her major was not chosen by herself; it was decided by the High Education Bureau of Shanghai, a local branch of the Ministry of High Education of China, which had planned the number of students for each professional training program. The decision was based on the National Development Plan, a five-year plan designed by the State Planning Committee.

She graduated as a planner and was sent to Beijing. Again, this was not her choice. She would have preferred to stay in Shanghai with her parents, but the university said that the country's capital had more construction activities and needed more city planners, and the decision was made based on the nation's need. She became a planner in the Municipal Planning Bureau of Beijing. Her main task as a city planner was to design site plans for residential areas. The Beijing Municipal Planning Committee decided the number of new residential units and community facilities for every fiscal year. All of this scheduling was based on the City Development Plan, a five-year plan similar to the one at the national level, so there was little involvement in decision-making required of the planner, residents, and current land users—land was "free," every piece being owned by the public.

She was assigned to a dormitory room, shared with two other girls, and paid a token rent of less than 1% her salary. The dormitory was built and managed by her work unit (the planning bureau) with a subsidy from the public sector. After several years, she had a boyfriend, an architect, and she wanted to marry him. She submitted an application for housing to the work unit. Three years later, she was given a one-bedroom apartment. The rent was about 2% of her salary. The construction of the apartment was planned by the city, and it was built with a public subsidy. She received a planned promotion, based on the government's quota system and her seniority; it had little to do with her job performance. She was going to have a child under the family plan. Finally, she would repeat the story of her parents, who retired with about 80% of their wages, full health-care coverage, and an apartment owned by their work unit—all were planned years ago before their retirement. When they died, their funerals would be arranged by their work unit and paid under the factory's subsidy, again a planned cost.

That was the story under the planned system in the pre-reform era. Almost every crucial decision in a person's life—birth, education, job, promotion, housing, retirement, and death—were made by the state. The loss of personal autonomy could be viewed as the cost paid for benefits provided by the planned system. The system significantly reduced the uncertainty of life. What would happen, and when, could be explicitly planned. The combination of the automatic provision of basic necessities (although at a low level) and the futility of individual involvement in the decision-making process had significantly discouraged ordinary people toward participation.

IV. DECISION-MAKING IN CHINA: AFTER THE REFORM

With the introduction of the market-oriented reform in 1978, the concept of "a small government, a big society," a typical market-oriented principle, was adopted. Local governments have received more freedom on financial decisions from the central government, and individuals have seen more money in their paychecks. At the same time, responsibilities are gradually being transferred from central to local government, and from the public sector to individuals. Coupled with government downsizing, government at various levels has released decision power on production issues to enterprises, and has started to share decision power on some social issues with communities.

Table 2B outlines the decision structure after the reform. The public sector still controls decisions on public affairs, but reduces its involvement in production and people's daily lives. Since the reform is a gradual incremental process, there is a coexistence of two parallel systems: the planned system that still remains in practice, although weakened, and a market-based system that is becoming stronger but is still at an early stage.

Formally, the decision structure as a whole has undergone no change. At the municipal level, the four power groups still hold the main decision power. But in supervising production, government control has been reduced to the macro level (tax policy, interest rates, and regulations); and in managing people's daily lives, the public sector has significantly reduced its involvement in providing basic needs to urban residents. It is largely individuals' responsibility now.

To enterprises, with the birth of various forms of ownership other than state-owned, the nonpublic sector has become more influential on issues related to urban development. The private sector has made significant contributions to the national industrial output (from 0% in 1978 to 22% in 1992 and 60% in 1999), and has a stronger voice on production-related decisions, including land disposal.

To communities, the role of Neighborhood Committees, the foundation of China's urban society, is changing. For a better understanding, we may start from the institutional setting of community organizations in China.

A city consists of several districts; the four power groups, as discussed at the city level, are replicated in each district. The lowest level administrative unit in China's urban area is the Street Committee (SC) (*jiedao weiyuanhui*), which officially represents the district government. Staff members of the SC are paid government officers at the lowest level, and they are appointed by the district government.

Each SC supervises several Neighborhood Committees (*jmin wueiyuanhui*), the basic cells of urban communities in China. An NC has a population from 1,000 to 5,000. The NC has various functions, which are reflected in the composition of the committee. A typical NC has seven staff members: party secretary, chairperson, deputy chairperson, and four division leaders in charge of programs for neighborhood security, public health, women's affairs, and social welfare. The NC party secretary's main responsibility is to ensure that the party's political decisions are being followed. The chairperson is responsible for small businesses and services managed by the NC. The security division works closely with the district security and police departments. The public health division manages a family practice clinic providing basic care. The women's affairs division handles family planning and issues relating to infants and children. The welfare division provides services to elderly, disabled, and other disadvantaged people (based on author's interviews June, 1997; also see Chen 1994).

NC staff members are elected by the residents of the neighborhood, but the nomination process is heavily influenced by leaders of the SC. Attendance rates for neighborhood voting were lower before reform, usually with one person (usually elderly) representing a household. NC staff members are unpaid government officers, retired seniors in most cases. While they do not receive a salary from the city government, they are subsidized by the businesses and services managed by NCs and SCs. As retired citizens, NC staff members receive the standard Chinese pension of 70–80% of their preretirement salary, plus the subsidy equaling 20–30% of their pension amount, plus a bonus—bringing their retirement income to at least the same level as before retirement. There have been important changes occurring with NCs in recent years, although the institutional setting remains the same.

First, bonuses and other nonsalaried income are becoming increasingly important. This extra income basically comes from the profits of small businesses and services managed by NCs. According to a 1997 survey, 70% of NC staff income came from small business (Wang 1997). The economic incentive makes NCs more active in the decision-making process in urban development projects because these projects may affect directly their benefits.

Second, younger people are joining NCs. The 1997 survey reported that

40–50% of NC staff members were in their working age, much younger than NC members several years ago. With the streamlining of factories and downsizing of government institutions, more working age people have been laid off, and many have become NCs staff. They have received better education, have more experience on public affairs, are more open-minded, and are eager to play a more active role in the decision process. (The party newspaper *People's Daily* [*Renmin Rebao*] has reported some stories about the change.)

Third, NC election voting attendance is becoming higher because the district government is giving more local businesses to NCs, which ties NCs more directly to their residents (based on author's interviews June, 1997; also see *People's Daily* 1997a). The 1997 survey found a 60% attendance rate in NC voting nationwide in 1996.

However, all these changes occurred just recently, and the government is not really ready to share decision power with average urban residents through NCs, especially not on major issues such as urban development. Here at the community level, the main decision-making structure is still the product of, and reflects the nature of, the planned economy.

Enterprises, on the other hand, have received more decision power on development issues from the government. More important, land has entered the market with the establishment of the market system. Today, a factory's planning for expansion may start from negotiation with a village from the outset, because as the current user of the land, the village has more to say in price determination. Land prices vary depending on location and future use. In 1995, for example, the price of land for residential development varied from US$33,335 per Mu in remote areas, to US$183,342 per Mu in the Special Economic Zone (SEZ) (Shanghai Land Use Reform Office and Shanghai Statistical Bureau 1996), about ten times the price in 1988. Land for commercial use is more expensive, but for manufacturing use is less costly. After drafting a proposal with the village, the factory registers for approval with the same government bodies as in the pre-reform age. Land use and building permits and construction license are still a must, but financing of the project is much less of a concern because the municipal government (the planning committee and the industry bureau) has released decision power to factory managers. If the land has been officially assigned for manufacturing use in the city's master plan (functioning as zoning), it is not difficult to get a land use permit and license, especially with support from the local village. Land administration issues (land records, deed changes) are under the control of the Municipal Land Bureau, a new institution established in 1985 after the start of urban reform. The main function of the bureau is to protect farmland by supervising changes in land use and controlling urban growth.

So there are changes in the decision making process: villagers have some power in the process of land acquisition, and factory managers can make decisions on construction funding. At the same time, changes in land management and the high price of real estate have affected every urban resident. Since housing responsibility has been transferred to work units, and high land prices directly cause increased housing costs, it has become more difficult for work units to provide housing to their employees. Housing projects for ordinary workers are forced to be located on the city's periphery, where land is less expensive, causing long employee commutes. Also, employees have to pay more for rent and for the "right of use" to work units who own housing properties. About 50% of the urban housing stock has been privatized, meaning housing costs over 10% of most owners' salary, much more than they paid on rent before. Population segregation caused by the housing affordability problem is another social consequence. Although more high-quality houses have been built in better neighborhoods, only rich people or well-connected government officials can afford them. Education is no longer free. For average people, such as the planner mentioned in the example, education from kindergarten to college is quite expensive. The total tuition for a college student alone is about two year's average salary. A co-payment is required to see a doctor or stay in an hospital. Moreover, the young planner may have to find a job after graduation. Not only do college graduates have to find their jobs, but unemployment becomes a looming threat to employees of state-owned enterprises. Since the government is dropping some housing and critical welfare programs and the market is not going to replace them, people will have to seek to provide urban services and facilities for themselves. Changes such as these in the public sphere are increasing the range of decisions urban residents must make in their personal lives, and are, by necessity, creating a different kind of relationship between residents and their local government.

V. THE TWO CHANNELS OF DECISION MAKING IN URBAN DEVELOPMENT TODAY

Because of the co-existence of the planned and the market system, there are two decision-making channels in practice today: a formal channel and an informal channel. The formal channel features a centralized hierarchy similar to the one before the reform and approvals from low to high government institutions under laws and regulations. The informal channel is operated either outside of the formal system but within government rules and policies, or outside the boundaries of current laws and regulations. Each of the channels has two approaches: bottom-up and top-down models (see Table 3). Three characteristics are examined in defining formal and informal decision-making channels: (1) adherence to the existing regulatory regime, (2) degree of openness to external monitoring, and (3) degree of consultation across sectors and concerned groups, including community organizations. Participation of various forms occurs at both the bottom-up and

Table 3 Two Decision-Making Channels in Urban China

Type	Formal	Informal
Top-down	1. Close adherence to regulatory regime, guided by laws and regulations, within existing administrative hierarchy or political structure	1. Within existing administrative structure, but often disregards laws and regulations due to the nature of dealmaking.
	2. Limited openness to external monitoring.	2. No exposure to public on grounds of legitimate excuse, most frequently "economic growth."
	3. Some consultation with community and quasigovernment groups; certain degree of consultation with other government institutions.	3. No consultation across sectors, institutions, stakeholders, or community groups.
Bottom-up	1. Within guidelines of laws and regulations, but with no initiative by the official administrative system.	1. Initiatives are innovative, with no reference to current laws or regulations, nor are they initiated by existing administrative system.
	2. Fully open to external monitoring.	2. Fully open to external monitoring.
	3. When initiative adopted by existing administration, mobilization across all sectors will be supported; then top-down structure may start functioning to take over or replace bottom-up approach.	3. If existing structure appreciates initiative, it may allow initiative's existence or even absorb it into a renewed official structure; more likely initiative may be turned down.

top-down approaches of formal channel, and at the bottom-up informal approach. There is no participation with the informal top-down decision making process.

The formal process refers to decisions made based on laws or regulations and approved by official government institutions in charge of the particular issue. There has been some public participation in the formal process, especially with the bottom-up approach. Participation usually occurs through representation and information, such as surveys, public exhibitions, or use of the public media. But real decisions are often made within the formal decision-making structure before being made known to the public. This formal process is essentially the same today as it was during the era of central planning. What differs now is the co-existence of an active informal structure with the formal one.

Informal decision-making is the antithesis of the formal process, and it has two models: top-down and bottom-up. The top-down approach begins with the most senior officer in a decision structure, the mayor for instance, disregarding laws or regulations in urban development and influencing the lower government institutions in charge of issuing the necessary paperwork. Money for the mayor is sometimes, but not always, part of the deal. More often, the mayor just wants to show his contribution to the city's economic growth by attracting more investment, no matter how or where. In the name of speeding up economic development, planning laws and land use regulations are ignored, making this process informal by nature. In this top-down model, there is no room for public participation, and openness is nonexistent.

The bottom-up approach refers to development activities initiated by ordinary people with no official government involvement and no knowledge of current regulations. For example, an unplanned retail market in a newly developed residential area is proposed based on need; it is to be funded, managed, and supported mainly by local residents, vendors, or concerned groups. This approach is participatory, ordinary people become involved in the whole process of decision-making. If the innovation is considered acceptable by the formal decision-making structure, it may create space to absorb the innovation. For example, a market building may be built. However, more often the unplanned project will be turned down.

Both models of the informal approach need formalization to become legitimate. In the top-down model, the mayor's decision needs to be legitimized by the completion of paperwork by relevant government bodies. To formalize the bottom-up model, residents' proposals need government approval. Financial and legal aspects are the main concerns in legitimizing informal decisions. For example, without formal approval from the Bureau of City Planning, no construction license will be issued, and no subsidized infrastructure or utilities will be provided if appropriate approvals from government agencies are not in place.

While the formal decision-making process is a product of the planned system, the informal process reflects the shared presence of the market system. Economic reform has created a vacuum in decision-making power: the government is downsizing by clearing away such responsibility as housing provision, but neither nonprofit organizations nor the market could takeover. It is this vacuum that creates space for informal decision-making channels, meaning people do it by themselves. Although informal development activities, such as illegal buildings in urban areas, did exist in the pre-reform era, cases were rare and small-scale.

Today's informal top-down approach is largely the result of combining the legacy of the old central planning system that authorizes decision power to one senior official, with the new decentralization that gives local officials more power without public supervision. On the other hand, the informal bottom-up model shows public reaction to government discontinuing the provision of some basic needs. Here, however, the fate of decisions initiated from the bottom depends on the nature of the issue and the political climate at the time. In most cases, this kind of initiative is presently not considered legitimate in the eyes of the authorities. Reform does open the possibility for some transfer of decision-making power, such as decentralizing financial decisions, but not much on noneconomic issues.

VI. PARTICIPATION IN FORMAL AND INFORMAL GOVERNANCE

Various forms of participation could be found in practice, from "nonparticipation" to "degrees of tokenism" to "degrees of citizen power," based on Arnstein's criteria (Arnstein 1969).

A. Participation in the Formal Decision-Making Process

Public participation takes place at three levels within the formal decision channel: municipal administration, planning institution, and neighborhood. At the municipal administration level, the 1989 City Planning Act requires examination and approval of development plans by the city's People's Congress before submission to the city government. The representatives of the People's Congress and the Political Consultative Conference thus have the legal right to examine the plans and give suggestions. This participation is representative in nature. The five cities interviewed all report the presence of this form of participation. For example, a bill to rebuild the landscape around Yuandong Lake was raised by representatives of the Xiamen People's Congress in the spring of 1996. The Municipal City Planning Bureau, supported by city government, had spent 300 million Yuan (US$36 million) on the project since then. Today the lake is the city's most attractive new public park.

With the spread of reform in the field of urban development, land use, real estate, infrastructure, transportation and environmental protection have become hot topics in all cities and towns in China. More bills on these issues are being proposed locally as well as in the state congress. The party's official newspaper, *People's Daily*, reported in March 1997 that about 30% of all bills in the 1997 National Congress were related to urban development (*People's Daily* 1997b).

However, there is no mechanism to tie the election of representatives to an awareness of their constituents' needs. Both the nomination and election process should be improved to better reflect voters' concerns. Some changes did occur recently. Rural villages have experimented with direct voting for local representatives and village leaders. The Ministry of Civil Affairs reported that 60% of Chinese rural villages had established autonomy system. (*People's Daily* 1997c) A more interesting case was reported in Shanghai. During the district election of 1997, the Huangpu District People's Congress denied the re-election of a former district director nominated and supported by the city's Party Committee. This case indicates that a new role in decision-making is emerging for the People's Congress. Although the effectiveness of these new experiments needs to be reviewed, this development shows the changing face of the decision-making structure.

Public participation also takes place at the planning institution level. The main channel of interaction is through consulting expert groups. An expert group consists of professionals and experts from all fields and functions as a consulting task force on important development projects. Experts are nominated by various professional organizations and appointed by the city planning committee. This type of participation is widely practiced in China. All five cities have established institutional channels to access expert groups.

The mechanism of expert consulting is rooted in the role of professionals in China, a developing country where experts are viewed by ordinary citizens as society's elite. However, because they are not elected by urbanites, their accountability might be questioned by some Western scholars. Experts selected into the group could experience damage to their reputation if their judgment is not professionally correct. This mechanism has certain accountability and it seems workable, as has been seen in Wuhan.

In 1995, the City Planning Committee of Wuhan adopted a new method of expert group consultation. The committee asked for nominations of experts, specifying that they should be under the age of 50 so as to possess updated knowledge of their fields, have earned at least a bachelor's degree, and be considered a leader in their fields. The committee then selected 75 professionals from the areas of economics, urban sociology, environmental science, infrastructure development, and city planning. The members were divided into small teams according to specialty, where they participate in discussions of projects related to their backgrounds and produce policy recommendations.

Many Chinese planners interviewed said that expert consultation is the most meaningful participation in China today. First, experts receive more attention from government officers because of their social and professional reputation. Expert policy recommendations therefore have greater probability of being adopted by the government. Second, experts are selected from a variety of professions, thus a relatively comprehensive picture of urbanite concerns regarding the issue at hand is provided. Moreover, because experts are technical and not political representatives, they have better relations with and are more trusted by ordinary people. This form of participation is politically feasible and subjectively workable in today's China.

The third level of public participation involves ordinary people, and it takes on three forms. The first is informative: it includes exhibition of plans and planning documents, description and explanation of plans through the media, and other propaganda-oriented activities. The purpose of this kind of participation is to inform people of government decisions and to mobilize people for better coordination. Psychologically, showing "the blueprint of the city's future" builds civic pride and stimulates community spirit. For city government leaders, an exhibition is a show of their achievements. All cities have organized city planning exhibitions, and have distributed surveys to visitors to get feedback in the last couple of years. Hongzhou's exhibition in 1997, for instance, lasted for three weeks and was attended by 65,000 people.

The second form of ordinary people's participation involves gathering their opinions on development projects through planner interviews, surveys, and open discussion in the media. Shanghai City Planning Bureau conducted a social services survey to revise community facility standards in new residential areas. NCs have played an important role in collecting public opinion. In urban renewal projects in Suzhou, members of NCs organized door-to-door interviews to collect inhabitants' comments to better meet the needs of the users.

There have been changes in NCs' attitude toward opinion-gathering. Before the reform, NCs were involved in opinion surveys, but were relatively passive, spending more time in convincing residents to cooperate with government decisions. Today, NCs pay more attention to people's concerns than simply following the dictum of local authorities. NCs want decision-makers to understand local needs. This change in attitude is largely due to changes in the financial status of NCs. Today, NC staff pensions are less important compared to other income, such as from bonus pay from small businesses and workshops run by NCs. (A recent survey in Shanghai found that only 51% of family income is from fixed salary or wages; the other 49% comes from various sources such as bonus pay and savings or stock interest. See *People's Daily* 1997d.) Small businesses and workshops did previously exist, but were small-scale and limited to certain service businesses. Now there is more variety in the types of businesses owned by NCs, especially in retail, which the reform allowed as an area of private enterprise. These businesses are located in the neighborhood and related directly to its residents, so any development plan affecting the neighborhood also affects the interests of every NC member. The changes in the neighborhoods' economic base have led NCs to change their attitude toward public opinion.

However, it is not unusual that despite the fact that residents express their desires and planners do listen, large amounts of public subsidy may be required—a decision coming only from a very high level. This shows the limits of local community participation. In some cases, no matter how active an NC may be, changes can be made only by actions at higher level.

Public-opinion collection is still the main form of participation practiced in China today. Senior Chinese planners thought it progressive to display plans and take people's opinions into consideration in making development plans compared to methods of the pre-reform era when decisions were made by a very small group, and planning data were even considered confidential. Today the data are a matter of public record, but if a questionnaire does not cover an issue that is critical to residents but not the government at that time, little protest would be heard, and public concern on that issue could be ignored. Therefore, while the exhibition approach is informative, the survey and interview approach is passive, because people do not fully participate in their own initiatives.

The third form of public participation, spontaneous action taken by residents, is not widespread. It varies from residents' initiatives to public appeal, petition, and demonstration. This form is bottom-up in nature and practiced in both formal and informal channels.

The most productive participation found within the formal bottom-up decision-making process involved people working with local government on issues of public interest (based on author's interviews). Shanghai Hongkou District's "Cultural Basket" program is one example. In recent years, many new residential developments have been built on the city's periphery, housing about 20% of Shanghai city residents (a total of 9 million). Physical conditions have been improved in these new areas, but the social network of the old residential areas dissolved as residents dispersed to the new housing. Also, the social services and NCs that played an important role in old neighborhoods have not yet been established in the new areas.

The Cultural Basket program provided cultural resources for and organized cultural activities in communities, especially the new ones and aimed to promote resident interaction through community cultural events. Having experienced the weakness of the market system in allocating cultural resources to ordinary people, local residents expressed a desire for local cultural activities. The district planning bureau and the culture bureau followed this initiative and supported cultural events organized by SCs and coordinated with NCs. Another well-received activity was free professional consulting. Four times a week, experts visited communities and provided consulting services on cultural, health, scientific, and recreational issues. Last year, 58,000 residents availed themselves of this community service.

Public appeal and petition is a different form of bottom-up formal participation. In this form, the public strongly expresses dissatisfaction on a development issue or policy and pushes local government to take action for improvement. While most interviewees did not mention this form of participation, there have been cases and reports of it in local newspapers. Shanghai's *Xinming Evening*

News (*Xinming Wanbao*) published a number of reader letters regarding dissatisfaction with some development projects. *The Xiamen Daily* (*Xiamen Rebao*) reported that from 1994 through June 1997, there were 1,454 petitions and appeals on urban physical development issues sent to the city government. This was 22.3% of all petitions received by the government in that time period (*Xiamen Rebao* 1997).

Most city governments provide channels for public appeals on urban development or socioeconomic issues. Telephone hotlines to the mayor's office and to the director of the planning bureau are open to the public. The majority of hotline calls are complaints on the quality of new housing projects and displacement. The planning bureau will be informed of these concerns, but action will be taken only when the bureau or other government body thinks the problem is important enough to put it on their agenda.

Some cities have an open house day for concerned citizens to discuss development issues with the mayor and senior decision-makers. There is an inspection office in each city to handle public appeals and complaints. City governments especially encourage citizens to supervise and report violations of planning regulations and building codes (*Zhongguo Shirong Bao* 1997). All these channels are reported to be effective. For example, the planning bureau of Beihai (population 400,000) averages over 10 telephone calls per day, 200 written reports per month, and a considerable number of visitors reporting concerns on urban development issues. However, the extent to which people's concerns and policy suggestions are accepted and translated into government action heavily depends on the prevailing political climate, the mayor, and the issue involved.

Some cases are not publicly reported. In Shanghai, residents have gone to the streets in protest of eviction from their homes to make way for urban renewal projects. In Ningbo, angry residents destroyed an electroplating factory that was causing pollution in their neighborhoods. Local authorities knew of these problems, but no serious effort was made to solve the problem before the public protest. However, situations such as these, in which citizens take radical action against official top-down decisions, are not considered legal and are strongly discouraged by local government. Sometimes these actions may even result in punishment of those involved. On the other hand, these events may draw enough attention to the problem to sensitize officials and planners to take preventive action in the future.

In summary, various degrees of participation take place at three levels in the formal decision-making process. Participation at the municipal administration level is representative and its function is limited. The expert consulting approach at the planning institution level is also representative, but offers more possibility for meaningful public involvement. There are several forms of participation at the neighborhood level: informative, passive, and active participation initiated from ordinary citizens.

B. Participation in the Informal Decision-Making Process

Participation practices have also been reported in the informal decision process, although not for the top-down model. In that case, only persons holding the highest political or administrative positions make final decisions. These decisions are unchecked by either the public or the internal inspection division because a unified leadership system makes the party secretary omnipotent, hence he or she can supervise the inspection division. No room is left for participation in this process.

Since 1990, the central government has pushed municipal government to decentralize decision-making on certain issues, including local revenue and development decisions. For example, the Shanghai Municipal Government adopted a dual-level financial system, that allows district government to share city tax revenues while sharing the responsibility of providing infrastructure. The Xuhui District received RMB 1 billion Yuan (US$120 million) in 1996, but it had to provide local infrastructure, such as street maintenance for its population of 800,000. Local districts now have final approval of development proposals for small and medium-sized projects. In regard to community development, the Shanghai Government issued The Community Reinforcement Act (Shanghai Municipal Government Document Number Seven, 1996), which asks district government to transfer decision-making power to SCs and NCs, especially on re-employment, senior citizens, and neighborhood physical improvements. These new regulations are changing participation at the local level.

Local governments welcome increased power in decision-making but also feel the pressure of increased financial responsibility. Moreover, the top local officers (party secretary and mayor) are assigned by the superior government, not elected by local constituency; their promotion relies heavily on their records in meeting the demands of the superior government—with current emphasis on economic performance. This combination results in the main decision-makers putting the present economic benefits at the top of their cost-benefit analysis. Planning, on the other hand, is based on the interest of all citizens in the long run by nature, so a potential conflict of interest between top decision-makers and planners is created.

During surveys in the five cities, planners complained that site selection for major projects was being decided by city leaders without regard for the comprehensive plan that was officially approved by the People's Congress and city government as a legal document. One Shanghai senior planner said:

> The most critical planning problem today is that decision-makers have a lot of power but little knowledge of planning. They give land to developers with no reference to planners. We were told to issue approval licenses to developers but have no idea what's going on for the project. Sometimes we said no to the developer, but the developer came back with a note from the city

(mayor's) office; the note asks our planning bureau to give the land to the project for comprehensive political and economic reasons (Author's interview 1997a).

Another senior planner at the Hangzhou Municipal Planning Institute pointed out:

A serious problem in city management is illegal construction activity. The causes of the problem include the division of financial responsibility between the city and the districts and decentralization. The real force driving these illegal activities is economic interest, the combination of power and money. Illegal activities are related to governments at all levels, including NCs in urban areas and village communities in rural areas, and to those businessmen who have close connections with power holders (Author's interview 1997b).

A similar comment was found in an essay by a senior planner in Xiamen:

Under the current decision system, the more the power holders ''care'' about development issues, the more their willingness would rule over decisions on development issues, and the public's wishes and citizens' control are almost zero (Author's interview 1997c).

The rationale of central government's pushing for decentralization of land use administrative power is to encourage districts to attract more projects to their areas to speed economic growth. During interviews, district and county leaders made clear that they appreciate decentralization. However, no supervision mechanism has been established in the decentralization process. Local power holders, such as a district director or county head, may ignore land use regulations and people's needs, and make decisions based on potential economic profits or even personal desire. There are examples of power abuse at district and county levels. Jin-Xian county, south of the city of Ningbo, has a national nature preserve that is open to the public. The Director of the County Planning Bureau had abused his land use administrative power, given to him under decentralization, by approving two high-rise apartments in the center of the nature preserve. David Rusk argued that decision-makers of smaller units tend to base their decisions on the narrow view of the interests of their small unit, while leaders of larger units have a wider view in understanding the interests of the whole area and can make better decisions (Rusk 1993). Whether, or how, decentralization could improve participation is still a controversial issue in China. The top-down informal decision-making process will not change overnight.

Participation in bottom-up informal decision-making is contrary to the top-down model: proposals are initiated by ordinary people or their organizations. In general, it takes place in areas where the government does little because of budget constraints or loosened controls. The government's limited involvement also results in existing laws and regulations governing these issues being too vague in practice or too outdated to meet current needs. Therefore, initiatives of the bottom-up approach sometimes force the government to revise existing regulations or create new ones.

The bottom-up model of the informal decision-making process has two versions. The first involves decisions initiated and made by people with limited government involvement, but within the guidelines of laws and regulations. The second is that decisions are made without government involvement or legal reference. Examples of both versions follow.

1. Informal Decision-Making Within Governmental Systems

Ningbo is a city with a 7,000 year history of civilization. It is rich in historic buildings and landmarks. The number of buildings awaiting preservation versus limited public funding presents a dilemma to planners. Citizens of the city have organized a fundraising movement for historic preservation with the support of the city planning bureau. NCs and local culture stations, the basic facility of community culture, have organized volunteers in the movement. About 1,100 volunteers have participated in finding historic objects, preserving landmarks, and restoring historic buildings.

This kind of bottom-up informal decision-making provides the best channel for public participation. However, participation generally occurs in areas not so critical to people's lives, such as in amenity creation or not entering government's "right of way." In more crucial areas, such as housing, this form of participation has not been very active. Cultural institutions such as museums and culture stations are free from governmental management in the postreform era and are able to enter the market, allowing for greater public participation.

2. Informal Decision-Making Without Government Involvement

The second form of bottom-up informal decision-making is more complicated. Decisions are often initiated by ordinary people with no government support, or even against current governmental laws and regulations. This form is a consequence of the market economy creating a vacuum of government control.

Rural-to-urban migration has been a serious problem in China since the reform. The estimated number of rural migrants in cities varies from 50–100 million (based on Author's interview 1997d; Day and Ma 1990; Nam 1990; Dai and Chen 1996). Big eastern coastal cities, such as Beijing, Shanghai, Guangzhou, and Shenzhen, are the main attractions for rural migrants. Most rural migrants find work on a contract basis with enterprises. A considerable number of migrants are self-employed. Until 1995, migrants were not recognized as legal city residents according to Chinese resident registration regulations. Housing and social services were not available to them, except for some benefits provided by employers, which were far less than those given to official employees, or legal urban residents. This situation caused a migrant crisis: limited infrastructure and social services were drained by more people in cities. Urban communities had to protect their privileges by building barriers against migrants, which caused tensions between the two groups. The migrants eventually moved to peripheral areas of the city, where they found affordable housing and a less hostile atmosphere. They gradually established a system of social services to fit their needs, such as medical clinics and retail shops. These settlements are not slums because there is a shared infrastructure, and their residents are not squatters because residents rented the land from local villages or communities (based on Author's interview 1997d).

From a planning perspective, migrant settlements in cities are the result of two errors. A city's planning bureau often neglects remote areas such as the periphery of urbanized areas. These areas could be considered part of the urbanized area that under the control of the city planning bureau, or they could be classified as rural area under the control of the county government. Institutionally, there is no administrative body in city government handling the migrant settlement problem. Thus, the geographic location and an institutional vacuum yield migrant settlements in cities.

As China's capital, Beijing, has attracted about 2 million migrants (based on Author's interview 1997d; also see Wu 1997; Dai and Chen 1996). The migrants gradually built settlements at the city's edge, especially concentrated in two areas. In the beginning, the local peasants and Village Committee (a neighborhood organization, similar to the NCs of urban areas) had no complaints about the migrants, as they were paying rent to the peasants. Nor were there problems with the city government, which was unaware of the existence of the migrant villages. However, by 1994 the villages were experiencing growing pains. Population had increased significantly. More services had been established exclusively for residents of the villages, such as delivery of money and goods to and from migrant hometowns. These developments meant a separation of the villages from the surrounding communities. Moreover, the villages were reported to have gradually fallen under the control of several gang organizations. There was no authority in charge of the migrant settlements, so the crime rate increased and organized crime emerged. The municipal security bureau and city police finally put a spotlight on village crime from the end of 1996 to January 1997. (*The Beijing Daily, Beijing Rebao*, carried a number of reports on the events in December 1996.) City planners did suggest absorbing migrants into the city in the development plan of 1992, but the mayor turned down the proposal due to the possible attraction of more migrants to Beijing.

VII. CONCLUSION

Public participation in planning in third world countries has attracted researchers and practicing planners since the 1950s. Some scholars believed that self-help or self-improvement practices, or "slums of hope" (Turner 1967, 1968), in less developed countries (LDCs) might shed light on the participation strategies of developed nations. Others argued that given the low educational and literacy levels in many LDCs, trained professionals are the only people possessing the required expertise to make judgements and reach decisions (Potter 1985). How should one evaluate participation practice in China, the largest LDC? What are the factors bringing the changes to the relationship between local government decision-making and citizen participation after the reform? Some findings are worthy of discussion.

1. Public participation can make a difference in improving decision quality, even in a country that has had limited experience in participation, such as China; but awareness of the importance of participation is still a problem. Many city planners interviewed have not yet recognized the importance of public participation in planning, or they consider informative and representative participation as the only forms. Planning is viewed as a series of technical decisions better involving elite actors. Decentralization is understood only within the administration system, that is, from cities to districts, with no intention to share decision power with the public.

Some researchers argued that "public participation in planning is at best a luxury and at worst entirely unnecessary" due to the situation facing LDCs (Potter 1985). Similarly, planners view participation as something good but not realistic under the current decision-making system in China. One planner said: "Even planners are struggling for the possibility to participate in decision-making on city development issues, not to mention the public. Important development decisions have never been made by planners, but are always under the control of senior government officers" (Author's interview 1997a). There is still a long way to go before reaching a meaningful participation in terms of redistribution of decision-making power.

2. Public participation may take various forms. Several factors are influential in defining forms of participation. An appropriate participation form first depends on the economic-political structure of a society. As discussed by many researchers, participation takes on various forms (Dalton 1988; Stiefel and Marshall 1994). Factors influencing forms of participation include economic development status, adopted political system, and culture. The most crucial factor is the economic-political structure of a society, namely the planned economy, the market economy, or their co-existence.

For instance, a planned economy has concentrated decision-making power, which gives limited allowance for bottom-up participation. However, if this limited allowance is used appropriately, public involvement can still make a difference, although only to a certain degree. Under a heavily centralized decision-making system, representative participation may be a feasible form. In China, expert group participation has proven to be very effective. Since many professionals work for government institutions, improving participation may start from improving intergovernmental coordination via professional participation in expert groups. This could be the beginning of integrated planning, and is ad hoc at present.

The economic-political background of a society defines the particular form of participation for the particular society during a particular time period. The search for an appropriate form of public participation in China remains a topic for future research.

3. Meaningful participation needs institutionalization and legalization. Public participation in China is still at the beginning stage. Existing decision-making structure and laws do not encourage people's direct involvement on important decisions. There are no institutional or legal requirements for public participation in the decision-making process. Also, a mechanism is needed for residents' right to follow up. Ordinary people may lose their enthusiasm for responding to surveys if they feel disappointed by city government's reaction to their expectations. We may conclude that there is still a long way to go to reach a better level of participation. However, many cases give cause for optimism.

ACKNOWLEDGMENTS

This research was supported by a grant from the United Nations Research Institute for Social Development (UNRISD) in 1997; an earlier version of the paper was presented at the 1998 ACSP annual conference. Thanks to David Westendorff and Charles Hoch for their support and comments on the article.

REFERENCES

Altschiller, D. (ed.) (1994). *China at the Crossroads*. New York: The H. W. Wilson Company.

Arnstein, S. (1969). A ladder of citizen participation. *Journal of American Institute of Planners 8*:3, July.

Author's interview with Chief Planner W. Zhao, in Shanghai, May 27, 1997a.

Author's interview with Director Z. Li, in Hangzhou, May 30, 1997b.

Author's interview with Deputy Director W. Ma, in Xiamen, June 6, 1997c.

Author's interview with Chief Planner Y. Gun, in Shanghai, May 23, 1997d.

Buck, D. (1984). Changes in Chinese urban planning since 1976. *Third World Planning Review, 6*:1, February, 5–26.

Chen, X. (1994). Determinants of urban industrialization in China: A human ecological and political economy analysis. Paper presented at the International Sociological Association Annual Conference, Spain.

Chen, X. and Parish, W. (1996). Urbanization in China: Reassessing an evolving model.

In J. Gugler (ed.), *The Urban Transformation of the Developing World*. Cambridge, England: Oxford University Press.

Dai, Y.-C. and Chen, D.-Q. (1996). *Employment and Income of a Labor-Surplus Economy* (*Laodong guoshen jingji de jiuyi yu shouru*) (Chinese). Shanghai: Shanghai Far East Press.

Dalton, R. (1988). *Citizen Politics in Western Democracies*. NJ: Chatham House.

Davis, D. (1995). *Urban Spaces in Contemporary China: The Potential for Autonomy and Community in Post-Mao China*. New York: Cambridge University Press.

Day, L. and Ma, X. (eds.) (1994). *Migration and Urbanization in China*. New York: M. E. Sharpe.

Haggard, S. and Kaufman, R. (1995). *The Political Economy of Democratic Transitions*. Princeton, NJ: Princeton University Press.

Huang, W. D. (1996). *The Hidden Economic Activities in China* (*zhongguo de yinxing jingji*) (Chinese). Beijing: China Business Press.

Li, L. (1995). Subjective well-being of Chinese urban elderly. *International Review of Modern Sociology 25*:2, Autumn, 17–26.

Link, P. (1993). China's ''core'' problem. In D. Altschiller (ed.), *China at the Crossroads*. New York: The H. W. Wilson Company.

Ma, R. (1992). Town residents and rural-town migration in Inner Mongolia, People's Republic of China. In C. Goldscheider (ed.), *Migration, Population Structure, and Redistribution Policies*. Westview Press.

Ministry of Construction of China. (1991). *City Planning Act of the People's Republic of China*. Beijing, China: Department of City Planning, Ministry of Construction of China.

Nam, C. Serow, W. and Sly, D. (eds.) (1990). *International Handbook on Internal Migration*. New York: Greenwood Press.

Ogden, S. (1989). *China's Unsolved Issues: Politic, Development, and Culture*. Englewood Cliffs, NJ: Prentice-Hall, Inc.

People's Daily. (1997a). New Jobs for Laid-Offs, July 26.

People's Daily. (1997b). People's Congress Reps Care About Development, March 10.

People's Daily. (1997c). Direct Voting in Rural Villages, November 25.

People's Daily. (1997d). Survey on Family Income in Shanghai, June 15.

Portes, A. and Itzigsohn, J. (1994). The party or the grassroots: A comparative analysis of urban political participation in the Caribbean basin. *International Journal of Urban and Regional Research 18*:3, 491–509.

Potter, R. (1985). *Urbanization and Planning in the Third World*. London: Croom Helm Ltd.

Price, E. (1993). Healthy cities movement spurs citizen participation. *Nation's Cities Weekly, 16*:47, November 22, 5.

Rusk, D. (1993). *Cities Without Suburbs*. Baltimore, MD: Johns Hopkins University Press.

Shanghai Land Use Reform Office and Shanghai Statistical Bureau. (1997). *Shanghai Real Estate Market 1996*. Beijing: China Statistical Publishing House.

Shanghai Municipal Statistics Bureau. *Shanghai Statistical Yearbook, 1986, 1990, 1995, 1996*. Beijing: China Statistical Publishing House.

Sit, V. (1995). *Beijing: The Nature and Planning of a Chinese Capital City*. Wiley Co.

Smith, H. (1989). *The Citizen's Guide to Planning*, third edition. Chicago: Planners Press.

Solinger, D. (1991). The place of the central city in China's economic reform: From hierarchy to network. *City and Society 5*:1, June, 23–39.

Solinger, D. and Perry, E. (1994). China's transition from statist legacies and marketing reforms. *Journal of Politics 56*:3, August, 869–871.

Stiefel, M. and Wolfe, M. (1994). *A Voice for the Excluded: Population Participation in Development: Utopia or Necessity?* London and Geneva: Zed Books Ltd. and UNRISD.

Tsui, M., Huang, H.-Y., and He, Q. (1995). The status of elderly women and men in the Chinese urban family. Paper presented at the American Sociological Association Annual Conference.

Turner, J. F. C. (1967). Barriers and channels for housing development in modernizing countries. *Journal of the American Institute of Planners 33*, 167–181.

Turner, J. F. C. (1968). Housing priorities, settlement patterns, and urban development in modernizing countries. *Journal of the American Institute of Planners 34*, 354–363.

Wang, Y. (1991). A comparative study of urban land use planning system in Scotland and China: with case studies in Edinburgh and Xian. Dissertation. *Dissertation Abstract International*, Vol. 53/04-A, p. 1292.

Wang, J. (1997). The functions and reform of China's Urban Neighborhood Committee. Paper presented at the UNRISD's ''Comparative Perspectives on Decentralized Governance in a Globalizing World,'' Shanghai, China.

Wu, W. (1997). The case of China. In U. Kirdar (ed.), *Cities Fit for People*. UNU Press.

Xiamen Rebao. (1997). Residents' Concern on Housing Quality, June 5.

Ye, B. (ed.) (1993). *Shanghai Housing (1949–1990) (Shanghai zhuzhai 1949–1990)* (Chinese). Shanghai: Shanghai Kupu Press.

Zhongguo Shirong Bao. (1997). Implementing Planning Regulations, April 27.

Zhu, Y. (1993). Urban land market development in China: Implication on the urban planning practice. Dissertation. *Dissertation Abstract International*, Vol. 54/06-A, p. 2350.

14

Social Development Amidst Economic Reform

Family Policy in a Changing Vietnam

Steven K. Wisensale
University of Connecticut, Storrs, Connecticut

With a population of more than 70 million, half of whom were born after the end of the war with the United States, Vietnam finds itself not only navigating a path between egalitarian socialism (*che do moi* was initiated in the late 1940s) and free-market capitalism (*doi moi* was adopted in 1986), but also attempting to blend the best of both worlds. To what extent the Vietnamese family in particular has been affected by these stresses and strains over the years, and to what degree the government has put forth specific marriage laws amidst dynamic social change, is the subject of this chapter.

This presentation is divided into five major sections. Part one consists of a brief discussion of the methodology employed in this study. The second section will focus on the Marriage Law of 1959 and the role it played in Vietnam's women's movement under socialist rule. Part three is devoted to the Law on Marriage and the Family of 1986, which was passed to coincide with the nation's abrupt shift from socialism to free-market capitalism. Part four will explore the 1994 Decree on Marriage and the Family, which was designed to fortify the institution of marriage in a rapidly changing society and protect the Vietnamese family from foreign influences. And the final section will discuss the present status and future prospects of Vietnam's families.

I. METHODOLOGY

The information presented was gathered primarily through a two-week study tour of Vietnam in the summer of 1996 that included several personal interviews; an analysis of key government documents, including the Marriage and Family Law of 1959, the 1986 Law on Marriage and the Family, the 1994 Decree on Marriage and the Family, the *United Nations Human Development Report* of 1990, the Vietnam Living Standards Survey of 1992–1993, the Vietnam Life History Survey of 1991, Vietnam's census of 1990, and the 1991 *World Development Report* of the World Bank; and a review of numerous secondary sources, including a variety of books, journal articles, and monographs.

II. THE MARRIAGE AND FAMILY LAW OF 1959

In both traditional and modern Vietnam, the family is considered to be the foundation of society. To Ho Chi Minh, ''[i]t is correct to pay great attention to the family, because many families added together make up a society. The interests and happiness of the family totally depend on the interests and happiness of the society. And the happiness of the society is manifest in the happiness of each member of the society, of each family'' (Himmelstrand 1981: 23). Ho's views were clearly implanted in the constitution of the young Vietnamese Republic in 1946. Article 64 reads, ''The family is the cell of society. The State protects marriage and the family'' (Constitution of the Republic of Vietnam 1946: 26). Thirteen years later the first major piece of legislation regarding marriage and families would be passed by the National Assembly.

The Marriage and Family Law, passed in 1959 and implemented in 1960, contained four major provisions. First, for the first time in Vietnamese history, arranged marriages were abolished and both men and women were granted the freedom to make their own decisions. Second, polygamy was declared illegal, and monogamy was adopted as the official form of Vietnamese marriage. Third, equality between men and women was to be practiced both in the home and in society in general. And fourth, the basic rights of women and children, such as freedom from abuse and oppression in the home, were to be protected.

Of the four provisions, however, the most successful proved to be the first two. That is, between 1958 and 1962 the proportion of arranged marriages fell in North Vietnam from over 60% to under 20% of all marriages. Today the rate is near zero. A similar pattern emerged regarding polygamy. With the exception of a few rural areas where it may be difficult to apply the law, it is virtually nonexistent (Goodkind 1995). The most difficult provisions to implement, however, have been the latter two (Truong 1996). Both gender equity and the protection of children within families have been ongoing challenges for Vietnamese policy makers.

According to Thanh-Dam Truong, a specialist in Vietnamese women's issues, "the issue of gender equality has been debated and acted upon in Vietnam long before it became framed as the Women's Question guided by socialist theory and morality" (Truong 1996: 3). Although this topic has become particularly interesting since the adoption of *doi moi* in 1986 and the shift to free-market capitalism, the liberation of women was always a precondition for Vietnamese socialism. Ho Chi Minh, very much aware of the oppression of women during the feudal and colonial periods, emphasized that "[w]omen are half of society, and half of society will not be liberated until women are. If women are not emancipated, socialism is only half established" (Himmelstrand 1981). Article 21 of Vietnam's constitution, which was adopted in 1946, reads: "Women enjoy equal rights with men in all spheres. . . . The State guarantees to women workers and functionaries the right to be paid maternity leave before and after childbirth" (Constitution of the Republic of Vietnam 1946).

The issue of gender equity in Vietnam is particularly unique in that it has always been linked to the quest for national independence. To mobilize women against French colonialists and American capitalists, they were told that contrary to the Marxist-socialist paradigm that promised liberation, the "aggressor nations" fostered patriarchal families that guaranteed female oppression. Subsequently, over a period of 50 years the government in the North and the National Liberation Front in the South (before reunification in 1975) put forth three policy initiatives designed to address "the women's question" (gender equity).

First, the Marriage and Family Law Act of 1959 freed women from arranged marriages, polygamy, and prostitution. Also, barriers that prevented women from working in male jobs were removed—similar to the movement of American women into defense jobs during World War II. As a result of these changes, significant improvements were made in female literacy, level of education, and participation in decision-making that previously had been reserved only for males (Mai and Le 1978; Marr 1981; Truong 1996).

Second, with females playing a major role as producers in defense efforts, the state provided substantial support to women so they could also continue their role as reproducers. Child care was made available at all sites and all levels of production. So not only did such an approach ease the burden of producer/reproducer that women shouldered, it also provided the state with an opportunity to socialize their children (Lee 1991; Truong 1996).

And third, to facilitate the mobilization of women in all spheres of society, a special organization was created: the Women's Union. With historical roots that can be traced back to the 1930s, the Women's Union has played, and continues to play, a crucial role in the development and implementation of policies that affect women, children, and families. It was the Women's Union that assisted in the implementation of the Marriage and Family Laws of 1959 and 1986 and the nation's family planning policy since the 1970s. It is also regularly consulted on various legislative proposals (Goodkind 1995).

But perhaps the most interesting question concerning gender equity in Vietnam has yet to be answered. That is, if the ''women's question'' has been comfortably imbedded in socialist thought for more than half a century, how will the issue of gender equity fare under *doi moi*, or free-market capitalism? After all, is it not the capitalist nations that foster patriarchal families that ultimately suppress women? And, therefore, what role will marriage law play in this endeavor. In short, is there common ground to be found between economic efficiency (the free market) on one hand and equality (state-sponsored socialism) on the other? How Vietnam responds to these questions may ultimately determine the future of marriage, the profile of its families, and their general state of well-being.

Recent literature indicates that the shift to a free-market society in 1986 has contributed to gender inequality (Allen 1990; Goodkind 1995; White 1989). On the other hand, there is some evidence that the government is at least sensitive to this issue and has responded to some degree. For example, the revised Family Codes in 1986, to be discussed in greater detail in the next section, forbids domestic violence and states that housework must be viewed as a contribution to family income when assessing common property. In 1988 the role of the Women's Union was widened ''to monitor and suggest policies related to women and children'' (Council of Ministers 1992). The Labor Laws of 1994 were adopted, with Chapter 10 devoted to the rights of women employees. Article 110 of that chapter gives special tax deductions to employers who hire women in large numbers. And Article 117 gives leaves of absence to women workers who adopt infants (Truong 1996).

However, despite such initiatives on the part of the government, skepticism still prevails in some quarters. ''Once the national objective of reunification was achieved in 1975,'' writes Thanh-Dam Truong, ''patriarchal culture re-emerged through the trade-off between gender equality and economic efficiency. Thus, in spite of the rights and political space women gained through decades of struggle, as the reform deepens this trade-off is narrowing women's alternatives and options, and will likely further erode their socio-economic position'' (Truong 1996: 8).

III. THE 1986 LAW ON MARRIAGE AND THE FAMILY

The second major piece of legislation regarding marriage was passed by the National Assembly on December 29, 1986. The 1986 Law on Marriage and the Family, consisting of 10 chapters and 57 articles, is far more detailed than the

1959 law it replaced. For the sake of clarity, the discussion that follows is divided into three separate sections: the regulation of marriage, parental responsibilities, and divorce law. The key provisions of the law are summarized therein.

A. Regulation of Marriage

Chapters I through III of the law stipulate who may or may not marry, what are the specific obligations of marriage partners, and what rights and responsibilities they have as a married couple. For example, men cannot marry until age 21; women cannot marry until age 18. Cohabitation is illegal. Vietnamese from different ethnic or religious groups are permitted to intermarry, while those who are mentally ill, have a venereal disease, or are blood relatives are prohibited from doing so.

With respect to obligations, married couples are required to abide by Vietnam's two-child family policy (''Husband and wife shall have the obligation to implement family planning''), to raise their children in a wholesome manner (''a duty to make their children useful to society''), and to not ill-treat one's spouse, child, or parent (The Law on Marriage and the Family of 1986: Chapter I, Articles 2 and 4).

Concerning rights and responsibilities of married partners, the husband and wife shall have equal rights, ''the husband shall have the duty to create conditions for the wife to fulfill her mother's role'' (The Law on Marriage and the Family of 1986: Chapter III, Article 11), each partner shall be free to choose their respective partners, and, in selecting a domicile, the couple shall not be forced to follow customary rules under which the wife usually moved in with her husband's parents if he was the eldest son. Equally important is the law on property, which states that husband and wife shall have equal rights and duties with regard to their common property. ''Purchase, sale, exchange, borrowing or other dealings involving property of considerable value shall require general consent between husband and wife'' (The Law on Marriage and the Family of 1986: Chapter III, Article 15).

In many respects, other than its prohibition of cohabitation and its requirement that family planning (''the two-child family'') be practiced, the Vietnamese marriage code is not atypical when compared to marriage laws in more developed nations. More interesting perhaps is not so much the adoption of the 1986 law, but the fact that such a code, which grants many rights to the wife that did not exist before, came so late. However, that may be explained by at least two particular factors. One, the termination of long-term military conflict freed up the nation's resources for addressing important social issues. And, two, the shift to free-market capitalism has catapulted the nation into the modern global economy. Old marriage customs may not be tolerated.

B. Parental Responsibilities

Chapters IV, V, and VI of the 1986 law spell out the rights and duties of parents and children, present guidelines to be followed in determining parentage, and clarify the adoption process. The key components of these chapters are identified and discussed here.

It is clear that the family, far more than the state, is responsible for the care and well-being of its members. Parents are required to support their mature children who are incapable of earning a living. Parents are also responsible for paying any compensation for damages caused by illegal acts of their children under age 16. Minors aged 16 or over must pay compensation out of their own pocket for any damage they may inflict on the property of others. Such financial responsibilities also apply to children 16 or older who are living with their parents. Under law, they are obligated to contribute to the family's livelihood.

A more interesting component of the 1986 code is found in Chapter IV, Article 27, which identifies intergenerational responsibilities within families. "Grandparents shall be bound to support and educate under-age grandchildren if they become orphans. Vice-versa, grandchildren who have grown up shall have a duty to support their grandparents if the latter have no surviving children" (The Law on Marriage and the Family of 1986: Chapter IV, Article 27). Primarily because of decades of war, concern for orphans and isolated elderly run deep in Vietnamese society. And, as illustrated here, such concern is reflected in their laws.

Two other areas of the 1986 code that relate to parental responsibility are the issues of out-of-wedlock births and adoptions. The former is considered a major stigma; the latter represents at least one remedy for it. By law, individuals may request a determination as to whether they are or are not a child's parent. Children under age, however, have no right to request that such a determination be made. Only the mother, father, or foster parent may make a request. Otherwise, such a child is classified as illegitimate. Only a child born out of wedlock who has been recognized by one of his or her biological parents or by the People's Court is granted the same rights and duties as a child born in lawful wedlock.

With respect to adoption law in Vietnam, three features in particular are quite visible. First, only persons 15 years old or under may be adopted. However, if the adopted child is 9 years old or older, his or her own consent is required. Exceptions under this law include those over 15 who are invalid soldiers or disabled. Second, any adoptions require the consent of both adopting parents; single-parent adoptions may be possible but only under extremely rare circumstances. And, third, once an adoption is finalized the parents and the child shall have the same rights and duties of those parents and children with biological ties.

C. Divorce Law

Vietnam has one of the lowest divorce rates in the world. According to 1992 statistics, the ratio of marriages per 1,000 people was 5.9%, compared to a divorce rate of only 0.9% (Nhi 1995). However, with more modernization and the shift toward a market economy, it is likely that the rate of divorce will increase and thus run parallel to patterns in other developing Southeast Asian nations, such as Thailand, Singapore, Malaysia, and Indonesia.

Perhaps in anticipation of a problem in the future, The 1986 Law on Marriage and the Family includes a fairly lengthy chapter on divorce law. Couples may indeed seek and be granted divorces but the process is not designed for their convenience. First, there is no such thing as no-fault divorce under Vietnamese marriage law. A couple may file for divorce, but before they are granted their wish they must first show evidence that they made a serious attempt to reconcile their differences. Second, although it is not easy, divorce is certainly made more possible if both parties seek an end to their marriage rather than just one partner. If only one party wishes to terminate the marriage, the People's Court is more likely to require a continuation of reconciliation efforts before even hearing the case again. Such an approach can be particularly problematic for women in abusive situations. But even if a divorce is granted, more challenges lie ahead.

For women who are pregnant when a husband requests a divorce, Vietnamese law requires that the husband cannot file such a suit until one year after the birth of the child. This provision does not apply to the wife's request for divorce.

Concerning the division of property under a divorce settlement, the law is equally complicated. Personal property shall be kept by the owner, common property will be divided based on the contributions made by each party, and when a couple lives with parents or inlaws the property will be divided ''in proportion to his or her contributions to the preservation and enlargement of the common property and to the family's livelihood'' (The Law on Marriage and the Family of 1986: Chapter VII, Article 42). This latter provision speaks to the existence of the extended family in Vietnam, though it is expected to decline with an increase in industrialization (Binh 1996).

Two other key components of the divorce codes are financial support and child custody. With phrasing that smacks of Marxist doctrine (''from each according to his abilities, to each according to his needs''), financial support is determined by the two parties involved or, if necessary, by the People's Court. ''When divorced, if either party is needy and asks for support, the other party shall give support according to his or her abilities. If no agreement can be reached, the People's Court shall decide'' (The Law on Marriage and the Family of 1986: Chapter VII, Article 43).

Concerning the issue of custody, Vietnamese law fluctuates between the "best interests of the child" principle on one hand and "the tender years doctrine" on the other. Both approaches appear in sequential statements in the 1986 codes. "In consigning the couple's child or children to the care of either of the divorcees for guardianship, the children's interests in every aspect shall be taken into account" (the best interest model). "In principle, nursing infants shall be consigned to the care of their mothers" (the tender years doctrine) (The Law on Marriage and the Family of 1986: Chapter VII, Article 45).

IV. THE 1994 DECREE ON MARRIAGE AND THE FAMILY

In 1994, the year of the United Nations' International Year of the Family, the Prime Minister reviewed the effect the 1986 law on Marriage and the Family had on Vietnamese society. "During the past eight years of implementation, the Law on Marriage and the Family has contributed very positively to the building and consolidation of Vietnamese families, promoted the fine national traditions, abolished the backward practices of the feudalist regime of marriage and the family and prevented the bad influence of the bourgeois regime of marriage and the family" (Office of the Prime Minister 1994:1). However, he expressed disappointment that violations still continued, including ". . . precocious marriages, unregistered marriages, violations of the principle of monogamy, maltreatment of women and children, and failure to contribute to the bringing up of their children and to support their elderly parents" (Office of the Prime Minister 1994: 1). He then called for an ongoing review of the law to determine its positive and negative impact.

In response to the Prime Minister's concerns, the Vietnamese Ministry of Justice issued a special decree that had two primary objectives: one, to clarify those sections of the existing codes that were confusing, and, two, to focus on potentially harmful influences foreigners may have on Vietnam's families. The latter point is not surprising in light of the recent growth in international trade and the corresponding increase in foreign visitors. The decree, issued on September 30, 1994, consists of 7 chapters and 41 articles.

Chapters I through III of the decree pertain primarily to the regulation of marriage, with specific regulations concerning marriages between Vietnamese and foreigners. In short, any marriage on Vietnamese soil falls under Vietnam's marriage codes. Such marriages performed outside the country must be approved by the Chairman of Vietnam's provincial People's Committee if one or both parties wish to reside in the country. If the Law on Marriage and the Family is not violated and . . . "the recognition of the marriage is not at variance with the basic principles of the Law on Marriage and the Family of Vietnam," the marriage will be recognized.

Perhaps even more indicative of Vietnam's concern about foreign influences is their effort to control foreigners' access to the nation's children. In 1992 the Council of Ministers issued temporary regulations on the adoption of Vietnamese children by foreigners, limiting such adoptions of "Vietnamese children who are orphaned, abandoned, disabled, and are being institutionally-cared for" by government authorities (Council of Ministers 1992). Two years later these temporary regulations were made permanent and expanded to include rules that restricted the tutorship of Vietnamese children by foreigners (The 1994 Decree on Marriage and the Family). In short, by actions set forth in the 1994 decree, foreigners will be restricted by law in their attempt to either adopt or tutor Vietnamese children.

V. MARRIAGE LAW AND THE FUTURE OF VIETNAM'S FAMILIES

Whatever shape Vietnamese families take in the future will depend a great deal on how well it assesses and applies its experiences from the past. It will also depend on how well it can assess its present state of affairs and to what degree it can formulate realistic goals and objectives amidst major economic reforms. Most recently it has devoted much of its energy to reforming its laws on marriage, clearly indicating that Ho Chi Minh was correct when he described the family as the most important cell of society. Whether or not this is the appropriate strategy to employ in the future remains to be seen.

Clearly, the facts before us are indisputable. There are social and economic forces at work that may not be contained by simply reforming marriage laws. By all measures, from an assortment of internationally recognized indicators, Vietnam is an extremely poor country—so poor that it depends on foreign aid from Cuba! Based on data from the Vietnam Life History Survey (1991), the Vietnam Living Standards Survey (1992–1993), the *World Development Report* of the World Bank (1991), Vietnam's Central Census Steering Committee (1990), and the *United Nations' Human Development Report* (United Nations 1990), the following conclusions can be drawn about the present socioeconomic status of Vietnam's people.

First, despite deep-rooted poverty and a per capita income of less than US$200 a year, 84% of the female population is literate, the infant mortality rate is 54% per thousand, and life expectancy exceeds 65 years. The infant mortality rate compares favorably to countries such as Bangladesh (120 per 1000 births) and even more modernized states such as the Philippines (48 infant deaths per 1000 births). Not to be overlooked is the fact that almost 80% of children under five are, according to UNICEF, immunized against the five main childhood diseases.

Second, a fairly large number of females over the age of 15 are in the labor force. Based on the 1989 census, 73.6% of the female population was fully employed during the six-month reporting period. According to classic socialist theory, women entering productive work provides an escape from traditional oppression that occurs in the household. Thus, not surprisingly, the high female economic activity rate is close to 90% of the male rate.

And, third, according to the United Nations' Human Development Report, in 1993 Vietnam's human development rank was 113, and in 1995 this ranking had slipped to 120, out of about 150 countries. According to Kaufman and Sen (1993), women in particular are suffering more from this decline.

So in whatever direction Vietnam chooses to move with respect to women, children, and families, it has already established some fairly significant benchmarks in socioeconomic status that are visible to the entire world. What effect will the economic reforms under *doi moi* have on these benchmarks in general and Vietnam's families in particular? And, equally significant, how will its strong socialist roots either help or hinder the development of Vietnam's major domestic policies in the future?

At this stage, the answers to these questions are unknown. And although one may be tempted to explore how other countries responded to family issues under similar circumstances, such comparisons can become too simplistic to bear fruit of any value. China is a likely candidate for comparison because it too is attempting to introduce market forces into the economy without fundamentally altering its political system. However, some would argue that Vietnam is more similar to the East Asian newly industrialized countries (NICs) in the early stages of their development than it is to China (Dollar 1993). These include Taiwan (late 1940s), South Korea (early 1950s), and Indonesia (early 1960s).

Vietnam may also want to compare itself to Malaysia, Thailand, and Singapore. However, here again the histories differ as do the social fabrics. Even more troubling, perhaps, are recent reports from these market-oriented nations that their family structures are beginning to unravel. ''Traditional family networks, touted by regional governments as the core of the indigenous social value systems, are breaking down under the weight of economic growth and the resulting migration and changing behavioral patterns'' (*Far Eastern Economic Review* 1996:38). Statistics support this statement.

Divorce is on the rise throughout all economically advanced Southeast Asian nations, particularly in urban areas. For example, in Thailand divorce rates are holding at 10% in rural areas but in urban regions they are at 26% and climbing. For every 1,000 Singaporeans, according to government statistics, 1.3 of them had experienced a broken marriage in 1990, up from 0.7 ten years earlier. In Malaysia, records from Kuala Lumpur courts indicate that the number of divorce cases processed by the courts increased from 506 in 1991 to 909 in 1993 (*Far Eastern Economic Review* 1996).

Children are also vulnerable in economically advanced Southeast Asian countries. A survey in Thailand revealed that 9.3% of urban men reported that their spouse's relatives were caring for children under three years of age, and almost 11% of urban women said that other people were taking care of their children. A 1995 survey of Malaysian young people between the ages of 13 and 21 revealed that 71% smoked, 40% watched pornographic videos, 28% gambled, and 14% took hard drugs. And juvenile delinquency is steadily increasing throughout the region. "The causes of these social ills are undoubtedly complex. But in the more developed Southeast Asian countries, politicians and academics are quick to blame drug abuse, moral decadence, and divorce for the erosion of traditional family structures. They have shrunk from extended family networks, to nuclear families, and increasingly, single-parent families" (*Far Eastern Economic Review* 1996:39).

For Vietnam the challenge is clear. A rich cultural heritage, combined with more than 50 years of socialist teaching, is expected to share a berth with free-market capitalism. How this mix will ultimately affect families in Vietnam has yet to be determined. Whether or not changes in marriage codes will inoculate this developing nation against the decline of the family unit is an unknown.

ACKNOWLEDGMENT

The author is greatly indebted to Trang Van Lee for his time and patience in translating documents and journal articles related to this research project.

REFERENCES

Allen, S. (1990). *Women in Vietnam*. Hanoi: Swedish International Development Authority's Policy Development and Evaluation Division.

Constitution of the Republic of Vietnam. (1946). From *An Outline of Institutions of the Democratic Republic of Vietnam*. (1974), p. 26. Hanoi: The Socialist Republic of Vietnam.

Council of Ministers. (1992). "Decision of the Council of Ministers on temporary regulations on the adoptions by foreign people of Vietnamese children orphaned, abandoned, disabled living in feeding institutions managed by the labor, invalids and social affairs authorities." Hanoi: Council of Ministers, Socialist Republic of Vietnam, No. 145-HDBT, April 29.

Binh, D. T. (1996). Interview by author, July 29, Hanoi.

Dollar, D. (1993). Vietnam: Successes and failures of macroeconomic stabilization. In B. Ljunggren's (ed.), *The challenge of Reform in Indochina*. Cambridge, MA: Harvard Institute for International Development, Harvard University Press.

Far Eastern Economic Review (1996). Whatever happened to family values? *Far Eastern Economic Review*, August 1, 38–42.

Goodkind, D. (1995). Rising gender inequality in Vietnam since reunification. *Pacific Affairs 68*:3, 342–359.

Himmelstrand, K. (1981). *Women in Vietnam*. Stockholm: Swedish International Development Authority's Policy Development and Evaluation Division.

Kaufman, J. and Sen, G. (1993). Population, health, and gender in Vietnam: Social policies under the economic reforms. In B. Ljunggren's (ed.), *The challenge of Reform in Indochina*. Cambridge, MA: Harvard Institute for International Development. Harvard University Press.

Lee, T. (1991). Women and their families in the movement for agricultural collectivism in Vietnam. In H. Afshar's (ed.) *Women, Development, and Survival in the Third World.* London: Longman.

Mai, T. and Le, T. (1978). *Women in Vietnam*. Hanoi: Foreign Language Publishing House.

Marr, D. (1981). *Vietnamese Traditions on Trial: 1920–1945*. Berkeley: University of California Press.

Office of the Prime Minister. (1994). ''Instruction of the prime minister on the review of eight years of implementing the law on marriage and the family.'' Hanoi: The Socialist Republic of Vietnam, No. 482/TTG, September 8.

Truong, T. D. (1996). Uncertain horizons: The women's question in Vietnam revisited. *Working Paper Series*, No. 212. The Hague: Institute of Social Studies.

The Marriage and Family Law of 1959. (1959). Office of the Prime Minister. Hanoi: The Socialist Republic of Vietnam.

The 1994 Decree on Marriage and the Family. (1994). Office of the Prime Minister. Hanoi: The Socialist Republic of Vietnam.

The Law on Marriage and the Family of 1986. (1986). Office of the Prime Minister. Hanoi: The Socialist Republic of Vietnam.

Nhi, T. X. (1995). Vietnam's families. In A. Gafurov's (ed.) *Worldwide State of the Family*. Tashkent, Uzbekistan: Institute of Strategic and Interregional Studies.

United Nations. (1990). *United Nations Human Development Report*. New York: United Nations.

Vietnam's Central Census Steering Committee. (1990). *Vietnam Population Census 1989 Sample Results*. Hanoi: Central Census Steering Committee.

Vietnam Life History Survey. (1991). Ho Chi Minh City: Institute for the Social Sciences.

Vietnam Living Standards Survey. (1992–1993). Ho Chi Minh City: Institute for the Social Sciences.

White, C. (1989). Vietnam: War, socialism, and the politics of gender relations. In S. Kruks, R. Rapp, and M. B. Young (eds.), *Promissory Notes—Women in the Transition to Socialism*. New York: Monthly Review Press.

World Bank (1991). The challenges of development: Country economic reports on Vietnam and Laos. In *World Development Report*. Washington, DC: World Bank.

15

Nations and Minorities

A Conceptual Comparison Between the Western and the Islamic Understanding with a Case Study

Andrea K. Riemer
ARIS Research and Consultancy Office for Security Studies, Vienna, Austria

I. INTRODUCTION

Minorities have always been part of the international landscape. They are often the result of movements of people due to political and religious persecution, economic deficiency, and the drawing of borders after wars. One can say that minorities are a natural part of society and its historical development. Systems evolution implies that there are majorities and minorities—regardless of scientific definition—due to perceptions by oneself and the other.

The rising of nations and states was one of the results of the Westphalian Peace. Since the end of the eighteenth century the process of nation-building has become a crucial factor in Europe—but not only in this region. During the nineteenth century a unified nation-state was the thriving idea.

Ethnic, political, and ideological borders fixed during the nineteenth century, after World War I and World War II, did not necessarily coincide. One could say that there was and still is an immanent and sometimes manifest contradiction between nations/states and minorities. Especially after the decay of the former Soviet Union, a number of ''old new'' minorities came on stage. A shift in interest brought a shift in perceptions as well. The minority issue became a realistic potential for crisis.

The purpose of this chapter is to provide a linkage between the concepts of nation, state, and minorities from the point of view of a historical sociologist. The following questions are guidelines. Is the existence of nations and minorities on the same territory a potential for crisis?[1] If yes, can both concepts nevertheless exist together? The answers will be given by a multidimensional theoretical framework on the triangle of nation—state—minorities, and a case study on the Kurds is presented with a special focus on the situation in Turkey.

II. THE TERMINOLOGICAL TRIANGLE OF NATION, STATE, AND MINORITIES

Nations, states, and minorities are strongly interconnected concepts on different societal levels. All three concepts are key ones in international law, but not only there. Social, historical, economic, and political aspects are also very important, although one has to admit that those facets are often not seen at first glance.

The historical roots for the three concepts can already be found in the Westphalian Peace Agreement in 1648. Nations, the nation-state, and nationalism are terms that came up during the Age of Modernity, the creation of civil society and the Industrial Revolution. The terms became leading ones in connection with political integration. The minority issue has always been part of the game. During the creation of the nation-state in the nineteenth century the issue became more and more relevant. Democratization and the right to vote increased in importance. The breakdown of empires, the changes in the political landscape after World War I, the end of colonialization, and the reshaping of borders, which in many cases was done without taking settlement areas into account, all led to problems between minorities and majorities.

Defining the three interrelated terms—nation, state, and minority—is a difficult procedure because in most cases a common definition or understanding does not exist. This is due to the fact that an agreed definition implies a number of far-reaching consequences in several societal areas. The concept of nation and the one of state will help find a way to define the term minority a little easier.

A. The Concept of Nation: Between Philosophy and Hard Facts

For the term nation, a number of definitions exists. Some of them are more philosophical; others refer more to international law. For years a broad debate has been going on over whether more focus should be placed on objective or subjective criteria in defining a nation. Karl R. Popper mocked the concept when he said that a nation is a number of people being held together by a common misperception of their history. Which are the defining features of a nation? We will face a number of problems to figure them out. Qualitative aspects, or soft facts, dominate. Hard facts are rarely found. One could even ask provokingly whether the concept of nation exists only in our minds. Nevertheless it is a very important concept in society—covering on one hand subjective aspects like a sense of solidarity; a common culture; a national consciousness, self-awareness, and self-perception and on the other hand objective aspects like a certain territory; a shared language, religion, and culture; and common descent. There is obviously something—a blend of objective and subjective criteria—keeping people together. It is not only a common misperception of their history. The concept of nation is one of the leading organization principles in the international system and provides a benchmark for orientations.

B. The Concept of State: More Hard Facts?

The concept of state, which refers more to structural issues, is a little bit easier to define because factual features can be made out. According to international law, a state shows at least four features (Malanczuk 1997:75): a defined territory, a permanent population, a government, and the capacity to enter into relations with other states. Those features point to quite hard facts that can easily be identified and compared. Although there is discussion among scholars of international law about those features, we will use them as a benchmark in the case study.

C. The Concept of Minority: A Multidimensional Approach for a Multidimensional Issue

1. Definition Efforts

The term minority is the key term in the chapter. In international law, but also in other relevant areas, the term minority is considered to be a very vexed one. The key reason for blurred definitions is quite simple. The subject to be defined is such a broad one that the definition procedure is like squaring the circle.

A minority can be defined as an ethnic minority, a religious minority, and/or a cultural minority. Moreover the term minority can comprise a group standing politically in opposition to a majority (political minority) or as a group in society feeling itself to be in a disadvantaged position. Another approach is a legal one. The legal term minority refers to the subjective consciousness of identity, to the cultural conception of oneself. There is no reference to a geographical territory. The definition of the United Nations for minorities is by far the broadest one. According to UN, a minority is ''a group numerically inferior to the rest of the population of a State, in a non-dominant position, whose members—being nationals of the State—possess ethnic, religious or linguistic characteristics differing from those of the rest of the population and show, if only implicitly, a sense of solidarity, directed towards preserving their culture, traditions, religions or language,'' (Malanczuk 1997:106).

2. Minority Protection—Making Equals More Equal?

The different approaches to the definition show the multidimensionality of the issue of minorities. Another way of definition is via minority protection. Minority protection focusses on the following questions. Who is protectable as a minority? What are the rights of a minority?[2] In a democracy, are not the rights of all citizens automatically covered? Do minorities really need an additional protection, respective to specific rights?

Those questions impel one to find a definition. Minority protection had come up in the nineteenth century. One later milestone was the Treaties of Paris 1919–1920. The international community tried to establish and protect minority rights by drawing up a network of treaties under international law and by including the League of Nations as an arbitrator after World War I. Some of the individual members of ethnic, linguistic, or cultural minorities were granted the right to have their language and identity respected by the state as part of the process of the development of human rights in general. But nation-states with minorities existing on their territory basically remained quite reluctant to take any significant step that might increase the danger of claims to independence and/or secession by minorities (Malanczuk 1997:105).

After 1945 individual rights based on human rights were preferred simply because the experience after World War I was that negative. Today one is aware that neither way serves the purpose of solving minority problems. Protection of minorities has several key targets. First, it intends to keep the potential for conflict or crisis down. Second, it aims to contain the potential for conflict or crisis and to regulate it. Third, in the long run minority protection seeks to settle disputes. Most probably, legal constructions (especially those based on collective rights) are not suitable to protect minorities from majorities. The complexity created by domination, suppression, competition, identity problems, and disadvantages makes it impossible to find a legal approach covering that network. We can say that so far legal provisions have been one method to regulate conflicts. But the conflicts themselves could not be solved and the disputes could not be settled.[3]

3. Minorities and Their Multidimensional Consequences

There are at least two consequences resulting from the complexity and multidimensionality of minority issues: a legal consequence and—much more complex—a political consequence. The legal aspect is related to a possible intervention of a mother country in favor of its minority. The political aspect refers to the issue of the meaning and the legal consequences of self-determination. From the state's point of view self-determination is always related with secession of a minority. This may lead to a loss of territory and the control over at least a part of the population. Consequently, legal provision could only be one of the supporting tools to solve minority problems in a sustainable way. Society itself— covering the majority and minority(ies)—has to make efforts to create harmonious relations. Minority protection is a task for society as a whole and not an area of specialists and of law. This means that the minority issue is a social one and not a legal problem. Legal provisions can only give a kind of guideline or framework to act within, but they can not solve the problem itself.

D.   Minorities—A Potential for Crisis?

Different and unclear definitions, vague international regulations, agreements ratified by only some states, and a huge number of minorities are reasons enough why minorities are a potential for crisis. Apart from definition problems, there are three main reasons or groups of conditions, which refer to the relations between members of the social system, that tell us why minorities can become a potential for crisis: First, the minority group is not accepted as a religious or ethnic or national minority and does not have any legal protection. Second, the minority group is not granted special rights (use of language, education, free exercise of religion and traditions). Third, the minority group is not granted autonomy, at least protection from the majority or social emancipation.

From a historic point of view, it was already clear during the Paris Peace Treaties that the minorities had to be protected from the majorities. Obviously it was the majority who had (and sometime still has) problems with the minority and not the other way around. One has to make the following differentiation between two types of society. In a democratic system with an open, pluralistic society minority–majority relations are part of the daily liberal and free interplay of forces. The change between minority and majority is always possible. A relation under crisis is never necessarily a longlasting or a permanent one. However, in an ethnically determinated system the tensed minority–majority relation may be very longlasting. The problems will last as long as the majority is defining itself and the state via ethnicity. Relations are rigid. There are only two ways out: either a separation or secession of the minority by taking the right of self-determination, which can lead to the creation of separate state. Usually this target can only be reached by a violent change of the majority–minority relation, or ethnic pluralism, of the society and state. The state is seen as a political one and not as an ethnic one. All citizens are equal.

Ethnic nationalism creates permanent new groups of minorities by excluding ethnically different groups either already living on a territory or coming in due to migration. Exclusion combined with specific measures of suppression in conflict with minorities' loyality or identity, or the combination of existing economic, social, and cultural disadvantages represent the potential for crisis. Nevertheless, it is the subjectivism of the majority that is the root for the crisis. The subjectivism of the majority makes use of history and of mythology for its political program. Nationalism becomes justification for everything.

Most minorities have so-called mother nations. Majorities are often afraid of minorities because the status of minority can vary due to changes in borders. Minorities could be made instruments of their mother nations and bring pressure on the nation where they are minority.

As long as ethnic nationalism exists, and in some cases is even part of the constitution, the potential for conflict and crisis will not decrease but increase. Protection of minorities will have no positive future. Escalation of conflict is inevitable, and ethnic radicalism on the one hand and ethnic cleansing on the other may not be mutually exclusive, but rather will provide the conditions for each other.

III. ISLAM, MINORITIES, AND THE CONCEPT OF NATION—A PERMANENT CONTRADICTION?

Minority issues in the Middle East can be understood only by explaining the basic differences between Islam and the Western world. The search for a new world order is not a new phenomenon. Both the Western world and the Islamic community have been trying to implement their world order for centuries.[4] The basic problem in connection with the ideological differences is a multilayered and complex situation. It is characterized first by the search of a new world order by modern cultural movements (Pax Americana versus Pax Islamica) and second by the simultaniousity of globalization from a structural point of view and cultural fragmentation from a cultural position.

What we call today Pax Americana (synonymous with the Western world) has its roots in European history. The Westphalian Peace Agreement (1648) marked the end of the then-dissolving sacred order. It was the beginning of a modern, secular, and international system of nation-states. The cultural framework for this development was provided by the modern age.[5] The divine dominated order lost its magic touch. The Ages of Reformation and of Enlightment and the French Revolution are cornerstones in the development of Western society. Events still have a strong impact on the Western understanding of basic elements of, for example, the civil society, democracy, human rights, the duties and rights of citizens, the nation-building process, and the relation between state and religion.

Nizam Islami (revival of Islam) does not accept history, existing political structures, or institutions. If correspondence with Islam is missing and a deviation from the Koran exists, it can not be accepted. Nizam Islami requires Islamic legitimacy, the *umma* (community of people in faith) to underpin this legitimacy, and political power to keep the Nizam Islami. In a first step the Nizam Islami has to be established on a national level.[6] After a certain period of time the tool of globalization will be used to make the ideas and ideology applicable on the world level.

Nizam Islami—although a very vague concept—is seen by many political Islamists as a means to solve political, economic, and social problems that evidently exist in the Muslim countries. Religious aspects are not the driving force for establishing Nizam Islami. Nizam Islami is often assessed as an answer to a crisis of meaning in the Islamic system itself. It is seen as the answer of a preindustrial culture in a rational, secular, technological, and scientific age (Tibi 1992: 86).

Dis-orientation and a structural and a meanings crisis are often seen as results of clashes with Western civilization and as the fueling ingredients for establishing Nizam Islami. Religious values are reinterpreted to a political doctrine to solve a multidimensional intrasystem crisis caused by internal and external factors. The target is to establish an Islamic system on the national and international level instead of the refused secular one.

Which are the significant differences between the two cultural movements? Three issues are chosen to demonstrate the irreconcilability. All of them are non-solvable components of each system.

First, the principle of subjectivity is compared with one of collectivity. The principle of subjectivity, targeted at the individual who is self-responsible, is closely connected with individual human rights and is in sharp contrast to one of collectivity. Collectivity is represented by the umma. In this approach the individual stands below the community.

Second, the concepts of nation-state and of umma are considered. The nation-state is a key product of European history. After the French Revolution the sovereignty of the people became the legitimate basis of a state. The modern international system corresponded more or less with the society of the European states. Sovereign dynastic states became national states (Tibi 1992:71). Islamic countries have had the impression that they have been forced to use the nation-state concept through colonialization. The Muslim world was not a closed area any more, although Muslims of today see themselves as an exclusive part of the world. The concept of the nation-state was a twofold innovation for the Muslim countries. First of all, the concept is based on inner sovereignty (citizenship, national identity, loyalty). The second part is the existence of external sovereignty (mutual acceptance of territorial integrity and noninterference in the domestic affairs of other states). Tribal structures stood in sharp opposition to the nation-state. Those structures have not been overcome so far, not even by the umma concept. The clan spirit has been modernized but not substituted by the nation-state. The decay of the Osman Empire is considered as the end of a sacred order. After 1924 (end of the Caliphate) the Arab countries tried to implement the nation-states idea to their countries. What they had in their minds was not a region of artificial Arab countries, but one of a big Arab nation within the existing international system of nations. It is the idea of pan-Arabism, or of a "universal Caliphate." The term nation became a new element. The restriction of the concept of nation to the Arab countries was in sharp contrast to the universalism of Islam. After the Six Days War in 1967 the secular pan-Arab nationalism was substituted by political Islam and the concept of a worldwide community of Muslims called umma (Faksh 1994:184). The secular concept did not bring the expected success and was assessed as not adequate. The umma concept targeting a world-embracing community does not take the classical concept of nation into account.

Universality versus universalism is a third distinguishing facet between the two societal approaches. Universality is primarily a Western philosophical principle that accepts variety in society. Several societal concepts are possible and acceptable. Universalism is the leading principle in Islam (as well as other belief systems[7]). Only one model for the whole society is accepted. It is generally valid and refers to the whole of mankind.

Globalization is one of the buzzwords at the end of the twentieth century. It refers to unification of processes and structures (Rosenau 1990:247). Although we do not have a common definition of globalization, we have something like an unspoken image of features for this phenomenon. It refers to certain conditions, to an end state, and to a process covering a large part of the world. Fundamentals of structure are increasingly existing on one common worldwide level. On the other hand we face an obviously contrasting trend, the one of cultural fragmentation. People who are structurally quite close together diverge in their cultural perception drastically. Cultural fragmentation creates the need for common values, guidelines, and rules. They are the cement for a working international system. A common agreement to settle conflicts must exist. Culture can be such a cement. We know that cultures are local phenomena. A universal culture does not exist. World orders like Pax Americana or Pax Islamica (the Islam-dominated and -guided way to organize society) are only two of several possible options for a restricted area. They do not represent the philosopher's stone. On the other hand it is obvious that fundamentalism and repolitization are two key consequences of these overlayering and controversial developments (Tibi 1992: 20–23).

The era of modernization—a process of adaption which is still going on for Islamic countries—brought many Muslim leaders to fight to get back to the roots, back to the basic values of Islam. The influence of the Western world has to be controlled. This is a kind of policy of containment in a new sense of the word. Western influence stands in close connection with technological, military, economic, and scientific superiority. In the Western world a separation of state and religion (secularism [8]) was necessary to solve the question of modernization. Islam did not bring enlightenment or revolution. In the Western world absolutist governments were substituted by parliamentary ones. In Islam the parliamentary principle is against the separation of religion and state. Moreover Arab countries picked out values of modernization fitting into their pattern to maintain power, for example, modern weapons, surveillance technology, and consumer goods. It was a process of selective adaption, or of sorting out. The system of values and the culture of modernization, which are key elements of progress, were not adopted, not even accepted. Only a very small part of the Arab population could benefit from this way of modernization. A large number became poorer than they were before and felt inferior in many ways. Modernization and Westernization are still considered to be moral decay.

The clash of two societal organization approaches generally provides a potential hotbed for crisis. The specific framework for the different perceptions of how to handle the minority issue in society represents the potential for crisis per se. There is a complex network of societal issues determining the status of minorities in a society. Religion and ideology play important roles in this determination process. Values, in a very general understanding, determine the position of minorities as such. The perception of what is society (an individual or a community) determines who is perceived as minority. States/nations on a crossroad of cultural areas and religious communities are in a very specific situation simply because they are influenced by both sides.

Those incompatibilities between the two approaches cause special problems for a state that is for several reasons in an interface position. Turkey and the Kurdish question are a good example of the problems arising from the different understanding of minorities and all the related consequences.

IV. TURKEY AND THE UNSOLVED KURDISH QUESTION

The following case study will first give an overview on the historical development of the understanding of the term minority in Turkey. Second, an effort to define the Kurdish tribes as minority will be undertaken. The third part will analyze the origins of the Kurdish question, the relevant international agreements after World War I, and the different obstacles for a rapprochment between Turkey and the Kurdish tribes as well as spillover effects. Finally, an outline for a framework of conditions leading toward a possible solution will be presented.

A. The Road from the Osman Empire to Turkey and the Understanding of Minorities

Turkey is the successor state of the Osman Empire. The history of both is inseparable. The influence concerning the understanding of minorities is still present in contemporary Turkey. For the reason, one has to analyze the situation during the Osman Empire, where a fixed order called *millet* came into being. Millet refers to church and other religious groups. Moreover the term and the concept stand for people and nation as well. In the terminology of the Osman Empire every religion created a people. When one referred to minorities, one applied this term only to non-Muslim minorities, especially to Armenians, Greeks, and Jews. Muslim minorities did not exist because this would have been a self-contradiction.

At the end of the nineteenth century during the *Tanzimat*[9] period the structures of the Osman Empire became loose. After World War I the empire was dissolved. Instead of the multiethnic empire, nation-states came into being. Turkey is one of those new nation-states. It is a fact that none of the newly established nation-states were based on only one ethnicity or one religion. Two key antagonistic forces can be made out. First, a modern national state required the equal treatment of all its citizens. Second, the Islamic order, which is seen as integral part of Islam, assumes a hierarchic order of Muslims, who are *the* people in the state, and members of other religious communities (*Dhimmi*, or persons under protection).

Turkey lies on the crossroad of cultures and religions. It is divided between two value systems. For this reason Turkish society shows elements of both sides. Moreover history and negative political experience have led the country into a half-and-half situation. It is neither Western nor Islamic. Turkey is both at the same time. Those facts make the position of minorities in the Western understanding extremely difficult.

How did the Turkish nation come into being? Intellectual elites, military officers, and leading bureaucrats played a crucial role in replacing the Osman structures and rules by a new leading class with new principles. Their key target was the creation of a Turkish national identity. During the Osman Empire, religion provided the key definitional ground. After the decay of the empire Kemal Atatürk[10] and his followers intended a new approach. They promoted a Turkish national identity based on the features of a civic nation. On the other hand, the ethnic center of the Turkish nation was intended to be based on Turkish ethnicity with the Turkish language and culture. Atatürk created the state on the basis of the multiethnic Osman Empire. The Lausanne Treaty[11] and the creation of a single ethnic Turkey were the basis for neglecting other ethnicities like the Kurdish tribes.[12] The concept of Turkey is an artificial one and is rooted in the Kemalist nationalism. Nationalism is one of the six pillars of the Kemalist ideology.[13]

Where do we find the origins of Turkish nationalism or Kemalist nationalism? During the Osman Empire nationality was determined on the basis of one's membership in a religious community. In fact, this is similar to Western Europe in the sixteenth century. Then religion constituted the basis for one's individual identity. While the European powers referred to Turkey and the Turks, the Turks considered themselves as Muslims. Muslims belonged to the umma, the community of Islam. They were subjects of the Sultan and the Caliph. Religious affiliation dominated the thinking of Muslims. It was far more crucial than ethnic or national identity. Basically, the Turks were an ethnic group, easily distinguished from outside observers. They had their own language, culture, tradition, and history. The roots of the Turkish nationalism as a politically powerful concept are seen in the reformist movements of the late nineteenth century. Those movements tried to establish a nationalism going beyond religious and ethnic differences in the Empire. This form of nationalism was seen as a cement to keep the Empire together, despite the disintegrating power of nationalist uprisings in the Balkans and the efforts by the then major powers in Europe.

The understanding of Turkish nationalism in the period from 1919–1923 targeted not the modern connotation but referred to the Nation of Islam, the reestablishment of the Osman Empire and the regaining of Osman territories.

Atatürk slowly pushed the religious component out of the public discussion and made it a private issue. The blend of religion and politics did not prove as successful. Turkishness replaced the Osman identity. The terms Turk and Turkishness had a new meaning, a functional concept, a basis for a new national identity. Turkishness became a kind a transformational vehicle to bring an old society based on Osman rules to a new and modern one, the Turkish society. Atatürk's key assumption was that within the Turkish borders only one nation, the Turkish one, exists. The persecution and suppression of members of the Kurdish tribes according to the Lausanne Treaty was ex post facto justified by Kemalism and the understanding of the terms nation, state, and minority.

The treatment of the Kurdish question in Turkey presupposes a discussion on the position of ethnic minorities in the Turkish Constitution and the legal system. It is necessary to understand the irresolvable connection between minority issues and the question of the ideological structure of the Turkish constitutional and legal system. Two key premises are fixed in the Constitution. First, Turkish citizenship automatically implies one is a Turk. Second, the state of Turkey is indivisible in its territory and people. The language is Turkish. People, language, and territory build a kind of troika of indivisibility. These are the guiding principles for any domestic assessment of the relation between Turkey and its Kurdish tribes.

B. The Kurds—a Minority?[14]

Since the second Gulf War the Kurds have become known to world. The Kurds are one of the oldest people in the world. For thousands of years they have been to many more of a legend than a reality. For decades they have been neglected and denied. Who are the Kurds? The answer is quite difficult and the picture is a complex one, simply because Kurds is a meta term for a number of non-Arab tribes living in an area stretching from the eastern Taurus region to the Zagros

Mountains in the west to the borders of Iran and the former USSR in the east. In the north it is bounded by the Pontic Mountains and in the south the borderlines are built by the Turkish–Syrian and the Turkish–Iraqi frontiers. This area is called Kurdistan. The term refers to a geographical, historical, and cultural area. It is not the name of an internationally recognized state.

The tribes have some common general features like their century-lasting will to become independent (self-determination and international recognition) from the states on whose territory they are living. The way to reach those goals, however, is still not agreed upon among them. Moreover, they show a high level of similarity in their cultural and traditional heritage. This may seem quite vague. Trying to make out features of those Kurdish tribes according to the contents of the different definitions of the key terms of this paper (nation, state, and minority), one faces a lot of difficulties and a heterogeneity one may not assume at first glance. Going according to the features of a state in international law, at least four of them can be made out (Malanczuk 1997:75): a defined territory, a permanent population, a government, the capacity to enter into relations with other states.

The control of a defined territory is seen as the core feature of a state. When one refers to Kurdistan one does not refer to a state in the sense of international law but to a quite torn area of living. "Kurdistan? Which one do you mean?" is a provoking but justified question. The Kurdish tribes do not live in a connected and homogeneous area. The area covers parts of Turkey, Iraq, Iran, Syria, and Armenia. We can say that, what is called Kurdistan, does not fulfill the criterion of the concept of territory. It is not a geographical area separated by borderlines from other areas and united under a common legal system.

Referring to the feature of a permanent population one has to admit that one does not have exact numbers on the Kurdish population. During censuses Kurds have often been put under pressure not the see themselves as Kurds but as citizens of the countries whose territory on which they are living. Although the term Kurd was indicated in the census in a very narrow interpretation. In consequence many Kurds did not regard themselves as part of this interpretation.

According to assessments we have the following distribution of Kurds: in Iraq, especially in northern Iraq live roughly 3 million; in Iran, primarily in western Iran, 5 to 6 million; in Syria 0.7 to 1 million, in the former Soviet Union approximately 200,000; and in Turkey, especially in the southeast and east of the country, live 10 to 12 million. In total a number of approximately 20 to 25 million members of Kurdish tribes seems to be a realistic assumption.

The two other features of a state—a permanent government and the capacity to enter into relations with other states—are also not fulfilled. Kurds founded a parliament some years ago, but a government accepted by all tribes does not exist. The last feature can also be assessed as missing.

Therefore it is clear that the Kurdish tribes are still far away from their common goal—to have their own state. Making out other possibly common features of the Kurdish tribes, like a common language or a common religion, we find the following. There is no common language in the sense of a standard language (high Kurdish), but rather a number of dialects exist. This development is due the facts that there has never been a Kurdish state promoting the development of common language or Kurd-based education and media. And in most countries where Kurds live, the use of their language has been prohibited. From an linguistic point of view the Kurdish dialects belong to the Farsi language group.[15] Those dialects differ markedly in pronunciation and in words. Communication between the Kurdish tribes is sometimes quite difficult. The language could not perform an integrating force for the Kurdish tribes. Moreover there are only a few instances of Kurdish written publications; rather, there is an oral tradition of the language. In most cases the written language is the language of the state on whose territory the tribes live. A rigid prohibition of using the dialects, especially in Turkey, Iran, and Iraq after World War I, had a negative and disintegrating effect. In consequence a north–south differentiation in cultural and social development arose. *Sorani*, the key dialect spoken in the southern regions, became the language for publications and indicates a higher social status. *Kurmançi*, the second key dialect, which has been used in the northern regions, points toward a lower social position. The language question is a very important one. The Kurds living in Turkey, in particular, have been confronted several times in the past decades with the question of language.

Religion, which can be an integrating force, also points more to Kurdish heterogeneity. Most of the Kurds are orthodox *Sunnits* in the so-called *Schaf'i* tradition.[16] Sunnits combine the Koran with the Sunna, which are guidelines and traditions given by Muhammed. Sunnits stand in contrast to the *Schiits*, who accept only the Koran as the single source of truth. Moreover the two big groups differ in the question of the legitimacy of religious leaders. Being Sunnits, the Kurdish tribes are put in opposition to their hosts and neighbors. However, Turks are Sunnits who ally with the *Hanafi* law school.[17] Apart from the Islamic groups, we also find Kurds who are followers of Christianity and of Judaism. The heterogeneity in religion has brought about a number of problems for the Kurdish tribes and their members. Some of them became a minority in a manifold senses of the word.

As already mentioned, one can not speak of the Kurds simply, because the name comprises a number of tribes or clans having a family tradition lasting several centuries. Clans determined the societal structure of the Kurdish tribes. Families, as a cell of the clan, are the center of interest. When Kurds talk of families they have a different approach in comparison to the understanding of the Western world. Usually they refer to an extended family covering several generations. The interests of clans go beyond individual interests. Sometimes they are in conflict. We also find conflicts of interests between the extended families. Clanism has been the key obstacle for creating an autonomous Kurdish state.

Summing up one has to state that there are a number of non-Arabic tribes living in the area delineated who are called Kurds. The members of these tribes have a multiple identity. Which one is chosen depends on the situation a Kurd is in. Thus a Sunni Kurd may be a Kurd, a Sunni Muslim, a citizen of Turkey, and at the same time a member of a certain social class, a tribe, or a village. The position depends on the specific context. The number of so-called Kurds is vague. Censuses does not provide the necessary information.[18] The clans as organizational units do not fulfill the features of a state in a legal understanding. So far they have not been able or allowed to create a common language. Religious heterogeneity is another splitting power. The clan's interests go beyond those of individual interests and the interests of other clans. There is a very strong will to become independent from the states on whose territory they are living. (At the least they want an integration within the state with guaranteed minority rights in the Western understanding.) And there is a cultural and traditional heritage providing a connection among the tribes.

Even though one faces some vagueness in definition, one can say that the Kurdish tribes are an ethnic minority, a religious minority, and a cultural minority. They are a group standing in opposition politically to a majority and a group in society feeling theirs is a disadvantaged position. Although they have a lot of definitional and feature deficits, they are doubtlessly a minority.

V.   KURDS IN TURKEY: A NATION VERSUS ITS BIGGEST MINORITY?

A.   The Origins of the Turkish Kurdish Question

The roots of the conflict between the Kurdish tribes and Turkey go back to the eighteenth century. They are connected with territorial shifts, border redrawings, and the solution of the ''Eastern question.''

The Eastern question dominated the late eighteenth and the nineteenth century. It involved the competition between the then great powers (especially Britain and Russia) for influence over the Osman Empire. After having suffered several military defeats and facing increasing internal problems in the Balkans, Russia had to take actions to solve these difficulties. In the aftermath, Russia constantly increased its political influence by expanding its territory to the southern regions at the expense of the British Empire. Moreover Russia gained significant power in the Balkans and even within the Osman Empire. Britain, on the other hand, performed a policy aimed at maintaining the Empire and balancing the Russian influence in the Near East.

By the end of the nineteenth century other great powers started to become interested in the Middle East territories of the Osman Empire. Germany became the third player. The Ottomans made use of this power and influence struggle and exploited the three countries by playing them against one other. This strategy supported the prolongation of the existence of the Osman Empire.

The decision of the Osman Empire to enter World War I on the side of the Triple Alliance altered the situation dramatically. Britain, France, and Russia decided to do everything they could to get rid of the Empire. Several agreements between 1915 and 1917 were clearly targeted at the partitioning of the Osman Empire. The Mudros Armistice in 1918 was the opener for the division. The Sèvres Treaty signed in 1920 between the Empire and the allies formally fixed the division of the Empire. The Eastern question was seen as settled.

The role of the Kurdish tribes in this power struggle was as follows. The Kurds had been part of the Osman Empire for centuries. Their area of living was and still is on a strategic crossroads between several regional powers. Border disputes between the Osman Empire and the Persian Empire brought the tribes to the center of regional politics. The Osman Empire often made use of the Kurdish tribes for border security purposes. The leaders of the tribes were aware of their importance, but they were unable to consolidate their power. The dynasties, looking toward their own advantages, were involved in local disputes. Decentralization of power made it impossible to speak with one voice on the Kurdish matter. The people has been split into several less powerful clans, which have been undergoing their own power politics. A common target was missing. This played directly into the hands of Turkey and the international community. It was used as excuse to not take any steps to solve the Kurdish question.

B.   Relevant International Agreements

In the following, international and national agreements and treaties concerning Turkish–Kurdish relations will be analyzed. The aim is to figure out the legal basis for the current situation. Basically there are two relevant agreements referring to the Kurdish tribes: the Sèvres Treaty (1920) and the Lausanne Treaty (1923).

The Sèvres Treaty is still seen as the key document for the integration or nonintegration of the Kurdish tribes in the states on whose territory they have been living, their opportunities for political activities, and the autonomy with respect to the foundation of their own state. The Sèvres Treaty was never accepted by the Turkish national independence movement headed by Kemal Atatürk. It was seen as a means by the allies to destroy the Osman Empire and to keep the successor countries as small as possible. Nevertheless many leaders of Kurdish tribes still consider this agreement to be a basis for a unique opportunity for them to found their own independent state. The Sèvres Treaty specified the preconditions for the foundation of two independent states, namely Armenia and Kurdistan. Within one year the Kurds had to claim autonomy. This wish had to be expressed explicitly. Moreover the tribes had to prove they were able to become autonomous. The preconditions for an autonomous state can be summed up by the readiness and the capability to form a new and independent state. This double condition could not be fulfilled by the tribes. The clan system was against the new state from the very beginning. Narrowmindedness made autonomy and an independent state impossible. A complex web of rivalries between the tribe leaders prevented the Kurds as a whole from gaining sufficient support to select a modern leadership and to organize a nationalist struggle with the target of becoming independent and to have their own state. Actually nothing has changed to the present day.

Moreover, the original separation of Kurdish tribes in Osman and Persian camps made the achievement of unity difficult. The further division in separate states was another imposition making the prospects for Kurdish unity more and more unlikely.

The Lausanne Treaty was the result of a restrengthening of the Osman Empire in terms of the newly created Turkey. Ataturk, the new Turkish leader, bargained a new treaty with Great Britain and France. This agreement brought an appreciation of the new state and its leader. For the Kurdish tribes the situation changed dramatically. The former Arab provinces were separated from the modern Turkey. They became mandates of the League of Nations. Later they were transformed into independent states. The Kurdish parts were left to Syria, Iran, Iraq, Turkey, and the Soviet Union. The reshaping of the areas, the redrawing of borders, and the strong personality of Ataturk gave the Kurdish question new dimensions and a totally different dynamic development. The Kurdish question became more and more complex by its trans-state nature.

The Treaty of Lausanne included the following provisions concerning minorities in general and the Kurdish tribes in particular. First, the Turkish government committed to keep up the life and the freedom of the people in Turkey, without any regard to birth, nationality, or religion. Second, it ensured the right of religious freedom and special protection of non-Muslim minorities. The Treaty of Lausanne extrapolates the Osman understanding of minorities. It refers only to religious minorities. Ethnic minorities are not covered by the treaty. The consequences of the treaty were as follows. The Kurds have been counted as Muslims and therefore have not been protected in a special way. Officially Turkey has a basis for refusing the acknowledgment of the Kurds' existence. The treaty did not provide an autonomous region for the Kurdish tribes on Turkish territory.

The agreement is still seen as the starting point for a decades-lasting diaspora in at least five countries. On the other hand it is the beginning of a desperate Kurdish nationalistic movement starting in the 1930s and lasting until the present day. Moreover, the treaty was the kickoff for a longlasting and intense assimilation campaign by Turkish governments as well as a parallel ongoing Kurdish refusal to assimilate.

C. Obstacles for a Rapprochment Between the Kurdish Tribes and the Turkish State

Apart from legal aspects there are at least three areas of problems making a coming together of the Kurdish tribes and the Turkish states difficult, if not impossible.

First, the economic situation in eastern and southeastern Anatolia is, compared to other parts of Turkey, very poor. Second, the years-lasting expulsions from eastern and southeastern Anatolia by the Turkish government and the Turkish army have led to a sustainable domestic migration. Third, the war with the Kurdish Workers Party (PKK) led to far-reaching destruction in the area. These issues are strongly interconnected, which makes an assessment of a future development more difficult.

The economic situation in the region is one of the worst in Turkey. The Kurdish tribes have been the key settlers there for centuries. The area is characterized by agricultural dominance in the economic structure. This, combined with very dry soil and water problems, has created a situation that requires very high investment by the state. Anatolia has been a traditional agricultural area for centuries. The feudal system (5% of the families own 65% of the area, and 70% of the population has to live off 10% of the land), which has grown over the past centuries, caused a sorting-out process. Many people had to leave the area for survival. Lack of capital to improve the agricultural performance was an additional factor. Few educational opportunities forced people who wanted to achieve high-level jobs to go to cities in the west. Expulsion due to the Great Anatolia Project (GAP), which started in the late 1980s and will be completed in the early 2000s, led to a high level of domestic migration. One of the world's biggest irrigation projects (covering the Eurphrates and Tigris) forced many Kurds to leave because their villages were flooded during the construction of dams. Resettlement activities already launched by the Turkish government have not been very successful. The decades-lasting economic disinterest and negligence by the Turkish government has brought sustainable damage which will be very difficult to repair. Anatolia, the former core part of the country, has become the poorhouse and developed into one of the most crucial areas.

The fifteen-year war between the PKK and the Turkish army was for many Kurds the trigger to leave the area for the cities in the west of Turkey. This led to a regional shift of the problem. Today Istanbul is one of the cities with a high proportion of Kurds potentially causing social and economic crises. The role of the PKK in the civil war against the Turkish government was a result of the repressive policy of Turkey after the military coups in the 1960s, 1970s, and 1980s. After the military coup in 1971 the Kurdish tribes started to revolt against the heavy suppression. One of the revolting groups led to the foundation of the PKK. It was founded in 1978 by Abdullah Öcalan. The key goal of this movement is to free the Kurdish people from suppression and to lead it to autonomy and to a Kurdish state. The PKK was the first movement to say explicitly that violence and the use of weapons against the Turkish state (government and army) are justified means to reach the goal of an independent state.

The situation in southern and southeastern Anatolia complicated by the PKK and its followers led to the declaration of martial law in several provinces and to the establishment of a state-sponsored village-guard system. Kurds were paid by the Turkish government to protect their villages against PKK-led raids. This strategy splitted the Kurdish tribes and provoked a high level of distrust. Members of the village-guard system were seen as traitors. Although the village-guard system was declared to be finished during 1997 and the state of emergency has been lifted in some provinces, the situation is still very tense. The PKK remains synonymous for Kurds, terrorists, and the key enemy of the unified Turkish state. This led to a number of misperceptions and damaged the Kurdish matter.

D. Spillover Effects to Other Political Realms—the Internationalization of the Kurdish Question

As already mentioned the Kurdish question is a complex and multidimensional one, going beyond the country's borders. Until 1991 Turkey and the world could ignore the international dimension of the Kurdish question. The exodus of refugees in the wake of the Gulf War in 1991 forced the world to pay attention to the Kurds. Turkey as well had to deal with a people which it had ignored for decades. Since then, the unsolved Kurdish question has complicated Turkey's relations with Syria, Iran, and Iraq.[19] The decay of the Soviet Union brought another aspect to the question. International society became very interested in the human rights situation as the number of clashes between the PKK and Turkish security forces increased constantly.

On the other hand Turkey has tried several times to play intermediary in the conflict between several Kurdish tribes in northern Iraq. The peace haven (''Northern Watch'') installed after the Gulf War to protect Kurdish refugees proved to be a flop. The Kurds were not in a position to keep up a quasiautonomous zone. Fights within the Kurdish clans, especially between Barzani and Talabani,[20] destroyed the dream of Kurdistan. The disaccord and division between the leaders of the two biggest Kurdish tribes and parties can be seen as an example of the still-dominant thinking in terms of clans. The behavior was seen as proof that the tribes are not in a position for self-determination or their own Kurdish state. Several efforts during the 1990s failed to bring the Kurdish tribes together. Neither in Iraq nor in Turkey are the prospects positive. The clans still dominate everything. In the past five years they have been used for the individual purposes of countries on whose territory they are living. Alliances have been coming and going. But the Kurdish question is still on the diplomatic table—unsolved.

The member states of the European Union especially had problems understanding the Turkish position, the regular interventions by Turkish security forces, and the very negative human rights record connected to the Kurds. The unsolved Kurd question has become one of the key problems for Turkey's joining the European Union. The agreement on the customs union has been delayed several times. The approval of the agreement by the European Parliament in December 1995 was given only by setting preconditions. One of them is the settlement of the Kurdish question. In the past five years, critiques by the European Parliament increased and led to a strong polarization between Turkey and the European Union. However, Turkey was still grounded in candidate status as of December 1999. The degree of participation of Turkey in the European integration process is still open—as open as the solution of the Kurdish question is.

VI. SETTLING A DISPUTE AND SOLVING THE CONFLICT: A TARGET FOR THE RELATION BETWEEN TURKEY AND THE KURDISH TRIBES

At the beginning of this chapter we had the following guiding questions. Is the existence of nations and minorities on the same territory a potential for crisis? If yes, can both concepts nevertheless exist together? The answers to be given have to be split into general ones and in those concerning the Kurdish question specifically.

Generally, one has to admit that the two concepts stand in a multidimensional contradiction. This fact provides a fertile ground for the arising of several potentials for crisis. In many cases it is difficult or even impossible to say what is cause and what is effect. The first step toward the outbreak of a crisis might be a very small one. When one combines the basic situation of contradiction and tension with the meta level of religion or of ideology, the spin toward an outbreak of a crisis or the realization of the potential for crisis might even be increased.

Moreover, it is clear that legal provisions are only a framework, not a solution in themselves. An accorded effort from society covering legal aspects and political steps in the broad sense of the word is required. In any case, all parties in dispute have to be flexible and bear a clear and accorded target in mind. This is a very first step toward a sustainable solution, but only the very first step and, again, not a solution in itself.

Concerning the specifics of the Kurdish question and possible solutions, one has to become aware which aspects are involved. The official Turkish perception is that a minority problem does not exist, but a social and terror problem has to be faced. The PKK is seen as synonymous for Kurds and for terror. This problem has been fought by military means. So far those means have turned out to be unsuccessful. Slowly, Turkish politicians have promoted a political solution and a solution to the big social problems. But there is still a quite antagonistic situation between government and army, between political solution and military solution, as well as between official recognition (and all its consequences like becoming a more privileged group than the Turks themselves) and denial of societal reality.[21] The trans-state dimension of the Kurdish reality makes a settlement and solution even more complicated.

After drawing a very complex picture of the Kurdish reality, one has to ask whether the Kurdish question in Turkey, but not only in this country, can be solved in a satisfying and sustainable way. The answer is, ''Yes—but.'' As it is a complex, trans-state issue covering several areas of society the solution cannot be a simple and fast one. Moreover it requires a dramatic turnaround of old points of view. What is required is a multilevel solution approach, whereas the start has to come at all three levels at almost the same time.

First, several premises on the international level have to be fulfilled. A clear strategy, instead of jockey politics by the European Union as well as by the United States, is required. A clear policy does not mean the use of pressure politics toward Turkey. In the past this way turned out to be very counterproductive and promoted the Sèvres syndrome.[22] A clear strategy of the international community implies that management by fire-brigade politics has to be substituted by a continuous strategy. Moreover a clear stressing of democratic standards and human rights is necessary. In case of nonaction, appropriate and predefined sanctions have to be applied.

Second, premises on the national level have to be taken into account and fulfilled. If Turkey wants to be part of the Western community, it has to adapt its understanding of minorities to Western standards. This would require a distance from the Treaty of Lausanne and a redefinition of the term minority, that is, in a Western understanding and interpretation. Moreover an inclusion of moderate Kurdish leaders in the political process is absolutely necessary. Additionally, the official Turkey has to step down from criminalizing people intervening for the Kurds. Moreover it has to stop forcing measures in southern and southeastern Anatolia. Finally, a thoroughly prepared dialogue could be the initial step for a resolution process.

Third, a number of premises on the level of the tribes have to be fulfilled.

The tribes also have to have a clear strategy—whether they want an autonomous state, a federal solution, or the provision of special rights. It is still unclear what the Kurdish tribes really want and who their negotiation head is on the bilateral and the international stage. With their vague claims and their jealousies about who is entering into talks, they are not taken as a serious negotiation partner. This requires the formulation of a common political and societal target, the harmonization of the interests of the different clans, and the fixing of the level of integration in the society. Moreover the tribes have to keep a distance from terrorist groups like the PKK and others.

The Kurdish question, perhaps more than any other problem, has damaged Turkey's international reputation sustainably. The role of Kurdish dissidents in Turkey as well as abroad led to a continuous preoccupation of political decision-makers and to a resource-consumption effect going far beyond politics. The persecution of Kurdish political parties has cut down responsible political activities and undermined the formulation of a political middle ground. Moderates have been kicked out of the circle of political decision makers; consequently moderate solutions are still missing.

It is obvious that all parties to the dispute still have big deficiencies in questions concerning the acceptance and integration of minorities. The complexity of the problem makes a solution even more difficult and challenging. A solution is unlikely to be achieved soon, but it seems to be achievable.

ENDNOTES

1. The phrase ''potential for crisis'' refers to the fact that there is a constellation of facts that might lead to the outbreak of a crisis, i.e., a crucial phase in the development of society. The outbreak is possible, but it is *not* a must.
2. The range of rights of minorities is one of the most discussed issues. It is still not agreed whether it covers, apart from cultural rights (like language, performance of tradition and culture, religion), self-determination also. This would mean that a minority can obtain its own state or join another state (e.g., its mother nation).
3. Although several international agreements have been signed (e.g., UN Declaration on the Rights of Persons Belonging to National or Ethnic, Religious and Linguistic Minorities in 1992), institutions for minority protection have been created (e.g., High Commissioner for National Minorities in the CSCE), and initiatives have been launched (e.g., the European Charter for Regional or Minority Languages in 1992 and the Council of Europe Framework Convention for the Protection of National Minorities in 1995), there are still a number of ''white spots on the minority protection map.''
4. When we speak of world order, we refer not only to politics but to a network of politics, economics, culture, and religion.
5. According to Habermas, the ''Modern European Age'' is a combination of culture,

technology, and science in a very specific way. It is characterized by the following features: individualism, right for critique, autonomy in action, and reflexive faith (man is the oneself knowing idea).

6. This sounds like a contradiction as nations in the Western sense of the term do not exist in the Islamic system.

7. Communism has the same basic assumption of a universality principle.

8. Literature does not provide a single definition of the term *secularism* or the French rooted pendant *laicism*. We go according to the most used understanding of a strict separation between state and religion. Religion is seen as a private matter and does not affect the state's affairs like the legal structure and education.

9. The Tanzimat Movement was a political movement at the end of the nineteenth century. It promoted modernization and reforms in the Osman Empire.

10. Kemal Atatürk is the founder of Turkey.

11. The Lausanne Treaty (1923) is the basis for the foundation of modern Turkey. It substituted the Sèvres Treaty (1920) which marked the end of the Osman Empire.

12. According to several reports, close to 50 identifiable ethnic groups live in Turkey.

13. The six principles or pillars are:
    Laicism/secularism (*laiklik*): strict separation between state and religion.
    Republicanism (*çumhuriyetçilik*): Turkey is a republic according to the Western understanding.
    Populism (*halkçilik*): politics has to be done according to the wishes of the people.
    Nationalism (*milliyetçilik*): there is only one indivisible Turkish nation.
    Etatism (*devletçilik*): economy is state-controlled.
    Reformism/revolutionism (*inkilapçilik*): progress in society is continuously sought.

14. This part is mainly based on Smutek-Riemer, A. (1996). *Die Kurden: Eine nicht ausreichend integrierte Minderheit als regionales Krisenpotential? Eine ethnische Genese der kurdischen Stämme im Irak, Iran und in der Türkei und ein Versuch einer Krisenpotentialabschätzung für die Türkei*. Frankfurt: Peter Lang, and Riemer, A. (1998). *Die Türkei an der Schwelle zum 21. Jahrhundert: Die Schöne oder der Kranke Mann am Bosporus*. Frankfurt: Peter Lang.

15. The Farsi language group is also called Persian. The Turkish language belongs to the Altai languages (like Finnish or the Hungarian language). Similarities can be found in new words used in the Kurdish dialects. They have been taken from Turkish and Arabic and are called paronymous words. This development does not justify the assumption by Turkey to call Kurdish dialects a Turkish dialect. From an etymological point of view it is totally mistaken to say that Kurdish, which is accurately described as a number of dialects, is a Turkish dialect.

16. The *Schaf'i* tradition is one of the four accepted Islamic law schools.

17. The *Hanafi* law school is the more liberal of the four accepted law schools.

18. In many cases minority self-identification is not asked. This is done on purpose because the census is still seen as one important basis concerning ethnic issues. Turkey performed this way in its latest census from 1997.

19. The PKK has been several times the basic trigger for Turkish security forces to intervene in the area and to cross the border to Iraqi territory. The fights against

PKK have been costing Turkey roughly $7bn per year, which is a lot for a country with chronic economic problems. Moreover these crossover actions caused a lot of international critique.

20. Massud Barzani is the leader of the Kurdistan Democratic Party (KDP). Jallal Talabani heads the Patriotic Union of Kurdistan (PUK). Both party leaders have been changing alliances several times in the past years causing further misunderstanding of the Kurdish matter on the international level. Due to the tensions between PUK and KDP, the PKK has been able to extend its influence in northern Iraq over the past seven years.

21. The political Kurdish groups have become very frustrated in the past few years. Many of them have been banned from all political activities. The continuing frustration played more and more in the hands of the PKK and other radical groups.

22. Sèvres syndrome refers to developments in Turkey, arising especially since the spring of 1995, making the perception of Turkey as a loser on the international stage as was done by the Sèvres Treaty after World War I.

REFERENCES

Malanczuk, P. (1997). *Akehursd's Modern Introduction to International Law*, 7th rev. ed. New York: Routledge.

Rosenau, J. N. (1990). *Turbulence in World Politics: A Theory of Change and Continuity*. Princeton, NJ: Princeton University Press.

Tibi, B. (1992). *Die fundamentalistische Herausforderung der Islam und die Weltpolitik*. Munich: Beck.

16

Russian Nationalism and Nation-Building in the Russian Federation

Implications for Russian Foreign Policy in the Near Abroad

Susanne M. Birgerson
University of Illinois, Urbana, Illinois

Roger E. Kanet
University of Miami, Coral Gables, Florida

I. INTRODUCTION

In this chapter we propose to examine the ways in which the Russian regime and its domestic opposition perceive the former republics of the Soviet Union in the context of state- and nation-building in the Russian Federation. Increasingly the Russian Federation is taking a more assertive position toward the newly independent states (NIS), or ''near abroad,'' resulting in part from a growing Russian nationalism that stresses the importance of the former territories of the Soviet Union for Russia's national self-interests.

The principal arguments of the chapter include the following. First, the importance of the near abroad to Russia results from a growing Russian nationalism that perceives these territories as crucial to the well-being of the Russian nation because they are either ''Russian lands'' or land areas vital to Russian security. The continuing significance of the near abroad in the context of nation building in the Russian Federation results from Russia's imperial past and its former central position in the Soviet Union.

Second, the Russian minorities living in the near abroad are a key ingredient, not only in the redefinition of a Russian national identity, but in providing the justification for a continued Russian presence in the near abroad.

Third, despite the state-building efforts in the NIS, which their initiators expect to result in political systems independent from Russia, the latter still dominates the Central Eurasian region economically and militarily. Despite the formal dissolution of the Soviet Union and the creation of independent states in the former republics, many of the economic and security commitments that linked the former republics to the Russian center have endured. This has left Russia in a position of dominance not unlike the role the Russian Soviet Federated Socialist Republic (RSFSR) played in the former Soviet Union. Given this preponderance of power, Russia is likely to remain the dominant force in the region, at least in the near future, despite efforts of some of the NIS to diversify their economies by pursuing alternate sources of energy and raw materials and seeking new markets for their exports. In effect, the impulses that will shape the future of the region will flow from the Russian center to the near abroad, rather than the reverse.

This chapter is organized as follows. First, we will examine the debate over Russian nationalism, especially its foreign policy component, in order to illustrate the link between Russian nationalism and a growing involvement in the near abroad. As part of this discussion, we will outline the political and intellectual debate on Russia's role in the world, its national interests, and its foreign policy priorities. Second, we will survey the evolution of Russian foreign policy following the dissolution of the Soviet Union. We will focus on the early dissension and subsequent consensus over the importance of the near abroad for Russian national interests, as well as the increasing conservatism of the Foreign Ministry and the expanding number of individual and institutional actors that shape Russian foreign policy. Third, we will highlight the dominance of Russia vis-à-vis the NIS, to provide evidence of a continuing central role of Russia in post-Soviet trade and security regimes. Lastly, we will consider future trends in relations between Russia and the NIS, especially the future integration of the NIS into a common economic and security space.

II. RUSSIAN NATIONALISM AND THE FOREIGN POLICY DEBATE

The breakup of the Soviet Union resulted in the formation of fifteen separate states along the formerly internal political borders of the Soviet Union—borders that had little to do with boundaries between ethnic groups or with boundaries of historic political units. The rise of nationalism and related attempts to define national identity have been integral to the process of establishing statehood in the NIS. Nowhere has this process been more difficult than in Russia, the former center of the Soviet Union. The reason for this stems from the fact that the development of Russian nationalism coincided with, and was often equated with, the

Communist Revolution and the rise of the Soviet state. Today the people of the Russian Federation struggle to define Russia and a Russian identity apart from the old Tsarist and Soviet one. While there is no consensus on what the Russian national idea should include, there has been since 1993 or so, an emerging consensus regarding the importance to Russia of the territories of the former Soviet Union, or what the Russian press refers to as the "near abroad."

The breakup of the Soviet Union caused a crisis of identity concerning the meaning of being Russian. Key to Russian national identity has been the issue of territory.[1] Notions of which territories should be included in Russia range from all of the lands of the near abroad to just the Slavic lands (the Russian Federation, Ukraine, and Belarus) to only the territory of the former Russian RSFSR. Nationalism is not static; the way in which members of a national group perceive themselves and their nation's place in the world changes over time, particularly in the wake of a national disaster. Vladimir Shlapentokh has noted the transformation and re-evaluation of the Russian national idea following Russia's losses in the Crimean and Russo-Japanese Wars, both of which ushered in monumental reforms transforming the relationship between state and society.[2]

National self-identification involves, among other things, perceptions of a territorial homeland that may or may not correspond to political borders. Even where the sovereignty of states is formally recognized, more powerful states typically exert influence over less powerful ones (especially in the absence of transnational organizations such as economic unions or political alliances that might mitigate such behavior) and in fact may consider the exercise of such influence as vital to national interests. Hence, relations between states do not always signify relations between equals and are typically a reflection of another's national interests, which are themselves a consequence of national self-identification. The ensuing debate over Russia's future borders and the ideas underlying various positions on the subject are indications of a nation attempting to adjust to the loss of its state, which in this case was a multiethnic empire.

A. The Debate Framed: Westernizers Versus Eurasianists

In the immediate aftermath of the breakup the intellectual debate over national self-identification and the future of the Russian nation split intellectuals and political leaders into two broad categories: Westernizers and Eurasianists. The debate over self-identification centered around the question whether Russia should be oriented toward Europe or whether it should follow its own unique path based on its geographic position as a nation straddling both Europe and Asia. Foreign policy became central to the debate because of its close link with national security and national interests.

As was the case with the earlier dichotomous concepts of nineteenth century Slavophiles and Westernizers, the development of broad categories of Westernizers and Eurasianists provides a way to conceptualize the debate about Russian national identity by representing two opposing positions on a spectrum. They do not represent an exclusive either/or position taken on this issue, nor are the views of political leaders and intellectuals so easily pigeonholed. In addition, this dichotomy does not reflect changes in individual beliefs over the course of the six years since the breakup of the Union. Nevertheless, it is possible to identify the general political leanings of individuals, not to mention Russia's foreign policies, as tending toward one or another pole.

Westernizers argued that Russia should accept the dissolution of the Soviet Union and define a new role for Russia within the borders of the former RSFSR. In this endeavor Russia should concentrate its energies on improving the quality of day-to-day life, not on restoring the empire nor on a preoccupation with Russia's historical past as a great power.[3] In fact, Russian intellectuals initially viewed the dissolution of the Soviet Union and the creation of the Commonwealth of Independent States (CIS) as a positive development, because it signaled the orderly demise of a defunct system. Westernizers, also labeled liberals, greeted the establishment of the CIS with enthusiasm, because it ostensibly provided a noncompulsory forum for the continued economic and political cooperation between Russia and the former republics, excluding the Baltic States.[4] Yeltsin's former adviser, the late Galina Starovoitova, had spoken of the CIS in terms of a "future confederation," while the head of Russian Television's First Channel, Egor Yakovlev, referred to the CIS as the beginning of a new Union.[5] In this arrangement, the coercive ideological underpinnings of the old system were to be replaced with a legal, voluntary organization in which the sovereignty of member states would be recognized.

The position of the Westernizers suggests a repudiation of the Soviet past. The tenets of liberalism, as expressed by Westernizers—democracy, human rights, free trade, rule of law—are incompatible with authoritarianism, the command economy, and coercion of the type practiced against the Soviet republics and the Eastern bloc countries. Hence, Westernizers regarded the Soviet period as somehow illegitimate and emphasized the need to define a new role for Russia based on Western democratic models.[6]

In defining a new role for Russia, Westernizers see the West as the model upon which Russia should be economically restructured and, thus, tend to support continued economic reforms, as well as improving relations with Western countries. In the post–Cold War era they consider the West a natural ally of Russia, especially since they share the same values as well as the same threats, for example, immigration, terrorism, and militant Islam.[7] In this regard, Andrea Kozyrev, Russian foreign minister until he was replaced in 1996, was the chief proponent of a foreign policy oriented toward the West. Kozyrev viewed Russia as belonging to the advanced industrialized states of the North and saw the eventual inclusion of Russia in the Group of Seven industrialized countries as the ultimate goal of Russian economic reforms.[8]

Soon after the collapse of the former Soviet Union it became evident that there was a need to define Russia's national self-interests apart from those of the West. This represented the Eurasianists' point of departure from the Westernizers. The Eurasian position stresses Russia's connection, not only with Europe, but also with Asia. Eurasianists feel that Russia has a special role in history and, therefore, needs to follow its own path, a path determined indigenously and not by imitating the foreign culture of the West. While Westernizers emphasize Russia's connection and commonalties with the West, Eurasianists stress the differences between the two and the uniqueness of Russia's Asian tradition.

As for the borders of the Russian Federation, Eurasianists tend to regard them as artificial. There are differing opinions about the Soviet era. Some accept it and consequently call for recreating the Union, while others, such as monarchists who view Orthodoxy as the path to national salvation, reject the Soviet legacy. Yet, the latter can be considered Eurasian in their outlook because of their belief that certain areas of the near abroad—usually identified as Belarus, Ukraine, northern Kazakstan, and perhaps Moldova—are Russian lands, and any notion of Russian statehood is incomplete without their inclusion. Although there are variations concerning the redrawing of the borders, the following generalization applies: the former territories of the Soviet Union are areas in which Russia should and must exert influence, if not outright control.

In the sphere of foreign policy, this position is manifest in declarations that the near abroad, rather than Europe, should be the highest priority in Russian foreign policy. Neither is the West viewed as an unconditional ally of Russia. Russia, because of its unique geographic position, has national interests apart from, and in some instances in opposition to, those of European countries. Despite the end of the Cold War, the United States would continue to be the principal rival (though not necessarily a hostile one) of Russia.

Although the recent debate is related to earlier, nineteenth-century debates between Westernizers and Slavophiles, there are differences in their respective orientations. In the earlier debate the controversy centered on the question of which set of traditions Russia should draw upon for inspiration and a plan of action. Westernizers believed that Russia should look to the West (that is, Europe), while Slavophiles believed that Russia should draw exclusively on its own experience, in particular the Russian Orthodox religion and peasant traditions such as the commune.[9] But both Westernizers and Slavophiles shared a belief in the empire. Differences between the two were more a matter of strategy; neither group necessarily questioned the existence of the empire itself, nor did they question the legitimacy of Russia's political borders. Today, however, Westernizers believe that Russia should accept the dissolution of the old imperial practices and adjust to the present borders of the Russian Federation. In adopting this position they divorce themselves from the Westernizers of the nineteenth century, and hence have no historical tradition with which to buttress their position. They are left to argue that Russia, great power pretensions aside, simply cannot afford, materially or spiritually, to forcibly re-establish the former Union.[10]

To Eurasianists such a view is practically treasonous, and they point to the lack of historical precedent for current borders, as well as for the independence of the former peripheral territories. A Russian withdrawal from the near abroad, they maintain, is more in the interests of the West than of Russia. In repudiating Russia's past, including the Soviet period, and looking to the West to provide the model for Russian statehood, Westernizers are regarded as rejecting Russian values and denying Russia a national identity, patriotic pride, and the right to protect its national interests.[11]

It is important to add here that the terms of this debate have shifted appreciably over the course of the past three or four years. The positions outlined largely characterize the positions laid out in 1992–1993. Although the general outlines of the debate remain largely in place, the center of gravity has shifted very noticeably toward a nationalist perspective. The Westernizers of 1992 have evolved into moderate nationalists. For example, former Foreign Minister Alexei Kozyrev, while denying any shift in his policies, responded to the increasingly powerful domestic nationalist pressure with a more assertive policy toward the countries of the near abroad and the assertion of Russia's legitimate interests that conflicted with those of the West.[12] The primary focus of the most violent criticism of Russian foreign policy was, however, Moscow's moderate position toward other Soviet successor states based on the respect for their sovereignty.[13] As former Vice President Aleksandr Rutskoi put it, "the historical consciousness of the Russians will not allow anybody to equate mechanically the borders of Russia with those of the Russian Federation and to take away what constituted the glorious pages of Russian history."[14] As we shall see in the following discussion, nationalist pressures have impacted visibly on Russian foreign policy.

B. Westernizers, Eurasianists, and Russian Foreign Policy

In the sphere of foreign policy Westernizers prevailed in the initial period following the August 1991 coup attempt in Moscow. Then Russian Foreign Minister Andrei Kozyrev directed a foreign policy aimed at cooperation with the West. To this end Russia had already accepted the reunification of Germany and the extension of NATO into the territory of the former GDR and voted in the UN Security Council for the use of force against Iraq in the Gulf War without attempting to extract concessions from the West. As evidence for the success of a Western-oriented foreign policy, Kozyrev and Yeltsin pointed to the West's recognition of Russia as the legal successor state to the Soviet Union, a fact which carried with it the retention for Russia of the Soviet Union's permanent seat in the UN Security Council. Most importantly, in accepting without resistance the independence of the former Soviet Bloc countries and the former republics, and in renouncing the coercive elements of Soviet foreign policy (Kozyrev uses the word imperialistic), Russia managed to avoid the tragic fate of Yugoslavia.[15] Kozyrev further viewed the creation of the CIS as the beginning of the creation of a common post-Soviet space on the territory of the former Soviet Union. Within the framework of the CIS and without using intimidation tactics, Kozyrev expected the CIS to provide a forum for greater economic and political integration.

The Westernizers' influence, although the prevailing force in Russian foreign policy from 1991 to mid-1992, began to decline after 1992. For one thing, Russian foreign policy drew considerable criticism from the political opposition. Even President Yeltsin began to distance himself from the controversy surrounding Kozyrev's foreign policy. Among the policies criticized were his emphasis on cooperation with the West and the lack of a coherent policy toward the near abroad. He was accused of acting contrary to Russia's national interests by neglecting the near abroad and the situation of the 25 million Russians living there. As early as October 1992, only a little over a year after the coup attempt, Yeltsin publicly blamed the Foreign Ministry for not having a distinct, consistent policy toward the near abroad, especially in the defense of the Russian minorities.[16]

Russia's national interests, as defined by Kozyrev in a Foreign Ministry document submitted to parliament in response to this criticism, included the following objectives: economic recovery, observance of human rights, democracy, and integration into the world economy. To this end Russia welcomed multilateral diplomacy within such transnational organizations as the Conference on Security and Cooperation in Europe (CSCE), the EC, and the Western European Union, among others.[17] The reference to maintaining ties with the Russian minorities living in the near abroad was vague. Kozyrev had stressed the need for the general adoption by CIS member states of a human rights treaty based on internationally recognized standards endorsed by the United Nations and the CSCE that would apply to all minority groups, including the Russians.[18] This universal approach to the Russian minority issue was generally considered ineffectual. Its perceived failure (as witnessed by the restrictive citizenship laws of the Baltic states and the conflicts in Moldova, Georgia, and Tajikistan, and the clashes between Russians and Kazaks in northern Kazakstan) provoked criticism not just from the political opposition, but from members of Yeltsin's government as well.

Andranik Migranian, then a member of the Presidential Council of Experts, summed up Russia's national interests as very definitely including the near abroad, which was in fact central to those interests. The reason for the incoherent policy toward the near abroad stemmed from the lack of experience and tradition of establishing bilateral relations with these areas.[19] For this reason, according to Migranian, it was wrong to expect the CIS to be able to preserve the economic and political space previously maintained by the Soviet Union. Similarly, it was erroneous for Russia to turn inward within the political borders of the Russian Federation and to renounce any special position in the near abroad. Even if Russia were inclined to do so, it could not for at least three reasons: Russia can not ignore events taking place in the near abroad because of its central role in these conflicts; the international community was not about to take on the task of resolving or containing these conflicts; and events, whether open fighting or political and economic strife, impact to varying degrees the domestic political process in Russia.[20] An obvious example of this development was the migration to Russia of refugees from conflict areas in the near abroad. Uncontrolled mass movements of people strain limited government resources and provoke popular resentment as migrants are generally regarded as competition for scarce jobs, housing, government benefits, and so on.[21]

The Eurasian position on Russia's national interests differed sharply from that enumerated by Kozyrev in the Foreign Ministry document. The document was rejected by the Russian parliament on several grounds. First, it ignored the state of Russia's bilateral relations with non-Western states and did not take into account those states with strong bilateral ties to Russia, which deserved special attention. Second, the document was vague in its references to the near abroad, and that vagueness complicated relations with the NIS. Negotiations with the Baltic States over troop removal, borders, and the Russian minorities were cases in point.[22] Third, Kozyrev's notions of Russian national interests ignored the multinational character of the Russian Federation itself. Here Eurasianists drew a distinction between Russkii and Rossiiskii. The first term refers to ethnic Russians while the second refers to all inhabitants who call the Russian Federation their home. Eurasianists recognize Russia as the product of centuries of combined Slavic, Turkic, and other cultural traditions. In fact many non–ethnic Russian traditions contributed to the development of what later became Russia. What all Russian and non-Russians have in common is a "Eurasian geographical and cultural space."[23]

C. Consensus over Russia's National Interests in the Near Abroad

The shift toward a Eurasian conception of Russia's national interests is an obvious manifestation of growing Russian nationalism. The shift was not the result of one group prevailing over another. Rather, it resulted from a shift in the position of the Westernizers themselves, as the failure of economic reforms became evident. Disillusionment with the process of reform was compounded by the perceived inadequacy of Western assistance and political support. Intellectuals and academics in Russia, formerly the most vocal proponents of liberal, Western values, have increasingly shifted to a more conservative, Eurasian orientation. Journalist and political commentator Vladimir Razuvaev noted this marked defection to the Eurasian camp during a conference on Russian foreign policy held by the Russian Foreign Ministry.[24]

The emerging consensus on the nature and objectives of Russian foreign policy was reflected in the growing conservatism of the Foreign Ministry and in criticisms of the ministry by members of parliament, of the President's Council, and of the Security Council. This growing criticism of the Foreign Ministry's pro-West orientation had two results: the shift toward a more conservative policy orientation within the ministry and the increasing activism of other organizations in the sphere of foreign policy. Kozyrev responded to domestic pressure about increasing Russian activism in the near abroad with the appointment of a deputy foreign minister, Fedor Shelov-Kovedyaev, who was responsible for handling foreign policy in the near abroad. But soon after Shelov-Kovedyaev presented to Yeltsin a report advocating a restrained policy vis-à-vis the near abroad that included ''gradual integration taking into account the interests of other [CIS] states,'' he resigned from the post, apparently because of Yeltsin's own shift to the right.[25] In line with a more activist foreign policy in the near abroad, the next deputy foreign minister, Boris Pastukhov, pledged to increase the level of performance at Russian consulates that were established in the countries of the near abroad in order to service the visa needs of the Russian minorities and generally to act as intermediaries between them and the Russian government.[26]

Kozyrev toured the near abroad for the first time in April 1992, after he had made several trips to Western countries and began to advocate a more activist Russian policy toward these countries. Though originally hoping to promote greater integration within the structure of the CIS, Kozyrev began to rely more on bilateral arrangements between Russia and respective CIS members. This shift is significant in that it resembles the pattern of interaction during the Soviet era. Bilateral relations between Russia and each respective country in the near abroad are reminiscent of the center-republican relations of the Soviet Union—or of Soviet relations with the countries of the Warsaw Pact.

Kozyrev also began to adopt a tougher line on protecting the Russian minorities in the near abroad. He stated that protection of these minorities was Russia's duty and that the use of force under certain circumstances could not be ruled out. He noted that the existence of a ''wide range of options to defend compatriots living abroad, beginning with the expression of a slight dissatisfaction by an anonymous representative of the Russian Foreign Ministry and ending with sanctions of a political economic nature.'' He went on to name as an option the use ''of a direct armed force in some cases.''[27] This remark provoked a storm of protest among Western countries as well as those in the near abroad who feared that this statement indicated the beginning of a more aggressive foreign policy.[28] It strained relations with the Baltic States, especially Estonia and Lithuania. Estonian Foreign Ministry press secretary Mari-Ann Kelam indicated that such statements hinder the normalization of Estonian–Russian relations, and made clear that the Estonian government regarded the statement as threatening. Lithuania, which had expressed a concern about being surrounded by a heavily militarized Kalinin Oblast and Belarus, was similarly critical, noting Russia's penchant for threats which were ''incompatible with norms of international law.''[29] Kozyrev's statement also elicited similar negative responses from Tashkent and Dushombe.[30] However, Latvian Foreign Minister Valdis Birkavs and the chairman of the Saeima Commission on Foreign Affairs basically viewed Kozyrev's statement as political rhetoric to satisfy the more chauvinistic elements in Russia that had been critical of his policies.[31] Likewise, Kazak president Nursultan Nazarbayev dismissed Kozyrev's comments as electoral rhetoric.[32] It is notable that the Speaker of the Crimean parliament, Serhiy Tsekov, publicly applauded Kozyrev's statement and appealed to the Russian president to ''adopt measures according to international commitments, protecting the rights of compatriots living on the territory of the Crimea and representing a national minority in Ukraine.''[33]

Despite the hardening line of the Foreign Ministry, Kozyrev was still drawing criticism. His tough rhetoric on defending the rights of the Russian minorities and not ruling out the use of force as an option, although welcome to some hardliners such as General Alexandr Lebed, seemed to others to be motivated by electoral politics rather than a change of heart.[34] Domestic skepticism is not surprising considering the sanguine reaction of some NIS leaders who believed that Kozyrev's career was in jeopardy, and therefore viewed his statements as election rhetoric. Moreover, shortly after Kozyrev's statement, Grigory Karasin, an official spokesman for the Russian Foreign Ministry, was quoted as saying that the Ministry has ''so far failed to considerably improve the situation with ethnic Russians' rights in the CIS and the Baltic states.'' The reason for this was summed up in the conclusions of a collegium meeting of the Foreign Ministry, which attributed the failure to inadequate staffing of the Russian consulates.[35] In a long-awaited move, Kozyrev resigned his position as Foreign Minister in January of 1996, after having been elected to the Duma in the December 1995 elections.[36]

At the same time that the Foreign Ministry began adopting a more aggressive stance toward the near abroad in 1992 and 1993, at least rhetorically, other organizations began to exert growing influence over foreign policy. Parliamentarians such as Speaker Ruslan Khasbulatov and Vice President Alexandr Rutskoi were outspoken about the need to protect Russians in the near abroad. Others, such as Nikolay Ryzhkov, openly advocated reunification with Ukraine.[37] The individual voices of politicians aside, government bodies such as the Defense Ministry, the Presidential Council of Experts, and the Security Council became more involved in the making of Russian foreign policy. Defense Minister Pavel Grachev took a hardline position toward the near abroad regarding the protection of the Russian minorities in a speech given in a meeting with Tajik representatives addressing the dangerous situation of Russian servicemen there.[38] Andranik Migranian, member of the Presidential Council of Experts, wrote several influential articles on Russian national interests in the near abroad and the need for greater Russian activism in protecting the rights of Russians. Even more significant was the appointment of Sergei Stankevich to the position of political advisor to the president, since Stankevich was outspoken in his views on Russian policy in the near abroad and the need to take concrete measures to protect the Russian minorities.[39]

While these organizations certainly have exercised considerable influence over Yeltsin and others involved in formulating foreign policy, their role was more informal than that of the Security Council. In fact their influence was directly related to the ambiguous position of the Foreign Ministry over policy toward the near abroad. The Security Council, which encompasses intelligence and security agencies, gained greater powers at the expense of the Foreign Ministry and in specific cases took over substantial areas formerly within the jurisdiction of that agency.

In July 1996, as part of President Yeltsin's attempt to strengthen his position for the second round of the presidential elections, Alexander Lebed, well-known for his uncompromising stance toward the near abroad, became the Secretary of the Security Council. After Lebed took the post, the Council was given expanded power. Among its duties were included defining state and societal interests (national interests) and identifying internal and external threats to security; constructing strategies to deal with these threats, including imposing states of emergence, the use of the military, and so on; and submitting recommendations to the president on these matters, as well as on domestic and foreign policies that impact Russian security. A subsequent statute on the expanded powers of the Security Council omitted mention of the participation of Security Council members, especially in the submission to the Council of alternative decisions. This provoked questions about the boundaries of the Secretary's powers.[40] The extension of broad powers to the Security Council in all areas of national security has clear implications for policy in the near abroad. By any measure, the near abroad falls within the sphere of Russia's national interests. Indeed, the Foreign Ministry's ambiguous role in constructing policy toward the near abroad was noted obliquely by Lebed in his reply to a question about the expanded powers of the Security Council. When asked ''at the expense of which government struc- tures'' did the expansion of powers take place, Lebed answered that the Security Council was filling a vacuum.[41]

After Lebed's appointment, the Security Council officially condemned Latvia's declaration of its own occupation during the Soviet period, viewing the declaration as a potential threat to Russia's territorial integrity. The Council also took control over the issue of the Black Sea Fleet in negotiations with Ukraine. The significance of both issues lies in questions of national security. In the Latvian case, accusations of occupation are potential preludes to territorial demands and border adjustments; while in the Ukrainian case, the key to the issue of the Black Sea Fleet is the joint defense of the Caspian–Black Sea region.[42] With primary jurisdiction over national security issues, the Security Council exerts significant power over Russian foreign policy in the near abroad. It is not clear what impact General Lebed's firing as Secretary of the Security Council after only several months in the position had on the day-to-day relations between the Council and the Ministry of Foreign Affairs or on Russian policy toward the near abroad. What is evident, however, is the fact that the Security Council and its role in policymaking are no longer as prominently covered in the media.

As for General Lebed, he is well positioned to contend for leadership as Yeltsin's power wanes in the wake of the collapse of the Russian banking system and the Russian ruble during the summer of 1998.[43] Lebed came in third in the presidential election of 1996; after his appointment as Secretary of the Security Council his backing of Yeltsin in the following runoff election was crucial to the latter's victory that year.[44] And as Russia's regional governors act increasingly independent of Moscow, Lebed, as the elected governor of Krasnoyarsk, is un- likely to be pulled down with Yeltsin and his supporters. To the contrary, his new power base in Siberia bolsters his image as a strong leader, unaffected by the corruption of Yeltsin and his entourage. What effect Lebed might have on foreign policy in the future remains unclear, as he has been deliberately vague regarding his ideological views.[45]

III. STRENGTHS AND LIMITATIONS: RUSSIAN ACTIVISM IN THE NEAR ABROAD

What are the implications of the political consensus about the importance of the near abroad to Russian national interests for Russian policy toward the countries of the region? The answer lies in Russia's capacity to influence events in the near abroad and in the domestic limitations on the implementation of certain policies. The strengths and limitations of Russian foreign policy toward the near abroad are evident in the actual strategies that Russia has employed in its relations toward the former republics.

Economically and politically Russia is still very powerful in comparison with the countries of the near abroad and is able to exert considerable influence over them. Economically Russia easily dominates Central Eurasia (meant here as the territory of the former Soviet Union). Despite economic difficulties, Russia is in a far more advantageous position than most of the countries of the near abroad for several reasons.

First, the countries of the near abroad are dependent on Russia and other CIS countries as a source of imports and for export markets. Despite a decline in inter-republic trade following the collapse of the ruble zone in 1993, a considerable percentage of NIS exports go to the former Soviet republics, which also represent a primary source for raw materials and inputs for local industries. In the Baltic countries, where progress away from dependence on the former Soviet republics is most advanced, Russia alone (not counting other NIS) accounted for 23.1% of all Estonian exports and 16.2% of total imports in 1994.[46] Corresponding percentages for Latvia in the same year were 28.1% and 23.6%, while in Lithuania trade with Russia amounted to 28.2% of all exports and 39.3% of all imports.[47]

The dependence on Russia and the former republics for export markets and imports is much higher in Central Asia, although the statistics are not always available. For example, the latest trade statistics complied for the Kyrgyz Republic show that in 1992 trade with former Soviet republics totaled 87.8% of exports and 95.5% of imports, while in 1991, the numbers for Turkmenistan were 85.8% and 83.8%, respectively.[48] In 1994 Tajikistan, the most dependent on Russia because of the civil war, exported 77.6% of its products to the former republics, while 54.6% of total imports came from them.[49] Comparative numbers for Uzbekistan in 1995 were 49.5% and 44.4%, respectively. While these statistics are formally based on trade with all the former republics, in fact Russia continues to be the dominant trade partner. Remaining inter-republic trade is by and large restricted to other Central Asian states. While not strictly comparable because of annual changes and the lack of recent data, the statistics on Central Asia illustrate the general decline in the percentage of trade being conducted with former Soviet republics, but they do not take into account unregulated cross-border trade.

In Kazakstan, dependence on trade with NIS states other than Russia declined, while trade with Russia increased from 37.7% in 1994 to 43.9% in 1995.[50] The level of dependence on Russia for both export markets and imports is especially high for Ukraine and Belarus, both of which have instituted only limited market reforms.[51] Belarusian trade with Russia totaled 47.8% of exports and 59.7% of imports in 1995.[52]

Second, the countries of the near abroad are still heavily dependent on Russia for energy resources especially petroleum. Although Turkmenistan is increasing its production of natural gas—which it exports to other former republics such as Uzbekistan, Kyrgyzstan, and Ukraine—Russia remains the principal source for fuel. Lithuania and Belarus receive virtually all of their gas and oil from Russia, Latvia gets all of its natural gas from Russia, and Ukraine receives 86% of its oil and 52% of its gas from Russia.[53] Electricity is also an important Russian export to the near abroad. Apart from a form of barter, most of the near abroad cannot afford to pay for fuel in hard currency, which Russia now demands for these exports. As a result, many of these countries have become heavily indebted to Russia. Debt rescheduling and negotiations over energy deliveries give Russia considerable political leverage over the near abroad. This leverage can be, and has been, used to extract political concessions. Ukraine's acceptance in 1994 of the provisions of the START Treaty in exchange for, among other things, the cancellation of Ukraine's fuel debt to Russia is a case in point.

Third, the Russian ruble, while weak compared to European currencies, is much stronger than the currencies introduced by the countries of the near abroad following the collapse of the ruble zone—with the exception of those of the Baltic states. Russia's refusal to underwrite the old Soviet rubles of the former republics and the introduction of tightened monetary policies (for example, instituting central control (by the Russian state bank) over the money supply) effectively drove the CIS countries, with the exception of Belarus and Tajikistan, out of the ruble zone. Provisions for a ruble zone, in which a single currency would be used to conduct trade on the territory of the former Soviet Union, were originally established under CIS agreements. However, conducting trade in rubles meant that the new states, especially Russia, were exporting goods at below market prices, prompting the re-export of such goods to "far abroad" countries (countries other than the NIS).[54]

Such practices persuaded Russia to tighten monetary policy and stabilize the ruble. The NIS have since established their own currencies. Although Belarus has established its own ruble and Tajikistan has done the same, they are parallel currencies tied to the Russian ruble.[55] Thus, detached monetarily from the former republics, Russia has refused to accept payment in rubles and instead demanded payment in hard currency. These tightened monetary policies bolstered the Russian ruble and placed Russia in an advantageous position vis-à-vis other CIS states on the strength of its currency as determined by the relative purchasing power of each of the currencies.[56]

Lastly, the sheer size of the Russian economy as compared with those of the former republics makes Russia a formidable economic power despite its many problems. The gross domestic product of Russia in 1995 totaled $677.7 billion. The second largest economy of the near abroad, that of Ukraine, had a gross domestic product during the same period totaling approximately $150 billion, less than one-fourth of Russia's GDP.[57] After Ukraine came Uzbekistan, Kazakstan, Belarus, Azerbaijan, and Moldova, with GDPs of approximately $58, $55, $45, $17, and $15 billion, respectively.[58] The remaining NIS countries have still smaller economies.

Politically Russia is considerably more powerful than its neighbors. Internationally Russia was recognized as the successor state of the Soviet Union, and, as previously mentioned, took the place of the Soviet Union in the UN Security Council. As a result of this recognition and because of its size, the international community has in several ways paid far more attention to Russia than to the other former republics. The current banking and currency crisis in Russia has not changed this fact.

First, Russia receives the lion's share of foreign investment. Kazakstan does not fare too badly in the area of foreign investment, although most of this investment has centered around extractive industries and has run into numerous administrative difficulties stemming from unclear and ill-defined state business and investment procedures.[59] Likewise Turkmenistan and Azerbaijan have attracted some foreign investment, although most of it goes to develop their petroleum and natural gas reserves. CIS countries without substantial mineral and energy reserves have not attracted significant foreign investment. Foreign investors tend to be cautious about investing in countries (with the possible exception of those with substantial mineral and energy reserves) that lack political and economic stability and clearly established laws and procedures in matters of investment, taxation, and property ownership. Russia, too, has its own problems in the area of political stability, but relative to many other countries of the near abroad, it does comparatively well.

Second, despite rhetoric from Europe and the United States in support of NIS sovereignty, very little tangible support has flowed to these countries, with the exception of the Baltic states. As noted, most foreign investment (with the exception of that for the oil and mining industries) is concentrated in Russia. Furthermore, in dealing with certain countries in the near abroad, especially Ukraine, Western countries do so through Russia. For example, concerning the issue of nuclear weapons, the United States made known its preference for dealing with only one nuclear power on the territory of the former Soviet Union, namely Russia. To this end, negotiations centered around transferring nuclear missiles from Ukraine and Belarus to Russia and dismantling those military assets that cannot be moved, such as ICBM silos in Kazakstan.[60] The determination of the United States to consolidate Soviet nuclear forces within the borders of the Russian Federation was evident in promises to Ukraine of developmental aid in return for relinquishing its nuclear weapons to Russia.[61] As for Belarus, the need to remove nuclear weapons to Russia was made redundant by the security union between Minsk and Moscow, which placed Belarusian security under Russian control.

Third, Russia enjoys the political advantage of being a power broker in Central Eurasia. This results not only from the sheer size of the Russian Federation, but also from the relatively undeveloped state of relations among the NIS themselves. Linkages generally run through Moscow, as they did during the Soviet period. Multilateralism, as attempted via the CIS, has by and large failed to emerge as a significant form of interaction; and bilateral agreements on trade, quotas, licensing, and so forth have become the modus operandi— bilateral agreements largely between Russia and individual NIS.[62] Political agreements, such as the establishment of consulates and accords guaranteeing the protection of the rights of Russian minorities, have similarly been concluded bilaterally.[63]

Where linkages among near abroad countries do exist, they are usually limited to countries of the same region (as among the countries of the Baltics, the Caucasus, and Central Asia) and are contentious at best (for example squabbles between Lithuania and Latvia over maritime borders) and hostile at worst (warfare between Armenia and Azerbaijan). Furthermore, many of the NIS face internal threats to unity (for example, Georgia, Kazakstan, Tajikistan, and Moldova), which weakens their position vis-à-vis Russia. It can further be argued that Estonia, Ukraine, and Kyrgyzstan also suffer from potential threats to unity, as in the case of the Russian minorities in Narva, Crimea, and the North/South divide, respectively. Such political weaknesses provide Russia with opportunities to intervene, as currently in Moldova, Tajikistan, and the Caucasus, under the guise of peacekeeping.[64]

Russia faces certain limitations in the strategies it employs toward the NIS. For one thing, the ability or willingness to provide economic assistance to the countries on its periphery would substantially enhance Russia's position in the near abroad, especially in Central Asia. Politically, however, there is little domestic support for providing assistance, since Russia herself has immense economic and financial problems. Another perception hindering Russian involvement in the near abroad involves the widespread belief that Russia is much better off without the near abroad. This belief was shared by international financial institutions, which advised Russia to stabilize and privatize its own economy without the cooperation of its CIS partners.[65] Since the independence of the NIS, Russia is no longer responsible for subsidizing industrial development in the form of free or low-cost energy supplies and raw materials.

The most notable limitation on Russian policy in the near abroad is widespread public resistance to the use of military force. Despite rising Russian nationalism and an increasing interest in expanding Russian involvement in the near abroad, support stops short of outright military intervention. Moldova and the Caucasus are exceptions, in that the 14th army in Moldova, now largely the product of the self-proclaimed Dnestr Republic, does not recruit from Russia and is not controlled by Moscow. Russian intervention in the Caucasus, both in the Georgian civil war and in the Armenian/Azerbaijani conflict involved large numbers of renegade soldiers and mercenaries who may or may not be acting according to Moscow dictates.[66]

The public by and large does not support large-scale military intervention. According to polls taken in 1992 and again in 1994, most Russians felt that Russia should "protect the rights of Russians" living in the near abroad. Yet, only 6.8% polled in 1992 supported military intervention in support of this objective; that number dropped to 2% in 1994.[67] Even more telling, 65.2% in another poll answered that the only way Russia can regain its former great power status is through the successful development of the Russian economy.[68] As of 1996, the most pressing problems faced by Russia, according to polls, did not include matters of foreign policy nor the near abroad. Sixty-three percent of Russians and 72% of Muscovites cited rising crime as among the most disturbing problems Russia faces. Rising prices and the economic crisis (falling agricultural and industrial production) were among the top three concerns of both Russians and Muscovites, with percentages of 74% and 70%, and 50% and 52%, respectively![69]

Still, if current economic and political trends continue, the situation could change if democracy were to fall by the wayside, with future leaders being less concerned about public approval. The recent murder of Galina Starovoitova, Yeltsin's pro-democratic advisor, is the latest political incident that suggests a growing political trend that leads away from democracy and market reforms. In early December two apparently hired killers, who have yet to be apprehended, shot Starovoitova in the stairwell to her apartment in St. Petersburg.[70]

Russia's economic and political dominance in Central Eurasia, as well as domestic opposition to certain policies, especially, the use of military force, have determined the strategies Russia has thus far employed to keep the near abroad within its sphere of influence. These strategies are economic and political in nature, although they have differed according to region.

In the Baltics, Russia continually linked troop withdrawal with concessions by the Baltic states on the issue of the Russian minorities living in the region. The withholding of energy deliveries was used periodically against the Baltics. Moreover, Russia was able to call on the Conference for Security and Cooperation in Europe to condemn Estonian citizenship laws.[71] In Ukraine, a similar strategy has been employed. In the Caucasus, the military option has been exercised, with Russia mediating the conflict between Armenia and Azerbaijan and supporting the Abkhazi separatist movement in pressuring Georgia to join the CIS. In Central Asia security agreements concluded between Moscow and the individual states have meant, in effect, that Moscow will continue to provide for the security of the southern border dividing the former Soviet Union from Iran, Afghanistan, and China.

IV. PROSPECTS FOR A NEW UNION

Some existing trends suggest that Russia and the near abroad, excluding the Baltics, are moving closer together. This development results primarily from the severe crises occurring in the former republics that have deepened their dependence on Russia. While Russia has made headway in economic stabilization, at least until the current financial crisis, most of the other CIS states have not. The prospects for a union vary according to region.

Belarus, Ukraine, and Kazakstan are often regarded as the core Slavic states that have the greatest opportunity for close economic and security integration. A long common political history and their close cultural affinity with Russia distinguish these countries. In the case of Kazakstan this applies to the northern half of the country, which is inhabited predominantly by Russians.

While the CIS failed to provide a framework for continued economic integration, the collapse of the ruble zone triggered a severe decline in trade that was itself the result of a steep decline in production. This has aggravated the economic crisis in several states, especially Belarus and Ukraine, which are the most dependent on trade with Russia. Belarus already has a military and customs union with Russia, and the Belarusian ruble is linked to the Russian ruble. Hence Belarusian military defense and its customs service are under the jurisdiction of Russia. Ukraine is not only dependent on Russia for fuel and raw materials for its industries, but the state is so weak that it does not have effective control over portions of its own territory, especially the Crimea. The border between Ukraine and Russia exists on paper only. And, although there is a vocal Ukrainian nationalist voice in the western areas of Ukraine, there is also a significant Russian and Russophone minority in the eastern and southern part of Ukraine that favors closer cooperation with Russia and, in fact, looks to Russia rather than westward for future security guarantees.

In Kazakstan the impetus for cooperation stems from the presence of a large Russian population living in northern Kazakstan. This territory is largely viewed as Russian land, both among the Russians living there and Russian nationalists in Russia. In order to stave off territorial demands, President Nurusultan Nazarbayev has maintained cordial relations with Russia. He has been the most consistent supporter of the CIS and economic integration with Russia. Nevertheless, accusations by Cossack groups against the reported mistreatment of the Russian population persist and could incite a reaction from Russia or the Russian population in northern Kazakstan on the border with Russia.

In Central Asia and the Transaucasus, the emphasis on Russian policy stems from security concerns. These include exclusion of the strong influence of other powers on the territory of the former Soviet Union and preventing military conflicts along the border states.[72] In Central Asia, the concern is with the influence of countries such as Turkey, Iran, Afghanistan, and China.

V. CONCLUSION

Russian activism in the near abroad is the result of a growing Russian nationalism that views the territories of the former Soviet Union as being within Russia's sphere of influence and forming the basis for Russian national interests. Russia's continued position of economic and political dominance has ensured a continued Russian presence within the near abroad without a heavy reliance on the military. Despite the centrality to Russian interests of the near abroad, there is little support in Russia for armed intervention and the use of force to bring about political dividends. Any union between Russia and individual countries of the near abroad will likely be the result of failed state-building in the NIS.

NOTES/REFERENCES

1. Robert J. Kaiser develops this argument in his book, *The Geography of Nationalism in Russia and the USSR* (Princeton, NJ: Princeton University Press, 1994).
2. Vladimir Shlapentokh, ''How Russians See Themselves Now: In the Aftermath of the Defeat in Chechnya.'' unpublished manuscript; Michigan State University. Available on ''Johnson's Russia List,'' January 11, 1997, djohnson@cdi.org.
3. Tolz, V. (1992). Russia: Westernizers continue to challenge national patriots. *RFE/RL Research Report 1*:49 December 11, 3.
4. Tolz, V. and Teague, E. (1992). Russian intellectuals adjust to loss of empire. *RFE/RL Research Report 1*:8, February 21, 4–5.
5. Tolz, V. and Teague, E. (1992). Russian intellectuals adjust to loss of empire, *RFE/RL Research Report 1*:8, February 21, 4.
6. Shenfield, S. D. (1994). Post-Soviet Russia in search of identity, p. 10. In D. W. Blum (ed.), *Russia's Future: Consolidation or Disintegration*. Boulder, CO: Westview.
7. Rahr, A. (1992). Atlanticists' versus 'Eurasians' in Russian foreign policy. *RFE/RL Research Report 1*:22, May 29, 18. On the foreign policy debate, see also Light, M. (1996). Foreign policy thinking, pp. 33–100. In N. Malcolm, A. Pravda, R. Allison, and M. Light (eds.), *Internal Factors in Russian Foreign Policy*. Oxford: Oxford University Press, for the Royal Institute of International Affairs.
8. Rahr, A. Atlanticists' versus 'Eurasians' in Russian foreign policy. *RFE/RL Research Report 1*:22, May 19, 18. *FBIS-SOV 4*:31, March 4.
9. See Gleason, A. (1978). *Young Russia*, p. 37. New York: Viking Press.
10. Tolz, V. (1992). Russia: Westernizers continue to challenge national patriots, *RFE/RL Research Report 1*:49, December 11, 1–3.
11. *FBIS-SOV*, p. 20, April 13, 1995. For a discussion of Russian national interests, see Shearman, p. (1997). Defining the national interest: Russian foreign policy and domestic politics, pp. 1–27. In R. E. Kanet and A. V. Kozhemiakin (eds.), *The Foreign Policy of the Russian Federation*. Houndmills: Macmillan Press. See also Pikayev, A. A. (1996). The Russian domestic debate on policy towards the ''near

abroad,'' pp. 51–56. In L. Jonson and C. Archer (eds), *Peacekeeping and the Role of Russia in Eurasia*. Boulder: Westview Press.

12. Bohlen, C. (1994). ''Nationalist vote toughens Russian foreign policy.'' *New York Times*, January 25.

13. Checkel, J. (1992). Russian foreign policy: Back to the future? *RFE/RL Research Report 1*:41, 17–18.

14. *Pravda*, February 30, 1993.

15. Kozyrev, A. (1994). ''Ne partiinye a natsionalnye interesy.'' *Rossiiskaya gazeta*, February 2.

16. Lough, J. (1993). Defining Russia's relations with neighboring states. *RFE/RL Research Report 2*:20, May 14, 54.

17. Crow, S. (1992). Russia debates its national interests. *RFE/RL Research Report 1*: 28, July 10, 44.

18. Kozyrev, A. (1994). ''Ne partiinye a natsionalnye interesy.'' *Rossiiskaya gazeta*, February 2.

19. Migranian, A. (1994). ''Roseau I Blizhnee Zarubezhye.'' *Nezavisimaya gazeta*, January 12.

20. Migranian, A. (1995). ''Roseau I Blizhnee Zarubezhye.'' *Nezavisimaya gazeta*, January 12. See also Kanet, R. E. (1996). The Russian Federation, pp. 60–86. In E. A. Kolodziej and R. E. Kanet (eds), *Coping with Conflict after the Cold War*. Baltimore: Johns Hopkins University Press.

21. Kobishchanov, Y. (1995). ''Kto budet zhit' v Rossii XXI veka.'' *Nezavisimaya gazeta*, February 10.

22. Crow, S. (1992). Russia debates its national interests. *RFE/RL Research Report 1*: 28, July 10, 44.

23. Chinyaeva, E. (1996). A Eurasianist model of interethnic relations could help Russia find harmony. *Transition*, November 1, 34.

24. Crow, S. (1992). Russia debates its national interests. *RFE/RL Research Report 1*: 28, July 10, 46.

25. Lough, J. (1993). Defining Russia's relations with neighboring states. *RFE/RL Research Report 2*:20, May 14, 56–57.

26. Andreyev, I. (1998). ''Mid Nameren Aktivnee Zashchishchat' prava Russkikh za Granitsei.'' *Izvestiia*, April 30.

27. *FBIS-SOV*, p. 72, April 20, 1995.

28. *FBIS-SOV*, p. 8, April 21, 1995.

29. *FBIS-SQ*, p. 74V, April 20, 1995.

30. *FBIS-SOV*, p. 62, April 20, 1995;

31. *FBIS-SOV*, p. 73, April 20, 1995.

32. *FBIS-SOV*, p. 59, April 21, 1995.

33. *FBIS-SOV*, pp. 45–46, April 21, 1995.

34. *FBIS-SOV*, p. 15, April 20, 1995.

35. *FBIS-SOV*, p. 12, May 31, 1995. For a discussion of integration in the CIS, see Webber, M. (1997). *CIS Integration Trends: Russia and the Former Soviet South*. London: The Royal Institute of International Affairs.

36. Gornostaev, D. (1996). ''Andrei Kozyrev predpochel deputatsii mandat ministerskomy portfeliu.'' *Nezavisimaya gazeta*, January 6.

37. *FBIS-SOV*, p. 4, November 20, 1995.

38. *FBIS-SOV*, p. 12, April 25, 1995.

39. Melvin, N. (1994). *Forging the New Russian Nation*, p. 38. London: The Royal Institute of International Affairs; Crow, S. (1992). Russia prepares to take a hard line on "near abroad." *RFE/RL Research Report 1*:32, August 14, 22.

40. Malkina, T. Trofimov, A., and Volkov, D. (1996). "Alexander Lebed zapolniaet vakuum." *Sevodnya*, July 12.

41. Malkina, T. Trofimov, A., and Volkov, D. (1996). "Alexander Lebed zapolniaet vakuum." *Sevodnya*, July 12.

42. *FBIS-SOV*, p. 5, September 6, 1996; *FBIS-SOV*, p. 11, September 9, 1996.

43. Hiltzik, M. A. (1998). Virtual banking. *Russia Review*, November, pp. 24–25.

44. "Russia's crisis: Could it lead to fascism?" *The Economist*, July 11, 1998, p. 20.

45. "Russia's crisis: Could it lead to fascism?" *The Economist*, July 11, 1998, p. 21.

46. The Economist Intelligence Unit (1997). *Country Report: Estonia, Latvia, Lithuania: Annual Profile*, p. 22 London: The Economist Intelligence Unit.

47. The Economist Intelligence Unit (1997). *Country Report: Estonia, Latvia, Lithuania: Annual Profile*, pp. 45, 65 London: The Economist Intelligence Unit.

48. The Economist Intelligence Unit (1996). *Country Report: Kyrgyz Republic, Tajikistan, Turkmenistan, Uzbekistan: 4th Quarter*, pp. 6, 29. London: The Economist Intelligence Unit.

49. The Economist Intelligence Unit (1996). *Country Report: Kyrgyz Republic, Tajikistan, Turkmenistan, Uzbekistan: 4th Quarter*, p. 58. London: The Economist Intelligence Unit.

50. The Economist Intelligence Unit (1987). *Country Report: Kazakstan: Annual Report*, p. 46. London: The Economist Intelligence Unit.

51. Boss, H. and Havlik, P. (1994). Slavic (dis)union: Consequences for Russia, Belarus, and Ukraine. *Economics of Transition 2*:2, June, 239–240.

52. The Economist Intelligence Unit (1996). *Country Report: Belarus, Moldova: 4th Quarter*, p. 6. London: The Economist Intelligence Unit.

53. Kosikova, L. and Mikhalskaya, A. (1982). Problems of state regulation of trade between Russia and the near abroad countries. *Foreign Trade 11–12*, 40.

54. Kosikova, L. and Mikhalskaya A. (1992). Problems of state regulation of trade between Russia and the near abroad countries. *Foreign Trade 11–12*, 41.

55. The Economist Intelligence Unit (1996). *Country Report: Russia: 4th Quarter*, p. 36. London: The Economist Intelligence Unit.

56. The Economist Intelligence Unit (1996). *Country Report: Kyrgyz Republic, Tajikistan, Turkmenistan, Uzbekistan: 4th Quarter*, pp. 66–67. London: The Economist Intelligence Unit.

57. The Economist Intelligence Unit (1997). *Country Report: Ukraine, 1996–97: Annual Report*, p. 20. London: The Economist Intelligence Unit.

58. The Economist Intelligence Unit (1997). *Country Report: Ukraine, 1996–97: Annual Report*, p. 20. London: The Economist Intelligence Unit.

59. Geyer, G. A. (1994). *Waiting for Winter to End: An Extraordinary Journey Through Central Asia*, pp. 59–60, 65–72. Washington-London: Brassey's.

60. *FBIS-SOV*, pp. 3–4, September 12, 1997.

61. Birgerson, S. M. and Kanet, R. E. (1995). East-Central Europe and the Russian Federation. *Problems of Post-Communism 42*:4, 34.

62. Kosikova, L. and Mikhalskaya A. (1992). Problems of state regulation of trade between Russia and the near abroad countries. *Foreign Trade 11–12*, 40. See also Anderson, J. (1997). *The International Politics of Central Asia*, esp. pp. 188–212. Manchester and New York: Manchester University Press.

63. *FBIS-SOV*, p. 10, March 30, 1994.

64. See, for example, McNeill, T. (1997). Humanitarian intervention and peacekeeping in the former Soviet Union and Easter Europe. *International Political Science Review 18*:1, 95–111. See also Kozhemiakin, A. V. and Kanet, R. E. (1998). Russia as a regional peacekeeper, pp. 225–239. In R. E. Kanet (ed), *Resolving Regional Conflicts*. Champaign, IL: University of Illinois Press.

65. Boss, H. and Havlik, P. (1994). Slavic (dis)union: Consequences for Russia, Belarus, and Ukraine. *Economics of Transition 2*:2; June, 243.

66. See Goltz, T. (1993). Letter from Eurasia: The hidden Russian hand. *Foreign Policy 92*.

67. *The Current Digest of the Post-Soviet Press 46*:30, 1994, 13.

68. Payin, E. (1994). ''Konsolidatsiia Rossii ili vosstanovlenie soiuza.'' *Sevodnia*, July 22.

69. Saveliev, O. (1997). ''Rossiian kusaiut tseny Moskvichei dostali vgolovniki.'' *Sevodnia*, February 23.

70. ''Ia znal, chto opasnost' iskhodit iz pitera.'' *Komsomol'skaia Pravda*, December 4, 1998; *The Economist*, p. 92 (Obituary: Galina Starovoitova), 28, November 1998.

71. In response to Russian pressures and the criticisms of the West, Latvia has liberalized its citizenship laws, and Estonia is in the final stage of approving similar legislation. See, for example, ''Moscow Welcomes Estonian Citizenship Law Changes . . . Says it Will Cease Rhetoric on Russian-Speakers in Baltics.'' *RFE/RL Newsline 2*:239, Part II, December 14, 1998.

72. Parrish, S. (1996). Will the union be reborn? *Transitions*, July 2, 33.

17

Forming a New Nation-State and the Repression or Protection of Ethnic Minorities

The Case of Slovenia

Miran Komac
Institute for Ethnic Studies, Ljubljana, Slovenia

I. INTRODUCTION

From the beginning of the Slovene ethnic revival, ethnic relations between the Slovene nation and the neighboring nations were contaminated with ethnic tension. The competition for exclusive possession over some ingredients of ethnic peculiarities (territory in the first place) had marked the interethnic relations with disjunctive processes. Without sufficient organization (in the political reflections of intelligentsia recognized in the State) the members of the Slovene fledgling nation lacked crucial institutions to protect their ethnic diversities.

In the theoretical thoughts about the Slovene ethnic issue, the creation of the State was proclaimed to be the cornerstone of the final solution of the Slovene national problem. Accumulated historical experience, additionally (re-)elaborated through cultural elites' considerations, has constructed the main purpose for the creation of the new State—the State is the fundamental organization to protect and promote the ethnic peculiarities of the Slovene nation and to defend members of the Slovene ethnic realm, without regard of their national status, that is, having legal Slovenian citizenship or forming Slovene ethnic minorities in neighboring countries.

The formation of the new State was (and still is) escorted with emphasized ethnic homogenization. This process allowed scarce possibilities for expression of non-Slovene ethnic identities. The societal citizenship is often connected with silent assimilation.

The main hypothesis of this chapter is that the model adopted in the Slovene nation-state formation has many parallels with the nineteenth century nation-building processes. The processes of ethnomodernization, encouraging ethnocultural pluralism, have been mostly cast aside. With this approach we have, perhaps, lost the opportunity to rebuild the concept of *le citoyen* in his or her entity, recognizing the natural fact that the individual has, at least, a national, ethnic, and civic part of identity.

II. FROM THE NATIONAL MINORITY TO THE NATIONAL MAJORITY

The founding of Yugoslavia in 1918 gave birth to Slovenia, a small state (16, 197 km^2). If we regard it as a realization of the ideal national program, known as United Slovenia,[1] its success was about 67%. The territory populated by Slovenes in the middle of the ninetieth century comprised about 24,000 km^2

The emergence of the state of Slovenia (within Yugoslavia) at the meeting point of a considerable group of nations (Italians, Friulians, Germans or Austrians, Hungarians, and Croats), who were the Slovenes' competitors for the same territory, signified that the operation, which would adjust ethnic and political borders in every detail, was doomed to fail. Or, to put it differently, the determining of state territory would primarily be the result of the proportion of powers in international relations and the (above all, military) power of the pretendents to the territories, which, upon the bases of various national programs, were to be incorporated by various nations into their own nation-states. In this game, the Slovenes' starting point was extremely bad. Without their own state institutions, they could only rely upon the democratic spirit of international bodies, having forgotten the ancient Gypsy wisdom that justice, blind as it is, clings to the rich man's table. Their wealth was sadly limited; defeats and failures were therefore a natural hallmark of the realization of the Slovene national program.

This failure resulted in the emergence of national minorities and the remains of Slovene ethnicity in the neighboring countries (Italy, Austria, Hungary) as well as those of the neighboring nations in Slovenia (Germans or Austrians and Hungarians). With regard to the prevailing concept of the function and role of the state at that time, which was based upon the ideas of the French revolution, or its Jacobinical derivative with often-present Vendée methods, it was clear that these very ethnic remnants would become generators of future ethnic conflicts. Perhaps, however, the statement on national minorities being generators of ethnic conflicts and destroyers of states is a bit too narrow, since they have often become that only after two, frequently opposed policymaking groups have tried to realize themselves through ethnic minority issues: those of the state in which the minorities are settled and those of the state populated by the majority population to which the minorities belong ethnically.

Soon enough, these starting points resulted in phrases which carried in themselves a seed of conflict: parent nation, parent nation-state, or even parent homeland. These notions usually relate to the neighboring ethnic population and the neighboring state where minorities are concerned. States in which minorities lived were regarded almost as foreign countries, and historic circumstances which had caused minorities to exist were deemed unjust and thus required correction as soon as possible. Minority status is undoubtedly a temporary condition for minority members, a period which demands a thorough preparation for the new rearrangement of state borders. Apart from this, a special state of mind should be mentioned which was gaining ground among national minorities members in Slovenia:[2] the sense of frustration on the one hand and of xenophobia on the other, since members of the up-to-then ruling nations (Germans, Hungarians) transformed almost overnight into minorities; this blow could be softened by the vitalization of the idea on the temporary character of political and state-territorial solutions.

Outside the borders of the Slovene (Yugoslav) state remained approximately 426,000 Slovenes (350,000 in Italy, 70,000 in Austria, and 6,000 in Hungary), about 30% of Slovene population on its recognized territory of settlement, a fact that must have caused a feeling of incredible injustice having been done to Slovenes. However, the Versailles agreement did not cause dissatisfaction only among Slovenes; members of new minorities (Germans, Hungarians) were convinced of just as harsh an injustice. At the very birth of a new state after the end of the World War I, interethnic relations were contaminated by ethnic distance and the negative charge of nationalism. Ethnic conflict thus inevitably became the motive power of events.

III. CONQUERORS AND CONQUERED

Repulsion against the newly emerged "Slovene" state was simultaneous to the reduction of members of the until-then ruling nations to minority status. Concerning the Hungarian minority, two-level behavior of its members was characteristic: on the one hand resistance of townspeople, joined by the *madžaroni* (Hungarophiles)[3] and all Jews,[4] and on the other political apathy and inactivity (regarded by some as loyalty) of the Hungarian peasant population. This was probably also due to the fact that the new authorities did not perform brutal, violent assimilation. They permitted the basic national rights, press and education included. The number of Hungarian minority schools started to diminish more noticeably after the population census of 1931, when many Hungarians declared themselves to be Yugoslavs.[5]

A similar reduction of the social status also awaited the Germans after the founding of a new state. The German population consisted of peasant and working classes along with a layer of tradesmen, craftsmen, industrialists, and members of liberal professions. With the exception of "Germans in Bosnia and Herzegovina, Germans in Slovenia represented the smallest German national minority in the new state, but they were economically and nationally by far the strongest, best organized, with a rich cultural and political tradition, and a strongly emphasized national awareness."[6] They owned many industrial plants, banks and loan societies, and appartment and other buildings (in some towns up to 60% of them all); particularly strong were German estate owners. Owing to its economic power and abundant organizational experience, the Germans of Slovenia had a decisive impact upon the building-up of German minority organizations in Yugoslavia. A rather extensive territory was settled by the Germans in the region of Kočevsko in central Slovenia.[7] The founding of the state of southern Slavs did not suit the German population. First they strived for the annexation to the German Austria, then they demanded their own Kočevsko Republic that was to be under American protectorate. But the attitude of the authorities toward the Kočevsko Germans was similar to that of Austria toward the Carinthian Slovenes. Reciprocality showed in the dissolution of associations, schools, and students' hostels. In Slovene elementary schools, Slovene was introduced as an obligatory subject. The public use of German was limited; German toponyms were substituted by Slovene ones. It was therefore understandable that they strived to introduce national autonomy. "Every more extensive treatise of theirs compares the Kočevsko region to small European states. Each ascertains that Kočevsko, with its nearly 780 km², is more spacious then many of them, and thus perfectly suited for independence. Since today's Germany [after 1938, when Austria was annexed to Nazi Germany] is only 70 km away from Kočevje, and only 28 km of air distance from the sea, Kočevsko is by some people regarded as a strong pillar of the German bridge towards the Adriatic."[8] It is quite possible that all of these "contributed in many ways to the fact that [the Kočevsko Germans] in the 1930s so quickly and in such multitude became followers of Nazism."[9] This can also be ascertained for practically the entire German minority in Slovenia.

The course of events in the neighboring countries, where Slovenes had become national minority members, further emphasized the awareness that the entire Slovene ethnic group was caught among nations, the political elites of which increasingly expressed aggressive and totalitarian nationalism. The slovene place on the Nazi/fascist scale may have been a trifle above the Russians and the Poles, but the fate they had in mind was not essentially different from theirs.

By having become citizens of the first Austrian republic, not only the actual but also the legal status of Slovenes in Austria was changed. Among the former legal regulations, "the new state adopted the well-known Article 19 of the December 1867 constitution, which guaranteed equality to all nationalities of the Austrian part of the Habsburg monarchy. However, it is well known how this regulation was implemented in practice before 1918; things did not improve after 1920. Apart from this, the legal practice was ever since the middle of the 1920s of the opinion that the regulations contained in this article were cancelled by the minority articles determined by the Saint-Germain peace treaty. This opinion was in the 1930s also adopted by the Austrian constitutional court."[10] In spite of international legal obligations, the status of the Slovene minority in Austria remained difficult. The period of the first Austrian republic was one of general pressure of the Carinthian German nationalism upon the Carinthian Slovenes. This was evident in the sharp opposition against the settling of the Slovene minority status in Austria by introducing the so-called cultural autonomy. It was shown in the colonization of German families to the territory of uninterrupted Slovene settlement, as well as in the intensive enforcing of the "Windische theory."[11] The annexation of Austria to Nazi Germany (1938) furthered the latent assimilation processes. Minority regulations which, at least formally, bound Austria to protect its minorities were by the annexation to Germany even formally extinct. They were replaced by aggressive nationalism with elements of ethnocide.

Unlike Austria, Italy as a member of the winning coalition was not required to adopt any international legal obligations for the protection of its minorities. Nevertheless, the first Italian postwar governments at least recognized the existence of minorities and granted their right to preserve their ethnic specificalities, albeit merely on the declarative level. Despite the declaratively benevolent dealing with minority issues, Italian nationalism was becoming more and more aggressive. The emergence of fascism in 1922 raised aggressive nationalism to the level of official state doctrine, the most important part of which was brutal and violent assimilation of the "non-Italian" population.

Regardless of different points of view, it is an indisputable fact that the fascist regimes of the neighboring countries destined ethnic death for the Slovene nation. World War II, which was to be the final chapter of the Slovene national existence, ended by bringing about a completely contrary ethnic result. The Slovenes not only managed to survive and enlarge their state territory,[12] but the war also helped "clean" the Slovene territory of settlement of members of all those nations that had previously been making attempts on their lives—Germans[13] and Italians.[14] The only minority to have emerged from the wartime and postwar conflicts relatively unmodulated was the Hungarian one.[15] This seems unusual since the Hungarian fascist regime also took part in the wartime division of Slovenia, and the Hungarians could, analogically with the fate of the Germans and Italians, have expected a similar fate. But the number of the Hungarin minority members remained almost unchanged. Their postwar existence was probably influenced by the wartime conduct of the Hungarian minority members, since the Hungarian population took a passive standpoint.[16] The Slovene tolerance toward the Hungarian population was certainly further influenced by the ideological proximity of the political regimes in the two states. After 1948 all plans to adjust political and ethnic borders (if they had ever existed) were prevented by the Iron Curtain, a part of which was also the Slovene (Yugoslav)–Hungarian border.

Accumulated knowledge on (and experience of) interethnic relations, adequately (re-)elaborated through the activity of humanistic and cultural intelligentsia and incorporated into many media of (political) socialization, was, in the opinion of many researchers, the decisive influence upon the formation of the Slovene national character. Which elements within the Slovene national character are supposed to (co)shape the attitude of the Slovenes toward members of other nations? The smallness of the territory of settlement and the even smaller state territory represent to many a starting point for reflection about the Slovene national character. The Slovene psychologist A. Trstenjak has named it a ''border nation.'' The smallness of the territory of settlement means that members of the Slovene nation incessantly encounter state borders. Limitation by borders signifies that members of this nation dwell in perpetual ''assimilational exchange with the outside world. . . . A border person unintentionally constantly adapts to his neighbors. In a number of ways. One is undoubtedly the competition. . . . This competitiveness can itself be expressed in at least two different directions: it either conforms and thus loses its originality and self-assurance (phenomenon of national renegation, *nemčurstvo*—Germanophilia, *madžaronstvo*—Hungarophilia), or its independence is enhanced to the degree when it refuses any adaptation, but gradually turns into antagonism and finally hatred generating tension and similar negative behavior.''[17]

In the Slovene national character, elements of negative self-portrayal are often explicitly emphasized: the Slovenes are presented as a humble, nonaggressive, even servile nation. Nonaggressiveness might signify a greater degree of tolerance in relations toward other nations or ethnic minorities. However, contrary to this stereotype, many research studies ascertain with the Slovenes high degrees of aggressiveness, dominance, aspiration, tendency to manipulate others, adventurousness, dogmatism, and machismo. What could have caused a comparatively high degree of psychoticism? Could it be the distrust of members of the nation, ''defined by Trstenjak as a border nation which, more than other nations, feels threatened, surrounded by strangers, jealous of its freedom and independence? Or is it perhaps the fact that with the Slovenes as a comparatively small national group, more aggressive, hard and obstinate individuals were better preserved through generations, while those more gentle and compliant were assimilated to a greater extent? Did a kind of natural selection also function in this case?''[18]

In order to relatively round up the accumulation of elements that should be taken into account in the analysis of ethnic and minority issues in the period of the creation of the new Slovene state (after 1990), consequences of the one-party state system ought also to be mentioned. The gradual postwar evolution of the ''solving'' of ethnic issues in Yugoslavia (and analogically in individual republics) culminated in the new constitution adopted in the middle of the 1970s. In the Slovene Constitution of 1974, the Italian and Hungarian minorities were raised to the level of constitutive elements of the Slovene state.[19] In accordance with this perception, the Constitution itself guaranteed special collective and individual rights to minority members.[20] It is certainly possible to conclude that such an ideal minority protection model could be realized partly because the one-party political model only allowed selected and limited participation of citizens in the process of political decision-making. For the forming and implementation of the minority protection model, this usually implied that all majority members who expressed any second thoughts about the regulation of minority protection, or overemphasized their devotedness to the Slovene ethnic community, were excluded from this process. However, these conflict-devoid interethnic relations were not preserved merely owing to dictated processes of tolerance and coexistence. Many media of socialization (primarily the school system) contained linguistic and cultural elements of both the majority nation and the minorities; mass media were freed of biased nationalistic information; and the open state border enabled communication between minorities and their parent nations. All of these were bound to have positive reflections in interethnic relations.

The supervised and directed implementation of national minority rights probably contributed to the restraint of ethnic tensions in the ethnically mixed territories also because the changing of state borders was accompanied by intensive migrational processes.

The area along the Slovene–Italian border, once the autochthonous territory of settlement of the Italian population, was being settled by numerous immigrants from inner Slovenia. Later on, a considerable number of members of other nations and national groups from other regions of Yugoslavia joined them. Such immigrant populations, consisting of members of ''constitutive'' nations, are frequently the bearers of an accented expression of loyalty to their own ethnic group, often even of ethnic distance and ethnocentrism. The legally commanded nonconflict state did not, however, do away with interethnic tensions resulting from contemporary migration processes; it solely derogated them to the level of latency, where they were ''safely'' swept under the ideological carpet of ''brotherhood and unity.''

IV. RISE OF THE NEW NATION STATE: THE "PARENT NATION STATE" IS BORN

The gradual ripening of the idea on the formation of the Slovene nation-state was taking place at the time of an increasing Yugoslav crisis, when a threat (intention) of the loss of previously acquired postulates of national development was often present. The solution could be seen in a new form of state system. The rising opposition saw the basic sense and purpose of the forming of an independent state in the establishing of autonomous defence mechanisms of the Slovene ethnic community, for the creation of which the Slovenes were supposed to have had enough of relevant political, cultural, and military traditions.[21] Countless proofs can be found in various materials originating from that time to support the above thesis. For example, in the document prepared by the united opposition in May 1989 under the title ''May Declaration,'' the introduction reads: ''Misunderstandings, provocations and open hostilities which the Slovenes nowadays encounter in Yugoslavia have convinced us of the turning point of the present moment in history, and oblige us to clearly express our will which will result in future actions. The signers of this declaration announce: 1. that we wish to live in a sovereign state of the Slovene nation''.[22]

At the beginning of the violent disintegration of Yugoslavia a new state was born, Slovenia. Considering the simultaneous ascent of the political opposition to power it could be expected that the key documents of the Slovene state would contain the greater part of the national defensive vision which had been crystallized in the 1980s. The Constitution of the Republic of Slovenia contains a number of regulations which confirm this expectation. The preamble states, among other instances: ''Acknowledging that we Slovenians created our own national identity and attained our nationhood based on the protection of human rights and freedoms, on the fundamental and permanent right of the Slovenian people to self-determination and as a result of our historical and centuries-long struggle for the liberation of our people, be it hereby enacted by the Parliament of the Republic of Slovenia THE CONSTITUTION OF THE REPUBLIC OF SLOVENIA.'' The first paragraph of Article 3 states that ''Slovenia is a state of all its citizens and is based on the permanent and inalienable right of the Slovenian people to self-determination.'' The role of the state in the preservation of ethnic diversity of the newly founded state can be found in Article 5.[23] At the center of the Slovene statesmanhood there is the protection of the Slovene nation in all its many-sidedness together with the protection of the two classical (territorial) national minorities.[24]

But this almost ideally conceived concept of defence of Slovenehood is limited by the relics of the aforementioned accumulation of experience and knowledge on interethnic relations. The attitude of the Slovene state toward members of the Slovene minorities settled in the neighboring countries (Italy, Austria, Hungary) remains captured at the mental starting point, according to which Slovene minorities in the neighboring countries represent extensions (remnants?) of the nation outside of the nation-state. In order to support this perception of the national minority issues, even a special vocabulary has been formed: it comprises phrases such as "parent nation," "parent nation-state," or even "parent nation homeland," which often bring to mind the existence of centers deciding the fate of national minorities from without and, more dangerous still, from abroad—from a neighboring state. Perhaps it was this kind of dealing with the national "remains" outside the state border that indirectly influenced their dropping of the original ethnic identity. Intensive dependency upon the parent nation-state evoked convictions about irredentistic tendencies of minority groups in the state of their actual settlement, which often triggered assimilative pressures. It is also true, however, that the "help" offered by the parent nation-state was frequently merely an answer to the brutal assimilation policies of the neighboring countries toward Slovene minority members, which were mentioned at the beginning of this chapter.

If the newly founded state wishes to fulfill the vocation written down in its fundamental law, it requires a new definition of relations between the parent nation and the minorities. Starting with the definition of minorities: they are (ethnically) a part of the Slovene parent nation living in the neighboring countries, but because of the intertwining of ethnic elements with influences/pressures from the part of majority nations, as well as from the part of the parent nation, they change into comparatively independent national units. National minorities are neither an authentic copy of the parent nation (even though they have common linguistic, cultural, and some anthropological characteristics), nor a mirror image of the social and ideological stratification of societies within which they live. National minorities change, owing to the intertwining of the two aforementioned levels, i.e., the national (autochthonous) and the adopted characteristics, into specifics idiosyncratic national organisms, the development of which is not determined only by the external but also by internal principles shaped in the process of two-track socialization. The new relation that ought to be formed between the parent nation and minorities could also be a step toward recognition of subjectivity of minorities. Subjectivity is a synonym for the global recognition and acknowledgement of two different communities who nevertheless share ethnic origins and many cultural characteristics. However, life in different sociocultural and political spaces has created (independent) national organisms with their own visions of development. Without this recognition, the (often feigned) lamenting for the lost part of the nation will continue, together with the concept of dealing with minorities as formations in a permanent phase of adolescence, which stagger painfully after the bright future of the Slovene (parent) nation. It is precisely because of this lagging behind in progress that they should be helped. These were the viewpoints that generated, to a considerable degree, the opinion that Slovene minorities in the neighboring countries should be assisted in their development problems! Once this principle was looked upon through political glasses, there was only one step to guardianship and tutelage.[25] Perhaps it was this perception of forced equalization, insisting upon transplantation of criteria of ethnodevelopment from the parent nation to an entirely different surroundings, that contributed to the dropping of their original identity with some members of Slovene national minorities in the neighboring countries.

The discussion on notions such as homeland, parent nation, and so on vitalizes the perception of the state as the exclusive guarantor of a nation's ethnic specificity. This applies to the part of the nation within nation-state borders as well as to the "ethnic remnants" without the state territory. The romantic perception of the relation between the parent nation and its minorities, a mixture of charity and protection, often conceals a distorted perception of national issues. The use of the phrase "parent nation" recalls a beelike organization of a nation, within which everything is in one way or another subjected to the preservation of the parent—the queen bee.

V. NEW NATIONAL COMMUNITIES: THE DEEP GAP BETWEEN LEGAL AND SOCIETAL CITIZENSHIP

As mentioned, the territory on which the independent Slovene state was founded in the beginning of the 1990s was never ethnically homogeneous. The number of ethnic minorities, their extent, and their real economic and political power were, in different historical periods, changing in accordance with the changing of political borders. The last changing of borders left in Slovenia a rather diverse collection of members of non-Slovene ethnic groups (see Table 1). They can be classified into two categories: the classical (territorial) minorities and a collection of newly created minorities (mostly members of nations which had formed the former common Yugoslav state), which are a result of contemporary economical immigration processes.

Two different concepts of minority policy correspond to two minority categories: (1) a relatively complete legal protection of traditional (territorial) ethnic minorities, comprising, apart from constitutional regulations,[26] about eighty laws and legal provisions, and (2) a completely nonelaborated attitude of the Slovene state toward the newly formed national minorities, within which many elements of silent assimilation can be traced.

The emphasis of the newly founded state upon the defence of the Slovene nation is reflected in the changed concept of the protection of classical ethnic minorities: unlike the former standpoint, which raised the Italian and Hungarian minorities to the status of constitutive national elements of the Slovene state (see note 19), the new constitution again "degrades" them to the level of mere national communities. Perhaps it was this very reduction of their status, along with explicit stressing of Slovenehood, that contributed to the occurrence of a considerable gap between the extensive legal regulations and the minority members' opinions regarding their perfection. The change of the political system, which was announcing a general increase of human rights, did not bring any positive alterations in the field of national minority communities protection. This is confirmed by the data in Table 2. Results of research studies[27] performed in 1992 and 1994 indicate that the frequently expressed conviction about the model system of minority protection in Slovenia cannot sustain empirical examination. Results of the 1994 research in Slovene Istria show that most members of the Italian minority feel they have no influence in political life, that Italians of Slovene Istria have no adequate role in the shaping of their own fate, and that the Republic of Slovenia pays more attention to Slovene minorities abroad than it does to minorities in its own territory. It is interesting to note that even the degree of positive opinions on the adequacy of legal protection of the Italian minority is much lower than might be expected with regard to the extent of protective standards (for more details, see Table 3). The causes of this probably lie in a series of events and processes which turned the period following the formation of the independent Slovene state into a "period of measured insecurity" for minority members. Reduction to the status of classical minorities, explicit stressing of Slovenehood, and political tensions between Slovenia and Italy during the first years of independence are important ingredients of the insecurity period. A number of lawsuits against national minority legislation, taken to the Constitutional Court of the Republic of Slovenia by various organizations as well as individuals, should be added to the list. These lawsuits relate to the question of the guaranteed minority mandate in the state parliament, or the competencies of the minority representative; to the issue of obligatory bilingual identity cards for all population of the nationally mixed communes; to the use of national symbols of national minorities (primarily the national colors); and to the field of obligatory bilingual education. Up to this moment, the Constitutional Court has not reached a final decision on any of these issues.

The number of members of classical national minorities is 11,567 persons (or 13,860 persons, if we include members of the Romany community), i.e., 0.59% (0.70%) of the entire population of the Republic of Slovenia; the state grants them the status of national minority and guarantees relatively complete legal protection. Besides the Slovenes and the other mentioned minorities, there

Table 1 Population by Ethnic Nationality According to 1953, 1961, 1971, 1981, and 1991 Censuses

	1953[a]		1961		1971		1981		1991	
	Total	Share (%)	Total	Share (%)	Total	Share (%)	Total	Share (%)	Total	Share (%)
Republic of Slovenia	1,466,425	100	1,591,523	100	1,727,137	100	1,891,864	100	1,965,986	100
Nationally defined										
Slovenes	1,415,448	96.52	1,522,248	95.65	1,624,029	94.03	1,712,445	90.52	1,727,018	87.84
Italians	854	0.06	3,072	0.19	3,001	0.17	2,187	0.12	3,064	0.16
Hungarians	11,019	0.75	10,498	0.66	9,785	0.57	9,496	0.5	8,503	0.43
Romes	1,663	0.12	158	0.01	977	0.06	1,435	0.08	2,293	0.12
Albanians	169	0.01	282	0.02	1,281	0.07	1,985	0.1	3,629	0.18
Austrians	289	0.02	254	0.02	278	0.02	180	0.01	199	0.01
Bulgarians	49	0.00	180	0.01	139	0.01	105	0.01	169	0.01
Czechs	807	0.06	584	0.04	445	0.03	433	0.02	323	0.02
Montenegrins	1,356	0.09	1,384	0.09	1,978	0.11	3,217	0.17	4,396	0.22
Greeks	24	0.00	50	0.00	24	0.00	18	0.00	23	0.00
Croats	17,978	1.23	31,429	1.97	42,657	2.47	55,625	2.94	54,212	2.76
Macedonians	640	0.04	1,009	0.06	1,613	0.09	3,288	0.17	4,432	0.22
Muslims	1,617	0.11	465	0.03	3,231	0.19	13,425	0.71	26,842	1.36
Germans	1,617	0.11	732	0.05	422	0.02	380	0.02	546	0.03

	Count	%	Count	%	Count	%	Count	%	Count	%
Poles	275	0.02	222	0.01	194	0.01	204	0.01	204	0.01
Romanians	41	0.00	48	0.00	43	0.00	94	0.01	116	0.01
Russians	593	0.04	295	0.02	302	0.02	194	0.01	170	0.01
Rusinians[b]	46	0.00	384	0.02	66	0.00	54	0.00	57	0.00
Slovaks	60	0.01	71	0.00	85	0.01	144	0.01	141	0.01
Serbs	11,225	0.77	13,609	0.86	20,521	1.19	42,182	2.23	47,911	2.44
Turks	68	0.01	135	0.01	53	0.00	87	0.00	155	0.01
Ukrainians[b]	—	—	—	—	143	0.01	192	0.01	213	0.01
Vlachs	9	0.00	6	0.00	5	0.00	17	0.00	38	0.00
Jews	15	0.00	21	0.00	72	0.00	9	0.00	37	0.00
Other	352	0.02	449	0.03	307	0.02	577	0.03	1,178	0.06
Nationally undeclared										
Undeclared per Art. 214 of Slovenian Constitution	—		—		3,073	0.18	2,975	0.16	9,011	0.46
Yugoslavs	—		2,784	0.18	6,744	0.39	26,263	1.39	12,307	0.63
Regional affiliation	—		—		2,705	0.16	4,018	0.21	5,254	0.27
Unknown	211	0.01	1,154	0.07	2,964	0.17	10,635	0.56	53,545	2.72

[a] Territory at the census date.
[b] In 1953 and 1961 censuses the Rusinians and the Ukrainians apper under one item.

Table 2 Results from "Interethnic Relations in the Slovene Ethnic Territory" Research Project (*Question*: To what extent did, in postwar periods, Italian national community in Slovene Istria have the opportunity to influence the regulation of its legal status?)

	Municipality of Izola					Slovene littoral Italians		
	Slovenes	Italians	Others	No answer	Together	Italians	Other	Together
A. From 1945 to 1954								
None	16.7	6.7	16.9	4.5	15.6	30.9	22.9	29.0
Little	20.4	23.3	9.2	18.2	19.0	25.7	20.8	24.5
Considerable influence	6.0	13.3	4.6	—	6.0	7.9	10.4	8.5
Much influence	4.2	13.3	3.1	—	4.4	2.6	6.3	3.5
Don't know, no answer	52.7	43.3	66.2	77.3	55.0	32.9	39.6	34.5
N	383	30	65	22	500	152	48	200
B. From 1955 to 1974								
None	4.7	—	6.2	—	4.4	25.0	12.5	22.0
Little	25.1	40.0	15.4	13.6	24.2	31.6	29.2	31.0
Considerable influence	18.0	10.0	9.2	13.6	16.2	9.2	14.6	10.5
Much influence	5.0	13.3	6.2	—	5.4	2.6	4.2	3.0
Don't know, no answer	47.3	36.7	63.1	72.7	49.8	31.6	39.6	33.5
N	383	30	65	22	500	152	48	200

C. From 1975 to 1990

None	1.8	—	3.1	—	1.8	13.8	8.3	12.5
Little	9.9	30.0	7.7	9.1	10.8	31.6	25.0	30.0
Considerable influence	35.0	43.3	20.0	27.3	33.2	29.6	35.4	31.0
Much influence	13.1	6.7	7.7	—	11.4	5.3	2.1	4.5
Don't know, no answer	40.2	20.0	61.5	63.6	42.8	19.7	29.2	22.0
N	383	30	65	22	500	152	48	200

D. After multiparty elections

None	2.1	—	3.1	—	2.0	11.8	6.3	10.5
Little	8.9	33.3	9.2	4.5	10.2	32.9	22.9	30.5
Considerable influence	30.5	33.3	18.5	22.7	28.8	20.4	29.2	22.5
Much influence	17.5	13.3	7.7	4.5	15.4	9.2	2.1	7.5
Don't know, no answer	41.0	20.0	61.5	68.2	43.6	25.7	39.6	29.0
N	383	30	65	22	500	152	48	200

Note: All figures are percentages except *N* rows.

Table 3 Results from "Interethnic Relations in the Slovene Ethnic Territory" Research Project (*Question:* We shall give a few statements on life of Italians in Slovene Istria. Please tell us whether you agree or disagree.)

| | Municipality of Izola | | | | | Slovene littoral Italians | | |
	Slovenes	Italians	Others	No answer	Together	Italians	Other	Together
V1. Italian minority has no influence in political life								
completely agree	14.1	26.7	12.3	22.7	15.0	40.5	20.4	35.6
mainly agree	24.5	26.7	21.5	18.2	24.0	24.8	32.7	26.7
neither agree nor disagree	14.1	13.3	16.9	4.5	14.0	19.6	28.6	21.8
mainly disagree	18.0	10.0	21.5	9.1	17.6	3.3	4.1	3.5
completely disagree	17.0	13.3	12.3	9.1	15.8	8.5	10.2	8.9
don't know, no answer	12.3	10.0	15.4	36.4	13.6	3.3	4.1	3.5
N	383	30	65	22	500	153	49	202
V2. Italians in Slovene Istria do not have adequate role in the creation of their own fate								
completely agree	5.7	16.7	4.6	4.5	6.2	39.2	22.4	35.1
mainly agree	11.2	33.3	15.4	9.1	13.0	24.2	16.3	22.3
neither agree nor disagree	12.0	16.7	15.4	4.5	12.4	17.0	24.5	18.8
completely disagree	27.2	13.3	18.5	18.2	24.8	7.8	16.3	9.9
don't know, no answer	13.1	3.3	15.4	31.8	13.6	2.6	8.2	4.0
N	383	30	65	22	500	153	49	202

V4. Republic of Slovenia pays more attention to Slovenes in neighboring countries than to minorities in its own territory (Italians, Hungarians)

completely agree	7.8	16.7	7.7	4.5	8.2	37.3	18.4	32.7
mainly agree	7.0	13.3	1.5	4.5	6.6	17.0	10.2	15.3
neither agree nor disagree	20.6	20.0	35.4	4.5	21.8	18.3	18.4	18.3
mainly disagree	19.3	13.3	9.2	13.6	17.4	8.5	18.4	10.9
completely disagree	25.3	20.0	12.3	40.9	24.0	6.5	20.4	9.9
don't know, no answer	19.8	16.7	33.8	31.8	22.0	12.4	14.3	12.9
N	383	30	65	22	500	153	49	202

V6. Italian minority in Slovenia is sufficiently legally protected

completely agree	50.9	33.3	33.8	50.0	47.6	24.8	30.6	26.2
mainly agree	31.1	30.0	29.2	18.2	30.2	23.5	22.4	23.3
neither agree nor disagree	6.3	13.3	13.8	9.1	7.8	16.3	20.4	17.3
mainly disagree	2.3	10.0	1.5	—	2.6	16.3	8.2	14.4
completely disagree	1.0	6.7	6.2	—	2.0	15.0	12.2	14.4
don't know, no answer	8.4	6.7	15.4	22.7	9.8	3.9	61.4	4.5
N	383	30	65	22	500	153	49	202

Note: All figures are percentages except *N* rows.

are 222,321 persons living in Slovenia (according to the 1991 population census), or 11.45% of the entire population, who belong to various other nations (see Table 1). To them, too, the Constitution guarantees free expression of their national appurtenance.[28] However, because of the very rudimental realization of the legislation in practice, these regulations remain, more or less, mere words on paper.

This population group consists mainly of members of nations and "nationalities" from the former common state. But before they could benefit from the new Slovene constitution, they—at least the majority of them—first had to become citizens of the Republic of Slovenia, in accordance with the Slovene legislation regulations. The Slovene parliament bound itself, in its statement on good intentions (*Official Gazette of the Republic of Slovenia*, No. 44/90), to enable naturalization to all members of other nations and nationalities with permanent residence in Slovenia who wish to become Slovene citizens. The law on citizenship of the Republic of Slovenia in its Article 40 only repeated the contents of this statement, but determined a six-month time limit during which applications would be accepted. This time limit expired on December 25, 1991, without the possibility of prolongation. By that time, 174,228 applications were put in, representing 8.7% of the entire population of the Republic of Slovenia. 170,990 applications were granted, thus creating a new category of citizens who are mostly holders of dual citizenship. Up to now, Slovenia has not succeeded in settling issues regarding citizenship with any of the newly founded states in the area of former Yugoslavia.

With the founding of the independent Slovene state, the status of the immigrant population underwent a radical change. Former members of constitutive nations of Yugoslavia, who (in most cases) migrated to other regions of the common homeland in search of employment, became practically overnight a statistically ascertained minority with all characteristics of economic immigrant communities.

How did ordinary people react to the issue of naturalization? Public opinion questionnaires show a considerably favorable attitude toward the benevolent solving of these problems. However, a certain degree of caution can be noticed; people also believe that some additional conditions ought to be fulfilled in order to obtain citizenship, such as, for example, a certain period of permanent residence or employment in Slovenia. The majority is opposed to dual citizenship. All these relations were studied in the research project of Slovene public opinion in 1990; the results of four of the questions are presented here:

Question No. 1: With the adoption of the new Constitution, the question of Slovene citizenship will have to be newly regulated. Who and under what conditions should have the opportunity to become a Slovene citizen?

	Yes	No	I do not know
a. Automatically all Slovenes, Italians, and Hungarians permanently settled in Slovenia and being Slovene citizens according to present law	86.4	4.6	9.0
b. Automatically all members of other Yugoslav nations permanently settled in Slovenia and being Slovene citizens according to present law	64.9	21.6	13.5
c. All Slovene emigrants, if they so desire	80.6	8.0	11.4
d. All members of other Yugoslav nations permanently settled and working in Slovenia, if they so desire	65.0	19.2	14.9

Question No. 2:   Ought workers from other republics and foreigners to comply with any of the below listed conditions to obtain naturalization?

That they had never been in close arrest	40.4
That they pass a kind of "citizens' examination"	20.4
That they understand Slovene	47.9
That they speak Slovene	56.9
That they have been regularly employed in Slovenia for a certain period of time	55.9
That they have been permanently employed in Slovenia for a certain period of time	59.3
None of these	7.3
I do not know	10.3

Question No. 3.   How many years of permanent residence or employment in Slovenia should be the necessary condition for naturalization of workers from other republics?

Average: 8.0

Question No. 4:   Can a Serb, settled in Slovenia and possessing Slovene citizenship, obtain also Serbian (dual) citizenship? Yes or no?

He can	23.3
He cannot	58.2
Takes no side, does not know	18.4

Whatever the causes of this relatively tolerant and benevolent attitude, it is a fact that this attitude radically changed after a few years. The Slovenes became convinced that the legislation enabled too liberal a system of naturalization. This can be seen in the results of the 1993 Slovene public opinion research. The question of naturalization was seen in this way:

Question: The Slovene state was too liberal in granting citizenship to immigrants:

I agree completely	50.7
I mainly agree	32.6
Uncertain	7.1
I mainly disagree	4.2
I completely disagree	1.2
I do not know	4.1

The founding of a new state caused radical change of conditions for the preservation of national identity of members of non-Slovene (immigrant) groups. Their language is losing its social value, it is reduced to the level of a means of communication between members of the same ethnic group. But this is not wholly the result of the emerging of a new state. In the 1991 population census, two questions were posed which indicated that the erosion of significance, social value, and use of languages of non-Slovene ethnic groups had already been diminishing in the former state. In this process, some of the elements of the aforementioned Slovene national character might also be found. Data indicate that Slovene prevails in ethnically mixed families. The majority nation language occupies an important position even within ethnically homogeneous families (Tables 4 and 5), to say nothing about the use of language outside of the home. These data present classical relations between immigrant communities and the dominating majority—the nondeveloped adaptation and nondeveloped cultural pluralism with limited possibilities for the expression and development of immigrant cultures. Processes of problematic diglossia are usually part of such a concept. This means "that ethnic minority members can only use their language in relations with family and friends, at primary level, while in secondary relations communication, i.e. in various institutions, while meeting different needs, they use the dominating language, which to them is the language by means of which social promotion is possible."[29] What course may processes of nondeveloped adaptation take in the future?

Seen from the viewpoint of Slovene public opinion (SPO) research it would seem that, at this moment, processes of nondeveloped adaptation are at a stand-

Table 4 Language of Communication in Families of Children Over 18 in Ethnically Mixed and Ethnically Homogeneous Families (Two-Parent Families Only)

	Total	Ethnically mixed families[a]											Ethnically homogeneous families[a]						
		Total	SLO ITA	SLO HUN	SLO CRO	SLO SER	SLO Other	ITA SLO	HUN SLO	CRO SLO	SER SLO	Other SLO	Total	SLO SLO	ITA ITA	HUN HUN	CRO CRO	SER SER	Other Other
Total	173,772	12,134	90	145	1,975	378	1,188	136	202	3,640	1,801	2,579	161,638	151,670	145	537	2,459	1,577	52
Slovene	162,074	10,842	38	67	1,838	332	961	64	112	3,475	1,629	2,326	151,232	147,000	9	13	1,726	565	19
Italian	227	36	15	—	—	—	3	16	—	1	—	1	191	30	113	—	2	—	—
Hungarian	492	45	—	26	—	—	—	—	19	—	—	—	447	6	—	429	—	—	—
Croatian	446	34	—	—	18	—	2	—	—	12	—	2	412	22	—	—	289	2	—
Serbian	248	8	—	—	—	3	—	—	—	—	5	—	240	9	—	—	—	185	—
Serbo-Croatian	1,143	59	—	—	1	12	15	—	—	6	14	11	1,084	100	—	—	30	345	6
Slovene and Italian	175	94	21	—	8	1	3	37	—	8	1	15	81	41	6	—	2	1	—
Slovene and Hungarian	—	—	—	—	—	—	—	—	—	—	—	—	—	—	—	—	—	—	—
Slovene and Serbo-Croatian	968	206	—	1	28	12	11	1	—	42	71	40	762	25	1	1	159	231	3
Slovene and other	455	76	—	3	7	3	26	1	3	6	7	20	379	279	—	1	11	8	—
Italian and Slovene	86	37	13	—	2	—	5	16	—	—	—	1	49	13	13	—	2	—	—
Italian and Serbo-Croatian	4	—	—	—	—	—	—	—	—	—	—	—	4	1	—	—	1	—	—
Italian and other	6	3	—	—	—	—	—	—	—	—	1	1	3	1	1	—	—	1	1
Hungarian and Slovene	65	19	—	11	—	—	2	—	5	—	—	1	46	6	—	31	—	—	—
Hungarian and Serbo-Croatian	3	—	—	—	—	—	—	—	—	—	—	—	3	—	—	—	—	—	—
Hungarian and other	26	8	—	4	—	—	—	—	3	—	—	1	18	—	—	17	—	—	—
Croatian and other	280	30	1	—	6	—	2	—	—	15	2	4	250	16	—	—	166	4	—
Serbian and other	236	26	1	1	15	3	2	—	—	12	17	2	210	7	—	—	9	120	3
Other language	965	93	1	3	19	2	26	—	9	23	9	16	872	462	1	12	15	48	3
Prekmurje dialect	2,598	93	—	6	2	2	8	—	—	10	10	17	2,505	2,490	—	—	2	1	—
Unknown	3,275	425	1	24	32	8	122	1	8	38	35	121	2,850	1,162	—	33	44	66	15

[a] Codes: SLO, Slovene; ITA, Italian; HUN, Hungarian; CRO, Croatian; SER, Serbian. First code given for each column refers to the father and the second code to the mother.

Table 5 Language of Communication in the Social Environment of Children Under 18 in Ethnically Mixed and Ethnically Homogeneous Families (Two-Parent Families Only)

	Total	Ethnically mixed families[a]											Ethnically homogeneous families[a]						
		Total	SLO ITA	SLO HUN	SLO CRO	SLO SER	SLO Other	ITA SLO	HUN SLO	CRO SLO	SER SLO	Other SLO	Total	SLO SLO	ITA ITA	HUN HUN	CRO CRO	SER SER	Other Other
Total	412,076	32,412	204	501	6,096	1,757	4,294	236	604	8,112	3,737	6,871	379,664	329,964	125	883	7,905	11,451	293
Slovene	381,947	29,592	87	219	5,757	1,654	3,818	113	252	7,775	3,557	6,360	352,355	319,961	17	59	6,283	7,853	181
Italian	114	36	17	—	3	—	—	13	—	—	1	—	78	8	38	—	1	—	—
Hungarian	240	29	—	15	—	—	2	—	12	—	—	—	211	—	—	185	—	—	—
Croatian	718	45	—	3	16	1	4	—	—	18	—	3	673	104	—	—	371	12	1
Serbian	435	9	—	—	1	—	2	—	—	—	5	1	426	35	—	—	4	321	—
Serbo-Croatian	2,433	46	—	—	8	6	16	—	—	3	7	6	2,387	333	—	—	94	621	14
Slovene and Italian	751	248	52	—	18	6	23	67	—	28	6	48	503	—	26	1	17	19	1
Slovene and Hungarian	—	—	—	—	—	—	—	—	—	—	—	—	—	—	—	—	—	—	—
Slovene and Serbo-Croatian	4,107	231	1	—	23	20	27	1	—	47	57	55	3,876	56	2	1	443	1,212	21
Slovene and other	986	110	—	5	18	6	20	7	24	9	3	18	876	370	2	14	46	66	3
Italian and Slovene	195	79	42	—	2	1	1	24	—	1	—	8	116	27	29	1	3	6	—
Italian and Serbo-Croatian	9	1	—	—	—	—	—	—	—	1	—	—	8	1	1	—	1	1	—
Italian and other	13	4	—	—	—	1	—	2	—	1	—	—	9	3	3	1	—	—	—
Hungarian and Slovene	545	126	—	72	2	—	—	—	50	2	—	—	419	30	—	348	1	—	—
Hungarian and Serbo-Croatian	—	—	—	—	—	—	—	—	—	—	—	—	—	—	—	—	—	—	—
Hungarian and other	71	20	—	4	—	—	—	—	16	—	—	—	51	4	—	42	—	—	—
Croatian and other	849	42	—	1	13	1	7	1	—	16	—	3	807	96	2	1	364	41	3
Serbian and other	1,037	28	—	1	—	2	7	—	18	—	—	—	1,009	11	—	1	27	490	4
Other language	2,706	306	2	9	81	22	77	1	28	43	1	42	2,400	1,250	—	37	31	256	8
Prekmurje dialect	4,787	232	2	17	47	4	39	—	—	42	43	38	4,555	4,478	—	1	11	8	—
Unknown	10,133	1,228	1	155	106	33	251	7	204	126	53	280	8,905	2,987	6	192	207	544	49

[a] Codes: SLO, Slovene; ITA, Italian; HUN, Hungarian; CRO, Croatian; SER, Serbian. First code given for each column refers to the father and the second code to the mother.

still, also due to the prevailing opinion on the acceptability of migrational policy one-sidedness, based upon immigrant societies interests, that is, upon processes of nondeveloped adaptation and nondeveloped cultural pluralism. This can best be seen when compared to the status of autochthonous minorities. Answers to questions posed in 1990 SPO research clearly illustrate this relation:

Question: Which of the below listed rights should be granted by the Constitution to the autochthonous minorities in Slovenia, mainly Italians and Hungarians, and which to immigrant citizens (Albanians, Serbs, Croats, Moslems . . .)?

	For autochthonous minorities		For immigrants	
	yes	no	yes	no
Free use of their own language	83.6	15.6	55.5	43.5
Expression of their own culture	85.8	13.2	67.4	31.4
Founding of their own organizations and institutions	77.0	22.1	56.2	42.9
Right to public use of their own national symbols	56.3	42.2	32.2	66.2
Develop their own economic activities	77.8	21.0	61.7	37.1
Organize their press, radio, TV	68.2	30.7	38.2	60.7
Form their own school system	53.8	45.1	24.1	74.7
Cultivate their contact with parent nation	89.8	9.0	78.9	19.9
Form special national communities in region of their settlement	62.2	36.4	35.4	62.
Have their own representatives in communes/municipalities	77.0	21.7	50.1	48.
Have their own representatives in parliament	72.2	26.6	41.9	56.
Found their own political parties	43.2	55.5	24.9	73.7

A similar question was posed two years later (SPO from 1992), and answers were similar:

Question: How should non-Slovene citizens ("from other republics"), who have been living in Slovenia for a longer period of time, behave?

Drop their own culture and language and accept the Slovene ones	12.9
Preserve their culture and language and live in isolation	2.2
After a certain period in Slovenia, they should return home	7.8
Learn Slovene and adapt to living conditions in Slovenia, but use their own language among themselves and cultivate their own culture	60.0
Have the opportunity of schooling in their own language and developing their own culture, but at the same time adapt to living conditions in Slovenia	8.9
Do not know, uncertain	8.1

The building-up of adaptation and developed cultural pluralism will evidently be a long-lasting process. We can hardly claim to have reached the line denoting the start. It seems that ethnic repulsion is still strong within the majority population. In SPO research projects, these relations can also be traced. The following standpoints, for example, are highly indicative:

Question: We shall list some words and notions; mark immediately, without much reflecting, whether your attitude toward them is very positive or very negative:

	Very negative	Negative	Neutral	Very positive	Positive	Don't know
Immigrants from the south:						
SPO 91	4.9	24.8	39.6	18.4	4.1	9.0
SPO 92	11.0	31.5	33.9	12.5	1.7	9.3
SPO 93	10.0	33.4	36.0	11.2	2.0	7.4
SPO 94	12.2	40.6	28.7	7.9	1.5	9.1

The entire cluster of relations falling under the category "negative attitude" will have to be further researched. Only thus will the first step be made toward an analysis of elements of ethnocentrism and xenophobia, which are also present in the Slovene society. Negative prejudice and stereotypes are often a sign of these phenomena. It is a common conviction that the number of criminal offences is increasing because of immigrants, that they are, in the economical sense, rather useless than useful. If we check again the results of SPO (this time for 1994), this is quickly confirmed in the responses.

Question: There exist different opinions on immigrants from other states, or republics of former Yugoslavia, who have settled in Slovenia (permanently). To what extent do you agree with the following:

		I agree completely	I agree	I neither agree nor disagree	I disagree	I completely disagree	I don't know
a.	Number of criminal offences is being increased because of immigrants	21.3	32.5	16.8	17.0	3.6	8.8
b.	Immigrants are generally useful to Slovene economy	3.0	15.9	23.6	36.4	10.0	11.1
c.	Immigrants occupy job which could be held by people born in Slovenia	21.3	34.6	17.9	16.5	3.0	6.8
d.	Owing to immigrants Slovenia is becoming more open to new ideas and cultures	4.2	22.9	19.2	30.5	7.3	15.8

The SPO data presented indicate that we probably find ourselves at the beginning of the building-up process, named by sociologists the process of adaptation and developed cultural pluralism. Processes of cultural pluralism are intertwined with processes of more developed adaptation, more complete adaptation. What it is all about is the preservation and development of "ethnic characteristics, ethnic identity, culture, by guaranteeing autonomy of cultures and tolerance towards the different. Processes of cultural pluralism belong among conjunctive processes which foster participation and self-management of ethnic communities. They are distinctly contrary to phenomena of ethnic stratification and forced assimilations, as well as to theoretical viewpoints which foretell the "overgrowing" and vanishing of ethnic communities. Cultural pluralism is based upon developed, more complete processes of adaptation and other conjunctive processes, but it is also connected to integrational conflicts."[30] This would therefore signify all-comprising respect for inborn ethnic characteristics, to which members of minority ethnic communities are tied, but at the same time consideration for the culturally different. It is probably the only way for a relatively scarce society, composed of different ethnic communities, to obtain suitable inner cohesion and integration. It is not quite clear how the Slovene authorities intend to solve these issues, since there is no existing document under the title "Slovene Strategy of Migrational Processes." But it will be difficult to avoid the regulation of the already cited Article 61 of the Slovene Constitution.

NOTES/REFERENCES

1. United Slovenia is the common name of the national program, prepared in 1848 by the Slovene intelligentsia and students. It postulated the abolition of old provincial units, and the shaping of new borders based upon national criteria; the newly formed territory would comprise all regions settled by Slovenes and would acquire the name of Slovenia. This new political unit would have its own parliament and its own administration within the Austrian empire. They were opposed to unification with the German empire. The Slovene language should become equal to German. There also appeared demands for the founding of a Slovene university.

2. In the period between the two wars, there lived in Slovene territory members of various, mostly small (in number) ethnic minorities: Serbs, Croats, Czechs, Slovaks, Rusinians, Poles, Albanians, etc. The most numerous were Germans: 42,514, or 3.9% of the population, and Hungarians: 14,429, or 1.4% of the population of Slovenia.

3. *Madžaroni* (Hungarophiles) were members of the Slovene nation to whom the xenophilic relation to Hungarians represented the motive power of their ethnic development. Analogically, the emphasized xenophilia toward Germans, and persons practicing it, were called *Nemčurji* (Germanophiles). This stratum of Slovenes in the northern regions of the Slovene territory of settlement claims that cultural progress is possible only with the help of German language and culture, and in political connection with Germans.

4. For more details on Jews, see Hudelja, M. (1991). Prisotnost židovske etnične manjšine v Prekmurju (Presence of Jewish ethnic minority in Prekmurje). In *Vzporednice slovenske in koroške etnologije* (Parallels of Slovene and Carinthian Ethnology), p. 7. Ljubljana; Küzmič, F. (1989). *Podjetnost Židov* (Jewish enterprise), p. 2. Ljubljana: Znamenja.

5. Nećak-Lük, A. (1981). Oris položaja madžarske narodne manjšine v Prekmurju v obdobju od 1918 do 1945 (Description of the sitation of the Hungarian minority in Prekmurje region in the period from 1918 to 1945). *Zgodovinski časopis 3* (Ljubljana), 279–286.

6. Biber, D. (1966). *Nacizem in Nemci v Jugoslaviji 1933–1941* (Nazism and Germans in Yugoslavia 1933–1941). Ljubljana, p. 114.

7. Settling of this scarcely populated region by German colonists began in the 1330s, when the Ortenburgers settled the first ones, originating from their lands in Carinthia. The main wave of colonization took place between 1349 and 1363. The territory of German colonization was gradually expanding through centuries, so that the island of German language reached about 800 km^2. Apart from economic privileges (peddling), the Kočevsko Germans enjoyed additional political rights. They had their representative in the provincial assembly of Kranjska, and in 1907 they even obtained a special mandate in the state assembly in Vienna. According to the 1921 population census, 12,610 Germans lived in Kočevsko.

8. Rus J. (1934). Jedro kočevskega vprašanja (Essence of the Kočevsko question). In *Kočevski Zbornik* (The Kočevsko Miscellany, p. 146). Ljubljana.

9. Ferenc, M. (1993). Kočevska—Izgubljena Kulturna Dediščina Kočevskih Nemcev (The Lost Cultural Heritage of the Kočevska Germans, p. 27). Ljubljana.

10. Zorn, T. (1984). Koroški Slovenci v prvi avstrijski republiki (Carinthian Slovenes in the first Austrian republic). In *Koroški Slovenci v Avstriji Včeraj in Danes* (Carinthian Slovenes in Austria Yesterday and Today, p. 40). Ljubljana.

11. Windische theory: under the guise of German nationalistic "science," politicians constructed in the 1930s this thesis about Carinthian Slovenes in Austria being a "special nation," speaking a special language. This language supposedly failed to develop into a special literary language only due to the small number of its speakers. That explained why "die Kärntner Windischen" use German as their literary language. Literary Slovene was said to be an artificial language, almost an assault against Carinthian dialect, incomprehensible to most Carinthians, and therefore renounced. German authors finally draw attention to particular national awareness which distinguishes "Windische" from "nationally conscious Slovenes."

12. The territory of Slovenia increased, after the 1947 peace treaty, by approximately 23%, and after the final determination of state borders in 1954 by another few hundred square kilometers; it thus comprised 20,251 km^2 and was for almost 25% larger from the old-Yugoslav one. It included about 85% of what was, in the most ideal national programs, called United Slovenia.

13. In 1948, three years after the war, there were only 1,824 Germans in Slovenia.

14. The western region of the territory which became part of Slovenia (Yugoslavia) after World War II was populated by a relatively large number of Italians. The October 1, 1945, census showed that in the area around Koper in zone B of the free territory of Trieste (annexed to Slovenia in 1954) lived about 22,000 Italians, mostly in urban centres Koper, Izola, and Piran. The final annexation of this territory to Slovenia in 1954 triggered massive migrations of the Italian population. According to the 1961 population census, there were only 3,072 Italians still living in Slovenia.

15. According to the 1953 population census, 11,019 Hungarians lived in Slovenia.

16. For more details, see Lük, A. N. (1981). Madžarska manjšina v Prekmurju 1918–1945 (Hungarian minority in Prekmurje region 1918–1945). *Zgodovinski časopis* (Historical review), 284.

17. Trstenjak, A. (1991). *Misli o Slovenskem Človeku* (Reflections on Slovene People), p. 13. Ljubljana.

18. Musek, J. (1994). *Psihološki Portret Slovencev* (Psychological portrait of Slovenes), pp. 71–72. Ljubljana.

19. Article 1 of the Constitution of the Socialist Republic of Slovenia (SRS): SRS is a state based upon the sovereignty of the Slovene nation and all people of Slovenia, upon the power of and self-management by the working class and all working people, and is a socialist self-management democratic community of working people and citizens, of the Slovene nation and the Italian and Hungarian nationalities.

20. Article 250 of the Constitution of the SRS: The Italian and Hungarian nationalities are guaranteed the right of free use of their languages, of expression and development of their national cultures, and for the same purpose of setting up organizations, making use of their national symbols, and realizing other rights determined by the Constitution.

       The Italian and Hungarian languages are equal in status to the Slovene language in all the areas populated by both members of the Slovene nation and members of the Italian and Hungarian nationalities.

In the areas populated by the Slovenes as well as members of the Italian nad Hungarian nationalities, the latter nationalities are guaranteed the right to be educated and instructed in their mother tongue. A bill may be enacted to establish bilingual education and instruction in education-cum-childcare institutions and schools, and to introduce compulsory instruction of Slovene in schools and education-cum-childcare institutions providing for the nationalities, simultaneously with compulsory instruction of the nationality language in Slovene schools and education-cum-childcare institutions.

The Socialist Republic of Slovenia takes care of the development of education and instruction, press and other mass media, as well as other forms of cultural and instructional activities on the part of the Italian and Hungarian nationalities; it also provides for the acquisition of qualification in the assignment of duties to the staff that are instrumental in realizing and implementing the status and the rights of nationalities; to this end, SRS also ensures the necessary means of support.

The SRS backs the growth of relations between the Italian and Hungarian nationalities and their mother nations, with a view to promoting the cultural and linguistic development of the nationalities.

The manner of realizing the rights of the Italian and Hungarian nationalities is to be stipulated by the law, by communal statute, and by self-management deeds of the organizations of associated labor as well as other self-managing organizations and communities.

21. In the suggestion for the new Slovene Constitution, prepared by the Slovene Writers' Association and the Slovene Sociological Association, one can also read: "In the *political* sense, the proposed theses for the Slovene Constitution are based upon the tradition of medieval Carinthia and Kocelj's principality, upon the demands for United Slovenia, upon the short-lived and internationally unrecognized state of Slovenes, Croats, and Serbs, upon the unification in the state of Serbs, Croats, and Slovenes, upon the program of the Slovene Liberation Front, upon the principles of the Antifascist Council of National Liberation of Yugoslavia, and upon experience gained in the socialist Yugoslavia; *culturally*, they are based upon the heritage of Trubar, Vodnik, Prešeren, Levstik, Cankar, Kosovel, Kocbek, and all branches of Slovene art which, lacking political organization or witnessing its precipitation and exaggerated conformity to foreign models, were taking upon themselves the essential responsibility for the preservation of the Slovene identity; in the *military sense*, they are based upon the traditions of anti-Germanic and anti-Christian rebellions in medieval Carinthia, peasant risings, anti-Turkish fights, heroic defence of the Western border in the WWI, military revolts in the Austrian army, military actions of the first modern Slovene army forces under General Maister, and above all the Slovene army during the National Liberation War, when organization of our forces was exclusively Slovene, and they were victorious despite the worst possible conditions." Rupel, D. and Menart J. (1988). *Gradivo za Slovensko Ustavo* [Materials for the Slovene Constitution], p. 6. Ljubljana: Časopis za kritiko znanosti).

22. Rupel, D. (1992). *Skrivnost Države* (Secrets of a State), p. 27. Ljubljana.

23. Article 5 of the Constitution of the Republic of Slovenia: Within its own territory, Slovenia shall protect human rights and fundamental freedoms. It shall uphold and guarantee the right of the autochthonous Italian and Hungarian ethnic communities.

It shall attend to the welfare of the autochthonous Slovenian minorities in neighboring countries and of Slovenian emigrants and migrant workers abroad and shall promote their contacts with their homeland. It shall assist the preservation of the natural and cultural heritage of Slovenia in harmony with the creation of opportunities for the development of civilized society and cultural life in Slovenia.

Slovenians not holding Slovenian citizenship shall enjoy special rights and privileges in Slovenia. . . .

24. It would be more accurate to speak of the protection of three ethnic minorities, since the Constitution provides for special protection of the Romany ethnic community (Article 65).

25. For more details, see Komac, M. (1995). Identitete nikar (Identity on no account). In *Teorija in Praksa*. Ljubljana.

26. Article 64 of the Constitution (Special Rights of the Autochthonous Italian and Hungarian Ethnic Communities in Slovenia):

The autochthonous Italian and Hungarian ethnic communities and their members shall be guaranteed the right to freely use their national symbols and, in order to preserve their national identity, the right to establish organizations, to foster economic, cultural, scientific and research activities, as well as activities associated with the mass media and publishing. These two ethnic communities and their members shall have, consistent with statute, the right to education and schooling in their own languages, as well as the right to plan and develop their own curriculae. The State shall determine by statute those geographical areas in which bilingual education shall be compulsory. The Italian and Hungarian ethnic communities and their members shall enjoy the right to foster contacts with the wider Italian and Hungarian communities living outside Slovenia, and with Italy and Hungary respectively. Slovenia shall give financial support and encouragement to the implementation of these rights.

In those areas where the Italian and Hungarian ethnic communities live, their members shall be entitled to establish autonomous organizations in order to give effect to their rights. At the request of the Italian and Hungarian ethnic communities, the State may authorize their respective autonomous organizations to carry out specific functions which are presently within the jurisdiction of the State, and the State shall ensure the provision of the means for those functions to be effected.

The Italian and Hungarian ethnic communities shall be directly represented at the local level and shall also be represented in the National Assembly.

The status of the Italian and the Hungarian ethnic communities and the manner in which their rights may be exercised in those areas where the two ethnic communities live, shall be determined by statute. In addition, the obligations of the local self-governing communities which represent the two ethnic communities to promote the exercise of their rights, together with the rights of the members of the two ethnic communities living outside their autochthonous areas, shall be determined by statute. The rights of both ethnic communities and of their members shall be guaranteed without regard for the numerical strength of either community.

Statutes, regulations and other legislative enactments which exclusively affect the exercise of specific rights enjoyed by the Italian or Hungarian ethnic communities under this Constitution, or affecting the status of these communities, may not be enacted without the consent of the representatives of the ethnic community or communities affected.

27. Research project: Interethnic Relations in the Slovene Ethnic Territory. A comparative analysis of national identity elements of the population in contact areas of regions in Slovenia, Austria, Italy, and Hungary (head of the project Albina Nećak-Lük).

28. Constitution of the Republic of Slovenia, Article 61 (Profession of National Allegiance): Each person shall be entitled to freely identify with his national grouping or ethnic community, to foster and give expression to his culture and to use his own language and script; Article 62 (The Right to the Use of Language and Script): In order to give effect to his rights and obligations, and in all dealing with State bodies and other bodies having official function, each person shall have the right to use his own language and script in such a manner as shall be determined by statute.

29. Klinar, P. (1986). *Etnične Avtohtone in Imigrantske Manjšine* (Ethnic Autochthonous and Immigrant Minorities), p. 51. Ljubljana: FSPN, RI.

30. Klinar, P. (1986). *Etnične Avtohtone in Imigrantske Manjšine* (Ethnic Autochthonous and Immigrant Minorities), pp. 48–49. Ljubljana: FSPN, RI.

18

Freedom Versus Equality? Some Thoughts About Attitudes Toward Gender Equality Politics in Eastern and Central Europe

Vlasta Jalušič
The Peace Institute, Ljubljana, Slovenia

I. INTRODUCTION

Since the first and second elections within most of the Eastern and Central European postsocialist states (so-called states in transition), there is still quite a low level of participation of women within the state and party politics. There are, on average, from 5–15% women representatives in the parliaments and even less in the governments of states in transition. In spite of this fact, these states have almost no mechanisms for the promotion of gender equality. Even more apparent is that among most of the newly formed parties, in public opinion and even among independent women's groups, a kind of general opposition to the introduction of legal measures for equal opportunity politics (quotas and similar) seemed to dominate, at least until recently. Therefore, not only are there poor mechanisms, but also no serious efforts to increase the participation of women can be detected at first glance.

However, this phenomenon does not seem to be a problem for general practical political nor for the most part, the theoretical reflections on the ''democratization stage,'' or of the successful transition of these countries toward democracy (both within these states and in the international elite political circles). There are few—mostly explicitly feminist—critics of this phenomenon and very rarely do analyses of the situations take into account the absence of women from political institutions.[1]

Political/public and theoretical discussions about the low political representation and participation of women after the first and second democratic elections
have only begun within some profeminist oriented circles in Eastern and Central
Europe (see, for example, Vodražka 1996; Butorova 1996; Nadace Gender Studies v Praze 1996; Ruže mezi trnim 1996). Some public opinion research in Slovenia, the Czech Republic, and Slovakia shows the public's inclination toward
the mechanisms of and for the political promotion of women (Klimešova 1996;
Butorova 1996). In the Czech Republic, the representation of women in parliament even increased after the last elections (in 1996) to 15%, but the analysis
does not pay any special attention to this fact. Some authors are even claiming
that this fact can not really reinforce the position of women in high level politics
and will not influence the development of a new women's agenda at all.[2] In
Slovenia, the opposite trend has taken place: the participation of women in parliament decreased after the last elections in 1996 to 8%, which is the lowest percentage since World War II (this was not the first loss, although these women were,
as in other East European countries, already ''defeated after the first democratic
multiparty elections'' [Antić 1996]). The rare or occasional analysis of the existing systems of political representation have claimed that one of the main reasons for this is the rejection of the mechanisms for the advancement of women
in politics by the newborn party elite (Antić 1996).

I would like to put forward and analyze some elements that are, in my
opinion, of structural importance for this situation and which might vary within
(1) the phenomenon of an almost notorious aversion to feminism, and (2) the
prevailing antistate and anti-institutionalist attitudes, originating in the perception
of politics within both the previous socialist and the new democratic system.
Both are likely to be connected with (3) the new liberal democratic legitimization,
which, by claiming the priority of freedom over equality, most likely supports
the nonparticipative sentiment and has a strong influence on what is going to be
the subject on the legitimate political agenda.

Of course, along with this structural setting, which influences the participation of women, there is also the major impact of the historical moment (the socialist past and tradition in general). There is also the impact of the spirit of the time,
which includes the international political agenda and surroundings. Besides, the
possibility for the higher representation of women in politics (parliament, government, and other political bodies) is influenced by a series of concrete institutional
arrangements. They can be seen as political methods of democracy (Pateman
1996): the voting system, party system, and their politics and possible special
measures among them, such as quotas or other mechanisms for the promotion
of women in politics. Each of these arrangements can effect specific trends; the
proportional voting system, for example, effects better electorate possibilities for
women. Women-supported party politics can result in a larger number of women
becoming candidates on the lists. The special measures—by both state and

party—in the form of so-called positive discrimination can and do influence the equal status of men and women in politics in general. But to be able to initiate such measures under the conditions of democracy, a certain shift in the consciousness of the majority is necessary.

Many analyses of the so-called transitional societies and the position of women within them, (so-called gender politics in postcommunism, Funk and Mueller 1993) confirmed the ''non-visibility'' and a ''spectacular loss of women representatives in the new parliaments'' (Janova and Sineau 1992). Some tried to find the reasons for this fact within the ''overpoliticized'' socialist past and in the antipolitical sentiment that comes from it (Dölling 1991). An ''allergy to feminism'' (Einhorn 1993) and the opposition to the concepts of equality (Lissjutkina 1992) might cause the nonexistence of the important ''organizational structures created by women's groups, especially voluntary organizations'' (Lovenduski 1986, Einhorn 1993). Mira Marody (1990) writes about the pronounced anti-institutional perception of politics, which has become, especially in the period of the oppositional activity within socialism, above all a moral attitude; this can also be understood as a consequence of the inherited notion of politics as a dirty business and as a result of the untransformed concepts of politics and political action (Jalušič 1997). Some Eastern and Western European authors have strongly criticized both attempts of merely transferring a Western-styled democracy model and the model of the Western women's movement to Eastern and Central Europe (Šiklova 1991; Marody 1993; Havelkova 1995; Sauer 1996; Kreisky 1996). What I consider very important are the analyses that connect the phenomenon of the nonexistence of both mechanisms and actions for the promotion of gender equality politics with the very nature of the political system in the transitional states (see Kreisky 1996; Ramet 1997). Of special interest are, in my opinion, those reflections that (1) emphasize the importance of the newly formed private–public relationships and (2) pay attention to a fact that has a distinctively negative influence on the structural position of women and on the possibilities of their participation in the public sphere: the fact that transition theory and practice ignore (in the style of the Western political tradition), but at the same time assume and build upon, the given gender relationships and family structures (Havelkova 1996a).

However, in this chapter I will not pay special attention to the institutional arrangements or to political systems only. Rather, my aim is to address the previously mentioned elements (antifeminism, antistate, and antipolitical attitudes and liberalism's valuing of freedom over equality) and to explore their possible connections with the problem of the absence of mechanisms and actions for the promotion of gender equality in some of the Eastern and Central European postsocialist states. This question regarding the absence of institutional mechanisms for gender equality politics—that is, of the institutional, systematic discrimination of women and the producing of new gender hierarchies—is closely connected with the very nature of transitional developments in postsocialist countries (both the factual developments within this process and the ideologies that carry it out). It sometimes rightly seems as if the role of the transitional ideologies is more important and more powerful than the question of the real events and developments within these systems. The powerful and effective transitional ideology of liberalism might also be the source of the Eastern European feminists' actual powerlessness and "inefficiency" in their attempts to change the situation. Besides, it is perhaps exactly the same phenomenon that can give the proper answer to the question of why women in these countries did not profit from the redistribution of the newly achieved power after the velvet revolutions. Only with this fact in mind can we understand what is going on in these societies: namely, the process that rapidly creates political and other gender hierarchic institutions can be marked as a kind of "transition automatism," with its typical ideology of complete reconstitution and with the enormous haste that prevails in all developments (despite the common claim that transition in these societies is going on too slowly).

II. THE AVERSION TOWARD FEMINISM: NEITHER COMRADES NOR FEMINISTS, BUT WOMEN[3]

The antifeminist sentiment can be the starting point of our survey. It can be considered as a symptomatic phenomenon, not only in itself, but because it contains (that is, is more or less saturated by) both other elements: the antistate, anti-institutionalist attitudes and the liberal transitional ideology, which sets up the political agenda that praises freedom over equality.

We can quite rightly say that the feminist movement, its various currents of thought, and the political activity of feminism had a strong influence in putting the equality of women on the political agenda of the Western European and North American democracies after World War. II. Furthermore, some questions—for example, of formal equality and the equal political participation of women— were in many ways granted political legitimacy by feminism. Not only in practical political activities but also within the framework of theoretical legitimacy, the introduction of gender issues to a large extent contributed to changes in political concepts and agendas. It contributed to the criticism of any concept of democracy that failed to include equal rights for women and to a greater openness on the part of political groups and political subjects (such as parties, associations, and the state) to women. Put more simply, the path toward legislation in Western Europe, comprising equality and equal opportunity, was cleared by years of feminist activity, a movement which developed as a grassroots movement and reached as far up as the state. This is also one of the reasons why it is possible for some Western European countries to speak about "state feminists" and "state feminism.'' The merit of these political activities carried out by women is the fact that feminism, as a social movement and as a mental and political current in the West, gained legitimacy; feminism became a term but also a political position. However, although it has laid down roots in the political consciousness of women, feminism as a set of political positions never managed to get itself internally connected to the very notion of democracy, therefore the Scandinavian authors use the concept of ''unfinished democracy,'' and the activists and some theoreticians used the saying ''democracy without women is no democracy'' (Russian feminists) or ''no state without women'' (East German feminists).[4] This I consider to be the crucial point.

Or we might reverse this: democracy as a system in most cases was not defined as a system granting equality to women (Pateman 1996). At this point I will allow myself a working description of feminism that should serve to support the statements in this chapter. I will say that feminism is above all a movement for the legitimization of political claims referring to the political equality of women and their implementation. The majority of the claims made by feminist movements were treated just like any other political claims. In the beginning they were laughed at, then tolerated, then eventually accepted. The feminist position has had the same fate as other political positions. Some time is needed before people accept it as legitimate position. Of course it becomes legitimate when it is taken up and defended by a large enough number of people and when the ideas about it become more or less convergent. This does not mean that the position needs to be entirely transparent and definable from the outside, that it needs to have absolutist, empirically scientific objective criteria. We can not objectively measure what feminism is and what it is not. As with any other political position, feminism has to be understood as pluralist. With its generality or its ability to convince, there has always been a thin line of consensus between what is generally accepted and the specific ideas and images of what it is supposed to represent.

I put this forward to avoid as many misunderstandings as possible. Namely, there are many misunderstandings, mainly in connection with what feminism in postsocialist countries means and to what extent women and men agree with it or not. First, as some authors put forward recently, women in Eastern and Central European countries are still not aware how much feminism contributed to the changing of the political agenda in Western societies.[5] Second, I would like to speak about feminism above all as a political phenomenon and political position that aims at political change, not as a social movement or cultural praxis only.

Soon after the so-called velvet revolutions the rumor went around, carried in literature and through discussions regarding the situation of women in Central and Eastern Europe, that Eastern European women (and men) did not want to hear about feminism. A series of articles concerning women in postsocialist Europe talks about the stubbornness of local antifeminism, about an ''allergy'' to feminism (Einhorn 1993), and, still more, about the conservatism of women in

Central and Eastern Europe (Šiklová 1991). Analyses have provided us with numerous reasons for this phenomenon, which are mainly based on the socialist past:

> The socialist experience, rejecting feminism as a bourgeois, capitalist phenomenon.
>
> The lack of a tradition of an independent women's movement lasting several decades.
>
> The nonexistence of a women's issue as a political issue under socialism.
>
> The equality and emancipation of women were already a part of the very legitimacy of the socialist system (also partly drawn up in the form of a law).
>
> The "emancipation" that came from the top (equal rights), which supported the equality of women, was not a result of a long-lasting struggle or of claims from the people.
>
> The role played by elite women belonging to the ruling party, the so-called state feminists. This elite has been, irrespective of its own intentions, unpopular and stigmatized. Usually it was specially organized: studies show that because of this, in socialist societies it was often equated with feminism in a pejorative sense.

Some analyses were developed from the presumption about the obligatory emancipation of women in socialism, which is said to have forced women into paid work, thus becoming part of a double burden.[6] They pointed out that women in socialism had had enough of equality and work and that they now wanted to have some sort of differentiation and household work (Marody 1993:859). They drew attention to the poor reputation of rights achieved under socialism. They showed how easily feminism could become a Western import which no one really liked or wanted. They sensed a tendency, a presumption, that democracy would spontaneously solve all the remaining (marginal) questions. In fact, democracy leaves them all at the margin, which is what actually happened to several issues such as class, minority status, and gender under socialism. The isolation of these systems, lasting several decades, prevented a circulation of ideas and this included feminism as well.[7]

While Western analysts of women's issues voiced their surprise and fear at the fact that there were neither feminism nor any mass self-organization of women, many of their counterparts in the East pointed out that women there were rightly rejecting feminism, alongside a kind of new unification of women that had been too strong under socialism. It often turned out that the image of feminism was too homogenous, and that the attitude toward it and toward feminist activities was defined through stereotype and prejudice—from both sides. A real "Feminismusstreit" was therefore created amongst women in both the East and West who were examining the situation of women. It appeared in discussions on the suitability and unsuitability of Western European feminist experience for Eastern Europe. The Eastern European answer to feminism ranged from the mild statement that Western feminists do not understand Eastern European women (Šiklová 1992) to its sharpest image in, for instance, Larisa Lissjutkina's text, with its provocative title ''Rather a Whore than a Feminist.'' Lissjutkina defended a position that said the postperestroika boom in pornography and prostitution added much to the liberation of women from the dry, desexualized image of women prevalent under socialism and that the image and appearance of a prostitute have a liberating role for women in the postsocialist world (Lissjutkina 1992).

The East–West Feminismusstreit began with a question about the origins of antifeminism in the East and continued with whether the East needed feminism at all, and, if so, what kind of feminism. Of course this was not a mere dispute and it was not always unproductive. This discussion reopened the question of the nature of feminism and the forms of political, economic, and social establishment relevant to women in different circumstances. In particular it opened up the issue of the ways of enshrining women's rights in law, the extent to which the legitimacy of claims for equality and equal opportunity can be ideologically supported, and the legitimacy that can be used for such support.

III. POLITICS AS WHORE: THE NOTION OF POLITICS

At this point the question of feminism and antifeminism is, of course, related to the issue of democracy and politics, to the very notion of democracy and politics in the postsocialist period, to what democracy is related to, and how politics are ''made.'' If we take a parallel look at the notions of democracy and feminism and the evaluation of them, which currently maintains a dominant position in the postsocialist period, we can draw the following quick conclusion: everyone wishes to live in a democracy and it ranks high on their list of values. But at the same time, there is a very small number who would identify themselves with feminism and who would accept it as their system of values.[8] Of course this is connected to the delegitimization and devaluation of the concept of equality in postsocialism as well as to the image that feminism is above all an excessive demand for the absolute equality of women that actually endangers real freedom.[9] The liberal democratic concept apparently became a kind of general link between the postsocialist societies. At the same time its general acceptability shows that the concept is so general that no subtopics or special interests can be articulated politically within its framework, since it seems that such an attempt would be rejected by the majority or would not be accepted by the majority at all. From its point of view one should not ''fragment the social agenda'' but ''form the united front'' (Butorova 1996:133). The female politicians who are not the mainstream politicians in this regard and would try to focus on women's agendas can be easily rejected by their environment: in the opinion of a few female politicians within Eastern and Central European Parliaments who are very conscious of the issues facing them as women, the representative of ''women's politics'' simply ''does not have a chance for success'' (see Vodražka 1996:9). This becomes quite clear if we take a look at the many voices of women, working in public functions in Eastern and Central Europe, who are publicly confessing themselves as not being feminists. Such confessions became almost a kind of a special ritual in these countries. The usual statement goes either through arguing about ''why I am not a feminist'' (feminism is usually equated with supposed militant American feminism[10]) or affirms the commonplace, that ''it is not important whether politics is made by women or by men. Important is . . .'' something else: either that politicians have good skills or that they are good professionals. Men can— so this opinion seems to state—represent women as well as they would represent themselves.

At this point we immediately come across some new issues: precisely who represents whom, who is the majority, how can it be defined, and what are the mechanisms that represent it? The fact is that the concept of democracy that prevailed in the East as a generally accepted everyday notion does not draw its legitimacy from a concept of women's equality, although a general prohibition of sexual discrimination exists in all the constitutions of these countries. This creates the feeling that equality is not an issue any more. Mira Marody wrote in 1993 that ''the simplest way to answer the question why there is no feminist movement in Poland would be to point to the habitual perception of gender differences as belonging to the biological rather than social realm. In this context a fight for gender equality seems as ridiculous as, for instance, a fight for the equality of blondes and brunettes as the beautiful and the ugly'' (Marody 1993:858). This quotation shows how much the difference concepts as a natural condition prevailed over the argument of equality. Hence, the concept of democracy is based on the value of freedom, understood in particular as a negative freedom and differentiation.

Empirical research into the images of democracy (within the political elite, which is for the most part composed of men) in Eastern and Central Europe shows that in their evaluations, the political elite put freedom above equality and that, in opposition to the social-democratic visions of Swedish or Austrian political elites, the prevailing values are those of capitalism and competition. And here we cannot find any big difference between the political and social strategies of the male and (much smaller) female part of the elite: ''The majority of women from Eastern Europe is convinced that the women's movement . . . is not an appropriate instrument to introduce the changes. Women . . . prefer the individual strategy of self-actualization, typical of professional women'' (Bunčakova, quoted after Butorova 1996:131). This position is, of course, in certain conflict with feminism as a political position, which nowadays exists above all through political and social solidarity and as a concept and demand for equal opportunities.

The values of the postsocialist, male-dominated political elite, transferred to the public space, are therefore automatically in conflict with the eventual claims of feminism. Not only do the data show a higher inclination against "women's poking into politics" among the male population,[11] there were also several examples which clearly point out this conflict: a proposed law against sexual harassment in the Hungarian parliament at the beginning of the 1990s was laughed out by the deputies; criticism of a sexist publicity by the Government's Office of Women's Politics in Slovenia was followed by a real media war and the unscrupulous mockery of the supposedly "ugly" feminists at the Office; a proposal on party financing in the new law on parties in Slovenia which depended on the equal representation of both sexes was rejected; and so on. The notion that freedom excludes equality is in some circles so strong that the proposals for special measures such as quotas or other mechanisms for "positive discrimination" of women are considered not only as something that would be laughed at, but also have been directly proclaimed as "egalitarian fundamentalism," "nonsense," or even as "racism"—the expressions borrowed from female representatives in the Czech parliament (see Vodražka 1996:11).[12]

Let us go back a bit and see how the current image of politics is connected with the past socialist images of politics and the very nature of the velvet revolutions. If we take a look at those groups who were in opposition in socialist times (those groups which in the majority of cases formed the parties in power in the new democracies), we can draw the following conclusions:

1. Opposition groups at the decline of socialism did include women, but in very specific positions. A whole range of reflections of this typical pattern exist today (see Kaldor 1991; Einhorn 1993; Funk and Mueller 1993; Matynia 1994; Šiklová 1997).

2. The concept of oppositional activity within socialism was the so-called antipolitical concept of the civil society. In a way, it was an answer to the idea that politics under socialism was a dirty, corrupt matter, and so was the state. Those who want to remain moral should therefore not be involved in this kind of politics; they are to remain outside as a special moral power. Under socialism the role of the moral dissident was ascribed to intellectuals, writers, and the like.

3. It is this image and attitude toward politics that suits exactly the split between public and private morality and, in accordance with this, between a public and a private woman (Elshtain 1974). Just as an intellectual socialist dissident remained morally clean because he had not been collaborating with the corrupt politics of socialism, so it was with women who remained apolitical after the velvet revolution. Besides, within the oppositional movements in socialism, a certain shift in the relationships between private and public happened. The private became, for a certain period, a space of relative freedom and different articula-

tion—a space for new political agendas. Women have, as we stated, taken part within this change. However, afterwards, with the creation of the new public space and liberal democratic institutions after the turning point in 1989 (actually with the new state), the places that have been the proper source of the velvet revolutions (more or less private or semipublic places) were either depoliticized again or even became spheres of constraint.[13] Men have left politics for the new places of power (new institutions); women were left out of it, somewhere within the social realm.

4. The image of politics and the attitudes toward it in postsocialism has changed very little if we compare it with socialism. The concept of antipolitics as a nonpolitical moral activity (society versus authority concept, Marody 1993) supported the presumption that there was too much politics and too much state in the former system. This is why the concept demanded a depoliticization of people's lives: as little politics as possible and as little state. The concept of as little politics as possible contributed a lot to the perception of politics in post-socialism and to the anti-institutionalist sentiment and still represents the very core of the liberal democratic attitude toward politics as above all "a vocation" in the sense of Max Weber.

The image of politics as amoral and scandalous, since it has to do with power, suits the image of a "public woman," that is, a woman who sells herself for money, a prostitute. This image is one of the most frequent and is being connected with the scandalous nature and corruption of the political elite in post-socialism: politics as a whore. Its message contains a moral tone, one which says keep your hands off politics if you want to remain moral. This message in particular refers to women. It is also one of the reasons why a number of the grassroots women activists in the postsocialist period do not want to enter high/official politics, why they do not want to become a part of the political elite, and why they are hostile toward political elites and institutions.

In relation to politics and political activity, we can therefore understand antifeminist attitudes as a certain reaction to the past, present, and future participation (of women) in public affairs and politics, and also as a reaction to their general and individual situations. Female antifeminism in Eastern and Central Europe is, on the one hand, a reaction to stigmatization. In many cases when women (politicians, scientists, reporters, and so on) proclaim themselves to be nonfeminists, such public rejection of feminism can also indicate a certain defense strategy, showing us a different starting point for postsocialist Central and Eastern European countries. It also seems that two kinds of antifeminist positions have to be distinguished: a principled and a pragmatic one, although they are both a reaction to changes and to claims from the outside. The principled position would be a general negative attitude toward the issue of the equality of women. The pragmatic position is about the relation toward images of what feminism is supposed to be. Although they are probably interrelated, it seems that the second, pragmatic antifeminism, is prevailing today because there is, in general, very little doubt expressed about the necessity of the legal equality of women.

This can be confirmed by opinion research that has been recently carried out in some of the Central and Eastern European countries: the public attitude regarding special measures for the promotion of women in the politics and quotas in the parliamentary elections is, as it turns out, quite inclined toward such measures. In Slovenia, at the beginning of 1996, more than 60% of respondents agreed with the statement that ''they would support the introduction of special measures for promotion of women in the politics.''[14] In the Czech Republic, 70% of interviewed respondents think that including more women in politics would be useful for the society (Havelkova 1996a:19). In Slovakia, 60% of women and 37% of men would support an introduction of the law that would reserve a certain percentage of parliamentary seats for women (Butorova 1996:119). This might be the sign of the nonelitist practical attitude toward equal opportunities for both sexes.

Despite this, antifeminism is, of course, an important indicator of the self-perception of women, their self-confidence, and of the lack of the initiatives which could work for the creation of equal opportunities and its mechanisms. This might be the most difficult point of our considerations, the point at which we probably have to ask ourselves the question of whether there is anything to be done with the antifeminist attitudes and with the denial of feminism. If antifeminism is not just a subjective, temporary defense reaction, but on the contrary has its roots in the denial of the legitimacy of the factual women's equality in the so-called new democracies, then it certainly creates many problems. As far as its pattern transfers itself, even if only discursively and symbolically, to the constant opposing of political activity, groups, and initiatives that would like to promote equal opportunities, and as far as it successfully deems them ''illegal,'' then it undoubtedly contributes a lot toward the existence of new democracies that exclude women. In this connection we can also question strategies which would be able to change this situation and could act in favor of the legitimacy of equal opportunity politics as well as leading from the consciousness of discrimination to a political reaction against it. The strategies will probably have to differ one from the other. I have already mentioned the necessity of pluralism in feminism (I have borrowed this term from Eva Kreisky). ''Feminismusstreit'' has shown the necessity of pluralism in order for the concept of feminism to prevail. Thus pluralism is already taking place on one side. However, quite some time will probably be needed. Pluralism is also one of the preliminary conditions for solidarity between women of different political beliefs. In this sense, this is political pluralism, which can also mean relativization of many existing concepts. Some women authors, facing the problems of differing interpretation of feminism, do incline toward a thesis that any coming together of women and their subsequent activity is already feminism. It seems, however, that in the case of such relativism, we could lose the distinction between activities with a political content and those based only on gender (Fabian 1996:93).

Such pluralism will necessarily happen (and already is happening) in a contradictory way. For if feminism is a movement for legitimacy and implementation of actual political equality, then it will, in different situations, present different arguments in favor of this equality. In some cases it will accept some forms of political organization and reject others. The already mentioned problem in the majority of Eastern and Central European countries is a rejection of almost any institutionalization of women's issues, a rejection of quotas (tokenism) as a means of political participation, and a supposed aversion toward state involvement in people's lives. Although, and this is a paradox as we have shown, there are indicators of not so massive public rejection of the mechanisms for the advancement of women in politics. This is to be underlined especially in face of the fact that the postsocialist state is no ''night guard,'' but—despite the antistatist ideology of the newborn elite—interferes strongly in people's lives through political, economic, and social reforms (Offe 1991).

So what are the possible ways to legitimize and to develop the path toward factual equality—equal opportunity politics or affirmative action within the newly formed Central and Eastern European political systems? A number of institutions existing in the countries of Western Europe can be an important legitimizing source, especially when the political subjects of the new democracies refer to Europe and are incorporated in the integration processes. At the same time, such legitimacy can also be unproductive: in some regards, women in some countries of Eastern and Central Europe had some very important social rights under socialism, including some rights women in most Western countries and especially in the United States had never before enjoyed (such as legislation on abortion rights, family law, divorce law, and social rights).[15] The gaze toward the West proved to be truly a double-edged sword, for instance, with the adoption of the Slovene constitution in 1991. Responding to the claim of numerous women and men that the right of free decision-making on birth control remain in the constitution as a special paragraph, the opponents of this right found a counterargument in the fact that no Western European country has such an article in its constitution, therefore Slovenia should not have it either.[16]

It has also been proven that women in Eastern Europe, although not used to the active political fight for their rights, organize themselves above all when their customary rights are endangered: reproductive rights, for example, as in Poland, Croatia, and Slovenia. Despite the liberation from above, reproductive rights in particular in many East European states, have been understood as customary women's rights, and in this sense the danger that abortion would be outlawed meant that women's equality (as equality of individuals) would be abolished—legally as well as symbolically. It is interesting that in the states in which abortion rights were not endangered directly after the 1989 elections (as in Czech

Republic, for example), the larger number of new critical women's and feminist groups emerged only later.

IV. LIBERAL IDEOLOGY AND POLITICAL AGENDA

What about internal legitimacy? The problem is, of course, manufactured by the popular ideology of democracy, which often contains a claim for a complete break with the socialist past. Thus the institutions which served as social mechanisms to bring together the different roles of women under socialism have been discredited in the new system. Women who are striving for equal opportunities in the new system often find themselves in a situation in which it is necessary to defend some of the old institutions, a very difficult and sometimes even suspicious activity. The traditional division between public and private is built anew. There exists a paradoxical split between the phenomenon of widespread and obviously obsolete gender ideologies that are circulating in the news media (together with the cleric and national representations) and the factual position of (still mostly working and, as Marie Čermakova (1992) put it, extremely adaptable) women, being active in almost all areas of life, but politically so very marginalized. It is quite obvious that the transitional ideology at the same time ''ignores'' but also assumes the unchanged family and private–public relationships in order to function successfully (Havelkova 1996a).

Another question arises at this point concerning the attitude toward a nation's past and the women's movement. Since, in comparison with the West, there are still very few studies that discuss women's history in these countries, it is difficult to find equality legitimacy within this otherwise rich resource. The past in the newly formed Central and Eastern European states is often wrapped up in a certain mythology of newly created statesmanship and heroes, which of course prevents a rational look into the past.[17] Of course, such an ideologized past dominates discussions about the future and blocks the development of new political agendas.[18]

Women are affected not only by the processes of building the new state institutions, but by the issue of integration into European institutions as well: higher budgets for sectors such as national security, the military, and foreign politics means at the same time minimizing the role of the state in the areas of social facilities. This has resulted in a new phenomenon, which I would call redundancy, of the whole strata of people who became unemployed or otherwise displaced and are not able to adapt themselves to the market and social competition. There exists no serious awareness about the possible social and political consequences of this phenomenon. The social and personal conflicts caused by it are mostly mediated within families. Women are therefore affected by the new situation not only directly (by their own unemployment and insecurity), but also through changes and additional conflicts within the family due to the insecurity of their partners or other family members; and they perform additional caring work. This is another demonstration of how the dominating theory of liberal democracy coexists and relies upon the given and unchanged private–public relationships, gender division, and patriarchal family and hence supports the efforts towards retraditionalization.

It is therefore extremely important to question a concept of politics that effectively excludes women in new democracies from the top levels of political decision-making. What is already happening (in some women's circles), as a result of certain sobering facts in relation to democracy, is a certain re-evaluation of the socialist past and not just a simple rejection. This is an element that can surely be very important, especially as far as establishing the attitude toward political institutions and the state is concerned. A question arises at this point whether the right way is really to focus only on the initiatives of civil society (on grassroots activities), or whether it would be necessary to pay more attention to the possible role of the state and its institutions. Hana Havelkova, who rightly pointed out the importance of introducing a women's agenda, also emphasized that, although the ''women's agenda'' was not articulated and introduced in the new system and in the political structures, it might be true that a ''traditional'' women's agenda is already ''theoretically'' transcended (Havelkova 1996a:23). Therefore, it would be very important to invest some energy into party politics and not only to work on the playground of an actually not-very-influential civil society: to bring so many women into the institutionalized structures (that is, parliament) as possible. And since most voting systems within the Central and East European states are either proportional (Czech Republic, Slovenia, Slovakia) or mixed (Poland, Hungary), there are still possibilities for more women to get into the parliaments through the party lists (this was the case in the last elections in Hungary). Some of the social-democratic parties of these countries have recently even gone so far as to introduce quota regulations. However, there exists a strong tendency among some circles (established elite) in these states to introduce majority voting systems, which—under the guise of state stability—would automatically diminish the electoral possibilities of women (this is the case in Slovakia and in Slovenia).

Sometimes it seems that Western feminists often give too much emphasis solely to the establishment of women's solidarity from the bottom up (civil society) and neglect the role of the state. This was, at least until recently, also the trend in the thinking of most Eastern feminists. But it is the state and its institutions (with a little help of strong liberal-democratic legitimacy) which in fact carry out the reforms in those Eastern European countries (Offe 1991). This is the point at which it becomes clear that it is not only antifeminism that can influence the deterioration of the position of women. One does not need the concept of a male conspiracy to miss the nuances and the seemingly minor details that relate to the situation of women in the process in which some 400–500 laws need to be changed in this period of reform (for example, 450 in Slovenia and 432 in Hungary in the period 1990–1994).[19] This is one of the reasons why the idea of introducing as many women as possible into the high politics of the parties and the state might be important.

I would like to close with this. I did not deal with questions relating to concrete institutional arrangements in different countries, which are also, of course, very important research areas. Instead I tried to show some general trends and similarities in the Eastern Central European countries that might be elements for understanding the attitudes toward gender equality politics. I also did not give practical suggestions as to how to change antifeminist attitudes and to promote institutional arrangements for the possibilities for equal opportunity. Of course there is no point in persuading Eastern European women and others on how feminism or quotas are (ideologically) sound. Although very many of them do not have a consistent concept of feminism, they already actually act as feminists, although they would not recognize it.[20] Thus far, this is a question of politics, one which always refers to the questions of action and not to the questions of epistemological truth.

V. CONCLUSION

Liberal-democratic institutions and the elite-building, along with the economic reforms, were the main activities and relevant political and research issues of the so-called transitional period of democracy in the Eastern and Central European countries. The main problem in connection with this process is that women, in spite of their mentioned readiness to adapt, were not a politically active part of this period. Even more, the main part of the new institutions were built under the assumption of the nontransformed and nontransforming traditional social–political divisions: nontransformed private and public relationships as well as the presupposed gender divisions within family and its functions for the state and economy. In this sense, the shift from socialist paternalism—which has built huge social facilities for ''solving'' the housework problem—to the situation of liberalism—with the factual relying on the ''good old family'' although denying it, without any equality measures—has shown that without the efforts to bring the question of political equality, representation, and active citizenship to the political agenda and without the efforts to change the traditional partner relationships, family conditions, and daily life, there is no serious chance for the active political participation of women. In the time of overall transformation and hyper-legislation, which is connected to many legal obscurities, the new institutions automatically produced(d) gender-hierarchic structures. Political institutions are the core of this process, and it seems that there is no explicit or additional sexism needed for the progress of this pattern, only a powerful enough gender-neutral ideology of freedom.

ACKNOWLEDGMENT

This work was supported by the Research Support Scheme of the OSI/HESP, grant number 1465/1997.

ENDNOTES

1. In this regard, see Carole Pateman's speech at the IPSA congress in 1994 (Pateman 1996) and the analysis of S. P. Ramet (1997), for example. See also Kreisky (1996) and Sauer (1996).
2. Hana Havelkova, for example, made the following statement: "its not clear whether these figures are something to celebrate. . . . Personally, I would have preferred a situation in which there were 10 fewer women, and no female Republicans or Communists at all" (McClune 1996).
3. See Matynia (1994:130), quoted after Butorova (1996).
4. See also S. P. Ramet (1997).
5. As Zora Butorova wrote for the Slovak example: "Very few women in Slovakia know that the feminist movement in the West has had a significant impact on political life in the past few decades. They do not realize that many problems and concerns that particularly affect women, and which previously may have seemed to be outside politics, are now central to political debates" (Butorova 1996:131).
6. There exists already vast body of analyses of women's legal and social statuses in socialism and their influence on the postsocialist developments (see, for example, Feminist Review 39, Feministische Studien 2/1992 (Autumn 1991); Einhorn 1993; Funk and Mueller 1993).
7. Šiklová, for example, maintains that feminism was the worst known stream of ideas in Eastern Europe: "We circulated, read and copied Orwell, Popper, Arendt, Dahrendorf, von Hayek, Althusser, Eurocommunistas, punk, pop music, porno, and so on. But feminists did not send anything!" (Šiklová 1997:260). However, there were big differences in circulation of feminist ideas among East and Central European socialist countries. In Yugoslavia, for example, an international feminist meeting already took place in 1978.
8. See also the data in Butorova (1996), which show that in Slovakia, 34% of women and 26% of men have positive and neutral conceptions of feminism. I think these data could be generalized for the whole of Eastern and Central Europe in many regards.
9. The mentioned Slovak public opinion research showed an interesting trend in opin-

ions regarding feminism: the higher an education women have, the more positive their relationship toward feminism. The trend among men is the opposite. Men with the university show the highest concentration of negative attitudes toward feminism. Zora Butorova, who conducted this research, claims that such negative evaluation of feminism is "based on the negative image that feminists have and to a lesser degree on the open rejection of the feminist movement itself" (Butorova 1996:129). Such insight is very interesting if we think of the postsocialist political elite as a male-dominated elite.

10. See the interview with the female politician Polonca Dobrajc in the Slovene daily *Delo* ("I do not approve ghettoisation." *Delo*, December 28, 1996). See also interviews with the female politicians in Vodražka (1996:88) and the analysis of Hana Havelkova in Vodražka (1996:30).

11. See Butorova (1996:115).

12. The Czech prime minister V. Klaus stated in 1996 that an introduction of promotion mechanisms for women in politics, such as quotas, could even be an "insult for women" (Vodražka 1996:12).

13. E. Matynia writes, for example, that "the only spheres of freedom available under Communist rule, those provided by the Church in Poland, by the so-called 'second economy' in Hungary and by the family in Czechoslovakia have now, for women became the spheres of constraint" (Matynia 1994:354).

14. The research carried out by the Slovene main daily *Delo*, March 2, 1996.

15. In Slovenia, for example, there existed a recognition of reproductive rights in the constitution since 1974, long parental leave for both parents, the opportunity to retain their family name after marriage, and so on.

16. See Jalušič (1994:135–137).

17. This is also a certain response to the empty liberal agenda. Empty in the sense that it puts forward the big questions such as progress, transition, democracy, and so on. This is the case especially in Poland, the Slovak republic, and also in Slovenia, but not so much in the Czech Republic and Hungary.

18. Marcin Krol writes for the Polish case that instead of discussing the factual problems, the "Poles seem to be totally immersed in the discussion of the past and its influence over the present" (Krol 1996).

19. This was the remark of the director of the Slovene governmental Office of Women's Politics, Vera Kozmik, in an interview (*Delo*, March 6, 1994).

20. This is what Hana Havelkova called "real existierender Feminsmus" (really existing feminism), playing with the ideological compound really existing socialism (Havelkova 1995), or postfeminism.

REFERENCES

Adamik, M. (1991). Hungary: A loss of rights. *Feminist Review 39*, Autumn 1991.

Antić G. M. (1996). Ženske in volitve v Sloveniji (Women and elections in Slovenia). In G. Slavko (ed.), *Volilni sistemi* (Voting systems), Ljubljana.

Arendt, H. (1993). *Was ist Politik? Fragmente aus dem Nachlaß*. Zürich: Piper, München.

Brown, B. (1993). Feminism. In R. Bellamy (ed.), *Theories and Concepts of Politics*. Manchester: Manchester University Press.

Butorova, Z. et al. (1996). *She and He in Slovakia: Gender Issues in Public Opinion*. Bratislava.

Čermakova, M. (1992). Tschechische und slowakische Frauen unter den alt-neuen Bedingungen der Welt der Arbeit. Materials for the sixteenth conference of Frauen-Anstiftung, October 16–19, 1992, Jiloviše, CSFR, pp. 45–56.

Delmar, R. (1986). What is feminsm? In J. Mitchell (ed.), *What is Feminism*. London.

Dölling, I. (1991). Between hope and helplessness: Women in the GDR after the "turning point." *Feminist Review 39*, Autumn 1991.

Einhorn, B. (1993). *Cindarella Goes to Market: Citizenship, Gender and Women's Movements in East Central Europe*. London, New York: Verso.

Elshtain, J. B. (1974). Moral woman and immoral man: A consideration of the public–private split and its political ramifications. *Politics & Society 4*:4, 453–473.

Fabian, K. (1996). Zur Artikulation von Frauenthemen in Zentral und Osteuropa. Ein Ueberblick. In Kreisky (ed.), *Vom Patriarchalen Staatssozialismus zur Patriarchalen Demokratie*. Wien.

Funk, N. and Mueller, M. (1993) (eds.), *Gender Politics in Post-Communism*. New York and London: Routledge.

Gross, I. G. (1994). *Constitutionalism in East Central Europe: Discussions in Warshaw, Budapest, Bratislava*. Bratislava: Czecho-Slovak Committee of the European Cultural Foundation.

Havelkova, H. (1995). Real existierender feminismus. *Transit-Europäische Revue 9/95*, 146–158.

Havelkova, H. (1996a). Ignored but assumed: Family and gender between public and private realm. *Czech Sociological Review 4* (Spring 1), 63–79.

Havelkova, H. (1996b). Ženy v politice a Ženska politika. In M. Vodražka (ed.). *Feministicke Rozhovory o Tajnych Službach*. Praha.

Jalušič, V. (1992). Zurück in den "Naturzustand"? Desintegration Jugoslawiens und ihre Folgen fuer die Frauen. *Feministische Studien 2/92*, 9–21.

Jalušič, V. (1994). Troubles with democracy: Women and Slovene independence. In J. Benderly and E. Kraft (eds.), *Independent Slovenia: Origins, Movements, Prospects*. New York: St. Martin's Press.

Jalušič, V. (1997). Die Geschlechterfrage und die Transformation in Ostmitteleuropa: Kann das Geschlechterparadigma zur Transformation des politischen Beitragen? In E. Kreisky and B. Sauer (eds.), Geshlechterverhältnisse im Kontext politisher Transformation. Politishe Viertel-jahresschrift, vol. 38, Special issue 28/1997, 450–474.

Jalušič, V. (1998). Socially adapted, politically marginalized: Women in post-socialist Slovenia. In S. P. Ramet (ed.), *Gender Politics in the Western Balkans: Women and Politics in Yugoslavia and Yugoslav Successor States*. Pennsylvania State University Press, forthcoming.

Janova, M. and Sineau, M. (1992). Women's participation in political power in Europe. *Women's Studies International Forum 15*:1.

Kaldor. (1991). Feminists and socialism. *Feminist Review 39*, Autumn 1991.

Klimešova, H. (1996). Kvoty—uplatneni v praxi v ruznych zemich sveta, nazory a doporučeni meziparlamentni komise. In *Politika s ženami či bez žen*? Praha: Nadace Gender Studies.

Konrad, G. (1984). *Antipolitics*. London, Melbourne, New York: Quartet Books.

Kozmik, V. (1994). Interview with *Delo* daily, March 6.

Kreisky, E. (1996) (ed.). Einleitung. In E. Kreisky (ed.), *Vom patriarchalen Staatssozialismus zur Patriarchalen Demokratie*. Wien.

Krol, M. (1996) Democracy in Poland. Paper for the project Democratization in Central and Eastern European Countries. Sussex European Institute, April.

Lissjutkina, L. (1992). Lieber hure als feministin. *Deutsches Allgemeines Sonntagsblatt*, May 8.

Makarovič, J. and Jug, J. (1994). How the new political elite in Slovenia understands Democracy. In F. Adam and G. Tomc (eds.), *Small Societies in Transition: The Case of Slovenia*. Ljubljana: special issue of Družboslovne razprave.

Marody, M. (1990). Perception of politics in Polish society. *Social Research 7*:2, 254–274.

Marody, M. (1993). Why I am not a feminist: Some remarks on the problem of gender identity in the United States and Poland. *Social Research 60*:4 (Winter), 853–864.

Matynia, E. (1994). Women after communism: A bitter freedom. *Social Research 61*:2 (Summer), 351–377.

Nadace Gender Studies v Praze (1996). *Politika s ženami či bez žen*? Praha: Nadace Gender Studies.

Offe, C. (1991). Capitalism by democratic design? Democratic theory facing the triple transition in East Central Europe. *Social Research 58*:4 (Winter), 865–892.

Pateman, C. (1991). Feminism and democracy. In J. Arthur (ed.), *Democracy: Theory and Practice*. Belmont, CA: Wordsworth Publishing Company.

Pateman, C. (1996). Democracy and democratization. *International Political Science Review 17*:1 (January), 8–12.

Ramet, S. P. (1997). Democratization in Slovenia—The second stage. In K. Dawisha and B. Parrott (eds.), *Democratization and Authoritarianism in Postcommunist Societies 2: Politics, Power and the Struggle for Democracy in South-East Europe*. Cambridge: Cambridge University Press, 189–225.

Rule, W. and Zimmerman J. F. (1994) (eds.), *Electoral Systems in Comprative Perspective: Their Impact on Women and Minorities*. Westport, CT: Greenwood Press.

Růže Mezi Trním, Ženy v politickém životě (1996). Sborník ze Semináře ženy a politika, Praha, 3–5 May.

Sauer, B. (1996). Transition zur demokratie? Kategorie geschlecht als prüfstein für die zuverlässigkeit von sozialwissenschaftlichen transformationstheorien. In Kreisky (ed.), *Vom Patriarchalen Staatssozialismus zur Patriarchalen Demokratie*. Wien.

Šiklová, J. (1991). Sind frauen in ostmitteleuropa konservativ? *Neue Gesellschaft/Frankfurter Hefte 11*, 1016–1019.

Šiklová, J. (1992). Versteht der Westen unsere frauen—Und warum nicht? Materials for the sixteenth conference of Frauen-Anstiftung, October 19, 1992, Jiloviště ČSFR.

Šiklová, J. (1997). Feminism and the roots of apathy in the Czech Republic. *Social Research 64*:2 (Summer), 158–280.

Tarasziewicz, M. (1991). Poland: Choices to be made. *Feminist Review 39*, Autumn 1991.

Vodrážka, M. (1996) (ed.). *Feministické Rozhovory o "Tajných Službách."* Praha.

19

Conceptualizing the German State
Putting Women's Politics in its Place

Birgit Sauer
University of Vienna, Vienna, Austria

> Scarcely had the right to vote been won, the Parliament had less to say than ever before; women had just barely begun to arise in lecture halls when the crisis of bourgeois science began (Bloch 1976:688).

This bon mot from Ernst Bloch can be interpreted in two ways. One way of reading it is that Bloch lays the blame for the decay of bourgeois institutions on the first women's movement. The other way of reading the phrase shows Bloch's intervention as astute analysis of the ambivalence of the feminization of public state institutions: inclusion of women in institutions can lend to the devaluation of the institution. The second reading, in my opinion, has a great deal of plausibility and quite a bit of empirical evidence. In Germany we have had an extensive and exhausting debate about the relation of feminist strategies to the state. For good reason the feminist movement in the 1970s positioned itself in opposition to state institutions: the German state was perceived as authoritarian, repressive, and primarily patriarchal (Kulawik 1991/1992). The feminist movement defined itself as autonomous, and women's groups were organized beyond state institutions. Feminist social science for example wasn't institutionalized within the universities; instead "summer schools" and feminist study centers were established independent from state-run academia.

With this strategy the feminist movement reproduced the strict separation of society and State and at the same time accepted the strong father State. In the 1980s state administration turned out to be the most important institution for the support of women's projects and women's equal opportunity politics. Feminist movements and feminist political science slipped into a dilemma: on the one hand, feminist politics aimed to develop and strengthen civil structures and to cut back the importance and influence of state institutions on women's politics; on the other hand, the feminist movement became more and more dependent on state funding. In the 1990s the neoliberal strategy of deregulation paralyzed feminist politics. One of the reasons for this blockade is the misleading and faulty concept of what the state is. In the following, I would like to formulate eight hypotheses for political science's treatment of the problem: state, equal opportunity politics, and feminist democratization strategies in the German context. My aim is to present a new analytic perspective on the state and on the interaction of state institutions and feminist politics.

I. EIGHT HYPOTHESES FOR FEMINIST POLITICAL SCIENCE

A. Hypothesis: Gender Research Must Conceptually Grasp the Contradiction and Dialectic of Feminist Politics

The talk about women's political roll back is both right and wrong at the same time: wrong when it dramatizes and alludes to a wire puller; right because there are, obviously, set backs to notice. The actual developments—the financial end of many autonomous, that is, non–state-affiliated, women's projects; sinking numbers of communal women's offices in the new states of Germany, and welfare state reforms at the cost of women—are better understandable when the incalculable, unintended results of feminist strategies and women's political achievements are brought in to the analytical horizon.

Feminist theory construction and political analysis should embrace the ambivalences and setbacks of feminist politics within theoretical constructions, rather than as counterstrategies of the state, of the business world, or of men. They should also be understood as (unintended) results of their own political demands, strategies, structures, and institutions. To name a few of these ambivalences: Men can take measures against discrimination in terms of gender (for example, quotas) as a basis for job claims. Women's support measures exclude certain women (for instance, on an ethnic basis) more permanently from the benefits of social policies. Bodily awareness and the health movement brought new forms of exploitation and marketing of the female body. The argument of pro-choice in the abortion debate provided protection for the argument that the fetus should also have a "choice." The debate on sexual harrassment is instrumentalized through "virtue apostles," and the pornography debate is instrumentalized through (male) censorship. Silvia Kontos insists that the development of the women's movement and women's politics should not be understood as an attack-and-counterattack movement but rather as an "interference-by-waves movement.'' ''The whole field of the women's movement and women's politics would then be a type of *large wave*, which at the end of the sixties received a series of impulses in a certain direction but, still remains in itself highly flexible, . . . a wave which tips, creates regressive whirlpools, spreads out to all sides, and is thereby constantly changing itself and its particular movements; it is a movement whose identity is, in the end, only identifiable by its dynamic'' (Kontos 1995:37, italics in original).

Neither democratization of society or institutionalization of women's movements are linear or monodimensional processes. Both are a bundle of completely different negotiation and strategy forms that are dependent upon the political context and the actors involved. This perspective has consequences for theorizing the relationship between the women's movement, the state, and democratic politics.

Respecting all ambivalences and paradoxes,the question of whether institutionalization and cooperation with state administration is a feminist strategy must be answered with a clear *yes*. Why? Institutionalization was, and is, an unavoidable feminist strategy and the women's movement was, and is, unavoidably a part of the state. This is in need of explanation and will be explained further.

B. Hypothesis: State and State Institutions Are, as Before, Blind Spots of Feminist Democracy Theories

Although six years ago Birgit Meyer mourned the nonrelationship of feminism and democracy and called for a feminist attention to democracy (Meyer 1992), today the term ''gender democracy'' rolls off our tongues easily, and the state question became, in feminist political science in Germany, more relevant. A second politicization of the women's movement and women's studies has apparently taken place; by that I mean the explicit reference to politically charged terms— those of *democracy* and *state*. Justified doubts of the performance of formal democratic institutions must not necessarily only lead to making state institutions tabu in feminist democracy theory construction. Feminist critique of the gender blindness of political science institutionalism and of Marxist functionalism, but also the connection to normative democracy debates under the heading ''Democracy and Difference,'' blend out fundamental bases of gender politics when the approaches are considered exclusive alternatives. But there still needs to be a clarification of the relationship between democracy and state, or state institutions. However, since the German-speaking debate on democracy theory discovered the civil society, the connection between democracy and state remains (once again) covered over, in hiding. Also the connection between a feminist democratization of the democratic state and given, professed state institutions remains too rarely taken up as a theme. There are unfillable gaps between the theoretical designs and democratic-political feminist critiques of Carole Pateman (1988), Anne Phillips

(1991), and suggestions of Iris Marion Young (1996) on the one hand and the political institutional structure and limitations of the German Federal Republic on the other. For example, an intense debate about forms of democracy in the context of the Europization of political structures is going on, but the feminist debates have until now searched for relatively few juncture points with these—admitedly conservative—ideas. Nonetheless, what could be worked out is, for example, the dimension of critique of basic principles of representative democracy such as representation, majority rules, and responsiveness.

A split is visible in feminist arguments and feminist interventions in political science debates. The "discovery" of new democratic feminist institutions is moved into the area of civil society as the institutions of the formal, or "real" democracy are granted no participatory expansion and absolutely no emancipatory potency in the sense of reaching feminist political goals such as autonomy *and* solidarity, freedom *and* care, female subjectivity *and* freedom from violence. At the same time, the terms participation and representation aim for participation of women in formal democratic institutions. It is valid to close the gap between the level of approach of feminist democracy theory and the political process as well as of political structures and political actors (therefore, the state) and the social relations, which implies, of course, the gender relations.

Democracy critique must also be state critique, not only because state institutions profess the procedure of democratic behavior, but also because democratic conditions are currently changing radically due to political transnationalization and "denationalization." State institutions must be analyzed as central institutions for the representation of interests and the performance of democracy in postindustrial societies. State institutions support or obstruct the representation of women; they construct, filter, and realize identities and interests. Therefore I would like to move to the question of the connection between democracy and state: How can "the state" and its "institutions" be conceptualized for a feminist debate, which means how can they be analyzed so that de-democratizing structures and strategies are made visible, however, also in such a way that democratizing opportunities—such as the participation of excluded groups, representation and realization of marginalized interests, and recognition of marginalized identities—can be carried out? An initial question is also included in terms of institutional shifts through social movements, specifically through the women's movement: Which new institutions were created permanently, and did they induce a change in handed down institutional, democratic behavior and regulation designs as well as bureaucratic structures?

With a grain of cynicism, one could now claim that just at the time that mainstream political science is formulating concepts about the erosion of the nation-state institutions, the feminist debate has discovered these institutions. However cynicism is not called for and in my opinion it is also incorrect. The attention given to state institutions has its feminist dimensions and justifications. It is, in the end, about evaluating and rethinking in a global context the succesful institutionalization of equal opportunity policies that have come of age.

C. Hypothesis: Necessity of Feminist Democracy, Institution, and State Critique

In scarcely any other political field was a social movement in connection with institutionalized women's groups so succesful in the establishment of new political structures as in equal opportunity politics (Roth 1994:234). Equal opportunity policies lead to the professionalization of women's politics with the chance of a more competent carrying through of women's interests (Sauer 1994:22), and it is not least through financial aid that feminist projects are permanently set up which would otherwise have scarce chances of survival and effectivity (see Roth 1994:252). Women's politics in communities or in semi–state institutions of the women's movement—such as women's shelters, women's emergency aid numbers, and girls clubs—is today no longer imaginable without equal opportunity posts in the community (Holland-Cunz 1995:16).

In the German feminist political science context, two contradictory perceptions of equal opportunity politics exist. One group of scholars and activists see equal opportunity politics as a pragmatic feminism that allows professionalization of feminist politics and with that also leads to a certain success. For others this feminism as profession necessarily means the loss of the women-moved charisma. The argumentation against equal opportunity policies can be bundled into four groups. First, institutionalized women's politics attempts to align women's lives to the daily lives of men, and with that they ignore and negate feminine difference. Through ''women's subventions'' women appear as the problem, as the deficient being. Second, equal opportunity policies are simply ineffective. Equal opportunity policies function as the fire brigade in precarious situations, yet can hardly change patriarchal structures. If equal opportunity works along at the same speed as at present, then we will reach gender parity in Germany in roughly 150 years. Moreover, equal opportunity policies serve only a particular clientele, namely, well-educated women. Third, equal opportunity policies are a trimming of feminist utopian and societally transforming politics and therefore a strategy of assimilating with the system. Fourth, equal opportunity policies depoliticize and take away the dynamics of the women's movement.

Institutionalized equal opportunity policy cannot offer a contribution to increase the quantitative representation of women, nor make possible a democratization of society. And actually, in deed, equal opportunity institutions are tainted with all the weaknesses of political institutions in representative democracies and the party democracy of the Federal Republic of Germany, such as the dominance

of proportional representation as a result of the representation principle, the juridi-
calization of political questions, the elitism of lofty administrations, and the problem of the majority principle.

In the context of these contradictory estimates of state women's politics,
it is necessary to assess perspectives of women's movement politics in interaction
with state political institutions, persons, and societal interests. The state should
not be either demonized or superelevated in terms of women's policies. In the
following argument I would like to re-evaluate the pros and cons of debates on
equal opportunity politics in light of a state critique debate, and, with the lens
of an institutional critique perspective, offer initial thoughts on theorizing the
state and institutions as a frame for the assessment of state-based women's policies. A new locus should be found from which feminist critique can be formulated
and, last but not least, where it is possible to rethink equal opportunity policy
and feminist political strategy in the current social, economic, and political transformation processes.

D. Hypothesis: State Institutions Have a Gender; Bureaucracy is Fate?[1]

Political institutions have internalized behavioral patterns and game rules for political interaction. They are fields of organization and standardizations "within
and by means of which the political actors behave" (Göhler 1987:8). Women's
movements and women's projects and networks are political institutions, if one
understands institutionalization as a form of stable and long-lasting regularity
of behavior and action. Erna Appelt provides an initial important definitional
contribution to the debate on institutions and institutionalization. She differentiates between "autonomous institutions" of the women's movement and "heteronomous institutions," which means state institutions (Appelt 1991:28), and
therefore emphasizes the fundamental structural similarity of institutionalizations
in modern societies: "The 'autonomous' institutions of the women's movements
must be analyzed as much in terms of their inner or outer dependence on patriarchal institutions as is the integration of women in 'heteronomous' institutions"
(Appelt 1991:30). Feminist state and democracy theory must therefore be about
how heteronomous state institutions can be analyzed.

The state-institutional organization and gendered arrangements which are
inherent, is, as before, the black box of democracy: the input and output can be
measured in terms of its gendering (actors, political programs, and measures),
but the "withinput" is unexplained. Simple consensus can certainly be reached
that the state is not gender neutral; it is not an empty shell, but rather is masculine.
But what determines the " heteronomy" and masculinity of state institutions?
Or, said in a different way, how does the patriarchal modus of equal opportunity
institutions work? How can the male-ladenness of state institutions be conceptual-

ized? How do political institutions define, filter, and realize interests in such a way that they are marked as male?

State institutions are male in a double sense. First, they are embedded with an "objectified masculinity"[2] in a Weberian sense, and second, in the actual sense of the word, they are manned. Witz and Savage (1992:37) call this "substantial" and "nominal" masculinity. Both aspects of institutional masculinity interact in a way that different forms of avoidance, averting, and defence techniques only admit a paradoxical and marginal institutionalization of equal opportunity policies. In the following I would like to give several clues as to the way in which institutionalized masculinity works. Substantial masculinity of state administration exists from a combination of hierarchical, supposedly nonemotional systems of rules, a gender specific division of labor, a hierarchical inside–outside topography, an institutionalization of women's interests as a "liminal" position, as well as a specific, closed thought style that hierarchizes knowledge and produces mystification. In short, bureaucracy as a principle of organization of state institutions is genuinely coded with masculinity. This implicit masculinity of state institutions came into being historically and has been handed down. Its gendering was bound into the bureaucratization of the state. The "expropriation" of the officeholders in modern state administration led to their promotion within the bureaucracy and to patriarchal compensation. Their maleness was of increased value and made a condition of their position, a state career was, for the time being, strictly a male career (Weber 1980). Max Weber's bureaucracy concept, thought to be progressive, described the *male* bureaucrat and not a genderless shell of obedience. His draft of instrumental rationality reads like the construction of masculinity: distance from the personal, from feelings and empathy, conceived of as against an ideological femininity which is placed in the world of chaos and disorder (Pringle 1989:88, 1992:161). State institutions define themselves as neutral merely in order to avoid prominently displaying their foundational gender.

As a result, through forms of recruitment, position, and workplace descriptions, through hierarchy and official channels, a hegemonial masculinity is institutionalized in the state bureaucracy (Grant and Tancred 1992:116; Kreisky 1992). Gendered hierarchies, principles of seniority, rigid roles and task distribution, as well as forms of finance allocation, are part of a masculine grammar of institutions. According to Rosabeth M. Kanter, men clone themselves to a certain extent within bureaucracies (Kanter 1977:58ff).

State structures and regulations therefore produce an internal gender division of labor and, with that, spheres of masculinity and femininity. Women are only integrated into the subaltern positions in the state bureaucracy, so that a dual system of unequal representation is created: women are assigned to the reproductive sector and women's departments are marginalized (Grant and Tancred 1992:114ff). A gendered system is created through the inclusion of men, the representation of their interests and lives, as well as through the exclusion or marginalization of women, their interests and identities. The state is not only masculinized but also defeminized. A discursively produced "feminization," which means the spread of the depoliticizing and privatizing dimension of women's traditional roles in the state and through the state, is, for Kathy Ferguson, that process through which women are excluded from state administration and held back from active political participation (Ferguson 1984:55f). It is also here that a state paradox is based: the bureaucracy is made the "other sex," because it is powerless and depoliticized; it is demasculinized just like the clients of state administration (Ferguson 1984:60ff).

In the following I would like to provide some clues as to the objectified masculinity within the political field of equal opportunity policies.[3] Equal opportunity politics is, in multiple ways, anchored as a temporary or liminal institution. One dimension of this threshold position is the claim that equal opportunity politics should be a "cross-section task," which means that they should act beyond departmental borders. This understanding of border crossing is difficult to fuse into the administrative workings, which are marked by department egoism. Such programs are—as also shown by policy analyses of other political fields—precariously institutionalized and underlie permanent questioning, for example, through financial cuts (Windhoff-Héritier, quoted by Holland-Cunz 1996:167).

The counterproductivity of this threshold situation shows itself at the cross-section of administrative inner, and political outer, realms. Here, the institutionalization forms of equal opportunity policy offer only suboptimal models, bound by rule to a gender-hierarchical labor division. In the political field of equal opportunity policy, the hierarchical formation of inner and outer orientation, as well as work considered public policy related and personal-private, is let in. Equal opportunity posts themselves, when created as staff posts, are primarily responsible for innovation and factual questions and normally work exclusively inner-administratively and are quite specialized; yet from equal opportunity officers, outer-oriented work is always demanded as well: publicity work, advice, helping work of a social and social-psychological type. The result of a study by Katharina Gröning is interesting: men who are responsible for the establishment and furnishing of equal opportunity posts place a special value on the visiting hours of the equal opportunity representatives (Gröning 1991:52). Qualifications assumed to be typically feminine are called for in the job outline.

The separation between inside and outside, between official state tasks within the core of the institution and personal activities with a link to the public, is attributable to the gender-specific division of labor within the administration. The significance of the "advisory duty" of the equal opportunity officers lies namely in that the contact with the public and regular visiting hours are status-lowering tasks within the administration (Gröning 1991). The masculine grammar of bureaucracy defines customer orientation as feminine, which means administrative work, which is far removed from the administrative apex located in the center. The edge of the institution, with the "clients," is considered feminized and of lesser value (Ferguson 1984). The patriarchal modus of integration in the masculine institutions implies the feminization and clientization of the affected women—the equal opportunity representatives as well as the group of women whose interests they look after.

Equal opportunity representatives are therefore tied into the gender-specific and emotional division of labor within institutions. Equal opportunity work is coded as emotional and disadvantaged, as opposed to the supposedly de-emotionalised administrative work. The marginal status of women representatives is perpetuated through the tabu on emotions within the administration. This conflict that the administration imposes and carries over onto the person of the equal opportunity representative is apparently at odds with the women's movement's understanding of self, in which the private is political. The desire is to erase the line of demarcation maintained by institutions between political and personal.

The precarious institutionalization of equal opportunity politics is supported by the "thought style" of the administration (Douglas 1991). The thought style primarily has the effect of maintaining the "thought collective" in its handed down form, making change unthinkable. The thought style evident in the methods, symbols, and traditions, in the inner-institutional habitus, is that embedded world of experience of men whose norms and values have shaped institutional practice for decades. The thought style of state administration is masculine. According to Mary Douglas, the thought style steers the "memory" of an institution, it creates the frame for how problems and tasks are defined and how decisions are made and it remains hidden from the members of the "thought collective" (Douglas 1991:121, 31). This is one reason why state administration is conservative in its structures and activities. Equal opportunity officers don't belong to this thought collective and were not able to inscribe a women-friendly narrative in the memory of state institutions.

To sum up; equal opportunity policy operates in the field of objectified institutional masculinity and is therefore paradoxical and marginal. However institutionalized equal opportunity policy can also be understood to be a politicization of this institutional sedimentary masculinity. Equal opportunity policy offers the chance to question gender, passion, and emotion, that means the unreflected underground—the masculine thought style of institutions. If negative or minimalist, the integration of equal opportunity representatives is also the permanent placing of critique within institutionalized masculinity; it is the integration of the "contradictions," the contradicting from within of a consensually masculine institution. With equal opportunity politics, the chance for permanent "de-ritualization" arises, or at least the obligation to justify masculinist inner-administrative rituals as, so to say, institutionally given. The physical presence alone of women's representatives makes the ritualization of masculinity apparent and no longer leaves the codes to be handed down at the discretion of the "secret" arrangements of the institution. Equal opportunity politics make, for example, the emotional household of institutions wobble.

E. Hypothesis: The Women's Movement Is a Part of the State

An ideal that is as seductive as it is false is that women were historically absolute "outcasts." Rather, they were, and are still, in a paradoxical way integrated into the state, especially in the welfare states of the late nineteenth and twentieth centuries. Women are integrated, and not least because there was a tenacious struggle by women for their integration in the state. Historically in Western democracy a constant increase in the quantitative representation of women in state institutions is discernable, for example, in politics, in the universities, in the military and police force. There are also feminized state realms, such as elementary schools, kindergartens, social administration, and naturally subaltern work relations in state administrations (Demirovic and Pühl 1998).

A polarization of state institutions and women's movements also does not correspond with reality, as both act on the same political terrain and both are part of a system logic—namely, the industrial capitalist gender regime, that is, the state in a comprehensive sense (Roth 1994:271). In order to analyze equal opportunity politics and feminist politics, the structure of this system's logic must be revealed and its transformation tendencies worked out.

This means conceptualizing state institutions not only as "the other" in terms of the women's movement, but taking into perspective the connection of the women's movement and state equal opportunity politics. Roth describes the behavioral repertoire of established institutions in interaction with social movements as threefold, and therefore more differentiated than the bipolar opposition of institution versus autonomy. One possible reaction of state institutions is *responsiveness*, which means that the institution takes on suggestions from the movement. A second strategy is the *exclusion* of the social movement and its themes—a common practice in Germany in the 1970s. The third strategy is the *co-optation* of themes, people, and institutions, which means the limited input of influence from movements into state politics. The creation of equal opportunity posts is, without doubt, such a co-optation of the women's movement (Roth 1994: 250). A co-opted women's movement operates in a state mined field and cannot imagine itself to be a system fugitive. The picture of opposition mechanics should be relativized for the benefit of an integral viewpoint—for the benefit of a state perspective which follows feminist insight on an individual level. The patriarchal gender order as a symbolic world is a component of the individual gender identity. A dichotomous opposition of state and society, of women's movement and state, in which the women's movement merely by virtue of its externality is awarded the ability to critique patriarchy (Eckart 1995:106), is not maintainable. Instead of this, a starting point must be a doubled, dialectical reference: negotiated free space *and* the dominance of discourses inside and outside of the state apparatus. This would mean that the occupation metaphoric must be revised, because the state cannot be theorized as an isolated, hermetic system, as a rigid, skeletal-like structure that the women's movement pushes against, or from which it is pushed, or by which it is absorbed. The women's movement was not "state-sated" through equal opportunity politics, rather there were also other active state appropriations from the women's movement.

This is not a hidden request to "join in" with the state, rather it is the attempt to find a new standpoint for feminist critique that does not imagine itself in a state-free space and end as a state-financed project. Democratization is only possible when the democratic, or actually the undemocratic, institutional arrangement of the state is recognized in its comprehensive structure. Only in this way is the political tangle possible, only in this way are the feminist bands so stretchable that they don't break under undemocratic unreasonable demands, so that women can bend back at any time into the state- and democracy-critique position. Such a state concept formulates the problem of a state women's movement in a way that there is space for the analysis of the gender regimes shaped by economic, political, cultural, and symbolic relations. I would like to give stimulus to such a state concept in the following.

F.   Hypothesis: Demystifying the State—Equal Opportunity Policy as Position for Negotiation

After decades of debates about the patriarchal or capitalist state, neo-Marxist, neo-Gramscian, and feminist state theories converge on many points (Sauer 1997). The state is not essentialized as an executive committee of capital or of the man, but also not understood as the Hegelian subject. The state rather is a "social power relation," a condensation of social contradictions, a compromise permanently negotiated (Poulantzas 1978). The state is therefore no unchangeable monolithic apparatus, as it tends to present itself and as it is perceived by feminist activists and scholars, but it consists of different groups of actors, fields of action, and spaces. The state is a "flexible" structure and a "strategic" relation (Jessop 1994:43ff). Gender relations are as much a part of the state as are relations of production and nationality definitions; and the corresponding actors build parts of the state discourse. Gender is an organizational pattern within state administration as well as a societal hegemonical relationship reproduced through institutions. The state possesses a structural gender as well as a strategic selectivity that privileges the formulations, articulations, and carrying-through of the interests of men as well as anchoring masculinity within society.

The crucial point of feminist state theory of the 1990s is that the state does not reflect a pregiven class or gender structure but rather is the result of powerful networks, relations, and alliances. It is a set of political, bureaucratic, and legal discourses and arenas (Watson 1990:112; Brown 1992:12), which are products of political confrontations. The state is therefore a ''field of hegemony'' (Demirovic and Pühl 1998), which means that it exists in and from discursive practices. The state is, in the words of Foucault, a power and control *dispositiv* that creates hegemonious conditions.

From this point of view, it follows further that the state is unallied, even unavoidably fragmented, so that no single-actor state exists behind individual politics. Its coherence is created in discourse or in changing temporally alternating interactions (Watson 1990:112). What appears to be intentionality in state behavior is not structurally given, but is rather a result of the success which various groups can bring in. Intentionality is therefore a result of diverse intentions, therefore always partial and temporary (Watson 1990). The state can thus act neither as a coherent agent of a specific societal group (the men, for example) nor with intentionality (as in the subordination of women) (Pringle and Watson 1992:55f). Friendliness as well as hostility toward women are both possible attitudes of the state, at times.

This implies that the analysis of state politics cannot begin with a given, consistent constellation of interests which already exist outside of the state and then influence *the* state or are embodied through it and realized. (Group interests are only constructed in state discourse in the confrontation within state arenas; they are ''practiced.'' Political interests and identities such as gender, class, and race do not exist beyond the state—they are also not represented, ignored, incorporated, or denied by the state. They are formed much more in confrontation, in discourse with state apparatus and agents. Pringle and Watson plea not to speak of female and male interests, but rather of (hegemonical) discourses. They grasp the marginalization of women as discursive (Pringle and Watson 1992:68). A state can, for example, be masculinist without representing the interests of men (Brown 1992:14). Through the construction of a framework of meaning, through the institutionalization of a discourse, and through the use of a specific language, chances for a political shift are opened or frittered away and prevented. It is here that the ''domination'' in and through the state is established.

This means that women's movements are not to be grasped outside of the state apparatus, but rather looked at much more in their paradoxical integration. This paradoxically marginal integration of women in the state is an effect of strategic negotiations from unequal negotiating positions. Gender hierarchy and masculinism of the state arise in state discourses. Gender is a central component in this hegemonous field, in these state practices and discourses: state discourse produces masculinity as hegemonous discourse. The state has a (denied) gender and it produces gender in that it opens and closes societal spaces, elevates male interests out of the private sphere, and lets female interests disappear in it. The state has, therefore, at its disposal the power to engender social processes and indeed to do so in an explicitly gendered or gender-neutral way. To decode the gender of the state it is next necessary to maintain that the state is male because it systematically produces male interests, especially interests of heterosexual men (Connell 1990:535; Hearn 1990:67). Altogether, through the history of the modern state it is possible to determine an "accomplice-hood" between state and male interest groups (see Elman 1996:13). The state organization showed a systematic gender-specific division of labor, or, more precisely, it facilitated easier access for men to the power of the state (Franzway et al. 1989:10). I would like to add to that two historical remarks. With the linking of the ability to handle weapons and citizenship the nation-state made masculinity hegemonial. Also the welfare state does not solve this problem of implicit masculinity; the class compromise reinstitutionalized "privacy" on a new basis and once again excluded women. The corporative structures of welfare state compromises in Europe institutionalized the class conflict but not the gender conflict (Dahlerup 1987:110). The welfare state and the male class compromise institutionalized a protected sphere of male gainful employment, but the needs of women remained outside of welfare state regulation in a newly measured field of the private.

From these premises we are able to draw the following conclusions for feminist politics and equal opportunity policy:

1. With such a vision of the state new actors come across the field of vision of feminist politics: the "corporate network" of administration, unions, economic groups, the financial world, the "power state," and the church as well as further projects and groups. Democratization must also be directed at these agents; they are possible opponents of feminist politics, but also potential allies of democratization. A feminist gender critique is therefore positioned *against* the state—if this critique is antipatriarchal and anticapitalistic—but it is also positioned *within* the state when practicing antipatriarchal or anticapitalist politics in alliance with other actors.

2. Equal opportunity policy is indeed the noticeable state marginalization of women, but it is also at the same time the noticeable occupation of a position in the state negotiation process.

3. For the evaluation of state equal opportunity policy, this concept of state means that there is no single uniform feminist interest which can be realized through equal opportunity policy or whose purity can be watered down through administrative control. Much more, feminists take on different strategies at different times and in different places (Holland-Cunz 1996).

G. Hypothesis: De-Nationalizing Feminist Democracy and State Critique

The question of state, democracy, and gender is at this time still related entirely to the nation-state. I think feminist democracy theory must confront the term globalization and ask what de-nationalizing, and the erosion of national political structures, and the de-territorialization of state (Sassen 1996) means for feminist politics and for democracy. Economic globalization, political internationalization, and the shift from a Keynesian welfare state to a Schumpeterian workfare state (Jessop 1994:57) change nation-state political patterns. To name some of the changes of nation-state democracy in the era of globalization, the state loses the monopoly on political-problem definition, agenda-setting, and problem-solving strategy- and decision-making. In the ''network state'' the central decision-making pattern in many political fields can be described as governance without (national) government (Scharpf 1992). But in spite of the change of the (welfare) state through globalization and internationalization, the nation-state has kept fundamental potencies, namely its ability to condense social contradictions. This function of condensing is also maintained by the state's apparatus in a multilevel system and in policy networks. Also in the future it will be the state which marks out the space, the framework, for negotiation networks, even when it no longer forms the dominant point in the negotiation system.

One consequence of the restructuring of the nation-state is that gender regimes will be restructured. This has direct consequences for democratization, but also for forms of institutionalization for women's politics. Therefore feminist state and democracy theories must reflect the change in political space and spread out to an at-the-same-time international and local space of thought and action.

H. Hypothesis: Transformation of the State in the Era of Globalization: More Democracy or More Masculinity?

Four tendencies of political development will make lasting influences on the conditions for feminist politics: (1) political deregulation, (2) the making of politics into economics (Koch 1995), (3) the erosion of traditional state institutions and the informalizing of nation-state policy and decision-making structures, as well as (4) internationalization of political decisions. All four developments let us predict a strong pressure on political actors concerned with women's issues. However, the coordinates of this transformation process, which build the new context for women's politics and the design for a re-vision of feminist politic strategy, are only roughly determinable. The four concepts are further discussed in the following paragraphs, respectively.

1. On the one hand, deregulation of welfare state institutions and redistribution residues devalue regulations fought for and won by feminists. Democracy appears to drift far away in the light of increasing social imbalance. At the same time, however, present distortions of welfare state regulations become clearer— for example, the employment bias of the welfare state. A breaking up of solidarity in welfare state discourse can also be interpreted as a jumping over of the inherited male welfare state compromises. Deregulation of institutional-bound mascu-

linity again contains the danger of the breakout of masculinity—if it is violence or misogyny (Kreisky and Sauer 1997).

2. The privatization and slimming down of state administration lets prospective women employees loose and brings equal opportunity policy into trouble as the "slim state" often cuts down on possible equal opportunity measures, defamed as bureaucratic baggage. It is to be assumed that the need for well-aimed women's support will rise due to the cuts in the social net, but that precisely those instruments of support will fall under the pressure for saving resources. Equal opportunity politics can increasingly degenerate to merely limit the damage so that women, in the course of economic and social restructuring, don't lose positions already achieved: active feminist structural and societal politics in the sense of "sustainability" (Jung 1997) possibly escape from this horizon of thought and action. Autonomous women's projects are also pushed to the edges of their financial existence. At the same time we can watch the increasing of the state's power monopoly, the classical male state terrains.

3. Informalizing of politics in several decentered networks brings indeed a leway for new political actors and for nonstate political networks. However it also contains the danger of intransparence, elitization, and de-democratizing. The thicker knotting of the corporate network, for example, operates against political movements outside of the network. Connected to the informalizing of politics is the increasing control of the executive in the political process with the possibility of an increase in masculinity, which is sedimented in executive structures.

4. Also at an international level, masculinization through globalization is probable. We already witness the development of new "expert brotherhoods" on international terrain (Demirovic and Pühl 1998). The global state will probably not be the nation-state in the handed down form but will continue as the gender state.

All four developments predict a strong pressure on actors in women's politics. Democracy, in the face of increasing social inequality and fragmentation, appears to be retreating into the distant background, and equal opportunity political institutions shrink to institutions which at the most can achieve improved status for a small clientele. In this situation, it is politically necessary that women and equal opportunity policy proponents, as well as the women's movement, clearly make the "social question" a theme. The demand for integration of difference, of class, race, and cultural background (which often degenerates into a fixed feminist phrase in gender research) can and must be politically demanded and realized. Women's politics must therefore intervene at the many locations of negotiation of a new welfare state compromise. Equal opportunity institutions are negotiation positions within the state negotiation processes, which should be used also when these positions in the "negotiation state" are "elitely" filled. Therefore, also the democratic political goal of a slim state and a growing civil society appears now to be relativized. An increased "civil societal" equality does not automatically let itself be realized in this way. More commonly, through state deregulation and under a pressure to save, many equal opportunity promises are shown to be what they (until then) were: lifeless bits of paper. Dangers to democracy lie now, in my opinion, not in too much state, but rather in too little, because state political functions are transformed into economic structures. Therefore societal democratization demands an, as it were, paradoxical intervention: namely, to carry out women's politics *with* the state apparatus *against* the state apparatus, which means against making politics economic and against the dominance of the economy. To see the women's movement as a part of the state apparatus does not mean, in any way, to assume naively that feminist politics can be realized simply through the state. The advantage of this concept lies in the fact that a politics of "interference" and of coalition is to be presented as indispensable, while at the same time the hierarchical cliff of these politics must be pointed out. A nobel distancing from the state gives all negotiation positions to other powerful actors within the state apparatus. On the other hand, the recognition of this position of "inclusion" is the prerequisite for a reformulated position of critique— a role which the feminist movement should take on.

The women's movement should find a new locus and a new role in conjunction with state equal opportunity policies in the recent political transformations. In order to give feminist demands emphasis, it is necessary to form coalitions within the state apparatus abuse with women's groups and women's projects that remain outside. Feminist research can and should again bring together theory and praxis of emancipatory politics and constitute a reflexive connection of theory and praxis.

ACKNOWLEDGMENT

The title of this chapter refers to Bob Jessop's book *State Theory: Putting the Capitalist State in Its Place* (Jessop 1990). I thank Lisa Rosenblatt for the translation.

ENDNOTES

1. See the title from Diamond et al. (1984).
2. At the universities, this sedimentation (Kreisky 1994) is institutionalized, for example, in the picture of the genial lonely scientist, in the master—student dyad, and in exclusionary transformation rituals such as graduation.

3. Mechthild Cordes analyzes the different models of equal opportunity institutions in Germany (Cordes 1996:85ff).

REFERENCES

Appelt, E. (1991). Zur transformation feministischer Anliegen im institutionellen Kontext. In M.-L. Angerer, E. Appelt, A. Bell, J. Rosenberger, and H. Seidl (eds.), *Auf glattem Parkett: Feministinnen in Institutionen*. Wien: Verlag für Gesellschaftskritik.

Bloch, E. (1976). *Das Prinzip Hoffnung* (3rd edition). Frankfurt: Suhrkamp.

Brown, W. (1992). Finding the man in the state. *Feminist Studies 18*:1, 7–34.

Connell, R. W. (1990). The state, gender, and sexual politics: Theory and appraisal. *Theory and Society*, No. 5, 507–544.

Cordes, M. (1996). *Frauenpolitik: Gleichstellung oder Gesellschaftsveränderung?* Opladen: Leske und Budrich.

Dahlerup, D. (1987). Confusing concepts—confusing reality: A theoretical discussion of the patriarchal state. In A. S. Sassoon (ed.), *Women and the State: The Shifting Boundaries of Public and Private*. London: Sage.

Demirovic, A. and Pühl, K. (1998). Identitätspolitik und die Transformation von Staatlichkeit: Geschlechterverhältnisse und Staat als komplexe materielle Relation. In E. Kreisky and B. Sauer (eds.), *Politik der Geschlechterverhältnisse im Kontext politischer Transformation* (special edition of the journal *Politische Vierteljahresschrift*). Opladen: Westdeutscher Verlag.

Diamond, S., Narr, W. D., and Hommann, R. (eds.) (1984). *Bürokratie als Schicksal?* (special edition No. 6 of the journal *Leviathan*). Opladen: Westdeutscher Verlag.

Douglas, M. (1991). *Wie Institutionen denken*. Frankfurt: Suhrkamp.

Eckart, C. (1995). Feministische Politik gegen institutionelles Vergessen. In M. M. Jansen, S. Barringhorst, and M. Ritter (eds.), *Frauen in der Defensive? Zur backlash-Debatte in Deutschland*. Münster: Lit-Verlag.

Elman, R. A. (1996). *Sexual Subordination and State Intervention: Comparing Sweden and the United States*. Oxford: Bogman Publisher.

Ferguson, K. E. (1984). Bürokratie und öffentliches Leben: die Feminisierung des Gemeinwesens. In S. Diamond, W.-D. Narr, and R. Homann (eds.), *Bürokratie als Schicksal?* (special edition No. 6 of the journal *Leviathan*). Opladen: Westdeutscher Verlag.

Franzway, S., Court, D., and Connell, R. W. (1989). *Staking a Claim*. Sidney: Allen and Unwin.

Göhler, G. (1987). *Grundfragen der Theorie politischer Institutionen: Forschungsstand–Probleme–Perspektiven*. Opladen: Westdeutscher Verlag.

Grant, J. and Tancred, P. (1992). A feminist perspective on state bureaucracy. In A. J. Mills and P. Tancred (eds.), *Gendering Organizational Analysis*. London: Sage.

Gröning, K. (1991). Den Frauen helfen . . . Der Balanceakt der Beratung in den Aufgabenkatalogen der kommunalen Frauenbüros. Eine empirische Auswertung. *Frauenforschung*, No. 3, 50–66.

Hearn, J. (1990). State organisations and men's sexuality in the public domain, 1870–1920. In L. Jamieson (ed.), *State, Private Life and Political Change*. London: Sage.

Holland-Cunz, B. (1995). Frauenpolitik im schlanken Staat: Die "Poetik" der lean administration und ihre Realität. *Zeitschrift für Frauenforschung*, Nos. 1 & 2, 15–27.

Holland-Cunz, B. (1996). Komplexe Netze, konfliktreiche Prozesse: Gleichstellungspolitik aus policy-analytischer Sicht. In T. Kulawik and B. Sauer (eds.), *Der halbierte Staat: Grundlagen feministischer Politikwissenschaft*. Frankfurt: Campus Polity Press.

Jessop, B. (1990). *State Theory: Putting the Capitalist State in Its Place*. Cambridge.

Jessop, B. (1994). Veränderte Staatlichkeit: Veränderungen von Staatlichkeit und Staatsprojekten. In D. Grimm (ed.), *Staatsaufgaben*. Baden-Baden: Nomos Verlag.

Jung, D. (1997). Nachhaltiger Sozialstaat: Frauen als Pionierinnen neuer sozialer Umverteilung und gesellschaftlicher Solidarität. *Kommune*, No. 3, 49–53.

Kanter, R. M. (1977). *Men and Women of the Corporation*. New York: Basic Books.

Koch, K. (1995). *Die Gier des Marktes: Die Ohnmacht des Staates im Kampf der Weltwirtschaft*. München: C. H. Beck.

Kontos, S. (1995). Jenseits des hydraulischen Bewegungsmodells: Einwände gegen das backlash-Konzept. In M. M. Jansen, S. Baringhorst, and M. Ritter (eds.), *Frauen in der Defensive? Zur backlash-Debatte in Deutschland*. Münster: Lit-Verlag.

Kreisky, E. (1992). Mit Frauen wurde kein Staat gemacht. Die Geschichte der Bürokratie als Geschichte des Frauenausschlusses. In Frauenreferat der Stadt Frankfurt (ed.), *Feminisierung des öffentlichen Dienstes—Bürokratisierung der Frauen*. Frankfurt: Stadt Frankfort.

Kreisky, E. (1994). Das ewig Männerbündische? Zur Standardform von Staat und Politik. In C. Leggewie (ed.), *Wozu Politikwissenschaft? Über das Neue in der Politik*. Darmstadt: Wissenschaftliche Buchgesellschaft.

Kreisky, E. and Sauer, B. (1997). Maskulinismus und Staat: Zwei Institutionen unter Globalisierungsdruck. *Neue Impulse*, No. 5, 4–11.

Kulawik, T. (1991/1992). Autonomous Mothers? West German feminism reconsidered. *German Politics and Society*, Nos. 24 & 25, 67–86.

Meyer, B. (1992). Über das schwierige aber notwendige Verhältnis von Feminismus und Demokratie. In E. Biester et al. (eds.), *Staat aus feministischer Sicht*. Berlin: FU Berlin.

Pateman, C. (1988). *The Sexual Contract*. Cambridge: Polity Press.

Phillips, A. (1991). *Engendering Democracy*. University Park, PA: Pennsylvania State University Press.

Poulantzas, N. (1978). *Staatstheorie: Politischer Überbau, Ideologie, Sozialistische Demokratie*. Hamburg: USA-Verlag.

Pringle, R. (1989). *Secretaries Talk*. London: Sage.

Pringle, R. (1992). Bureaucracy, rationality and sexuality: Case of secretaries. In J. Hearn and D. L. Sheppard (eds.), *The Sexuality of Organization. Organizational Behavior. Sexual Differences*. London: Sage.

Pringle, R. and Watson, S. (1992). "Women's interests" and the post-structuralist state. In M. Barrett and A. Phillips (eds.), *Destabilizing Theory: Contemporary Feminist Debates*. Stanford: Stanford University Press.

Roth, R. (1994). *Demokratie von unten. Neue soziale Bewegungen auf dem Weg zur politischen Institution.* Köln: Bund-Verlag.

Sassen, S. (1996). Toward a feminist analytic of the global economy. *Indiana Journal of Global Legal Studies 4*, No. 1, 7–41.

Sauer, B. (1994). Totem und Tabus. Zur Neubestimmung von Gleichstellungspolitik: Eine Einführung. In E. Biester, B. Holland-Cunz, E. Maleck-Lewy, A. Ruf, and B. Sauer (eds.), *Gleichstellungspolitik—Totem und Tabus: Eine feministische Revision.* Frankfurt: Campus-Verlag.

Sauer, B. (1997). ''Die Magd der Industriegesellschaft'': Anmerkungen zur Geschlechtsblindheit von Staatstheorien. In B. Kerchner and G. Wilde (eds.), *Staat und Privatheit: Aktuelle Studien zu einem schwierigen Verhältnis,* Opladen: Leske und Budrich.

Scharpf, F. W. (1992). Die Handlungsfähigkeit des Staates am Ende des Zwanzigsten Jahrhunderts. In B. Kohler-Koch (ed.), *Staat und Demokratie in Europa.* Opladen.

Watson, S. (1990). Unpacking ''the state'': Reflections on Australian, British and Scandinavian feminist interventions. In M. F. Katzenstein and H. Skjeie (eds.), *Going Public. National Histories of Women's Enfranchisment and Women's Participation Within State Institutions.* Oslo.

Weber, M. (1980). *Wirtschaft und Gesellschaft: Grundriß der verstehenden Soziologie* (5th edition) Tübingen: Mohr.

Witz, A. and Savage, M. (1992). Theoretical introduction: The gender of organizations. In M. Savage and A. Witz (eds.), *Gender and Bureaucracy.* Oxford: Oxford University Press.

Young, I. M. (1996). Communication and the other: Beyond deliberative democracy. In S. Benhabib (ed.), *Democracy and Difference: Contesting the Boundaries of the Political.* Princeton: Princeton University Press.

20

The Limits of Tolerance in a Liberal Society

In Search of Guidelines

Marlies Galenkamp
Erasmus University, Rotterdam, The Netherlands

I. INTRODUCTION

Over the last few years, most Western European societies have become multicultural societies due to the arrival of migrants and refugees. The conceptions of the good and the ways of life of ethnic minorities are sometimes at odds with the dominant ones. Take the so-called *hijab* affair or the discussion within the Netherlands on the admissibility of female circumcision. Recently there has been much noise in the Dutch media about two other issues: the wearing of a turban by a Sikh in the Amstelhotel in Amsterdam in pursuance of his job as a cleaner and the debate on the harmfulness of male circumcision.

Those discussions on practices of migrants are illustrative of topical discussions on the admissibility of minority groups' practices in general (like sects, subcultures, and lifestyle groups). Take the current "hunt" for members of the Scientology movement in some Western European countries like Belgium, Germany, and Greece. Or take the recent judgment of the European Court on the inadmissibility of sadomasochistic practices.

These examples—divergent though they may seem at first sight—yet raise the same kind of normative questions. First, the theoretical question whether, and to what extent, within a liberal-democratic society there should be room for the preservation of the identity of minority groups. Second, and more specifically, there is the question of admissibility. To what extent should uncommon practices of groups be accepted within a liberal democracy? Reformulated, this question amounts to a classic question of liberal political theory: what are the limits of tolerance that a liberal society can show for intolerant or illiberal groups—and, more importantly, why are the limits exactly there? Finally, there is the most practical question what is the justified scope for state intervention within illiberal groups.

Answering these questions is a hard job. Most of us will be led by a double—actually conflicting—intuition. On the one hand, it is generally acknowledged that within a liberal democracy there should be some room for tolerance and hence for the freedom to lead one's life as one prefers. This includes the freedom to associate, to form a dissenting group, and to stick to the idiosyncratic norms and values of the group. On the other hand, most of us will also agree that this room cannot be taken as absolute (in view of, for example, human rights violations). Consequently, there should be a limit to the group's freedom. The question is, however, where to draw the line. At harm done to others or done to oneself? At the free will and consent of the members of those groups? Or should we adhere to the statement that some practices—awful though these may seem from the outside—flow from a religious conviction and hence should be permitted in view of the constitutionally secured right to freedom of religion?

In this article, I will address the above normative questions. I will especially focus on the second question of admissibility of practices of minority groups. I use the broad terminology of "minority groups" in order to indicate that this question arises not only with respect to ethnic minority groups, but with regard to other identity groups (such as religious or lifestyle groups) as well. My assumption is that there may be a tension between preserving group identities on the one hand and individual autonomy on the other hand. One of the key questions in any liberal political order seems to be how to adjudicate instances in which associations collide with liberal-democratic values such as individual autonomy. In legal terms one may speak of a collision of rights. What is to be done when the right to freedom of association or the freedom of religion seems to be at odds with another right (for example, the right to equal treatment)? The question is whether a model can be developed wherein identity groups (of various kinds) are accommodated and, at the same time, individual rights are protected. And if so, what would this model look like? My intention in this chapter is to develop some guidelines that may help determine how we should balance these two values. This balancing will be done after having elaborated and assessed two divergent views on this topic. They are, respectively, Will Kymlicka's and Chandran Kukathas's.

Within the current political philosophical doctrine, both Kymlicka and Kukathas are known as liberal—instead of communitarian—scholars. They also share the intention to develop a liberal theory wherein minority groups are accomodated without abandoning the protection of individual rights. In spite of these similarities, there are some substantial differences as well. These differences originate from what both authors consider to be the core liberal value: is it autonomy or is it tolerance? For Kymlicka, the fundamental value is autonomy. In his view, minority group cultures may be protected only in so far and to the extent that they enhance the autonomy of the individual members of those group cultures. In contrast, Kukathas views tolerance as the key liberal value. According to him, as liberals we should even tolerate nonliberal groups. These two ''idealtypically'' liberal positions will be elaborated and assessed in, respectively, Sections II and III (on Kymlicka) and Sections IV and V (on Kukathas). On the basis hereof, I will draw some conclusions on both positions (Section VI), articulate some lessons (Section VII), develop some guidelines (Section VIII), and make some concluding observations (Section IX).

II. WILL KYMLICKA: AUTONOMY WITHIN A CULTURE

In order to answer the questions at stake here, I start with one of the currently most authoritative views on the relationship between individual autonomy and group identity, that of the Canadian political philosopher, Will Kymlicka's. Since he has written a lot on this issue(see also Kymlicka 1989), I will restrict myself to an exposé of his ideas expressed in his 1995 book, *Multicultural Citizenship*: *A Liberal Theory of Minority Rights* (Kymlicka 1995a).

As the title indicates, in this book Kymlicka develops an argument in favor of minority protection (in the form of ascribing special rights to those groups) within the liberal philosophical doctrine. According to him, special rights are sometimes needed in order to preserve the threatened group identities of minority groups (such as national and ethnic minorities). His argument is based on a specific view of cultures. According to Kymlicka, cultures should be seen as ''contexts of choice'' for individual human beings. That is, one's embeddedness within a culture is a precondition for individual autonomy. Before elaborating on the normative consequences of this perceived connection between freedom and culture, let me give a brief overview of the main strands of thought in the book.

Kymlicka's main proposition is that the issue of multiculturalism is often dealt with in overgeneralized terms. Therefore he proposes to distinguish between national and ethnic minorities. National minorities are ''territorially concentrated cultures, which were previously self-governing, but have been involuntarily incorporated into a larger state through colonialism, conquest or 'voluntary' federation'' (Kymlicka 1995a:10). A principal characteristic of those minorities is their wish to maintain themselves as distinct societies—or, more precisely, as ''societal cultures''—alongside the majority culture, which becomes evident through their demanding forms of autonomy or self-government. According to Kymlicka, minorities in Eastern Europe, but also native peoples and the French-speaking minority within Canada, fit within this category. Apart from these national minorities, cultural diversity within a country may also arise from individual and familial immigration. Kymlicka states that such immigrants or ethnic minorities—often coalescing into loose associations—typically wish to integrate into the larger culture and be accepted as full members (Kymlicka 1995a:10–11). In his own words: ''Immigrants are not 'nations' and do not occupy homelands. Their distinctiveness is manifested primarily in their family lives and in voluntary associations, and is not inconsistent with their institutional integration'' (Kymlicka 1995a:14).

According to Kymlicka, seen from a liberal perspective these two kinds of minority groups are qualified—although to different extents—to the ascription of special rights. Three of those rights may be distinguished: self-government rights (such as the well-known right to self-determination), polyethnic rights, and special representation rights. The second and the third are, respectively, concerned with financial support for certain practices of minorities and with guaranteed seats for ethnic and national groups within the central institutions of the larger state. The reason for ascribing these special rights to minorities is their need for the protection of their relatively vulnerable and threatened identity amidst a dominant culture. That is, special rights are ever externally oriented. Their main value lies in the protection of minority groups against the dominant society and hereby in the promotion of equality between groups.

Interestingly, Kymlicka sets up a rather huge distinction between ethnic and religious minorities. Whereas the first category should be qualified for a special treatment, the second should not. The reason for this has to do with his view of liberal states. To him (Kymlicka 1995a:111), though these states can be religiously neutral, they can never be culturally neutral. This implies that ethnic minorities are ever far more disadvantaged than religious minority groups. Consequently, they alone are qualified for special treatment.

Furthermore, in Kymlicka's book we can find a differentiation of special rights for ethnic and national minorities. Whereas immigrants should have at best some additional polyethnic and special representation rights, only national minorities may gain self-government rights. In an article some years ago, Kymlicka wrote:

> And I think this is a significant distinction. Surely immigrant groups cannot claim the same rights as national minorities. If I and others decide to emigrate to China, we have no right that the Chinese government provide us with public services in our mother language. We could argue that a government policy that provided English-language services would benefit everyone, by enriching the whole cultural environment. But we have no right to such policies, for in choosing to leave Canada, we relinquish the rights that go with membership in our cultural community. Public subsidization of the ethnic activities of voluntary immigrant groups is best seen as a matter of policy, which no one has a right to, or a right against (Kymlicka 1991:250).

According to Kymlicka (1991:252), this differentiation of minority groups, having different special rights is close to the actual practice and national consensus in both the United States and Canada. The laws in those countries give Indians, Inuit, French-Canadians, and Puerto Ricans a special political status that other ethnic groups do not have.

So far we have seen that in Kymlicka's view some special rights are needed in order to protect the identity of vulnerable minority groups. Having said so, it remains to be examined whether those groups have the right to preserve their own identity unconditionally or whether there are some limits to it. This brings us to a key issue of this article: what are the limits of liberal toleration and why are the limits exactly there? In Chapter 8, "Toleration and Its Limits," of his book (*Multicultural Citizenship*), Kymlicka enters into these issues. According to him, the endorsement of cultural identities is always a conditional and qualified one. As he notes, the demands of some minority groups exceed what liberalism reasonably can accept: "Liberal democracy can accommodate and embrace many forms of cultural diversity, but not all."

More specifically, Kymlicka distinguishes two limitations of minority rights, concerning "internal restrictions" and "external protections." To begin with the second, as mentioned, the main function of minority rights is the (external) protection of vulnerable minority groups against the larger society. Some external protections—legitimate though they are in order to reduce the minority's vulnerability to the decisions of the larger society—are yet forbidden. They are forbidden in case these protections result in a straightforward exploitation and oppression of other groups. In Kymlicka's own words: "Liberal justice cannot accept any such rights which enable one group to oppress or exploit other groups" (1995a:152). The background hereby is the aforementioned rationale of special rights, the promotion of equality between groups. External protections of a minority group are legitimate only in so far as they promote equality between the minority group and the majority.

Another precondition of minority rights is that the protection of a minority culture may not result in internal restrictions. One may think here of restrictions in the sphere of basic civil and political liberties of the members of those cultures. In other words, the individual rights of the members should always be respected. This limitation has to do with Kymlicka's previously elaborated "positive" view of cultures. Membership within a culture ideally enables autonomous choices of individuals about how to lead one's life. Even more, according to Kymlicka the fundamental reason for supporting cultural membership is that it allows for such meaningful individual choice. This implies that liberals can only endorse minority rights in so far as they are consistent with respect for the freedom and autonomy of the individual members. This precondition indicates Kymlicka's sensitivity to the threat of forced inclusion of individuals within their cultures. Not all minority cultures are worth respecting, since some of them are oppressive. As he himself notes: "Individuals should have autonomy, because communities can be oppressive." Thus in a liberal society a minority group may stick to its own practices, provided that these practices are not at odds with the autonomy of its members. That is, provided that this minority group is—to a certain extent—liberal itself.

By thus sticking to the liberal value of autonomy, Kymlicka seems to relativize the value of tolerance. Societies may consider tolerance of paramount importance, yet may be quite illiberal societies, since the value of individual autonomy is not respected. The so-called millet system during the Ottoman empire is a good illustration. This system was based on a large amount of respect and tolerance for different religious groups (based as it was on the axiom *cuius regio*, *eius religio*). Nonetheless, to him this system cannot realistically be viewed to be a liberal system due to the lack of individual autonomy and individual rights (for example, the right to change one's religion). According to Kymlicka (1995a: 158), as liberals we should not be committed to tolerance as such, but to a much more specific form of tolerance, that is, one wherein there is a commitment to autonomy.

Now one could question whether by thus sticking to the value of autonomy we do not force minorities to become liberal. Kymlicka answers this question in the negative. The fact that some practices of minority groups seem to be inadmissible from a liberal point of view (in the sense that they violate the rights of their members) does not automatically imply that the state should intervene into those illiberal cultures and forbid those practices. Here we arrive at the question of legitimacy of state intervention. In contradistinction to what we would expect, Kymlicka tends to be rather wary of such intervention. In his view, we have to distinguish two questions. The first is the question of identifying a defensible liberal theory of minority rights. This is the task which he, as a political philosopher, has set himself in his 1995 book. The second is the much more practical issue of imposing that liberal theory. To Kymlicka, there is relatively little scope for legitimate coercive state interference into an intolerant culture. As he contends: "In cases where the national minority is illiberal, this means that the majority will be unable to prevent the violation of individual rights within the minority community. Liberals in the majority groups have to learn to live with this" (Kymlicka 1995a:168). Nonetheless, intervention is justified in case of gross and systematic violations of human rights. Here, a number of factors are relevant. They include "the severity of rights violations within the minority community, the degree of consensus within the community on the legitimacy of restricting individual rights, the ability of dissenting group members to leave the community if they so desire and the existence of historical agreements with the national minority" (Kymlicka 1995a:169–170). Unfortunately, these factors are not elaborated in more detail.

Finally, the room that is created for intolerant and illiberal minority groups has to be qualified in another sense. Although his 1995 book is about both national and ethnic minorities, with regard to the issue of nonintervention Kymlicka seems to have in mind merely national minorities. With regard to ethnic minorities, things are completely different. As Kymlicka (1995a:170) notices: ''In these cases, it is more legitimate to compel respect for liberal principles.''

III. ASSESSMENT

How to evaluate Kymlicka's approach? There is much to comment upon. I want to restrict myself here to a review of those aspects that are relevant to the key questions of this article. They are, respectively, (1) the distinction that Kymlicka sets up between different kinds of minorities, (2) his autonomy-based conception of liberalism, and (3) his plea for non–state intervention into illiberal cultures.

   1. The differentiation that is set up between different minorities.   I want to start by expressing my sympathy for Kymlicka's attempt to differentiate. To date, in international legal circles, the topic of minority rights is still too often dealt with in rather unspecific terms. The broad definition of minorities forged almost twenty years ago by Capotorti (''groups numerically inferior to the rest of the population of a state, in a non-dominant position, wherein there is a common will of the members to preserve their distinctive characteristics'') is still in use as the most authoritative one. In order to put the discussion on minority rights on a higher level, differentiation and specification of the terms is called for. This does not imply, however, that I fully endorse Kymlicka's proposal for differentiation. It seems to me that the strength of his proposal is its weakness at the same time: the urge for differentiation ends in too large a difference between different kinds of minorities.

   Take, for example, the distinction between national and ethnic minorities. The main rationale for distinguishing these two groups lies in the diverging aspirations of both groups. Whereas national minorities want to be independent, ethnic minorities want to integrate. For one, this subjectivistic approach—focussing on the subjective wish of the respective groups and hereby neglecting objective circumstances—is too one-sided to be convincing (see Galenkamp 1996). Besides, it seems to be based on an unrealistic view of ethnic minorities. Most migrants in Western European countries do not merely want to integrate and assimilate into the dominant culture. They want to integrate, while at the same time preserving their own identity. Actually, a paradox arises here. Kymlicka is known as a defender of the rights of national and ethnic minorities. But with regard to ethnic minorities, he turns out to be a defender of a policy of forced assimilation with practically no room for the preservation of one's own identity. In the famous phrase of Shakespeare: ''When in Rome, do as the Romans.'' This plea for assimilation seems to be at odds with current migrant policy in most Western European countries. Consider the policy concerning minorities in the

Netherlands. Although migrants are urged (and currently more than ever) to integrate into the dominant culture, yet it is accepted that they may preserve, just like other minority groups such as religious or lifestyle ones, parts of their own identity.

Apart from this distinction between national and ethnic minorities, there is the distinction between ethnic and religious minorities. Also here the differences seem to me overstretched. For one, in actual practice this difference is difficult to uphold. Take the ethnic minorities in the Netherlands. Most of them are religious minorities at the same time. Even more, the problems that have been raised in the last few years with regard to those groups all have to do with their religious (that is, non-Christian and especially Islamic) convictions. That is, most of the discussions focus on the conflict between liberal-secular values (such as the equality of men and women) and Islamic values. By explicitly excluding those kinds of groups, Kymlicka's approach seems to have too little to offer in case of such religiously laden conflicts. Besides, in so far as the distinction between ethnic and religious groups can be upheld, it is unconvincing to do so since it may lead to some counterintuitive outcomes. Ethnic minorities would be qualified for special treatment, whereas religious minorities would not. This seems to be a far cry from state practice in most Western European countries, wherein the freedom of religion is constitutionally secured and the right to preserve one's own culture generally is not.

  2. The autonomy-based approach of liberalism. As we have seen, minority groups may stick to their own practices, provided that these practices are not at odds with the autonomy of their members, that is to say, provided that these minority groups are, to a certain extent, liberal themselves. But one could ask, does not Kymlicka get rid of the problems too easily by adding this provision (Galenkamp 1998:132)? It is easy enough to tolerate liberal communities. Far more difficult, however, is the question of what to do with nonliberal communities. Should we tolerate these communities, too? With regard to this question, a blurry picture emerges. For one, in day-to-day politics we should tolerate these cultures, and hence we should not intervene into those cultures (see the following discussion on nonintervention). But at the same time seen from the liberal and theoretical perspective, we cannot tolerate such groups, for they are likely to violate the autonomy of their individual members. But one could ask, what remains of the value of tolerance and respect for dissenters? Does not a liberal viewpoint also include the idea of what one could call "sphere sovereigny" and hence the freedom to choose autonomously for a nonautonomous life (for example, in case of certain orthodox religious communities)? We seem to have arrived here at a second paradox in Kymlicka's approach. As noted, Kymlicka has been known as a defender of minority groups and their right to live according to their own conceptions of the good. Looking in more detail to his approach however, the margins to live according to one's own values tend to be quite small indeed. In this respect, Kymlicka can be blamed for coming close to a—in the words of Freeman (1995:37)—"liberal imperialistic" attitude, in the sense that liberal norms and values are held out as an ideal to nonliberal groups. To say it in other words, Kymlicka seems to be inspired by strongly universalistic ideals. It is doubtful whether such universalism is a good basis for dialogue between different communities within society.

 3. *The plea for non–state intervention.* In view of the second remark, this plea comes as a surprise. It is surprising because Kymlicka views the violation and suppression of basic individual rights of group members by their own group as unjust from a liberal perspective. Nonetheless, he believes that the state has no authority to intervene in the practices of (nonliberal) minority groups. I wonder whether Kymlicka hereby does not detract from his autonomy-based liberalism. For, one could ask, does not the having of liberal principles commit one to stand up for them? If not, one's liberal principles are, so to say, put up for sale. More practically seen, the net result of nonintervention is that individual members of illiberal minority groups are rendered vulnerable to infringement of their basic rights (see Section VII). This plea for non–state intervention has brought us quite close to the tolerance-based approach of liberalism, which will be elaborated now.

IV. CHANDRAN KUKATHAS: TOLERANCE AND THE RIGHT OF EXIT

In his article "Are There Any Cultural Rights?" (Kukathas 1995, originally published in 1992), the Australian political philosopher Chandran Kukathas offers us a second liberal approach for coping with the potentially competing claims of the individual and his (or her) community. The intent of his approach is quite the same as that of Kymlicka's: how can we strike an appropriate balance between the claims of the individual on the one hand and the interests of the minority community on the other hand? In spite of this similarity, the differences between the two approaches could hardly be greater. These differences are mainly due to the primacy that Kukathas attributes to tolerance, instead of autonomy. His plea for tolerance stretches rather far. In Kukathas's view, liberals are even obliged to tolerate intolerant and illiberal minority (or, as he calls them, "identity") groups. Interestingly enough, however, this room for identity groups is not created by giving them special or collective rights. On the contrary, Kukathas takes pain to argue that the individual human rights approach will do. Let us have a look at his argumentation in more detail.

 Kukathas starts his article by criticizing current critics of mainstream liberalism (such as Kymlicka), who condemn it for having no room for cultural minorities and, hence, plead for special rights for those groups. As Kukathas (1995: 230) notices: ''. . . while we are right to be concerned about the cultural health of minority communities, this gives us insufficient reason to abandon, modify or reinterpret liberalism.'' To him, far from being indifferent to the claims of minorities, liberalism puts concern for minorities at the forefront. So there is no need to depart from the liberal language of individual rights to do justice to minorities.

Hence, Kymlicka can be blamed for giving too much recognition to cultural minorities (by ascribing special rights to those groups). But Kymlicka can also be blamed for giving too little recognition to those groups, insofar as he regards autonomy as the fundamental liberal value (Kukathas 1995:245). Hereby he tends to disregard the interests of cultural communities that do not value the individual's freedom to choose. According to Kukathas, any attempt to force minority cultures to reorganize themselves in accordance with liberal norms is intolerant and hereby illiberal. On this basis he makes a plea for bringing the value of tolerance—rather than autonomy—back in.

But why should we consider tolerance as the key liberal value? Here again we see Kukathas's ultimately individualistic mode of reasoning. We have to respect the minority's wish to live according to its own ways of life, not because its culture should have a right to be preserved, but because individuals should be free to associate (Kukathas 1995:238). Notice that Kukathas focusses on the freedom of association rather than—what far more often occurs—on the right to freedom of religion. According to Kukathas, a corollary of the freedom of association is that the individual should be free to dissociate from communities. Hence, the claims of the individual and those of minority groups are accommodated by merely two individual rights: on the one hand, the right of association and, on the other hand, the right of dissociation, or as Kukathas calls it, ''the right of exit.'' If you do not like the group practices anymore, you should be free to leave the group. This last right of exit is especially a guarantee that the individual's interests will ever be taken into account.

The resulting picture of the liberal state is one that is quite at odds with the one presented by Kymlicka. In Kukathas's article we find no requirement whatsoever that minority groups within such a state should be liberal themselves. On the contrary, in his view, minority groups may indeed be quite illiberal. Take, for example, the Amish. According to Kukathas, they have the right to live by their traditional ways. This implies, for example, the right of not sending their children to school. The wider society has no right to require particular standards or systems of education within such cultural groups or to force their schools to promote the dominant culture. In Kukathas's own words: ''If members of the cultural community wish to continue to live by their beliefs, the outside community has no right to intervene to prevent those members of acting within their rights.'' For the individuals within those illiberal communities this implies that ''as members of the greater society, they have—just like other citizens—individual freedoms and individual rights, but as members of the illiberal minority group they do not have'' (Kukathas 1995:248).

With regard to the topic of admissibility of uncommon practices of minority groups, the one relevant question to Kukathas is whether the individuals taking part in it are prepared to acquiesce to it. In any illiberal culture, individuals should have the choice between abiding by the wishes of the community or ceasing to be part of it. According to Kukathas, this primacy of the right of exit is consistent with our intuitions: ''If an individual continues to live in a community and according to ways that (in the judgment of the wider society) treat her unjustly, even though she is free to leave, then our concern about the injustice diminishes.''

Kukathas's far-reaching plea for tolerance is put in perspective at the end of his article, though. First, in order to prevent the right of exit being merely a paper formula, the wider society should be open to individuals wishing to leave their local groups. Furthermore, even illiberal groups are bound by some liberal prohibitions, concerning ''cruel, inhuman or degrading treatment'' (Kukathas 1995:249). Third, just like Kymlicka, Kukathas makes a difference between the (normative) position of national and ethnic minorities. As he notices: ''The acceptance of cultural norms and practices depends on the degree to which the cultural community is independent of the wider society'' (Kukathas 1995:251). Here Kukathas seems to have in mind traditional groups such as the Indians (Cree, Inuit, or Pueblo) or the Amish. In all those cases the cultural community lives rather independently from the wider society. This cannot be upheld in the context of ethnic minorities. This geographical condition fairly limits the room for tolerance for migrant's practices: ''The immigrant society, while entitled to try to live by their ways, have not right here to expect the wider society to enforce those norms against the individuals'' (Kukathas 1995:251–252).

V. ASSESSMENT

How should we evaluate Kukathas's approach? First of all, I think this approach is valuable since it sketches an interesting and stimulating (liberal) alternative to the one presented by Kymlicka. As we have seen, Kymlicka takes the value of autonomy as the key liberal value. But as Kukathas rightly contends, in many cultures and subcultures this liberal value of autonomy is not valued at all. We should beware of putting autonomy first. In the light of the current diversity within the world at large and within most nation-states, is it not better to focus on tolerance?

Another positive aspect of Kukathas's approach is its balanced outlook. Kukathas tries to solve the conflict between individual rights and communal interests, though from quite a different angle than Kymlicka. Kukathas himself sketches the balance as follows: "The theory advanced here looks to recognize as legitimate cultural communities which do not in their own practices conform to individualist norms. . . . Yet at the same time, it is a liberal theory, inasmuch as it does not sanction the forcible induction into or imprisoning of any individual in a cultural community" (Kukathas 1995:247). No doubt, his approach is individualistically oriented. The two main rights—the right to association and dissociation—are individual rights. Besides, groups (even national and ethnic minority groups) are seen as voluntary associations of individuals. These two individualistic starting points already imply a criticism of any communitarian thinking. Cultural groups as such do not have a right to self-preservation (contra, for example, Charles Taylor 1994). Ultimately, it is up to individual members to determine whether a (minority) group culture is worth being preserved. This individualistic outlook is not all, however. Interestingly (and paradoxically) enough, we end up with an approach wherein there is a lot of room for cultures in general and illiberal minority groups more specifically. Outsiders do not have the right to intervene into those cultures, even in the name of liberal values. The resulting picture is that of a liberal society composed of different groups, all having the freedom to govern themselves in purely internal matters with their own legal codes and with no threat of external interference. In a slogan, "live and let live." Could it be more beautiful?

I wonder whether this picture of group sovereignty is that beautiful however. Whereas Kymlicka's approach is vulnerable to the danger of liberal imperialism, Kukathas's approach is vulnerable to quite the opposite threat: the value of tolerance being stretched so far that ultimately our liberal values are put at stake. In the words of Freeman (1995:37), this may result in a situation of "non-liberal collaboration," or, in the words of Leslie Green, "local illiberalisms." Let me sketch three problems in more detail.

The first problem concerns the net result of Kukathas's analysis. As just indicated, we end up at a society wherein there are different—maybe illiberal—islands living quite separate from one another. There are some drawbacks to this picture. It will be clear that this island model of society is not a good basis for dialogue amongst different groups. Besides, the impression that is falsely made is that identity groups may exist as autonomous entities with no relationship whatsoever to the constitutional state. Groups are free to determine their own values and to live according to their own ways of life. Hereby, they are not restricted by the norms and values of the constitutional state. Hence, in the long run this model may even imply the end of the constitutional state itself.

Second, Kukathas not only tends to overlook the relationships between (minority) groups and the state, but also between individuals and their groups. By attributing a large amount of tolerance to groups, little scope remains for dissent of individual members. As we saw before, the two individual rights that are recognized are the right to association and to dissociation. But one may wonder whether the having of these two rights suffices in order to speak of a liberal society. According to Kymlicka, we have to answer this question in the negative. Kukathas's model of society cannot be viewed as a liberal model "for it does not recognize any principle of individual freedom of conscience" (Kymlicka 1995a:157). Consequently, individuals (and especially dissenting ones, in terms of Green's "internal minorities") are locked up into their community. As long as they are not willing to leave the group (see the following paragraph), they are forced to comply with the norms and practices of the group. Now Kukathas's solution to the tension between individual rights and communal interests has become much clearer: it is obtained by denying practically all individual rights!

No doubt, Kukathas could counter the former remark by contending that people always have the right of exit from their identity group. So what is the problem? In Kukathas's analysis the right of exit seems to function as a panacea that solves all tensions between members of a group and the group itself. This brings us to a third area of some serious drawbacks. First of all, it seems to me that the right-to-exit argument forces insiders into a cruel and unrealistic zero sum choice: either accept all group practices, including those that violate your basic individual rights, or leave. "Take it or leave it." Happily, in real life situations there are usually more options left than this phrase suggests. Second, one could ask what are the real prospects for exit from the groups concerned. Kukathas's view seems to obscure the real hardships of leaving one's identity group. The mere possibility of exit does not suffice to make it a reasonable option. The groups concerned are mostly not voluntary ones, but rather involuntary ones, such as national or ethnic minorities. Besides, by speaking of the right of exit and the condition of consent, Kukathas tends to presuppose adult human beings. Hereby he passes over the really difficult issues that are currently at stake, such as concerning the rights of children within illiberal communities. For example, what do we do with the practice of female circumcision of baby girls, currently practiced in the Somalian minority group within the Netherlands? The exit option seems to be out of the question here. Finally, the right of exit may be a necessary, though not a sufficient, condition to a liberal society. No doubt, when exit is unavailable, things are even worse. That does not prove, however, that when exit is available, things are all right. As Freeman (1995:39) notices: "For individuals to lead good lives in a complex world, a set of rights more . . . than the right to exit from oppressive groups is required."

Kukathas's approach may be used as a good illustration of what is left in case the room for tolerance is overstretched. We arrive at a society consisting of illiberal islands, wherein the rights of individual human beings are easily sacrificed. I think Green (1995:270) is right in his observation: "With respect to 'internal minorities,' a liberal society (in Kukathas's model MG) risks becoming a mosaic of tyrannies: colourful, perhaps, but hardly free.'' Although pluralism within a culture is a precondition of liberalism, Kukathas's pluralism of cultures seems to be quite at odds with liberalism!

VI. SOME MORE DRAWBACKS

So where are we now? Thus far, we have elaborated and assessed two kinds of liberal theories that, although they start from different angles, both try to do justice to the eventually competing claims of minority groups and their members. It will be clear by now that the dilemmas at stake have not yet been solved. Starting either from the value of autonomy or the value of tolerance seems to have a lot of drawbacks. In the words of Kymlicka (1995b:15): "Basing liberal theory on autonomy threatens to alienate these groups, and undermine their allegiance to liberal institutions, whereas a tolerance-based liberalism can provide a more secure and wider basis for the legitimacy of government. Yet basing liberalism on tolerance abandons the traditional liberal concern with individual freedom of choice, and threatens to condemn individuals or subgroups within minority cultures to traditional roles that may be unsatisfying and indeed oppressive." As we have seen, in both approaches the threat of illiberalism is lurking (either by forcibly inducing groups to be liberal or by leaving members of illiberal groups to their own devices).

Notwithstanding these two different angles, there are some striking similarities between Kymlicka's and Kukathas's approaches as well. First of all, both analyses are of little relevance to the migrant's policies of most Western European countries. This is due to the almost exclusive focus on national minorities. A second parallel is that both scholars are critical of state intervention into illiberal groups. I agree that both for practical and for principled reasons state intervention should be seen as an *ultimum remedium*. It seems to me however that a categorical rejection of state intervention is too much of the good. Especially Ayelet Schachar (1998:105) has made a good point here. According to her, such a categorical rejection of state intervention reinforces the previously elaborated myth that identity groups, if they only be given the chance, could exist as autonomous entities with no relation to the constitutional state. Besides, the application of the ideal of non–state intervention conflates the language of respect to groups (and their rights) with a license to subordinate group members and to violate their individual rights. In legal terms, one could say that a policy of non–state intervention actually denies group members their equal protection as citizens of the state and hereby degrades them into second-class citizens. In view of these criticisms, Schachar (1996:16) (I think rightly) concludes: "If individual rights are not to be an empty category, then some entity—that is, the state—must have the responsibility for intervening if those rights are violated."

VII. THREE LESSONS

On the basis of the two foregoing theoretical approaches, my assessments, and the parallels between them, we have now arrived at some insights that may be of help for the questions under review.

1. First, seen from an internal perspective, we should beware of a, what one may call, "forced inclusion" of individuals within their identity group (Galenkamp 1995:174; Galenkamp 1998:140). Doing justice to those groups may easily end up in the curtailing of the individual autonomy of their members. This was already indicated by Kymlicka. Even more, cultural tolerance may become a cloak for oppression and injustice within those groups. In legal terms one can say that the collective right to self-determination can be at odds with the individual right to self-determination. It seems to me that human rights do not lose their relevance within identity groups. Human rights ideally function as a shelter for individuals, not only in society at large, but also within minority groups!

2. A second lesson is externally oriented and concerns the exclusion and discrimination of outsiders. It can be formulated as follows: by doing justice to identity groups, we should beware of exclusion and discrimination of outsiders. This second lesson was already elucidated by Kymlicka in his second precondition to minority rights. As we noticed there, special rights for those minority rights are legitimate only in so far as and to the extent to which they promote equality between groups. They are not legitimate, however, in so far as they result in new forms of inequality. This second lesson already illustrates that minority practices may have consequences not only for members of the group itself, but may have external effects as well. Reformulated in legal terms: the right to self-determination of a group may be at odds with the right to self-determination of other groups or individuals.

3. Third, we should beware of society becoming a collection of illiberal islands, no longer being in touch with one another. This lesson is derived from the broadest, that is, national, perspective on the issue. It stresses the need for preserving the civic unity of the liberal state. This lesson was elucidated in my assessment of Kymlicka's approach. As we saw there, there are some dangers of presenting minority groups as autonomous from the state structure. It seems to me that identity groups—even the most independent ones—are ultimately not outside, but inside the state. In case we should view them otherwise, local illiberalisms are lurking.

VIII. IN SEARCH OF GUIDELINES

In Section VII, I rejected the nonintervention doctrine propagated both by Kymlicka and Kukathas. In my view, in some instances the state should intervene into minority groups and forbid some of their practices. This raises the question of when the state should intervene. How should we determine which group practices are legitimate and which are not, seen from a liberal perspective? In other words, what kind of criteria can be set up that may determine whether state intervention is legitimate or not? In our search for such criteria, I think the afore-elaborated lessons may be of help. They may make us attentive to the problems we may encounter in the case of a culture-based analysis. Hereby, they may give a first indication of the proper limits of tolerance to uncommon practices of minority groups. In this section, I will search for a correct translation of these three lessons into some guidelines.

Notice that my terminology is still broad. Rather than restricting myself to national or ethnic minority groups, I speak of minority groups in general. To me, the key question that arises in the context of ethnic minorities is ultimately quite the same as the one that arises in the context of other kinds of minority groups (such as religious or lifestyle groups): do subcultures within a liberal society have the room for preserving their own identity and, hence, for practicing this identity. If so, what are the limits hereof? Which practices are intolerable?

Even more, I think that a potential advantage of my three guidelines is precisely that they enable us to lessen the differentiation that is often currently set up between different kinds of minority groups. It seems to me that independently of whether it is the practice of a religious or a lifestyle or an ethnic or even a national minority group that is involved, in all those different cases quite the same question is at the center: should we tolerate this specific practice and, if not, what are good reasons for forbidding this practice? As to the question of admissibility of group practices, perhaps we should not look so much at the nature of the group (for example, is it a religious group and is the practice inspired by some deep-down and well-ingrained convictions?), but—much more basically— at the extent of harmfulness of the practice itself. Investigating the extent of religiousness of a group would be a hard job, which seems to be ultimately problematic from a moral point of view, and, besides, it has often led to a privileging of the older and established religions at the expense of the newer ones. I think it is high time we acknowledged that the argument of religious freedom of parents may sometimes be used as a license to subordinate their children and to violate their rights.

Before presenting my guidelines, however, let me give a first sketch of my own normative presuppositions. My starting point is the idea of "sphere sovereignty" (see also Weisbrod 1992:805). What do I mean by this? In my view the basis of any liberal order should be tolerance for dissenting groups. My reason for starting with this presupposition of sphere sovereignty is that it seems to lie at the basis of the Dutch constitutional system. Besides, this idea has been one of the motivating forces underlying the specific form of democracy as we know it in Holland, namely consociational democracy, or as we call it in Dutch, *verzui-*

ling. More specifically, the phrase originated from one of the founding fathers of the Calvinist movement in Holland, Abraham Kuyper.

To the attentive reader, it will be obvious that by choosing this starting point of sphere sovereignty, I depart from Kymlicka's approach. As we have seen, his approach is autonomy- rather than tolerance-based. My approach bears greater resemblance to that of Kukathas's. But there are some differences from his approach as well. In contradistinction to what is argued by Kukathas, in my view we should not take the axiom of group sovereignty as a conclusion. The three guidelines below can be seen as a threefold restriction of the axiom of group sovereignty.

1.   The first guideline concerns the potentially harmful effects of minority practices on individual group members. This guideline may be formulated as follows:

> *Minority groups may stick to their own practices, unless these cause serious physical or mental harm to the group members. Less serious harm is admissible, in so far as these members endorse these practices.*

Underlying this guideline, there are two kinds of normative considerations. First of all, there is the so-called harm principle, a classic principle within liberal doctrine since J. S. Mill. This principle expresses the thought that the freedom of citizens may only be limited in cases where their freedom would harm others. A second consideration concerns the idea of consent. In my view, members of a minority group should have the opportunity at any time to subscribe to (or to criticize!) a specific group practice. This consideration includes, of course, the right of exit as an *ultimum remedium* (see Kukathas). But it is more extensive: it includes democratic and participation rights within the groups. Freely rendered from Hirschman's famous 1970 book, *Exit, Voice and Loyalty*, one could call this the right to voice. In case group members do not endorse a practice, they are owed state protection against their own groups (that is, if needed, state intervention). The rationale of this first guideline will be clear by now: preventing that individual members will become a victim of group practices.

2.   On the second guideline we may be brief, since this guideline logically follows from the first. This guideline concerns the potentially harmful effects of group practices to nonmembers. In short:

> *Minority groups may stick to their own practices, unless these practices are harmful to outsiders (in the sense of discrimination and gross violation of their human rights).*

This guideline bears a lot of similarities to the second precondition that was formulated by Kymlicka. Here we see a second departure from Kukathas's approach (since he was silent on this issue). The reason underlying this second guideline is the presence of potentially external effects of group practices. In my view, the admissibility of group practices considerably diminishes in cases where these have strongly negative effects on the freedoms and rights of outsiders. Groups may be sovereign within their own sphere, but this does not imply that they are sovereign outside this sphere (Bovens and Witteveen 1991:48).

3. So far we have provided two sorts of restrictions to the idea of group sovereignty. But will these two do? I do not think so. A third guideline is needed that is related to the most abstract level of the (existence of the) liberal state itself. This third guideline may be formulated as follows:

> *Minority groups may stick to their own practices, unless these practices en-*
> *danger the fundamentals of our liberal-democratic state.*

What is the purpose of this third guideline? Generally speaking, one could say that the liberal state itself is the main precondition for the preservation of group autonomy. That is to say, the plurality of our society may merely last by the grace of the continuity and unity of the liberal-democratic state itself. This third guideline implies a third departure from Kukathas's way of reasoning. Important though the idea of group sovereignty may be in a liberal setting, it can never be the last word. Ultimately, within a liberal constitutional state the primacy should not lie within different spheres, but at the constitutional state as such. As noted by Koch (1993:154), the idea of sphere sovereignty should not be equated with the idea of ''one's sphere to be completely sovereign.'' For whereas in the first instance some kind of legal pluralism is tolerated (all this under the umbrella of a common set of liberal norms and values), in the second instance the idea of group sovereignty is overstretched, due to which this common set—and, consequently, civic unity—is at risk.

IX. CONCLUSION

In this chapter I have to tried to get a firmer grip on a highly topical subject: the relationship (but especially the tensions) between individual autonomy and group identity. More specifically, I have focussed on three questions. First, the theoretical question whether, and to what extent, within a liberal-democratic society there should be room for the preservation of the identity of (ethnic) minority groups. Between the lines the attentive reader may have read my affirmative answer to this first question. It seems to me that one of the main aspects of liberal thinking is tolerance of dissenting groups. Consequently, in my view liberalism can both accommodate minority groups (of various kinds) and at the same time protect the liberal value of individual rights.

The second question is how the potentially conflicting interests of individuals and groups may be appropriately balanced. Reformulated, this question concerns the topic of admissibility. To what extent should uncommon practices of groups be accepted within a liberal democracy? That is, what are—seen from a liberal perspective—the limits of tolerance that a liberal society can show for intolerant and illiberal groups, and more importantly why are the limits exactly there? Third, and related to this, there is the question of what is the justified scope for state intervention in those illiberal groups.

In order to answer the last two questions, I have sought recourse at two theoretical approaches: those of Will Kymlicka and Chandran Kukathas. Since both approaches seem to overlook some problems, I have tentatively formulated three guidelines that may be of help in determining the exact limits of tolerance toward practices of identity groups and, hereby, of state intervention. The first lies at the harm done to members of the group and the ''locking up'' of individuals within their subculture. Second, harm to outsiders (in the form of far-reaching discrimination and violation of their human rights) is proclaimed inadmissible. The third limit concerns the endangering of the liberal-democratic state itself. It seems to me that in all three instances, state intervention is called for. By following these three guidelines, perhaps we may skirt the Scylla of liberal imperialism and the Charybdis of nonliberal collaboration.

No doubt, the proposed guidelines raise so many questions that they seem to obscure rather than elucidate the issues at stake. For example, when should we speak of harm? Is this a universally valid norm, or is the content of harm culturally determined? Has the criterion of consent any feasibility? Who exactly are to count as outsiders? When is our liberal-democratic state in danger? And so on. Apart from these technico-philosophical issues, one could question whether these guidelines are of help in problems of daily life. Take the examples from the beginning of this article. As to the *hijab* affair and the wearing of a turban, it seems to me that these affairs do not violate any of the guidelines. For no harm is done and consent is implied. As to the indoctrination that seems to occur within the Scientology movement, the harm and the consent at stake are more blurry. The topic of female and male circumcision is problematic in view of the aspect of consent and also in view of its harmful effects (to a greater or lesser extent). Finally, the example of sadomasochistic practices. Here, consent seems to be implied (in the case of adult human beings), but the topic of harmfulness is much more difficult to answer. The answer to this last question depends to a large extent on whether one subscribes to a subjective or an objective definition of harm. It will not come as a surprise that a further elaboration of these issues is called for.

Notwithstanding these qualifications, I hope to have yet made clear that the three guidelines together provide a threefold qualification of Kukathas's idea of group sovereignty. Fundamental though this kind of sovereignty may be in a liberal state, it should never be taken as absolute and unlimited, since this would endanger the individual's freedom and his (or her) rights. Besides, the axiom of group sovereignty does not imply sovereignty outside the group. Finally, it does not mean to say that groups should be seen as independent from the larger state. Useful though the axiom of group sovereignty might be as a prelude, it cannot be the finale.

REFERENCES

Bovens, M. A. P. and Witteveen, W. J. (1991). Rechtspluralisme en gepassioneerde minderheden (Legal pluralism and passionate minorities). In M. A. P. Bovens (ed.), *Heftige Affaires: Absolute Overwegingen in de Rechtsstaat*. Amsterdam/Antwerpen: L.J. Veen.

Freeman, M. (1995). Are there collective human rights? *Political Studies 43* (special issue on politics and human rights), 25–40.

Galenkamp, M. (1995). Special rights for minorities: The muddy waters of collective rights. In T. van Willigenburg, F. R. Heeger, and W. van der Burg (eds.), *Nation, State and the Coexistence of Different Communities*. Kampen: Kok Pharos.

Galenkamp, M. (1996). The rationale of minority rights: Wishes rather than needs? In J. Räikkä (ed.), *Do We Need Minority Rights? Conceptual Issues*. Den Haag: Martinus Nyhoff Publishers.

Galenkamp, M. (1998). *Individualism versus Collectivism: The Concept of Collective Rights*. Rotterdam: Gouda Quint.

Green, L. (1995). Internal minorities and their rights. In W. Kymlicka (ed.), *The Rights of Minority Cultures*. Oxford: Oxford University Press.

Hirschman, A. O. (1970). *Exit, Voice and Loyalty. Responses to Decline in Firms, Organizations and States*. Cambridge: Harvard University Press.

Koch, K. (1993). Rechtspluralisme: Een politicologisch perspectief (Legal pluralism: a political scientist's perspective). In N. J. H. Huls and H. D. Stout (ed.), *Recht in een Multiculturele Samenleving*. Zwolle: W.E.J. Tjeenk Willink.

Kukathas, C. (1995). Are there any cultural rights? In W. Kymlicka (ed.), *The Rights of Minority Cultures*. Oxford: Oxford University Press.

Kymlicka, W. (1989). *Liberalism, Community and Culture*. Oxford: Clarendon Press.

Kymlicka, W. (1991). Liberalism and the politicization of ethnicity. *Canadian Journal of Law and Jurisprudence* 4:2(July): 239–256.

Kymlicka, W. (1995a). *Multicultural Citizenship: A Liberal Theory of Minority Rights*. Oxford: Clarendon Press.

Kymlicka, W. (ed.)(1995b). *The Rights of Minority Cultures*. Oxford: Oxford University Press.

Schachar, A. (1998). Reshaping the multicultural model: Group accommodation and individual rights. *Windsor Review of Legal and Social Issues* 8(January): 83–110.

Taylor, C. (1994). The politics of recognition. In A. Gutmann (ed.), *Multiculturalism: Examining the Politics of Recognition*. Princeton: Princeton University Press.

Weisbrod, C. (1992). Emblems of federalism. *University of Michigan Journal of Law Reform* 25:3 & 4, 795–836.

21

Back from the Edge

Rebuilding a Public Heritage—A Case Study of Dubrovnik, Croatia

Linda K. Richter and William L. Richter
Kansas State University, Manhattan, Kansas

> Those who seek paradise on earth should come to Dubrovnik.
> (George Bernard Shaw)
> Come to Croatia! The Coast is Clear! (Postwar tourism slogan)

I. INTRODUCTION

During the years 1991–1992, the ancient walled city of Dubrovnik—known as the Pearl of the Adriatic—was subjected for several months to relentless bombardment and devastation. Near the southernmost tip of the newly declared Republic of Croatia, Dubrovnik found itself the target of the destructive firepower of Serb and Montenegrin forces of the so-called Yugoslav National Army. Although the initial siege was broken in 1992, attacks continued with varying degrees of intensity until November 1995, when the Dayton Accords brought uneasy peace to the region. As a city that had been a cornerstone of tourism on the Dalmatian Coast, Dubrovnik has faced monumental challenges of rebuilding—its physical infrastructure, its economy, and its society.

Dubrovnik, Sarajevo, and other cities of the former Yugoslavia are not alone in facing challenges of reconstruction in the wake of natural or human-generated disasters. Wars, floods, fires, earthquakes, volcanic eruptions, and other forms of destruction have often wreaked havoc in human and economic terms as well as in crumbling buildings and disfigured monuments. The task of rebuilding is not an uncommon experience, however unanticipated it might be in each particular instance.

Much of the literature of public administration deals with situations of "normalcy," that is, with relatively stable conditions. When change *is* considered, it is generally orderly change, either positive (for example, development administration) or negative (for example, cutback management). Even the literature focussed on turbulent environments scarcely envisions administrators in the range of hostile artillery. There is, of course, a sizeable literature on emergency management, but that tends to deal primarily with delivery of services during and immediately after crises. Postcrisis reconstruction may be regarded as an area of public management that is broader and longer in duration than what is normally included in the concept of emergency management.

An easily neglected component of postcrisis reconstruction, especially in areas where tourism has been an important industry, is the rebuilding of cultural and social, as well as physical and economic, infrastructure. Traditionally, postwar recovery in most places focusses on rebuilding homes, bridges, and businesses, not in opening hotels, guest houses, museums, galleries, and restaurants, or in repairing palaces, churches, and decorative facades. Citizens' personal needs usually take priority. However, international tourism has increasingly assumed so central a role in national and regional economies that its restoration is sometimes deemed critical to overall recovery. Such is the case in Dubrovnik and in Croatia as a whole.

Heritage management in postcrisis reconstruction, like the overlapping field of heritage preservation, is typically a public sector responsibility, for several reasons. It is often public values and public heritage that are being protected, preserved, or reconstructed, and the general public may wish to have a share of responsibility for both process and outcomes. In a postsocialist society like Croatia, the private sector may not have enough resources to undertake the task, especially if it is on a large scale. However, even though heritage management may be a predominantly public-sector enterprise, that does not necessarily preclude public–private partnerships, as the Dubrovnik case illustrates.

Although restoration is an important component of postdisaster reconstruction, heritage management should not be seen just as replacement or restoration of the past. Heritage is a shared understanding of the past, but that understanding may be distorted or inaccurate. There may also be a considerable degree of "staged or reconstructed authenticity" (MacCannell 1994). Finally, the events of the intervening disaster, whether natural or human-generated, may be sufficiently compelling to be incorporated into the heritage. In short, heritage management draws upon a shared pool of experiences and images to create a common understanding of the past within a community or society. It is not unlike the processes of mythmaking and identity formation that are common to ethnicity and nation-building (Brass 1974).

Dubrovnik's experience provides a remarkable case study of these processes at work. The case illustrates the roles played by local, national, and international agencies, especially the World Heritage Program of the United Nations Educational, Scientific, and Cultural Organization (UNESCO). It also illustrates the process of heritage building, even drawing upon experiences of the war and devastation and incorporating them into the newly constructed heritage.

Before looking at the specifics of the Dubrovnik case, it will be helpful to review in greater detail some of the issues raised by heritage management in times of postcrisis recovery.

II. HERITAGE MANAGEMENT IN POLITICAL AND ECONOMIC RECOVERY

Any place recovering from disaster faces incredible administrative challenges. Bureaucrats grapple with tough decisions about the allocation of scarce resources and must balance physical, psychic, economic, and political needs. While food and shelter are basic requirements, repairing and restoring historic properties may both provide some housing stock but also begin the restoration of the sense of the community's endurance and the continuity of its identity. That is a form of sustenance to citizens, but it also allows for the community to reaffirm its survival and value by encouraging the development of tourism.

Some may regard tourism as a callous consideration at such a time, but in many places the economic benefits of tourism had been important to predisaster society. As such the restoration and recovery of that tourism base may be an important part of an emergency management strategy. The quicker debris is removed, buildings are stabilized, and heritage sites repaired and reopened, the sooner the economic and civic life of the community re-emerges. As Friedman noted in his book, *From Beirut to Jerusalem*, he knew there was hope for Beirut as long as people kept putting glass back in their windows after the shelling. When they started boarding up the windows, he knew they were losing that hope (Friedman 1989).

What is central here is the growing economic dependence and sense of political identity associated with being a premier tourist destination. This means that increasingly public managers are tasked with developing tourism not only for financial resources but as a way of building community solidarity. Following the shattering of personal and public identities in war, it is perhaps more understandable that the recovery and growth of tourism flows is often seen as a top priority of postwar public management.

This preoccupation with jumpstarting postwar tourism is especially critical in a region determined to redraw national boundaries at the point of a gun. A new nation—in this case, Croatia—finds in tourism an industry that markets the new country even as it reinforces and links the postwar identity to the great historic and scenic sites within its borders.

Recovery, be it from natural catastrophes or political turmoil, is an important public sector responsibility. Rarely, if ever, does the public administration literature include heritage recovery and preservation in the emergency management responsibilities of the public sector. Perhaps it should. Too rarely in such situations can the indigenous private sector do more than deal with its own problems. The common interest in heritage preservation is intrinsically a public responsibility in times of crisis.

Many of the trouble spots of the world are also places whose heritages are of great importance. In the short run, administrators facing the tasks of recovery must do a kind of cultural triage, determining what and how much can be saved, rebuilt, and preserved. What must be demolished may be clear from an engineer's perspective, but not from the standpoint of the community's attachment and identity.

In the long run, public and private planners face equally difficult choices about whose heritage gets restored, protected, promoted, and celebrated and how much can be done. In multiethnic societies like the United States, Canada, Indonesia, and the former Yugoslavia, scarce heritage funds and disaster relief must be allocated by criteria that reflect political considerations as much as intrinsic heritage values (Richter 1997a).

Reconstruction after turmoil may also raise questions of authenticity and interpretation. In Dubrovnik, for example, earthquakes and war have exposed different eras of the same city block. Churches had earlier church buildings exposed by the damage. Which should be saved? Does one automatically restore to the oldest, the most beautiful, or the latest?

Public sector tourism planners also need to consider the kinds and amounts of tourism appropriate in the recovery phase. Pompeii's residents do not have much choice concerning what type of tourism development features the burial of their city by Mt. Vesuvius, but residents in other natural and manmade disasters may well object to being scrutinized by leisured outsiders as they attempt to rebuild their lives.

In still other instances, there is a desire to showcase disaster, particularly that which affixes blame on a political enemy (Richter 1997b). Vilifying the destroyer allows one to use tourism for political advantage, for public relations, and for building domestic consensus for tourism's role in showing the world who the good and bad guys are.

It is also true that political turmoil is good box office. War and its aftermath have a long history of being a magnet for tourists (Seaton 1996:234–243). It is a real irony that while war almost immediately destroys tourism—there are always more serene alternative destinations—after the war the stories, battlefields, museums, prisoner-of-war camps, and cemeteries exert a powerful pull on the imaginations of travelers (Richter 1997a). In fact "milking the macabre" has become such a big business in cities like Hiroshima, Waterloo, Dunkirk, Gettysburg, and in literally thousands of other communities that there is a whole genre of tourism research now developing known as thanatourism (Dann 1994; Seaton 1996, 1997). Journals of heritage preservation, history, and tourism are increasingly chronicling our perhaps problematic fascination with visiting sites associated with appalling casualties. Thus, at the end of the twentieth century special intergovernmental, international partnerships of public and private organizations exist to help nations protect and restore those elements of their heritage important not only to them but to the entire world.

While heritage preservation is a global phenomenon that has both political and economic motivations, for this chapter the focus will be on a particular program, the World Heritage Program of UNESCO, and its role in the recovery of Dubrovnik, Croatia. This chapter also highlights the linkages between the public, private, and not-for-profit sectors and the roles they have played in using tourism development for economic and psychological recovery.

III. DUBROVNIK: TO THE EDGE OF DESTRUCTION AND BACK

A. Historical Background

The ancient walled city of Dubrovnik (current population 35,000) on the Dalmatian coast of Croatia provides a very contemporary case for the study of the reconstruction of a world historic site after it has come back from the edge of obliteration.

Once the rival of Venice, Dubrovnik is a very special city. Founded in the seventh century, it had a huge navy of more than 300 vessels by the tenth century. Though Dubrovnik fell under the control of the Venetians from 1205 to 1358, it began its public planning during that era! It abolished slavery in 1416, among the first political entities in Europe to do so (four centuries ahead of the British). Later the more liberal Hungarian-Croatian kingdom took over from Venice and allowed Dubrovnik to evolve into an independent city-state. When the Turks threatened that independence, Dubrovnik "bought" its self-rule by paying tribute to the Ottoman Empire (Hadley and Turner 1987:442–443).

Dubrovnik was a major trading center between the East and West throughout the Middle Ages and the Renaissance. Its wealth was lavished on spectacular palaces, churches, art and sculpture, moats, drawbridges, and enormous fortifications. Dubrovnik was a shipping center until a change in shipping routes and the catastrophic 1667 earthquake led to economic downturn. In 1806 the French under Napoleon ravaged the city. During 1815–1918 Dubrovnik was part of the Austrian Empire before becoming a part of Yugoslavia (Hadley and Turner 1987: 444).

In the twentieth century Dubrovnik became a tourist attraction, particularly for German and British visitors attracted by its heritage and idyllic locations on the warm, clear Adriatic Sea. World Wars I and II did not threaten the treasures of Dubrovnik and heritage tourism grew more central to the city's economy.

B.   The 1979 Earthquake and Its Consequences

However, disaster again struck Dubrovnik in 1979 when another huge earthquake damaged much of the city. In the wake of that emergency, policies and organizational infrastructure were put in place that have greatly enhanced Dubrovnik's ability to deal with the more recent and much greater devastation of war.

On the local level, the Institute for the Restoration of Dubrovnik was founded, with an initial commitment to ''the complete restoration of of the monuments most affected by the earthquake and an establishment of a system of budgeting that would merge the restoration with the tourist trade'' (Institute for the Restoration of Dubrovnik 1997:1). On a global level, the decision was made to include Dubrovnik on UNESCO's list of World Heritage Sites, in the company of such world treasures as the Taj Mahal and Borobadur.

The World Heritage List was established under the Convention Concerning the Protection of the World Cultural and Natural Heritage, adopted by the General Conference of UNESCO in 1972. To date, more than 145 political entities (termed ''States Parties'' under the terms of the Convention) have signed the Convention and more than 550 sites have been placed on the list. Selection is based upon a process that involves proposal by one of the countries and approval by the World Heritage Committee, a body of representatives from 21 States Parties, elected by the General Assembly of the States Parties of the Convention (UNESCO 1997:1–2).

In very practical terms, being on the World Heritage List meant global recognition of Dubrovnik's heritage value, as well as money, expertise, and coordination in the recovery from the earthquake.

C.   Tourism Before the War

Dubrovnik and the rest of Croatia forged a strong comeback from the earthquake's devastation. Tourism was soaring—so much so that even as the former Yugoslavia began to disintegrate in the late 1980s, most observers expected the good times to continue. As Croatia moved to independent status, a soft revolution was anticipated with internal political liberalization and external peace. By 1990 Croatia hosted more than 7 million tourists with Dubrovnik a leading attraction.

In late 1990 and early 1991 Dubrovnik and the rest of Central Europe were negatively impacted by the Gulf War. It was summer 1991, at the height of the tourist season, when war came to Croatia. Within days hundreds of tours were canceled, hotels abandoned, and the industry so key to Croatia's independence was nearly moribund (Ban 1997:1).

D.   The War

This savage ethnic war was unleashed by the Serb-dominated former Yugoslav Army on a nation without a real defense. While neighboring Bosnia-Herzegovina took the worst from Serbia, it would be Croatia, and especially Dubrovnik and environs, that suffered the greatest deliberate attacks on nonmilitary targets of historic importance.

In accord with the 1954 Hague Convention, citizens and public officials rushed to make blue and white flags to delineate protected historic sites and medical facilities. But this seemed only to make them better targets (Primorac 1991–1992:104).

All this came as a tremendous shock to Dubrovnik's citizens:

> Dubrovnik's perfectly preserved 15th century stone fortifications still lure foreign visitors, who . . . arrive with cameras rather than siege artillery. So when the Yugoslavian People's Army (JNA) charged over the mountains . . . annexed the hinterland and began lobbing shells . . . it came as a total surprise to residents (Woodard 1996:3).

Dubrovnik had neither barracks, military value, nor a Serbian minority to be "liberated." The Serbs, seeking to cripple Croatian's tourist industry destroyed without resistance the Dubrovnik airport and then proceeded to plunder the countryside.

Ironically, the hotels in and around Dubrovnik would soon be full with panicked refugees from the surrounding region. One luxury hotel near Dubrovnik housed hundreds, who lived for more than a year from resources stockpiled originally for the tourist season!

Dubrovnik itself was shelled mercilessly for six months. Between May–June, 1992, all fourteenth-to-eighteenth-century landmarks were hit. Thirty percent of the buildings had been damaged earlier. Ten percent were destroyed (Primorac 1991–1992:104). The Serbs cut off all electricity and water for several months but never invaded the city, ostensibly because they feared an ambush. There were in fact no soldiers and only four old cannons. But over 800 people huddled in the basements of buildings for months, uncovering ancient wells to drink from and surreptitiously drawing salt water at night for washing. The mayor recounted how the city's symphony schedule was even maintained—albeit shifted to afternoon for sunlight!

War is never tidy and the authors acknowledge their resources and travel were in Croatian rather than Serbian territory, but Primorac does put the Serb attack in historical perspective: "In the course of its long history, it [Dubrovnik] suffered from earthquakes, but none from its conquerors—the French, the Austrians, the Italians, the Germans—none ever shelled or burned it until the onslaught of the Serbs" (Primorac 1991–1992:104).

By October, the town and surrounding region had absorbed great damage. Dozens of fifteenth-to-eighteenth-century palaces were devastated. The arboretum, which had been cultivated continuously for 500 years, was completely burned. Those trying to put out the fires were shelled. (Primorac 1991–1992: 104). Even after the siege was lifted in 1992, the JNA would lob shells at the city or the airport every now and then to depress the tourism essential for Dubrovnik's recovery.

E. Restoration

Dubrovnik's ability to begin its process of rebuilding even in the midst of devastation was reflective in part of some special attributes that are not shared by all cities that fall prey to disaster. One is a long tradition of self-government as a political entity, accompanied by strong feelings of civic pride and identity. Related to this is a long tradition of town planning, from as early as the thirteenth century. In 1272, Dubrovnik enacted laws governing building codes and responses to natural disasters. Following a major fire in 1296, addition-building regulations were introduced, including prohibitions on balconies and wood construction. A major earthquake in 1667 led to further regulations that required the citizenry of the city to contribute to rebuilding (Jemo 1996). The major recent experience of relevance was the 1979 earthquake, out of which developed the major organizations that managed much of the reconstruction in the 1990s.

The most prominent of these organizations has been the Institute for the Restoration of Dubrovnik, established in 1979. Two associated entities have been the Institute for the Protection of Cultural Monuments, more recently renamed Public Administration for the Protection of Cultural and Natural Heritage—Commission Dubrovnik, and the Society of Friends of the Dubrovnik Antiques (Jemo 1996). At the national level, a Parliament Committee for the Reconstruction of Dubrovnik has provided coordination, supervision, and liaison for financial support to the restoration program.

A key factor in Dubrovnik's survival was the international support it received, especially through its ties with UNESCO. It survived because it was a place the world cared about. "World attention may have prevented the Serbs from attempting to capture the city and highlevel diplomacy . . . eventually broke the siege" (Woodard 1996:11). When the Serb attacks began, Dubrovnik was immediately listed as a UNESCO World Heritage Site in Danger and throughout the siege plans were already being formed to restore it. A UNESCO-sponsored booklet, ''The Plan of Action for Dubrovnik,'' was published in 1993, both to inventory damages and ''to mobilize financial aid worldwide'' (Obuljen 1995: 1).

Detailed inventories were made of structural and architectural features. Collaborative plans for Croatian institutions to work with UNESCO to identify donors and work out different types of contributions were made.

Among the first steps was to inventory the condition of those buildings protected on the World Heritage List. Second, a list was developed of human resource agencies and organizations at the municipal, national, and international level. Third, a strategy of restoration was developed. Fourth, there was a commitment to best practices in the restoration rather than emergency quick fixes. The whole idea was to insure that whatever was done would preserve the unity of the urban design. The fifth component was to activate national and international organizations. The final element was to communicate the project needs to decision-makers and to those shaping public opinion to help raise the funds and obtain the critical expertise.

UNESCO's objective was first and foremost preservation, but the priority that restoration assumed with community and national leadership was inextricably linked to the recovery of tourism and the economy in general.

F. Back from the Edge

It would be another five years before Dubrovnik in particular or Croatia in general would reach even 50% of its prewar tourism arrivals. Recovery was complicated by a number of obstacles. Despite immediate aid from UNESCO for repairing roofs and restoring damaged artifacts, plus energetic state and city preservation efforts, the recovery of tourism itself was slow.

First, transportation routes—both air and over land—had been severed by the fighting and new boundaries. Longer and more costly routes had to be substituted.

Second, whereas Yugoslavia had a known identity to the world's tourists, Croatia, which was the heart of the former Yugoslavia's tourism, did not. Except for Germans, Austrians, and Slovaks accustomed to visiting Dubrovnik, most of the world did not know where Croatia was. Building that image would prove difficult. Industry leaders wanted to have a blitz based on ''Croatia—Paradise on Earth,'' the winning and controversial tourism slogan coined by the Minister of Tourism's wife. Not only was it controversial for a close relative of the minister to win the contest, but it also seemed unlikely that ignoring the war and billing a war-torn nation as a paradise would build Croatia's credibility with tour operators abroad.

Third, though the fighting ended by late 1995, the region would still carry an international stigma of violence and danger. As a result, many lucrative markets—particularly the British and American—continued to avoid Croatia and Dubrovnik.

Fourth, tourist facilities long used for crowded housing needed considerable refurbishing before they could be brought up to an acceptable standard (Vukonic 1997:86). Beyond that, tensions elsewhere prevented some refugees from leaving. Their presence was a depressing reminder that the so-called paradise had recently been a war zone. As a consequence of infrastructure shortages and refugees, it would be cruise ships that first put Dubrovnik back on their itineraries.

Fifth, rebuilding and renovating were complicated by the process of privatization that had begun shortly before the war. Legal titles were often in dispute. Owners who were once simply Yugoslavian were now missing or living in other countries created by the war (Gosar 1997). Moreover the global enthusiasm for privatization made public urban planning more difficult. Sustaining a commitment to the public interest, public spaces and public treasures was probably facilitated by the commitment of international aid agencies responding to the crisis. Elsewhere in the former socialist societies, the transition in urban societies from socialist to private economies has tended to neglect the public spaces (Musil 1993:899–905).

Finally, the war in Croatia and especially in Dubrovnik meant the loss of critical tourism skills to other countries. The length of the conflict left the city and the nation bereft of much of its tourism expertise and capital.

G. Heritage Tourism

Despite the obstacles, Dubrovnik's recovery of its heritage tourism had many equally important advantages, not least of which was the steely determination of its citizens. The Serb attack on Dubrovnik was seen as a direct attack on the cultural heritage of the city and on its ability to prosper from tourism: ''cultural values are the basis of the nation's strength for survival . . . culture and all the values it has created in an area are the foundations of tourism. . . . That is the reason why culture is dangerous for the enemy and it only makes sense that it comes under attack first and most thoroughly'' (Vukonic 1997:93). Also, Dubrovnik had an 800-year tradition of urban planning and a pride of place second to none. Third, Dubrovnik had the public-relations advantage. Thanks to television and the Internet, Dubrovnik's heartbreaking siege was high drama for the entire globe. As a consequence, not only did Dubrovnik's plight engage world public opinion, but it also spurred massive and immediate aid for postwar recovery even as Dubrovnik's own citizens hid in unlit and unheated cellars month after month.

Amazingly, throughout the war the national tourism organization continued to visit trade fairs in an attempt to keep the new Croatian identity before the global tour operators. For both political and economic reasons, the tourism offensive never flagged.

War dismantled newer accretions to historic buildings—a Renaissance overlay no longer hid the art and architecture of the middle ages. That raised the issue of which era to restore. Once Dubrovnik began again to receive tourists (see Table 1), the siege itself became part of the city's new mystique. Dubrovnik perfected the story of heritage lost. Tour guides pointed out the damaged frescoes, drawbridges, churches, as well as the cement repairs that may take generations to weather until they match their surroundings.

Visitors were continually reminded that the Serbs did more damage than two world wars. ''[T]ourists saw damaged roofs, the burned out remains of the Festival, Martinusic, Sorkoveic and Dordic Palaces, rubble piled in front of the Jesuit seminary and the mortar scars on the marble pavements. For tourists it was a glimpse of a soft architectural form of warporn'' (Woodard 1996:3).

The question of how to integrate the war experience into Dubrovnik's redefined heritage was illustrated by issues of when and how to document war damages.

Table 1   Tourist Traffic in the Dubrovnik Region, 1979–1996 (Figures in Thousands)

Year	Domestic tourists	Domestic nights	Foreign tourists	Foreign nights	Total tourists	Total nights
1979	307.9	1796.1	375.7	2733.4	683.6	4529.5
1980	323.2	2049.5	399.2	2821.9	722.4	4871.4
1981	335.5	2051.2	413.6	3100.5	749.1	5151.7
1982	348.7	2142.8	394.2	2920.2	742.9	5063.0
1983	391.9	2320.8	379.7	2663.8	771.6	4984.6
1984	359.4	2078.8	466.4	3179.7	825.8	5258.5
1985	356.4	2213.9	548.7	3654.3	985.1	5868.2
1986	346.0	2069.0	505.4	3455.9	851.4	5524.9
1987	348.0	2003.4	544.6	3492.3	892.6	5495.7
1988	316.2	1806.9	537.9	3314.1	854.1	5121.0
1989	315.8	1830.1	489.6	3068.7	805.4	4898.8
1990	272.1	1529.5	484.7	2931.8	756.8	4461.4
1991	71.4	312.3	59.2	327.3	130.6	639.6
1992	2.5	8.5	1.5	6.2	4.0	14.7
1993	6.1	15.9	3.1	9.3	9.2	25.2
1994	23.9	96.0	14.1	58.4	3.0	154.4
1995	23.7	96.7	7.5	22.6	31.2	119.3
1996	56.3	261.7	39.3	158.3	95.7	420.0

Source: Ban and Borkovic-Vrtiprah (1997:3)

> Despite the initial disorientation, it soon became evident that traces of the
> crime would be wiped out forever unless damages are documented. People
> of Dubrovnik demanded even more to be done—damaged sites of the
> wounded Town should be permanently marked. The best solution was to be
> chosen at the open competition but the decision was not made then. We are
> aware of the requirements of the past; the reconstruction must contribute to
> the beauty of the Town. Our opinion is that the labelling of each wounded
> site would disrupt the existing harmony. Therefore we support a professional
> approach backed by documentary evidence. Records on damages should be
> published and permanently filed for the sake of generations to come (Jemo
> 1996).

In September 1997, when these authors toured the area, guides constantly remarked on what was no longer there—the villages leveled, the olive groves destroyed, the gardens burned. Visitors are taken to churches desecrated, wells pol-
luted, sites of torture and mayhem.

Even now there is uncertainty as to whether the war should be emphasized
for its public relations and fundraising value or de-emphasized to encourage rebuilding of tourism. One tourism slogan cleverly alludes to the recent war while
at the same time assuring visitors that they will be safe: ''Come to Croatia, the
Coast is Clear.'' Most in the industry—particularly those coming from abroad—
would rather downplay the war.

The future of Dubrovnik is vulnerable to the political situation in the region. Serb actions against ethnic Albanians in Kosovo have contributed to the
sense of tourist insecurity in Dubrovnik. Still the recovery has been impressive. Those looking for portents may well note the growing attraction just over
the Herzegovinian border in Medugorje where apparitions of the Virgin Mary
have lured more than 10 million visitors since the initial sighting on June 24,
1981. Many are combining a stay in Dubrovnik with the pilgrimage (Vukovic
1996:145–146).

IV. CONCLUSION

The case of Dubrovnik offers some important lessons for public administrators
faced with threats to heritage from political or natural disasters. It also provides
some interesting insights into the dynamics of heritage management in situations
of postcrisis recovery.

Heritage tourism was central to the economy of Dubrovnik and the Dalmatian Coast before the outbreak of war in 1991. It was also apparently central
to the otherwise senseless and incomprehensibly barbaric attacks of the Serb/
Montenegrin forces against cultural, religious, and historical sites during the

siege. Finally, heritage tourism has been central to the processes of physical, social, and economic recovery during and after the war.

Several factors in Dubrovnik's recovery may or may not be present in other postcrisis situations. Clearly, the city's strong civic tradition, dating back several centuries, was manifested in a will to resist the siege, to endure, and even to maintain as much dignity and culture as possible in the midst of the destruction. As the Mayor of Dubrovnik expressed it, the Dobrovnik Symphony's performance during the worst of the shelling was "an assertion of the forces of the human spirit against the forces which would seek to extinguish it" (comments at performance of Dubrovnik Symphony Orchestra, September 25, 1997). It was no doubt the same sort of spirit which led a single violinist to play openly in Sarajevo during the worst of the fighting there.

Dubrovnik was also fortunate in having used the experience of the 1979 earthquake to build organizational infrastructure that could be called into play when human-generated disaster struck in 1991. The Committee for the Restoration of Dubrovnik has mobilized worldwide contributions, utilized worldwide expert opinion, and guided recovery efforts, with support from Croatian government agencies and UNESCO's World Heritage program.

Heritage management is a complex and interesting area of administrative practice, especially during periods of postcrisis recovery. It requires that issues of physical restoration be balanced against cultural and economic considerations and that the opinions and advice of experts be balanced against the needs and interests of the people of the city.

The incorporation of the war experience into Dubrovnik's evolving heritage may serve several important functions. The recent addition to the heritage is not only a tale of bravery in the face of devastation and of culture in response to barbarism, it is also an experience that binds Dubrovnik to Croatia as common victims of Serb aggression. The Dubrovnik heritage is wrapped up in the Croatian national heritage, just as Valley Forge is in that of the United States.

Other cities and nations with rare historic treasures are continually jeopardized by disaster, but it is too seldom that conventional notions of emergency management extend to the protection of the sites and its treasures. The importance of having industry and the public sector work together on contingency plans for recovery is vital in an era when terrorism or slow civil wars can cripple the ability to protect heritage and restore the economy.

ACKNOWLEDGMENTS

A prior version of this chapter was presented as a paper at the American Society for Public Administration annual meeting, Seattle, Washington, May 9–13.

The authors wish to acknowledge support from the Kansas State University Office of Sponsored Programs, the Office of International Programs, the College of Arts and Sciences, the Women's Studies Program, and the Department of Political Science, as well as the Institute for Tourism of Zagreb, Croatia.

REFERENCES

Ban, I. and Borkovic-Vrtiprah, V. (1997). The influence of war on tourism in Dubrovnik. Paper presented at the War, Terrorism, and Tourism Conference, Dubrovnik, Croatia, September 25–27.

Brass, P. (1974). *Language, Religion, and Politics in North India*. New York: Cambridge University Press.

Buric, V. (1997). *Handbook for Foreigners in Croatia*. Zagreb, Croatia: Cakovec.

Cavlek, N. (1997). Tour operators gages of destination safety. Paper presented at the War, Terrorism, and Tourism Conference, Dubrovnik, Croatia, September 25–27.

Dann, G. (1994). Tourism: The nostalgia industry of the future. In W. F. Theobald (ed.), *Global Tourism, The Next Decade*. London: Butterworth Heinemann, Ltd.

Friedman, T. L. (1989). *From Beirut to Jerusalem*. New York: Farrar Straus Giroux.

Gosar, A. (1997). Reconsidering tourism strategy as a consequence of the disintegration of Yugoslavia—The case of Slovenia. Paper presented at the War, Terrorism, and Tourism Conference, Dubrovnik, Croatia, September 25–27.

Hadley, M. H. and Turner, A. (1987). *Eastern Europe on $25 a Day*. New York: Prentice Hall.

Hitrec, T. and Turkalj, K. (1997). Political aspects of tourism as a factor of peace and security with particular reference to Croatia. Paper presented at the War, Terrorism, and Tourism Conference, Dubrovnik, Croatia, September 25–27.

Hravatska, M. (1997). *Dubrovnik in War*. Dubrovnik, Croatia: Ogranak.

Institute for the Restoration of Dubrovnik (1997). (http://www.laus.hr/zod.html). September 15.

Ivandic, N. and Radnie A. (1997). War and tourism in Croatia—Consequence and the road to recovery. Paper presented at the War, Terrorism, and Tourism conference, Dubrovnik, Croatia, September 25–27.

Jemo, I. (1996). Experiences in the postwar reconstruction of the historic core of Dubrovnik. Paper prepared for International Conference on Settlement Revitalization in Postwar Reconstruction, Zagreb, April 26–27. (http://www.laus.hr/zod/ijhabeng/Welcome.html).

Jemo, I. Models of elaborations of documentation for the renewal of villages of the Dubrovnik region and the historical nucleus of Dubrovnik having suffered war destruction. Unpublished paper.

Keller, P. (1996). General trends in tourism today. In World Decade Secretariat, UNESCO, (ed.), *Culture, Tourism and Development: Crucial Issues for the 21st Century*, pp. 13–15. Paris, UNESCO.

MacCannell, D. (1994). Reconstructed ethnicity: Tourism and cultural identity in Third World communities. *Annals of Tourism Research, 2*:3, 375–391.

Musil, J. (1993). Changing urban systems in post-communist societies in Central Europe: Analysis and prediction. *Urban Studies 30*:6, 899–905.

Obuljen, N. (1995). ''At the Occasion of the Dubrovnik UNESCO/Organization of World Heritage Cities.'' (http://www.ovpm.org/ovpm/english/hour/dubrov2.html). September 11.

Primorac, I. (1991–1992). The war against Croatia: Salient traits. *Journal of Croatian Studies 32/33*, 91–110.

Pusic, V. (1998). Croatia at the crossroads. *Journal of Democracy 9*:1, 111–124.

Richter, L. K. (1997a). The politics of heritage tourism: Emerging issues for the new millennium. Paper presented at the International Academy for the Study of Tourism meeting, Malacca, Malaysia, June 24.

Richter, L. K. (1997b). After political turmoil: The lessons of rebuilding tourism in three Asian countries. Paper presented at the War, Terrorism, and Tourism Conference, Dubrovnik, Croatia, September 25–27.

Richter, L. K. (1992). Political instability and tourism in the Third World. In D. Harrison (ed.), *Tourism and the Less Developed Countries*. London: Belhaven.

Seaton, A. (1996). Guided by the dark: From thanatopsis to thanatourism. *International Journal of Heritage Studies 2*:4 (Winter), 234–243.

Seaton, A. V. (1997). War and tourism: The paradigm colossus of Waterloo, 1815–1914. Paper presented at the Conference on War, Terrorism, and Tourism, Dubrovnik, Croatia, September 25–27.

UNESCO (1997). ''About the World Heritage.'' (http://www.unesco.org/whc/intro-en.html). September 15.

Vukonic, B. (1996). Medugorje—A tourism case. In B. Vukonic (ed.), *Tourism and Religion*. New York: Pergamon.

Vukonic, B. (1997). *Tourism in the Whirlwind of War*. Zagreb, Croatia: Golden Marketing.

Woodard, C. (1996). Morning in Dubrovnik. *Bulletin of the Atomic Scientists 52*:6 (November-December), 11.

22
Human Rights, Civil Society, and the Guatemalan Peace Process

Scott Turner
University of Montevallo, Montevallo, Alabama

I. INTRODUCTION

Recent decades have witnessed the proliferation of thousands of nongovernmental organizations (NGOs) both at domestic and international levels. Such organizations vary widely in their functions, goals, and the scope of their activities. In some cases NGOs prefer a confrontational relationship with state institutions, while in others they work closely with both states and international organizations (IOs). Some NGOs have employed violence. In general, however, the emerging global civil society of grassroots political activism is characterized by nonviolent initiatives and progressive agendas, such as peace, ecology, and human rights.

This civil society represents a new sphere of action in the arena of world politics. It is neither the public sphere of state authority and institutional violence, nor the private sphere of market forces and corporate profits. It is both broader in scope and, in some respects, less centered around state institutions and processes than domestic pluralist systems—though needless to say there is considerable overlap between these two phenomena. It interacts with states and IOs at diverse points of contact, it challenges the legitimacy of established institutions at others, and in some cases it acts independently both of states and international organizations. It reinforces the central role of state institutions by appealing for laws that protect human rights and regulations that restrict corporate behavior, yet it ultimately may undermine the absolute sovereignty of states by constricting their range of legitimate action and extending the range of citizen action from the national to the global level. In the extreme, the state system and global civil society may be idealized as diametrical opposites: the state as institutional hierarchy with a monopoly of the legitimate use of violence and civil society as an anarchical realm of actors devoted to humanitarian causes.[1] Needless to say, reality is far more nuanced and problematic. Nevertheless, such a model of contrasting ideal types can be useful in generating theoretical clarity, and it is not without empirical support.

The case of Guatemala provides a particularly vivid illustration of such a contrast. It reveals a state for which, until recently, the exercise of power entailed the unrestrained use of violence and an utter disregard for human rights. It also reveals a multifaceted community of nongovernmental organizations arising in the shadow of institutional terror to confront state violence and demand an end to impunity for human rights abuses. This article assesses the effective role of human rights NGOs in the Guatemalan peace process. It concludes that that role has been considerable, but the results have been mixed. The case of Guatemala illustrates the persistence of human rights demands in the face of awesome terror; and over time that persistence has at least partially mitigated the culture of terror. Despite significant failures, the success of NGOs in promoting the peace process provides further evidence that the emerging global civil society is a politically significant sphere of human action. In as much as it also represents a stark contrast to state-centered violence, this vital sphere holds the potential to further erode the legitimacy of state action whenever it does not conform to generally accepted norms of human rights.

II. HUMAN RIGHTS NGOs AND THE STATE

Human rights NGOs are distinct both from governmental institutions and political parties. They do not seek direct political power and generally are not directly affiliated with groups that do. Rather, they serve a watchdog function of monitoring the behavior of governments and seeking to ensure their compliance with human rights standards. Such standards may include national laws and international agreements which prohibit torture, political imprisonment, forced disappearances, and extrajudicial executions.

In addition to NGOs devoted exclusively to human rights work, there is a plethora of political organizations which include human rights within a broader list of concerns. These include churches, trade unions, women's groups, indigenous peoples' organizations, development organizations, and environmental groups. Some of these organizations may be concerned exclusively with the rights of their own members or constituents, or human rights may be an ancillary concern.[2] But pure human rights groups seek to protect the common and universal rights of all people. They also abrogate the use of violence in pursuing their goals and refuse to ally themselves with groups that employ it, however noble their cause

The unwillingness of human rights organizations to embrace particular political causes or to choose sides in a given conflict has invited criticism from some corners that human rights work remains marginal to effective political struggle. This criticism is particularly salient in the Third World context, where western NGOs that urge respect for the rule of law, but neglect the structural environment that permits human rights abuses to continue with impunity, have been charged with perpetuating a "paradigm of dependency."[3] Western NGOs have focussed mainly on political and civil rights rather than economic and social rights. They have pressed for legal protections through publicity, lawsuits, lobbying, and occasionally demonstrations and civil disobedience. Yet national laws and court orders, not to mention international agreements, are routinely ignored by the most egregious violators. The exclusive emphasis on revising and enforcing legal standards may appear fruitless, if not cynical and suspect, to those engaged in struggles for the radical restructuring of societies. Yet even where such struggles have raged, there have been indigenous organizations that have refrained from violence and have maintained independence both from government and rebel groups. They have created new public spaces by pressing their demands through sometimes highly innovative strategies. Furthermore, some groups have taken initiatives to protect and promote human rights directly, acting independently of government altogether.[4]

The most prominent tactic of human rights NGOs entails information gathering and dissemination for the purpose of exposing human rights violations. This paradoxical strategy depends upon publicity to shame the main violators—states—into respecting and enforcing human rights standards. NGOs may relay their information and demands directly to states or international organizations, in some cases seeking to bring attention to a particular case of abuse, while in others seeking to revise human rights norms generally. Human rights groups often are engaged in proposing legislation and testifying before government committees. Such groups may also provide legal aid to victims of human rights abuses and promote human rights education, including training in public advocacy skills.[5]

An interesting innovation in the field of information gathering entails the application of forensic science to cases of suspected disappearance and extrajudicial execution. Forensic scientists have assisted NGOs in identifying bodies buried in mass graves and performing autopsies on people who have died under suspicious circumstances or while in police custody. This approach originated in 1984 with the investigation into Argentina's "dirty wars" in the 1970s. The American Association for the Advancement of Science sent several forensic experts to Argentina to teach doctors, students, and others how to identify suspected victims of disappearance. This approach has since spread to a variety of other locations, including the former Yugoslavia, where forensic science has provided the UN War Crimes Tribunal with vital information for prosecuting suspected war criminals.[6]

In addition to independent information gathering and educational functions, some human rights groups have engaged in public demonstrations to publicize their concerns. Jennifer Schirmer argues that such initiatives not only create public spaces for expression and publicity, but they also sharply juxtapose the NGO's nonviolent orientation with the state's reliance on force:

> These public demonstrations represent more than the capture of political space and a statement of political purpose: they also represent a temporary suspension of any kind of institutional control. Within a repressive state, which brutally eliminates all political opposition and defines as subversive all public displays and ceremonies which are not directed or controlled by the state itself, these protests in public squares and at public buildings are displays of a defiantly different social order. Indeed, the 'public' takes and occupies national buildings, supreme courts, cathedrals, plazas and streets in order symbolically to regain the rule of law and justice, while the government represents the institutionalization of death.[7]

The widespread commitment to non-violent political action in the NGO community challenges the state's legitimacy to the extent that the state's power rests precisely upon the application or threat of physical force. While NGOs frequently become the targets of state violence, such violence in itself serves to undermine the state's moral authority and to highlight the alternative theory of legitimacy that the victims represent.[8]

Despite the considerable tension that exists between the NGO community and the state, however, global civil society is not a purely anarchist realm committed to the state's destruction. Independent NGO initiatives and public demonstrations, as well as a widespread commitment to nonviolence and human rights, are anarchistic to the extent that state action is the central target of criticism and protest and the state represents institutionalized violence. But NGOs also interact cooperatively and institutionally both with states and international organizations. Indeed, Asbjorn Eide insists that "only in the context of an organized society with public authorities does the notion of 'human rights' make sense. . . . 'Human rights' refers to norms concerning the relationship between individuals (sometimes groups of individuals) and the state."[9] Thus in an important sense human rights NGOs seek not to dismantle but to strengthen state institutions as instruments for monitoring and enforcing human rights standards.

Among the most important mechanisms through which this goal is pursued are international conventions. NGOs have participated actively from the outset in forging international human rights standards through the United Nations.

Forty-two U.S. organizations were invited to the founding conference of the United Nations in San Francisco as consultants to the American delegation, and they pressed to make the UN Charter an instrument for promoting respect for individual human rights. Furthermore, a coalition of NGOs pressed for the adoption of an "international bill of rights" even before the San Francisco conference, which culminated in the adoption of the Universal Declaration of Human Rights in 1948. NGOs have continued to pursue the development of an international human rights system through formal consultative status with the Economic and Social Council as provided for by Article 71 of the UN Charter. In recent years human rights NGOs have even participated in the drafting of declarations and conventions at the level of working groups, as exemplified by their prominent role in the development of the UN Convention Against Torture and the UN Convention on the Rights of the Child.[10]

Additionally, UN conferences have routinely been accompanied by parallel NGO fora. At the 1993 World Conference on Human Rights in Vienna, thousands of NGO representatives participated in the official proceedings along with representatives of 171 governments. This has paved the way to institutional cooperation between the UN Commission on Human Rights and NGOs in human rights monitoring. The Commission has established a human rights hotline for reporting human rights violations. Amnesty International (AI) now reports thousands of cases through this mechanism every year.[11]

Indeed, Amnesty International's relationship with the United Nations well illustrates the institutional and state-oriented character of much NGO human rights work, while at the same time it highlights the normative contrast between business as usual in the state system and the reform demands of the NGO human rights community. In the movement to establish international standards and conventions against torture and disappearances, Clark finds that "AI was a leader rather than a follower of states on the normative front." It reported violations and connected domestic actors to the international human rights monitoring system. While AI's relationship with international organizations is defined by the rules made by states, "when normative issues are introduced that are represented by NGOs or other third party actors, largely through communicative mechanisms, they change the environment for action that states must anticipate in decision making. By advocating changing international human rights norms, NGOs have helped to mold expectations of international behavior and to demand that states conform."[12]

The institutional relationships that have emerged between NGOs and IOs possess a necessary tension and a degree of mutual apprehension. NGOs may exercise more effective influence over international standards and the behavior of states by moving beyond a confrontational posture and participating directly in the institutional decision-making mechanisms established by states at the international level. Yet the very idea of universal human rights militates against absolute state sovereignty and is likely to be met with hostility precisely from those states whose human rights practices are most subject to criticism. Furthermore, to the extent that NGO demands proceed from principles that are to some extent fundamentally antithetical to the state system itself (that is, universalism and nonviolence), institutional cooperation with states and IOs ultimately may prove to be not only futile, but threatening to the integrity of the principles themselves. Rather than NGOs bringing about a normative transformation of the state system, state institutions may force upon NGOs destructive political compromises. In other words, cooperation may lead to co-optation.

This danger is even more clearly illustrated by the direct relationship that sometimes exists between NGOs and states. On the one hand, NGOs have brought pressure to bear on national foreign policies toward abusive regimes by highlighting systematic human rights violations. This happened with Amnesty International's 1977 fact-finding mission to Argentina, which led to international publicity and outrage against the pattern of disappearances occurring there, and ultimately to concrete changes in government policies. Likewise, when the international human rights community in conjunction with domestic NGOs began to bring attention to Mexico in the 1980s, and Mexico became particularly sensitive to international opinion as a result of free trade negotiations with the United States, the government began to take proactive measures to improve its human rights record.[13] There are also cases of more direct institutional cooperation, as when the Washington Office on Latin America (WOLA) and the Quaker Friends Committee on National Legislation played an important lobbying role in the enactment of Section 116 of the U.S. Foreign Assistance Act, restricting economic aid to governments that are responsible for gross violations of international standards of human rights.[14] The cooperative relationship between NGOs and states has even extended to foreign aid. By the late 1980s more that $200 million in foreign aid, including bilateral aid, was flowing to NGOs every year. According to Peter Sollis, donors came to prefer NGO recipients over governments ''because external support was intended to impart a political as well as a humanitarian message.''[15] While such political messages may include demands for improved human rights practices, this cozy relationship between powerful states and NGOs may be a Mephistophelean bargain. NGO recipients of foreign aid could ultimately provide a supporting infrastructure for long-term foreign policy agendas that, on a broader scale, are quite antithetical to the NGO goals themselves. NGOs that become dependent on First World aid may indeed contribute to the paradigm of dependency mentioned earlier. Considerable compromises may ultimately be demanded of NGOs in exchange for access to policy-making processes both at state and international levels.

Nevertheless, Felice Gaer insists that ''Human rights organizations aim to be independent both of government and of partisan groups seeking political power.''[16] They are integral to an emerging global civil society that may possess an independent vitality that is not easily subject to co-optation and manipulation by state entities. Indeed, the integrity of the state system itself may be challenged by the patterns of interaction emerging among states, IOs, and the multifarious NGOs that make up civil society. According to Sikkink:

> Because sovereignty is a set of intersubjective understandings about the legitimate scope of state authority, reinforced by practices, the mundane activities of the human rights network can accumulate to question the idea that it is nobody else's business how a state treats its subjects. Every report, conference, or letter from the network underscores an alternative understanding: the basic rights of individuals are not the exclusive domain of the state but are a legitimate concern of the international community.[17]

Likewise, Melucci believes that the proliferation of NGO networks and the normative alternative they represent are generating a "transsocietal order" that "challenges not only the cultural shape of international relations but the logic governing them."[18]

The nature of the relationship between the state and civil society can be effectively explored through the case of human rights NGOs in Guatemala. There the decades-long civil war forged a state with one of the most nefarious human rights records in the world. But the 1980s also witnessed the emergence of an impressive human rights community in Guatemala. The role that that community has played in the Guatemalan peace process is illustrative of the dilemma faced by human rights NGOs and civil society generally in interacting with the state while preserving the integrity of its principles. It also highlights the dynamic relationship between human rights and the problem of peace. Before addressing these issues specifically, however, the following section provides a brief historical overview of the Guatemalan civil war and peace process.

III. THE GUATEMALAN CIVIL WAR AND PEACE PROCESS

It is today widely known that in 1954 the CIA orchestrated a rebellion against the popularly elected government of Jacobo Arbenz, which included an extensive U.S. bombing campaign against Guatemala. This was in response to the Arbenz government's nationalization of largely uncultivated land held by United Fruit Company, an American multinational, and the minor presence of Guatemalan communists in Arbenz's coalition government. Six years later, in 1960, the CIA again intervened to put down a coup attempt against the government of General Miguel Ydigoras Fuentes. Several leaders of this failed rebellion fled into the countryside and organized a guerrilla movement among Guatemalan peasants. Over the next 36 years the government's counterinsurgency campaign against these guerrillas would cost the lives of some 200,000 unarmed civilians, mostly highland Indians. Thanks in part to the guidance of U.S. military advisors, Guatemala would become the first of numerous countries in Latin America to experience death squads and disappearances. The height of the counterinsurgency campaign was reached in the early 1980s, when Indian support for the guerrillas triggered a government scorched-earth strategy, whereby some 440 villages were destroyed and between 100,000 and 150,000 civilians were killed or disappeared. Additionally, more than a million people were forcibly uprooted from their homes, many fleeing to Mexico. Beginning in 1983, the government set up forced resettlement camps in which the people's lives were tightly controlled by the army. Civilian self-defense patrols (PACs) were created by the military and as many as 1 million Indian peasants were forced to serve in them. These units would subsequently carry out numerous attacks against unarmed civilians.[19]

In the early 1990s, a series of events set in motion a process that has culminated in the establishment of a final peace accord between the government and guerrillas. The most important of these was the constitutional crisis of 1993. In an act of bravado modeled after President Fujimori's 1992 *autogulpe* (self-coup) in Peru, on May 25 Guatemalan President Jorge Serrano Elias dissolved the Congress, the Supreme Court, and the Court of Constitutionality, and suspended key parts of the constitution. The Court of Constitutionality immediately ruled the action unconstitutional, and various sectors of civil society condemned it. On May 27 the Clinton administration announced sanctions against the Serrano regime. Various NGOs and activists carried out protest demonstrations, including Rigoberta Menchu, recipient of the 1992 Nobel Peace Prize. On May 30 negotiations were held in the National Palace that included the church, business leaders, NGOs, the diplomatic corps, the government, and the military high command. On June 1 Serrano resigned, and on June 5 the Congress voted to install Human Rights Ombudsman Ramiro de Leon Carpio as president.[20]

The Carpio presidency opened the door to a series of agreements that have finally brought an end to Guatemala's nightmare. The first of these agreements was the Global Human Rights Accord, signed by the government and the armed opposition, the Guatemalan National Revolutionary Unity (URNG), in March 1994. This accord provided for the establishment of the United Nations Mission for the Verification of Human Rights in Guatemala (MINUGUA), which set up shop in November of that year. In June 1994, accords were signed on the resettlement of displaced populations and the establishment of a Commission for Historical Clarification of the Past, or Truth Commission, which is supposed to investigate and report on wartime human rights violations. In March 1995, an agreement was reached on the Identity and Rights of Indigenous Peoples. An additional agreement on the role of the army in a democracy has led to the demobilization of PACs, which began in August 1996. These confidence-building measures led up to a final settlement with the signing of the Accord for a Firm and Lasting Peace on December 29, 1996.[21]

The final hurdle to the signing of the peace accord, however, was the passage of a controversial amnesty law on December 18. The Law of National Reconciliation grants a general amnesty for human rights violations that occurred during the war. It excludes from immunity cases of forced disappearance, torture, and genocide, but there is no specific reference to extrajudicial execution. Thus human rights groups are concerned that persons responsible for such crimes may escape prosecution. The Truth Commission began its work in July 1997. Its mandate is limited to six months, with the possibility of a six-month extension. It has a caseload of more than 20,000 reported human rights violations to investigate during this time. While human rights NGOs have played an active role in shaping the character of the peace process at various pivotal stages, the persistence of impunity for human rights violations illustrates that NGO successes are significantly limited by institutional political constraints.[22]

IV. HUMAN RIGHTS NGOs IN THE GUATEMALAN PEACE PROCESS

Human rights activists have a rich history of involvement in Guatemala. Among international NGOs this involvement has included responding to human rights violations with ''urgent action'' letter-writing campaigns and conveying the concerns of human rights victims and activists within Guatemala to political leaders in the North.[23] During the 1980s solidarity networks were forged between Guatemalan progressives and international human rights organizations in the United States and Europe. This helped to bring international attention to acts of violence committed by the Guatemalan military against the civilian population.[24] The proliferation of Guatemalan NGOs was itself spurred by the influx of international disaster relief in response to the 1977 earthquake.[25] Additionally, the 500th anniversary of Columbus's voyage spurred the formation of many new Mayan organizations that declared ''500 years of marginalization is enough.'' These groups became involved in human rights work on behalf of Mayans as well as the general population. When negotiations between the government and URNG began, Mayan NGOs came together to form the Coordination of Organizations of the Mayan Pueblo (COPMAGUA) to facilitate unified participation in the dialogue.[26] MINUGUA asserts that human rights NGOs not only have played a significant role in the evolution of Guatemalan society, but they also have participated directly in the work of the UN mission itself:

> The role of human rights NGOs has been crucial in Guatemala's history. These organizations have managed to remain attuned to the expectations and concerns of Guatemalan society and have contributed to the process of social change in recent years. . . . The Mission has carried out activities to support

the strengthening of some NGOs through their direct participation in various research and consultancy projects on numerous themes of importance to human rights.[27]

Stephen Baranyi considers NGOs and the Catholic Church's Human Rights Office to be crucial interlocutors for the UN Mission. This role includes assisting MINUGUA to gain the confidence of communities affected by human rights violations and providing a mechanism for victims to communicate their allegations to MINUGUA. NGOs participate in regular consultations and periodic working meetings with UN offices.[28]

One of the oldest and most notable human rights groups in Guatemala is the Mutual Support Group for the Reappearance of Our Sons, Fathers, Husbands, and Brothers (GAM). It was founded by the mothers, daughters, wives, and sisters of people who were disappeared in the early 1980s. It is made up mainly of poor, indigenous women who had no previous political experience. The group emerged when women regularly met one another in morgues, cemeteries, police stations, and hospitals in search of their missing relatives. From there they began meeting at the local headquarters of an international NGO, Peace Brigades International (PBI). According to founding member Nineth de Garcia, the women formed the group "because we could not find support in any institution."[29] GAM began to document cases of disappearance that its members provided. It also has worked to end impunity for human rights violations and to free political prisoners, and it has mobilized thousands of Guatemalans in support of these campaigns. As a result, a number of GAM members were themselves disappeared in the late 1980s, despite their lack of association with URNG or any political party. In the wake of the military's counterinsurgency campaign, GAM pursued nonviolent but aggressive and innovative strategies for pressuring the government to investigate the disappearances. President Mejia Victores ultimately established a Tri-Partite Commission for this purpose, but GAM considered the gesture disingenuous. In 1985 it began petitioning the Commission to permit members to present their testimonies directly. Every Friday the women protested outside the Public Ministry, blocking traffic, playing flutes and whistles, and beating drums. They also occupied the National Constituent Assembly and demanded that the new constitution refer specifically to political prisoners. After President Cerezo was inaugurated in 1986, he reluctantly agreed to establish an independent commission to investigate disappearances. Yet in that same year the new Supreme Court assigned more than 2,000 habeas corpus writs, most of which were cases of disappearance supplied by GAM, to a single criminal court, and none of the findings held any security or military officials responsible.[30]

Another important group that has pressured the government to investigate and prosecute human rights violations is the National Coordination of Guatemalan Widows (CONAVIGUA), which is made up of Mayan women whose husbands were victims of political violence. The organization is funded by Community Aid Abroad, and it has sought to demilitarize Guatemalan society and end forced recruitment by the military. It has carried out a variety of initiatives, including a demonstration outside of Congress denouncing military repression, a mass media campaign on conscientious objection and nonviolent resistance, and local human rights education workshops. The Council of Indigenous Communities (CERJ, or ''We Are All Equal'') has also been very active in protesting forced conscription into the civilian self-defense patrols, and in the late 1980s at least 17 of its members were killed in a manner that suggested government involvement. In response to the danger faced by domestic activists, Peace Brigades International entered Guatemala in 1983 to provide unarmed protective accompaniment to individuals, organizations, and communities threatened by violence, under the theory that the Guatemalan army is reluctant to risk the international exposure that would be invited by the murder of foreign nationals. Such international cooperative linkages among NGOs demonstrate the potential of innovative nonviolent initiatives for bringing a unique kind of pressure to bear on even the most repressive of regimes.[31]

Amnesty International has documented hundreds of cases of extrajudicial execution, torture, and disappearance in Guatemala. Though it has met with the Guatemalan government, it has been frustrated by the persistent record of impunity within the country. Despite the signing of the Global Human Rights Accord in 1994, AI believes that members of Guatemalan security forces continue to be responsible for widespread abuses. It blames the persistence of human rights violations on the unwillingness of the government to investigate allegations of past abuses, in part because of personal connections between government officials and the accused. In one recent case, AI has called for an investigation into the arrest and possible disappearance of Juan Jose Cabrera on October 19, 1996, an operation reportedly carried out by Guatemalan security forces. Cabrera is believed to have been a member of the Revolutionary Organization of the People in Arms, a branch of URNG. As of May 1997, the government had made no response to the request, and it had rebuffed MINUGUA's request to interview the members of the security forces who allegedly participated in the operation.[32]

In addition to documenting allegations of human rights abuse, other NGO initiatives have generated forensic evidence to be used in any future judicial proceedings against the perpetrators of human rights violations. Even the technical and scientific investigative functions that ordinarily would be performed by a government interested in justice have been partially assumed by the private sector in Guatemala. In 1994 the Association of Families of the Detained and Disappeared of Guatemala (FAMDEGUA) and the Archbishop's Human Rights Office of Guatemala (ODHAG) enlisted the assistance of the Argentinean Team of Forensic Anthropologists (EAAF) in excavating a mass grave where more than 350 people were buried after they were massacred by the Guatemalan army in the village of Las Dos Erres in Peten in 1982.[33] A similar excavation was conducted in the village of Los Josefinos. No effort on the part of the government was made to identify the victims or prosecute those responsible for the massacres. While groups like EAAF and AI have helped to document violations and bring international attention to the persistence of human rights abuses and impunity in Guatemala, that persistence itself demonstrates that the results of such NGO efforts have been quite limited.

Some groups have taken other direct initiatives to respond to crises with little if any government involvement. NGO response to the refugee problem is a case in point. As a result of the scorched-earth campaign in the early 1980s, thousands of Guatemalan peasants were displaced from their homes. Many fled to Mexico, while others were resettled in army-run "model villages," where they were subjected to economic exploitation and severe living conditions. In at least one case, forced relocation has led to violent conflict among separate groups of indigenous peoples: the army brought in one group to occupy the land from which it had forcibly displaced another, and displaced persons trying to reclaim their land were met with violence by those now occupying it.[34] Yet some groups have managed to defy this divide and conquer strategy. For example, the Communities of Population in Resistance of the Sierra (CPR-Sierra) and the Committee for the Recuperation of Land in Chajul have entered into direct negotiations with one another and recognized their common condition as victims of government violence. The negotiations were assisted by Peace Brigades International, as well as the legal department of the Archbishop's Office of Human Rights and the Legal Counsel Office of the Chajulense Association. They developed a joint statement of demands for the government to provide land for the displaced communities of the CPRs and an assistance program for the people of Chajul until they are able to return to their own land, where the CPRs are currently living. Their efforts caught the attention of President Arzu, who visited Chajul only five days after assuming office.[35] In yet another case, the U.S.-based NGO Witness for Peace has accompanied displaced Guatemalans who have been able to return home from exile in Mexico since an agreement on the terms of their return was reached with the Guatemalan government in the early 1990s.[36] However, even where the government has made no provision for the peaceful resolution of land disputes, as in the case of the CPR and the people of Chajul, some NGOs have taken impressive independent initiatives to address the disputes and make specific demands on the government to help ameliorate the refugee crisis that it created.

A. Instancia

The role of human rights NGOs in the Guatemalan peace process was dramatically enhanced by the response of civil society to President Serrano's attempted *autogulpe* in 1993. Organized opposition to the coup was initiated by the business sector, but it was soon joined by representatives of popular organizations, unions, and political parties to form the Instancia Nacional de Consenso (Committee of National Consensus), or Instancia. McCleary[37] identifies five objectives of the Instancia:

1. To promote the participation of different sectors of civil society in the decision-making process
2. To demonstrate to the international community the Guatemalan people's commitment to democracy
3. To strengthen democratic political institutions by restructuring, cleansing, and reforming those institutions
4. To consolidate the peace process
5. To establish an intersectoral dialogue with the purpose of reaching consensus on the problems facing Guatemala and drawing up a national plan for the country

During the two-week crisis, the military and the Constitutional Court gave the Instancia the responsibility of identifying presidential candidates to replace Serrano. Among those selected by the Instancia was Human Rights Ombudsman Ramiro de Leon Carpio, who was installed by the Congress on June 5. The Instancia called on political parties to identify and expel corrupt members. While some party representatives were willing to participate in this process of self-cleansing, others such as the Christian Democrats refused. Instead of dismissing allegedly corrupt members of Congress, the parties worked out an agreement with the executive to elect a transitional Congress. Widespread resentment of such back-room dealing led to a split in the Instancia between the more conservative elements, which accepted the compromise, and popular sectors that continued to demand a thorough purge. A number of popular groups came together in the Foro Multisectorial, which defied the illegitimate government's ban on association with street demonstrations and public protests. Several months later it would continue its militant tactics with an occupation of Congress and circulation of a petition calling for the resignation of all its members. In the weeks following President Serrano's resignation, organized forces in civil society continued to press for political reform and justice, and they were able to pressure the government into replacing two ministers of defense who had been involved in the coup.

In the end, however, the Instancia had only limited success in purging political institutions of corrupt officials. The Carpio government's reforms were largely superficial and designed to maintain the existing concentration of power among elites. Furthermore, the willingness of key elements of the military to permit such initiatives from civil society must not be discounted—without it Serrano quite probably would remain in power today. Prado and Holiday argue that the military was willing to permit limited reforms only because the insurgents and those demanding more thoroughgoing social transformations were under control. Institutional reform was permissable only within the parameters defined by the military.[38]

Nevertheless, civil society's emergence and assumption of "moral legitimacy" during this period of political crisis effectively illustrates its potential capacity to serve as an important check on the illegitimate exercise of political power. The role played by the Instancia in undermining President Serrano's attempted *autogulpe* and replacing him with Ramiro de Leon Carpio helped to establish the political conditions for the subsequent peace process. This role highlights not only the level of legitimacy enjoyed by civil society in contrast to the oppressive state, but also the importance of legitimacy both for the exercise of power and the forging of peace.[39]

B. Assembly of Civil Society

The role of civil society in the peace process was officially recognized with the establishment of the Assembly of Civil Society (ASC) in 1994. The ASC includes representatives of a variety of social sectors, including campesinos, women, labor, human rights groups, indigenous people, religious organizations, and NGOs—but not the business sector, which chose not to participate. Its purpose is to give the various sectors of civil society an opportunity to develop and express consensus positions on negotiation and implementation of the peace accords. The decision-making process within the ASC has been compared to the decentralized mode of public participation in New England town-hall meetings. First, separate position papers are developed by each sector, then common positions are hashed out through give-and-take debate. Accordingly, unions and grassroots organizations are said to have found this forum more receptive than conventional electoral politics. Nevertheless, most sectoral organizations possess a vertical structure with centralized functions, thus limiting input from lower levels. The ASC produces an evaluation report on the implementation of the peace accords every three months, which is sent to the government and MINUGUA and communicated to the public.[40]

The women's sector was initially excluded from the list of ASC participants developed by the government and rebels, but it has proven to be one of the most successful sectors in persuading the government to agree to its demands.[41] The ASC was also highly influential in securing recognition in the Agreement on Indigenous Peoples of the need to eliminate discrimination against women and to secure their rights to land. Furthermore, in the Fall of 1997, a Women's Forum was established consisting both of government and civil society representatives. Its purpose is to oversee the implementation of those aspects of the peace accords that relate to women.[42]

In 1995 the ASC developed a set of proposals for implementing and monitoring international funding for the implementation of the accords. It sent a delegation to Washington, D.C., to promote its agenda with U.S. government officials, international financial institutions, embassies, and NGOs. Consequently, the United States included five ASC proposals in its agenda at a subsequent meeting in Paris of the Grupo Consultivo, a group of international lending institutions and governments which meets under the auspices of the World Bank. Among these proposals was the stipulation that aid be made conditional upon the inclusion of civil society in reconstruction.[43]

Yet, overall the ASC's influence over the negotiation and implementation process has been quite limited. The limited inclusion of civil society at the institutional level is likewise apparent in the makeup of the Commission to Accompany the Peace Process, charged with implementing the accords. The Commission's civil society representatives are limited to an economist, a businessman, a Mayan academic, and a member of the cooperative movement. In May 1997 the ASC issued a report on the first 90 days following the signing of the peace accords in December. The report criticized the government for ignoring its proposals and failing to promote the inclusion of civil society in the peace process. Though the report gained considerable international attention, the Guatemalan government and URNG sent only low-level officials to receive it, and no UN representative was present. As in the 1980s when the government responded to GAM's demands for investigations of disappearances by establishing an impotent commission, its agreeing to an institutional role for civil society through the establishment of the ASC seems largely to have been an empty gesture.[44]

Here again civil society is faced with the dilemma of institutional cooperation versus confrontation with government institutions. When the state offers little opportunity for institutional access and participation, NGOs find that a confrontational mode is the only means of expression. During periods of political crisis, such as Serrano's *autogulpe*, civil society may find considerable opportunity to influence the course of events through direct confrontation with the state, or through alliance with oppositional institutional agents, and this taste of power may lure it into institutional cooperation with the government once the crisis has passed. But the emergence of opportunities for institutional cooperation associated with reform may obfuscate the virtues of confrontation. Institutional processes possess an uncanny capacity to neutralize demands for substantive change through procedural tinkering and an illusory impression of participation and inclusion. Even a democratically inclined government may accept the institutional inclusion of civil society in decision-making processes only when it can effectively limit the extent of its influence. This is particularly true in Guatemala, where the military has long defined the limits of acceptable reform. On the other hand, a stubborn attitude of confrontation with a moderately reformist government could leave civil society on the sidelines when periods of crisis pass and the political process again becomes routinized. ASC member Sandra Moran argues that the accords have opened a space for institutional cooperation between civil society and the government. NGOs and civil society are still learning how to pursue this relationship, while remaining wary of the risk of co-optation. According to Prado and Holiday, "the extent to which the union and popular movement will be able to enhance its impact without giving up its democratic ideology will also depend on the existence of stable conditions of respect for human rights."[45]

Sollis warns that Guatemalan NGOs "are not fully prepared to deal with the processes that are inevitably propelling them into collaborative situations with the government." He insists that they need greater technical capacity and more effective coordination or they may "be unable to realise their potential contribution to development and democratisation."[46] Yet aside from technical issues, civil sectors—and especially human rights NGOs—must evaluate what they can realistically expect to gain from institutional cooperation and what sorts of compromises it entails. It is worthwhile to recall that NGOs have demonstrated considerable vitality in pursuing initiatives independently of government institutions. Where these initiatives have highlighted a fundamental contrast between civil society and the state, they have sustained a unique form of opposition and pressure for reform.

Such contrast is well illustrated by the differing positions of the government and human rights sector toward the issue of impunity. Recall that the Law of National Reconciliation passed in December 1996 originally was intended to grant immunity from prosecution to individual perpetrators of human rights abuses during the war. After protests from Amnesty International and other human rights groups, the original draft was amended to exclude from immunity acts of forced disappearance, torture, and genocide, but there is no specific reference to extrajudicial executions. Human rights groups were skeptical about the exclusion of genocide, since it will be difficult to prove that Mayans were targeted because of their ethnicity. Nevertheless, Anne Manuel of Human Rights Watch counts the revision of the law as a victory for human rights groups. She points out that since the law was passed, it has not been used as the basis for extending amnesty to human rights violators.[47]

Human rights groups continue to document persistent human rights violations carried out by security forces and PACs, which they blame on the culture of impunity. While some prosecutions have moved forward, others have collapsed. Despite strong evidence that one former military commissioner carried out as many as 35 killings, 44 kidnappings, and 14 rapes in the department of El Quiche in the early 1980s, he was absolved of responsibility. In a highly publicized case, charges brought by American Jennifer Harbury against 11 military personnel for the murder of her husband and U.S. citizen Michael Devine were dropped in 1997. Colonel Julio Roberto Alpirez, one of the accused, was subsequently reinstated in the military. Despite a reported decrease in politically motivated human rights abuses in 1996, GAM insists that the Law of National Reconciliation provides evidence that institutional terror has been replaced by a policy of impunity.[48]

In response to the perceived policy of impunity and the Truth Commission's limited mandate, resources, and time for processing its overwhelming caseload, a number of NGOs have taken it upon themselves to investigate and publicize the truth about human rights abuses in Guatemala. A coalition of NGOs called the Convergence for Truth has independently documented more than 25,000 cases to send to the Truth Commission. The Human Rights Office of the Catholic Archbishop has trained community leaders to record the testimony of victims of military violence as part of its Project to Recover Historical Memory. The project's aim is to "identify the victimizers in order to dignify their victims."[49] Approximately 800 volunteers have interviewed more than 5,000 people in small Indian villages. The interviews are taped, and most are conducted in Mayan languages and then transcribed into Spanish. They were scheduled to be published in a two-volume document in the summer of 1997. The project has documented almost 500 mass killings and has gathered information on the locations of more than 300 clandestine cemeteries. As mentioned before, other NGO initiatives have led to excavations of graves at the sites of mass killings.[50]

While Guatemalan NGOs persist in highlighting the illegitimacy of impunity and creating alternative public spaces through independent initiatives, Sollis argues that the presence of a large number of NGOs may actually deter much needed institution building on the part of the state, as "government responsibilities are jettisoned in favor of the NGO sector." While NGO activities "eroded repressive state authority" during the war years, "[i]n postwar conditions . . . NGO fragmentation is a liability when it prevents the organisation of strong representative bodies to promote their collective interests." He also insists that NGOs have been ineffective in influencing the distribution of resources toward poverty reduction and development.[51] Furthermore, Baranyi points to a lack of technical expertise on the part of some NGOs that has undermined the credibility of some of the information that they have provided regarding alleged human rights abuses.[52]

Yet human rights groups in particular not only helped to focus the attention of the international community on the government's miserable record of abuses during the war years, thus enhancing the pressure for peace negotiations and political reform, but they continue to highlight the relationship between human rights and the peace process. In their study of the role of civil society in the democratization of Guatemala, Prado and Holiday conclude:

> We are witnessing, therefore, a period of embryonic processes which favour
> the reconstruction of the social fabric. These include new forms of political
> opposition; new social actors with an interest in strengthening community;
> ethnic and gender-based organizations; and growing public opinion, spurred

on by the efforts of the human rights organizations, that is learning to monitor the legal conduct of the authorities and shows an interest in creating a practice of respect for the rule of law.[53]

Central to the reconstruction of the social fabric is civil society's ongoing struggle against impunity.

Not only does the struggle against impunity identify justice for victims and respect for human rights as a necessary foundation of lasting peace, but the work of human rights groups during the war and throughout the peace process can be understood in terms of a broader struggle to identify peace itself as a fundamental human right.[54] As Alston argues:

> From a human rights perspective, the struggle to achieve peace, and thus for realization of the right to peace, is very closely associated with the struggle against all forms of oppression, discrimination, and exploitation and other mass and flagrant violations of human rights of peoples and persons since such violations pose a direct threat to peace and constitute the negation of the spirit in which respect for human rights, including the right to peace, must be sought.[55]

The right to peace has likewise been recognized by the UN as ''an indispensable condition of advancement of all nations, large and small, in all fields.'' Furthermore, UNESCO has declared that ''no international settlement secured at the cost of the freedom and dignity of peoples and respect for individuals can claim to be a truly peaceful settlement, either in its spirit or in terms of its durability.'' Thus there exists formal international recognition not only of the fundamental right to peace, but also that genuine peace requires respect for the broad array of other recognized human rights. NGOs in Guatemala have persistently highlighted the integral connection between a climate of respect for human rights and a culture of peace.

V. CONCLUSION

The Guatemalan case suggests a number of tentative conclusions concerning the role of human rights NGOs in civil society and the broader relationship between global civil society and the state. When the state in Guatemala was most repressive during the civil war years, its relationship to human rights groups was decidedly adversarial. Human rights activists highlighted the illegitimate activities of the army and PACs, and as a result many became targets of military violence themselves. They were targeted in part because, through their links with other activists outside of Guatemala, the government was subjected to considerable international scrutiny and criticism. By the time of Serrano's attempted self-coup in 1993, civil society in the form of the Instancia would serve as an alternative source of legitimacy against which the government's actions were evaluated both by Guatemalan society and the international community. The illegitimate regime was unable to stand against such scrutiny.

Yet the role of civil society, especially human rights groups, has in some respects become more complicated and problematic with the progress of the peace process. By exploring the possibilities of cooperation with a reforming state, human rights groups and other NGOs must contend with the political reality of compromise, including the compromising of principles. Through institutional cooperation NGOs seek to have a voice within a more inclusive political establishment. Yet much of their legitimacy and vitality derive from their moral integrity, which can be difficult to sustain when they are too closely associated with institutional processes that require unacceptable moral compromises. On the one hand, human rights groups are naturally inclined to support the peace process by acknowledging the legitimacy of a regime that has demonstrated a commitment to a negotiated settlement. On the other hand, these same groups are disinclined to acknowledge the legitimacy of political outcomes that militate not only against human rights, but also against lasting peace to the extent that respect for human rights is viewed as necessary and integral to such a peace. Thus the relationship between civil society and the state, even a reforming state, entails a necessary tension.

Finally, NGOs must be wary of the risk of being co-opted or marginalized through institutional cooperation with the state, as may have happened with the largely impotent Assembly of Civil Society. This is related to the broader issue of formal NGO participation in international organizations. For example, while consultative status clearly provides activists with a unique and convenient opportunity to represent the diverse voices of civil society in international fora, it also means that states are ultimately defining the structure and limits of such participation. Additionally, while NGOs have played an impressive role in the development of bold international declarations of principle, these same declarations are routinely disregarded by the very states that casually endorse them. One wonders if NGO energies and resources would not be better directed toward a more direct and confrontational approach toward those states that routinely and blatantly violate the principles that they cynically celebrate through unenforceable international agreements. In the final analysis, superficial procedural reforms are no substitute for the substantive transformations that human rights groups and other activist elements of civil society seek.

Despite the dilemmas of interacting with institutions that, at least in their more perverse manifestations, are the source of the evils that many NGOs seek to subvert, the potential for reforming the institutional environment within which civil society must operate may justify the risk. By and large, global civil society is not anarchistic. Most human rights activists and similar crusaders do not seek to abolish the state. But they do seek radical reform of the state system's modus operandi. They seek not to destroy the sovereignty of states, but rather to transform sovereignty from a destructive and oppressive institution into an instrument for promoting broad human interests and protecting universal human rights. It is in this respect that civil society represents an alternative measure of legitimacy against which the behavior of states may be evaluated in the arena of global public opinion. The disparity between state behavior and the standard of legitimacy that civil society represents determines the degree of necessary tension between the two. As Guatemalan NGOs negotiate the evolving dynamics of this necessary tension, they effectively highlight the central dilemmas of a broader relationship between the turbulent state system and an emerging global civil society.[56]

NOTES/REFERENCES

1. This definition of the state is taken from Max Weber: see Gerth, H. H. and Mills, C. W. (eds. and trans.) (1946). *From Max Weber: Essays in Sociology*, p 78. New York: Oxford University Press.
2. For example, one Mayan caucus in Guatemala split when a member organization decided that too much emphasis was being placed on general respect for human rights rather than its particular concerns with cultural identity, autonomy, and linguistic integrity. Furthermore, a number of Guatemalan groups involved in human rights work have actively supported the electoral efforts of the progressive coalition party FDNG. This information is found in Prado, T. P. and Holiday, D. (1996). *Towards a New Role for Civil Society in the Democratization of Guatemala* (Peter Feldstein, trans.), pp. 62, 74. Montreal: International Centre for Human Rights and Democratic Development.
3. This charge was issued in the keynote address delivered by Dr. Abdullahi Ahmed An-Na'im, former prisoner of conscience in Sudan and current Professor of Law at Emory University, at the Southern Regional Conference of Amnesty International in New Orleans, November 2, 1996.
4. Wiseberg, L. S. (1992). Human rights and nongovernmental organizations. In R. P. Claude and B. H. Weston (eds.), *Human Rights in the World Community: Issues and Action*, 2nd ed. Philadelphia: University of Pennsylvania Press.
5. Gaer, F. D. (1996). Reality check: Human rights NGOs confront governments at the UN. In T. G. Weiss and L. Gordenker (eds.), *NGOs, the UN, & Global Governance* pp. 57–58. Boulder: Lynne Rienner; Wiseberg (1992), op. cit., p. 373.
6. Collins, N. (1995). Giving a voice to the dead. *Human Rights* (Winter), 28–29, 47–48; Snow, C. C., Stover, E., and Hannibal, K. (1992). Scientists as detectives: Investigating human rights. In R. P. Claude and B. H. Weston (eds.), *Human Rights in the World Community: Issues and Action*, 2nd ed. pp. 389–390. Philadelphia: University of Pennsylvania Press; Wiseberg (1992), op. cit., pp. 372–380.
7. Schirmer, J. (1989). Those who die for life cannot be called dead: Women and human rights protest in Latin America. *Feminist Review* (No. 23), 23.
8. For a fuller analysis of the normative contrast between global civil society and the

state-centric world system as alternative paradigms, see Turner, S. (1998). Global civil society, anarchy and governance: Assessing an emerging paradigm. *Journal of Peace Research 35*:1, 23–40.

9. Eide, A. (1986). The human rights movement and the transformation of the international order. *Alternatives XI*, 369.
10. van Boven, T. (1989–1990). The role of non-governmental organizations in international human rights standard-setting: A prerequisite of democracy. *California Western International Law Journal 20*:2, 217–218; Clark, A. M. (1996). The contribution of non-governmental organizations to the creation and strengthening of international human rights norms. Paper presented to the annual meeting of the International Studies Association, San Diego, California, April, 16–20, p. 16; Claude, R. P. and Weston, B. H. (1992). Human rights NGOs. In R. P. Claude and B. H. Weston (eds.), *Human Rights in the World Community: Issues and Action*, 2nd ed., p. 367. Philadelphia: University of Pennsylvania Press; Ghils, P. (1992). International civil society: International non-governmental organizations in the international system. *International Social Science Journal* (No. 133, August), 417–429; Gaer (1996), op. cit., pp. 51–52.
11. Gaer (1996), op. cit., pp. 55–58.
12. Clark (1996), op. cit., p. 18.
13. Sikkink, K. (1993). Human rights, principled issue-networks, and sovereignty in Latin America. *International Organization 47*:3, 411–441; Gaer (1996), op. cit., p. 54.
14. Claude and Westen (1992), op. cit., p. 367.
15. Sollis, P. (1995). Partners in development? The state, nongovernmental organizations and the UN in Central America. *Third World Quarterly* (September), p. 3.
16. Gaer (1996), op. cit., p. 57.
17. Sikkink, (1993), op. cit., p. 441.
18. Quoted in Lipschutz, R. D. (1992). Reconstructing world politics: The emergence of global civil society. *Millennium: Journal of International Studies 21*:3, 399.
19. Amnesty International (1997a). "Appeals against impunity." http://www. amnesty.org/ailib/aipub/1997/AMR/23400397.htm, April 22; Jonas, S. (1996). Dangerous liaisons: The U.S. in Guatemala. *Foreign Policy* (Summer), 2–3; Blum, W. (1995). *Killing Hope: U.S. Military and CIA Interventions Since World War II* pp. 74–75, 229–230. Monroe, ME: Common Courage Press.
20. Human Rights Watch (1994). *Human Rights in Guatemala During President De Leon Carpio's First Year*. pp. 126–129 New York: Human Rights Watch. McCleary, R. M. (1996). Guatemala: Expectations for peace. *Current History 95*:598, 89.
21. Amnesty International (1996). "Central America and Mexico: Human rights defenders on the front line." http://www.amnesty.org/ailib/intcam/cemenixo/guatem.htm, March; Amnesty International (1997b). Guatemala. In *Amnesty International Report 1997* p. 163. London: Amnesty International; "Peace in Guatemala." *Cerigua Weekly Briefs* (No. 1, January 2), http://www-personal.engin.umich.edu/~pavr/ harbury/archive/cerigua/cwb01_97.html#Head2; Jonas (1996), op. cit., p. 5; Peace Brigades International (1997a). "Organizations in Guatemala." http://www. igc.apc.org/pbi/guate.html.
22. Amnesty International (1997b), op. cit., "Truth commission ready to roll." (1997).

Cerigua Weekly Briefs (No. 9, February 27), http://www-personal.engin.umich.edu/ ~pavr/harbury/archive/cerigua/cwb09_97.html#Head4; ''Amnesty pact passed by congress.'' (1997). *Cerigua Weekly Briefs* (No. 1, January 2), http://www-personal.engin.umich.edu/~pavr/harbury/archive/cerigua/cwb01_97.html#Head2; Rohter L. (1996). ''Guatemalan amnesty is approved over opponents' objections.'' *New York Times*, December 19, p. A13.

23. Baranyi, S. (1996a). The challenge in Guatemala: Verifying human rights, strengthening national institutions and enhancing an integrated UN approach to peace, part II. *Journal of Humanitarian Assistance* (January 6).

24. Wilkinson, D. (1995/96). Democracy' comes to Guatemala. *World Policy Journal* *12*:14, 71–81.

25. Sollis (1995), op. cit.

26. Peace Brigades International (1995). ''Guatemala: Voices of the Pueblo Maya.'' http://www.igc.apc.org/pbi/cap95-03.html, October.

27. MINUGUA (1996). ''Fifth Report.'' http://www.un.org/Depts/minugua/fifthr.htm, January 1–June 30, p. 33.

28. Baranyi, S. (1996b). The challenge in Guatemala: Verifying human rights, strengthening national institutions and enhancing an integrated UN approach to peace, part I. *Journal of Humanitarian Assistance* (January 6).

29. Schirmer (1989), op. cit., pp. 3–29.

30. Amnesty International (1996), op. cit.; Schirmer (1989), op. cit.; Wilkinson (1995/96), op. cit.

31. Amnesty International (1996), op. cit.; Community Aid Abroad (1997), Protection from violence. *Horizons* (No. 19, January); Peace Brigades International (1997a), op. cit.; Peace Brigades International (1997b). ''Guatemala.'' http://www.igc.apc. org/pbi/guatemala.html, March.

32. Amnesty International, (1997c). ''Guatemala: 10 steps to end impunity and human rights violations.'' http://www-personal.engin.umich.edu/~pavr/harbury/archive/ai/ainews043097.html, April 24; Amnesty International (1997d). ''Guatemala: For over six months the government has turned a deaf ear to Amnesty International's calls for an investigation into the possible 'disappearance' of Mincho.'' http://www.amnesty.org/news/1997/23402197.htm, May 21.

33. Amnesty International (1996), op. cit.

34. ''Clash with villagers stops refugee return.'' (1997). *Cerigua Weekly Briefs* (No. 9, February 27), http://www-personal.engin.umich.edu/~pavr/harbury/archive/cerigua/cwb09_97.html#Head4.

35. Peace Brigades International (1996). ''The CPR-Sierra/Chajul dialogue: A great step forward.'' http://www.igc.apc.org/pbi/cap96-06.html, March.

36. Lloyd, R. (1994). *Journey Home: Accompaniment in Guatemala*. Videocassette. Burlington, VT: Green Valley Media.

37. McCleary (1996), op. cit., p. 90.

38. Prado and Holiday (1996), op. cit., pp. 5, 17, 19.

39. Blackmore, M. (1993). ''Guatemala: Political analysis by ROUG.'' http://www.stile.lut.ac.uk/~gyedb/STILE/Email0002040/m4.html, November 12; Human Rights Watch (1994), op. cit.; McCleary (1996), op. cit.

40. Frundt, H. J. (1995). Applying to Guatemala lessons learned in Haiti. *America 172*:

2, 5–7; telephone interview with ASC member Sandra Moran on November 7, 1997; Prado and Holiday (1996), op. cit., p. 34.

41. ''Women document their role in the peace talks.'' (1996). *Cerigua Weekly Briefs* (No. 7, February 15), http://www-personal.engin.unmich.edu/~pavr/harbury/ archive/cerigua/cwb07_97.html#TOC, p. 4.

42. Baranyi (1996a), op. cit., p. 1; Bauduy, J. (1997). ''Sandra Moran: At the forefront of women's issues.'' *The Siglo News*, June 26; ''Women document their role.'' (1996), op. cit.; ''Ten years of negotiations: A chronology.'' (1997). *Cerigua Weekly Briefs* (No. 1, January 2), http://www-personal.engin.umich.edu/~pavr/harbury/ archive/cerigua/cwb01_97.html#Head2; Frundt (1995), op. cit.; Holiday D. (1997). Guatemala's long road to peace. *Current History* 96:607, 68–74; Jonas (1996), op. cit., p. 5; Peace Brigades International (1997a), op. cit.

43. Prado and Holiday (1996), op. cit., p. 37.

44. ''Peace oversight commission established.'' (1997). *Cerigua Weekly Briefs* (No. 6, February 6), http://www-personal.engin.umich.edu/~pavr/harbury/archive/ cerigua/cwb06_97.html#Head5; ''ASC report given low profile.'' (1997). *Cerigua Weekly Briefs* (No. 18, May 8), http://www-personal.engin.umich.edu/~pavr/ harbury/archive/cerigua/cwb18_97.html#Head6.

45. Telephone interview with ASC member Sandra Moran on November 7, 1997; Prado and Holiday (1996), op. cit., p. 52.

46. Sollis (1995), op. cit., p. 14.

47. Telephone interview on November 3, 1997.

48. Amnesty International (1997c). ''Guatemala Peace Prize winners Arzu and Moran yet to demonstrate their full commitment to the peace agreement.'' http:// www.amnesty.org/news/1997/23402597.htm, June 25; Amnesty International (1997f). ''Guatemala: Human rights violations and impunity.'' http://www. amnesty.org/ailib/aipub/1997/AMR/23400897.htm, March; ''GAM: Violence has Roots in Impunity.'' (1997). *Cerigua weekly Briefs* (No. 5, January 30), http://www-personal.engin.umich.edu/~pavr/harbury/archive/cerigua/cwb05_97.html#Head7; Najarro, O. and Monroy, C. (1997). Military reinstates Colonel Alpirez, implicated in Devine and Bamaca cases. *The Foundation for Human Rights in Guatemala Newsletter* (July), http://homepage.interaccess.com/~dlindstr/fhrjul3.htm; Jonas (1996), op. cit., p. 9.

49. Rohter, L. (1997). ''Guatemalan rights group tracing abuses in war.'' *New York Times*, April 7, p. A8.

50. ''Truth Commission support group formed.'' (1996). *Cerigua Weekly Briefs* (No. 38, September 26), http://www-personal.engin.umich.edu/~pavr/harbury/archive/ cerigua/cwb38_96.html#Head8; ''GAM reports 834 violations in first half of 1997.'' (1997). *Guatemala Human Rights News Clips* (July 7), http://homepage.interaccess. com; Rohter (1997), op. cit., p. A8; Wilkinson (1995/96), op. cit., p. 80.

51. Sollis (1995), op. cit., pp. 12–13.

52. Baranyi (1996b), op. cit.

53. Prado and Holiday (1996), op. cit., p. 86.

54. In a telephone interview on November 3, 1997, Anne Manuel of Human Rights Watch stressed the importance of justice and accountability to the peace process. She argued that only by bringing to justice those persons found to be responsible

for human rights abuses can the cycle of violence be broken. Likewise, she insisted that national reconciliation in which victims lose hope for justice is not reconciliation, but frustration.

55. Alston, P. (1992). Peace as a human right, p. 205. In R. P. Claude and B. H. Weston (eds.), *Human Rights in the World Community: Issues and Action*, 2nd ed. Philadelphia University of Pennsylvania Press.

56. The reference to a turbulent state system is derived from James Rosenau; see Rosenau, J. (1990). *Turbulence in World Politics: A Theory of Change and Continuity*. Princeton: Princeton University Press.

23

Managing Diversity in Multiethnic Federations

The Case of Canada

Réjean Pelletier
Laval University, Ste-Foy, Quebec, Canada

I. INTRODUCTION

Federalism refers to the double notion of unity and diversity. It looks for *unity* by concentrating power in a central government in the name of efficiency. At the same time, it recognizes *diversity* by the diffusion of power to its constituent parts (such as provinces) in order to provide a greater degree of freedom and equity. This corresponds with the way in which Daniel J. Elazar (1987:12) defines federalism, namely, "self-rule plus shared rule": self-government of federate entities (or the capacity to govern oneself) cannot be absolute, it is shared with a central entity more encompassing, but not totally dominant.

Federalism, in effect, cannot be solely based on the idea of one concentrated power which threatens to topple the federal structure down on the side of the sole majority; it must modulate its organization of power according to the principle of equity that recognizes the multiple forms of pluralism and the presence of minorities. While it is often said that the federal system was created to accommodate minorities or different ethnic groups by according them a political status within the federation, several, if not most, of the federal systems, as Murray Forsyth (1989:3) underlines, were not put into place to reconcile different ethnocultural

This chapter is a revised version of a paper presented at the seventeenth World Congress of the International Political Science Association in Seoul, Korea, August 17–21, 1997 claims. One can cite the case of the United States, where the African-American population had at that time a subordinate status; those of the Federal Republic of Germany, of the Commonwealth of Australia, and of the former Dutch provinces, who had no well-defined and localized ethnocultural minorities within a certain area; and even that of the former Swiss Confederation (until 1815)— essentially germanophone, whereas the francophone and italophone communities were either allied or subordinate to the Swiss germanophone core.

In addition to the Swiss model that would progressively transform itself from 1815 on in such a way as to recognize the ethnic and linguistic differences, it would be necessary to wait for the Canadian experience of 1867 to witness the federative formula employed with the aim of not only uniting a people that shared a common language and culture but who were living in different political entities (as was the case in the United States, and later in Australia and Germany), but also uniting from then on one population—different in origin, language, and culture—seeking the advantages of belonging to one common political unit.

The Canadian experience also teaches that the federal formula only cannot entirely respond to the claims of some groups. Other means of action must be added to this formula to respond to the double need of unity and diversity. For example, to satisfy the recognition of linguistic diversity within a certain territory, some federations, such as Canada, adopt the principle of personality, according to which an individual benefits from linguistic rights which are extended to all federal territory; whereas others, such as Belgium and Switzerland, opt instead for the principle of territoriality according to which one language is protected within a certain territory (Laponce 1984; Lapierre 1988; Pelletier 1991).

Before approaching this study of the different means used by the Canadian Federation to reconcile the search for unity and the recognition of diversity, it is important to further clarify this notion of diversity within the federal context.

II. SOCIAL AND TERRITORIAL PLURALISM

Most, if not all, societies are crossed by diverse currents that use different channels of expression. Therefore, the multiplicity of political opinions normally translates into the creation of several different political parties. Similarly, a multiplicity of different religious beliefs gave birth to several different religions. Within such a society, different religious and political opinions can coexist as well as different social behaviors and cultures, which are recognized or tolerated by the political authorities and the society itself.

In a federal system, this diversity of opinions, beliefs, and behaviors can take two main forms, namely a *social* pluralism and a *territorial* pluralism. In the first case, the multiplicity of values, interests, and even identifying anchorages transcend the frontiers of the federate entities (province, state, canton). This social pluralism concerns questions just as important and diverse as the equality between men and women, the recognition of a language or a cultural group, freedom of religion, and so on. This social pluralism is of interest within the context of this chapter in that it leads to political debates and is often defined in terms of a certain constitutional recognition. In other words, we are looking to see how a federation, such as the Canadian Federation, can deal with social cleavages not limited to a specific federate entity, such as a province, but widespread within the whole territory of the federation, and to bring forward answers of a political and constitutional nature.

Territorial pluralism can address the same types of cleavages, this multiplicity of interests, values, and cultures. However, within a federation, it becomes territorial in the sense that the cleavage exists or has its point of origin in the territory of a federate entity, whether it be a province, a canton, or a land. Such pluralism is often the source of conflicts within a federal system and often has an impact on the survival of the federation. This is why analysts of federal systems usually fix their attention on studying territorial cleavages and the solutions, especially those of a constitutional nature, that have been brought out.

Social diversity and territorial cleavages are therefore important for studying federal systems, though the latter are more likely to threaten their survival. As Michael Burgess reminds us (1993:8), ''Territoriality—the sense of place— has always been a crucial mobilizing force for the assertion and reassertion of distinct values, interests and identities, but, so too, have non-territorial imperatives.''

In so far as the goals of the present text mainly concern the Canadian Federation, the chapter will only deal with one single dimension of territorial pluralism, that which affects ethnocultural groups defined by a common language and culture, however without approaching the complex and vast question of native peoples.[1] In a sense, limiting territorial pluralism to only an ethnocultural dimension allows us to attempt to respond to the question put forward by James Tully (1995: 1): ''Can a modern constitution recognise and accommodate cultural diversity?'' For the purposes of this text, this question will be approached in terms of the recognition of ethnic and linguistic minorities rather than that of a nationalist movement asking for an independent state, using the varying degrees of cultural recognition as defined by Tully (1995:2). This brings us to further define this notion of territorial pluralism in the case of federations confronted with multiethnicity.

To discuss territorial pluralism, there must be *territorialization* of ethnocultural groups,[2] that is to say a concentration of a community or an ethnocultural group on a portion of a national territory where it is the majority, while being the minority in the rest of the country. Such a situation has a tendency to accentuate conflicts as this group can use government resources of that particular territory (province, canton, *Länder*) Such is the case in Canada where the concentration of francophones in Quebec allows this minority to be a majority within the province and to control its own government. In fact, more than 88% of francophones in Canada live in Quebec, where they constitute the majority of the population (82.7% in 1991). This territorialization of linguistic and ethnic communities is supported by the new Belgian federation, which divided the country into Flemish and Walloon regions with the exclusion of the Brussels region. This is not found in the United States where the linguistic and ethnic cleavages do not coincide with the territorial divisions of the states, even if the majority of the hispanophone population is concentrated in the border states with Mexico and the African-American population is located especially in the deep South and in larger cities throughout the country. In neither case does the ethnocultural group form the single majority of the population of a state of which it would control the political institutions.

To this first factor, one can add another which is substantially related, that is, to what extent the linguistic and ethnic tensions and conflicts have been *institutionalized*. Institutionalization is normally preceded by a mobilization phase with regard to the conditions under which the group lives or perceives to live. However, ethnic, linguistic, or even religious mobilization is different from economic and social mobilization. In the last case, one can downplay or, in the best of all cases, make disappear the disparities between individuals and groups, in terms of economic status by the transfer or redistribution of wealth as well as in terms of social matters by appropriate social programs. In the first case, there is really no middle ground between one language or the other, for example, English or French in Canada, except by institutional or individual bilingualism, which is always favorable to the dominant language (Pelletier 1991). Nor is there a middle ground between religions, for example, in terms of whether or not to teach religion in the schools.

The mobilization of a community with regard to its collective identity or ethnicity will bring about institutionalization of conflicts when the community reclaims more power and uses the administrative and financial resources from the territorial government to accomplish these goals. This allows this government to become identified with the community and speak for it. From the simple notion of identity (who we are, how we define ourselves in our relationships with others), one moves on the necessary recognition of this identity by others. This leads to the transformation from an ethnic and linguistic identification to a territorial one, the territory which then reinforces the notion of ethnicity.

Conflicts become substantially more intense as they start to involve ethnic or community *bipolarization*.[3] This third condition is defined by the presence within the same territory of two communities where one is the majority that wants to affirm its number and its rights as majority and the other is the minority that wants special protection of its rights. It is possible to imagine different types of protection of which the recognition of the asymmetrical nature of the society can appear as an essential aspect. This bipolarization is present in Canada and Belgium, however not within the United States, nor even in Switzerland; this last federation is instead characterized by the absence of exact superposition between the territorial divisions and linguistic and religious cleavages, which mitigates the potential bipolarisation (if one considers as less important the italophone and Romansh-speaking representation). In Switzerland, no francophone or germanophone, catholic or protestant canton can pretend to monopolize the representation of the ethnic or religious groups and say that it speaks as the single voice for that group.

All three conditions are present in the Canadian case. Territorialization of an ethnocultural group within the limits of a province is present with respect to Quebec. Ethnic bipolarization is also a factor, where one of the poles of this polarization is the francophone minority that is concentrated within one territory. (The presence of Canadian native peoples adds a third pole.) Furthermore, there is institutionalization of conflicts because the governments of Quebec for about 50 years, and especially since 1960, have taken responsibility for defending its francophone majority.

III.   FROM THE IDENTIFICATION OF PLURALISM TO ITS RECOGNITION

Let us once again take the question put earlier by James Tully by looking how he explained somewhat later: ''the question is whether a constitution can give recognition to legitimate demands of the members of diverse cultures in a manner that renders everyone their due, so that all would freely consent to this form of constitutional association'' (Tully 1995:7). For the problem that concerns us within this chapter, that is, managing diversity in multiethnic federations, this idea of diverse cultures is defined by the double notion of social and territorial pluralism, the latter being important as the concentration of an ethnocultural group within a given territory in a federation takes on capital importance for that federation. This is particularly the case in Canada.

However, what forms can the recognition of ''the legitimate demands of the members of diverse cultures in a manner that renders everyone their due'' take? One can imagine two types of recognition: an *egalitarian* recognition allowing each culture the same treatment, or, more exactly, allowing all the people of different cultures the same rights; or a *differential* recognition in the sense that one recognizes the differences, what distinguishes ourselves, in such a manner as the constitution of the federation recognizes and protects these differences.

Behind these different forms of recognition, one can discern different types of logic at work. First of all, a logic of *obliged inclusion* in the sense that the constitution of the federation accords the same rights to all citizens in the name of the unity of the country. This logic erases diversity while opposing uniformity. These equal citizens possess as well a unique identity, that which confers to them their sense of belonging to a "nation," that is to say, "an imaginary community to which all nationals belong and in which they enjoy equal dignity [and one could add equal rights] as citizens" (Tully 1995:68). In short, it is important to recognize the equality of individuals, all having the same rights and being treated in an identical fashion, in such a way as to reinforce the unity of the nation, imposing therefore uniformity by opposition to the recognition of differences. The example of the American melting pot comes immediately to mind. Furthermore, as we will see later, the inclusion of a Charter of Rights and Freedoms in the Canadian constitution has also had an effect of making Canadian society more uniform and its citizens more homogenous.

Another approach to the problem of diversity in federal states is that of *consensual inclusion*. This approach goes further than the individual consent to integration, or, more exactly, assimilation to the dominant language and culture (with respect to this form of inclusion, it is important to recognize that it can often be more consensual than obliged). It implies the protection of cultural identities in order to reinforce national unity and avoid confrontation and conflict of all types. Conflicts are often born out of nonrecognition and lack of respect of different cultural identities of the members who make up the political community. Opposition then protests against a dominant cultural imperialism. If institutions and the constitution protect these cultures, instead of looking to destroy them, citizens of diverse cultures can more easily have an allegiance to that constitution and share with others a sense of belonging to, and identification with, that same constitution, as well as all the political institutions that stem from that constitution and which provide the basic values on which the country was founded. In Canada, there is wide recognition of the existence of the "cultural mosaic," which is often counterposed by Canadians to the American melting pot. This chapter will further analyze this recognition of multiculturalism within the Canadian constitution.

The third approach to managing diversity takes the form of *differentiated inclusion*. If the first two approaches applied more to the notion of social pluralism, this approach deals more with that of territorial pluralism. With regard to this form of inclusion, there is a recognition of ethnocultural diversity according to differentiated and diversified means, not necessarily according the same treatment to each group. The asymmetry formula corresponds well to the situation in the Canadian case, a formula that can apply to federate entities (provinces, cantons, *Länder*) and, more particularly, to an ethnocultural group concentrated within a given territory, as in the case of Quebec. This differentiated recognition of the cultural diversity can take many forms: it can be entrenched in the constitution, stem from differentiated practices permitted under the constitution, or be the result of administrative agreements. In all cases, it looks to respond to diverse needs.

To these three approaches, one can add two others that will not be discussed here, however, they are worth mentioning to give a complete picture of the Canadian situation. These two other approaches also imply the wish of an ethnocultural group to be recognized for its cultural identity within or outside a federal system. The *inclusion–exclusion* approach corresponds to the sovereignty-partnership agreement put forward by the Parti Québécois to the Quebec population at the time of the referendum on the future of Quebec in October, 1995. The sovereignty policy translates into a form of exclusion with respect to the Canadian Federation, while the economic partnership (and even political in certain respects) would be in the context of a Canadian common market. Finally, the approach of *exclusion* is defined by a complete separation from the rest of Canada, supported by a smaller group of hardline separatist Quebecois.

As this analysis deals with different ways of managing diversity in multiethnic federations, I will focus only on the first three approaches, which deal with the main forms of recognition of ethnocultural groups within a federal system.

IV. MANAGING DIVERSITY IN MULTIETHNIC FEDERATIONS

I will now attempt to explain and gain further knowledge with regard to the three different approaches that advocate the recognition of diversity in order to ascertain whether these approaches adequately meet the demands of social *and* territorial pluralism within a federation using the Canadian case as an example (see Table 1).

A. Egalitarian and Identitarian Federalism

To begin with, let me analyze the first manner in which diversity can be managed within the Canadian federation. All citizens must be accorded the same rights,

Table 1 Three Approaches for Managing Diversity in Multiethnic Federations

	Social pluralism	Territorial pluralism
Obliged inclusion approach	Yes or no	Yes or no
Consensual inclusion approach	Yes or no	Yes or no
Differentiated inclusion approach	Yes or no	Yes or no

whatever their sex, religion, language, or culture may be. Social diversity (or social pluralism) cannot therefore be a factor to consider; on the contrary, despite the differences that can characterize Canadian citizens, each one must benefit from the same rights according to the terms of an egalitarian federalism. In other words, while you may be different, you are equal under the law.

The Canadian Charter of Rights and Freedoms, entrenched in the Constitution in 1982, clearly bestows the same rights upon all Canadian citizens and defines them as having equal rights, or, more precisely, protects them from any government intervention that may restrict these rights (with the exception of the derogation clause as written in Section 33 of the Charter). It affirms that individual rights must be recognized indiscriminately and without regard to differences that may exist among citizens. Everyone has the right to freedom of thought, belief, religion, and association; to legal guarantees to protect him or her; and to school instruction in either official language (English or French) regardless of province. According to former Prime Minister Trudeau, it is the essence of liberalism that "all members of a civil society enjoy fundamental, inalienable rights and cannot be deprived of them by any community (nation, ethnic group, religious group, or other)" (Trudeau 1990:386–387).

The Charter was not only drawn up to protect individuals from arbitrary government action and ensure their rights in keeping with the purest principles of liberal individualism. It was also conceived as an instrument for fostering common values, particularly that of equality among individuals according to which everyone in the country has the same rights. As former Prime Minister Trudeau often said, it is the expression of a Canadian identity. More precisely, it is "the culmination of a political policy aimed at reinforcing Canadian unity through the pursuit of a just society based on liberty and equality" (Trudeau 1990:391. He goes on to say "the Canadian Charter of Rights represented a new beginning for Canada and sought to strengthen *unity* by founding the sovereignty of the Canadian people on a set of commonly held values, notably on the notion of *equality* among all Canadians" (Trudeau 1990:386, emphasis added). A vision such as this was, for a long time, entrenched in Trudeau's thoughts.

The Charter was thus just one component of a broader strategy of nation-building, of forging a Canadian nation opposed to all forms of provincialism excessively focussed on local interests, ultimately a way to foster a Canadian nationalism opposed to all other forms of nationalism, particularly Quebec nationalism. The Charter, according to Peter Russell (1983), provided a common reference point for all Canadians and gave symbolic expression to the idea that Canadians enjoy a collective political identity. Moreover, the uniform application of rights and freedoms and the definition of national standards by courts, especially the Supreme Court, that interpret the Charter can only lead to centralization and greater power for central authorities, to the detriment of the federated provinces and their greater emphasis on diversity.[4]

In short, the Charter was not only drawn up to protect individuals; its ultimate objective was to join all Canadians together to share the same rights and the same values. In this context, provincial boundaries would appear obsolete, or at least have no reason to exist in the face of a Charter that applies uniformly to all Canadian territories (Cairns 1991, 1992). That's why we call this kind of federalism an egalitarian (same rights for all Canadians) and identitarian (common values) federalism.

Such a type of federalism, which has the effect of making the society uniform and homogenous, meets the demands of an obliged inclusion approach in the sense that it hopes to make people forget differences, to propose a single identitarian vision in such a way that all citizens must adhere to the same set of principles. This is why it does not meet the needs of the recognition of social diversity and even less so of territorial pluralism. Its ultimate objective is to reinforce the unity of the country, not the diversity of the federation. But this strategy has failed. "In fact," wrote Kenneth McRoberts (1997:245), "rather than unifying the country, it has left Canada more deeply divided than ever before."

B. Multicultural Federalism and Bilingualism

The second approach which will be analyzed has for an ultimate objective the reinforcement of national unity as well. However, it puts more emphasis on the recognition of diversity. The recognition of two official languages in Canada as well as the recognition of different cultural communities give evidence of the great cultural diversity of the country. However, in both cases, it essentially amounts to the recognition of social pluralism and not the registering of this diversity within a precise territorial border.

With regard to linguistic rights, Sections 16 to 23 of the Charter, the Official Languages Act of 1969 and its replacement Act of 1988, reside on the absolute primacy of individual rights, that is, the right of individuals to demand federal government services in the official language of their choice (English or French) by virtue of the 1969 and 1988 acts and the Charter (Sections 16–22) or the right of their children, under certain conditions, to receive instruction in the official language of their choice by virtue of the Charter (Section 23).

The federal government had one important goal in imposing individual bilingualism throughout the country: to see to it that Quebec could not claim to be the sole voice of French Canadians or the only political authority empowered to speak in the name of the French Canadian nation. As former Prime Minister Trudeau declared in a 1968 address, "if minority language rights [in that case French] are entrenched throughout Canada then the French-Canadian nation would stretch from Maillardville in B.C. to the Acadian community on the Atlantic coast. . . . Quebec cannot say it alone speaks for the French-Canadians. . . .

Nobody will be able to say 'I need more power because I speak for the French-Canadian nation' '' (quoted in McRoberts 1993:259).

It is clear that this conception of linguistic rights is based on the principle of personality or individuality, making linguistic rights applicable throughout the federation under the same manner as the right to vote or the right of religious expression are applicable. It is a right that applies to the individual, whatever his or her place of residence within the federation. This opposes the principle of territoriality, which rests on intrastate borders, in reference to the separation of languages in contact ''as much as possible by means of fixed and secure borders'' (Laponce 1984:164; see also Lapierre 1988). The Canadian linguistic policy aims only at recognizing social diversity (more exactly, linguistic diversity), not a territorial border where it would be necessary to protect the language of the minority within the federation.

As for multiculturalism, the policy adopted in 1971 (and later recognized in Section 27 as a rule for interpreting the 1982 Charter) accords all Canadian citizens the legal right to the preservation and enhancement of their multicultural heritage, thus placing all cultures on equal footing and refusing to recognize a common Canadian culture. Until very recently, this was the signal sent to all new immigrants entering Canada, who were given a brochure entitled *How to Become a Canadian Citizen*, which read ''You do not have to renounce your past to become a Canadian, because even though there are two official languages in Canada, there is no official culture. You are thus free to live according to your own customs'' (cited in Burelle 1995:79).

In the case of multicultural communities (as well as native communities), the Charter does not look to define rights in terms of the individual so much as in the community, as Trudeau himself recognizes (1990:338). However, it does not do this in terms of a concentrated community within a given territory, as in the case of Quebec. In reality, the recognition of multiculturalism by dissociating culture (multicultural communities) from language (two official languages) provides a convenient alibi for refusing the distinct nature of Quebec society, and thus reducing the status of Quebecois or francophone Canadians to that of an ethnic group like any other.

On the whole, bilingualism and multicultural federalism allow the social diversity to be recognized within the Canadian Federation, however not its presence within a defined territorial boundary, for example, in a province such as Quebec.

C. Asymmetrical Federalism

The Canadian Federation used a third approach to deal with diversity within the country. Asymmetrical federalism refers to particular arrangements to accommodate the needs and demands of minorities or ethnocultural groups.

In the Canadian and provincial constitutions, there are several elements of asymmetry (Milne 1991; Pelletier 1996). Some apply only to Quebec, while others apply to Quebec and a few other provinces at the same time. Some provisions can be conceived as a type of protection, others as obligations imposed on governments of the provinces concerned. In some cases there is an increase in the autonomy of a province (for example, the civil law system within the province of Quebec), in others it means restrictions on this autonomy (for example, the bilingual legislative regime only in Quebec[5]).

On the whole, with the exception of the civil law system, it can be said that the asymmetrical provisions laid down in the Constitution do not affect the equilibrium of the whole federation. In other words, all the provinces were granted the same legislative powers under the BNA Act of 1867, with the exception of the Quebec civil law system, which represents the choice of an alternative legal system dating back to the Act of Quebec in 1774. However, some asymmetrical clauses—such as the bilingual requirement in political institutions or the protection of religious minorities within the various school systems—impose additional constraints on the provinces involved (such as Quebec) without increasing their powers.

The preceding provisions granting powers or imposing obligations on some provinces do not exhaust all forms of asymmetry within the constitution. Other constitutional measures allow asymmetry in practice, however without there being necessarily any asymmetry at all; it depends on the way in which it is used by the provinces. Such is the case of articles providing for the presence of the two levels of government in the same sector, however with a preponderance of provincial laws. As well, articles allowing provincial assemblies a right to withdraw or opt out with respect to constitutional amendments that affect their powers[6] or allowing them to derogate from some sections of the Charter, which results in a differentiated application of the Charter,[7] are all asymmetrical in practice.

The use by one province of either provision leads to an asymmetrical relationship between the provinces. For instance, Quebec has its own pension plan, while the rest of Canada has been accommodated with the plan put into place by Ottawa. Moreover, the conclusion of an agreement between Quebec and Ottawa on immigration leads to an asymmetrical relationship between Quebec and the other provinces, at least as long as these others do not avail themselves of the opportunity to conclude such an agreement with Ottawa.

One should note that asymmetry also plays a role at the institutional level in reference to the participation of the provinces in central institutions and the amending formula. For example, the provinces are not represented in an equal fashion in the Canadian Senate; regions, defined in a more or less arbitrary manner (both Quebec and Ontario forming separate regions) are the ones represented. Similarly, the agreement for most subjects of two-thirds of the provinces (7 out of 10), representing at least 50% of the Canadian population is provided for in the amending formula. Such a provision is in itself asymmetrical if one considers that it would be necessary to have recourse to the unanimity rule to have the provinces, whatever their respective populations, be on a truly equal footing.

On the whole, what can we draw from the Canadian experience in terms of asymmetry? First, we can note that the Canadian Constitution (the Constitution Act, 1867 as well as the Constitution Act, 1982 and the provincial constitutions) foresees a good number of asymmetrical provisions, not so much in terms of distribution of powers (the civil law system being a notable exception) than in terms of protections or obligations imposed on some provinces or particular resources allocated to them. Similarly, the Charter of Rights, by its notwithstanding clause (or legislative override of the Charter) and by its recognition of affirmative action programs, as well as the amending formula, both present in the Constitution Act, 1982, contain several asymmetrical provisions.

Second, in the Canadian case asymmetry eventually recognizes the existence of a social pluralism; however, it remains largely within a provincial territorial limit. Therefore, certain asymmetrical provisions protect Catholic or protestant minorities (in education matters) or the anglophone minority in Quebec or the francophone minority in some other provinces (such as Manitoba or New Brunswick), therefore recognizing the existing social pluralism. However, in all these cases, this recognition is in keeping with the territorial border of a province; the powers, the protections, the obligations, or the constraints are given or imposed to the legislatures and the provincial governments.

One may also add that a number of constitutional provisions of an asymmetrical nature only concern Quebec or have been used by Quebec alone. In certain cases, the possibility of bypassing the general rule has been offered to all the provinces, with Quebec being the only province that took advantage of it. This is not surprising when, as it has been previously underlined, only Quebec meets

Table 2 Managing Diversity in the Canadian Federation

	Social pluralism	Territorial pluralism
Obliged inclusion Egalitarian and identitarian federalism	No	No
Consensual inclusion Multicultural and bilingual federalism	Yes	No
Differentiated inclusion Asymmetrical federalism	Yes	Yes

the three conditions brought out earlier in this essay: the territorialisation of an ethnocultural group, the institutionalization of conflicts, and ethnic bipolarization.

In this sense, the Canadian example—and the particular situation of Quebec within Canada—shows how among the three options analyzed here to manage diversity within a multiethnic federation, only asymmetry responds at once to the recognition of social diversity and territorial pluralism. Therefore, one could answer the questions raised in Table 1 as I have done in Table 2.

V. THE THREE OPTIONS REVISITED

We may now extend our study and examine in greater details the three principal ways in which the Canadian government attempts to manage diversity within the federation. Egalitarian and identitarian federalism emphasizes equality among individuals and the sharing of common values that forge a Canadian identity. Such a unitary vision tends to ignore the differences in the Canadian Federation and to transcend provincial borders. In the end, this attitude can even overshadow the very meaning of federalism, which incorporates the recognition of diversity (Burelle 1995).

To this first fact one can add another. We cannot forget that there exists an important difference between the sharing of the same values and feelings of belonging to the same country. As was argued by Wayne Norman (1995:148), shared values ''do not necessarily give peoples and polities a reason to share a country.'' The simple sharing of common values is not a sufficient condition to create a national or political identity. Even if sharing values could reinforce identity, it cannot do it alone. It is also necessary to share a sense of solidarity with, and an identification to, the same political community.

These harmful aspects of egalitarian and identitarian federalism for the recognition of diversity are, however, lessened owing to the fact that the Canadian Charter of Rights and Freedoms conveys a double conception of the difference. The first is to ignore diversity: you are different, however you have the same rights. The second is to recognize it: because you are different, you have a right to a special recognition in the Charter. Such is the case for women, ethnic minorities, linguistic minorities, multicultural communities, native peoples, and all those who are expressly identified in Section 15 (those called the ''Section 15 Club'' by Knopff and Morton [1992]). In the end, this last conception accentuates more than erases differences between groups and individuals.

Furthermore, if the decisions of the Supreme Court can have a homogenizing effect on the whole of Canadian society, it is necessary to also consider other factors. In analyzing Canadian jurisprudence, Avigail Elsenberg (1994:20–21) concludes that ''the characterization of Canadian jurisprudence in terms of competition between individual and collective rights is inaccurate and misleading'';

on the contrary, "the identity related differences are the crucial values at stake." This notion refers to the "differences between people that play a constitutive role in shaping their identities [such as culture, religion, language and gender, which are] . . . amongst the cental differences that distinguish and help to determine the identities of people in Canadian society" (Eisenberg 1994:9).

If this conclusion is accurate, it is necessary to look again at the "identitarian vision" that stems from the Charter, reduce its effects, and conclude in accordance with James Tully (1995:173) that "a critic of rights has no reason to complain, for the alleged blindness [of the Charter] to cultural differences has been corrected, yet without abandoning rights." That's why we want to somewhat qualify our first conclusion with regard to the recognition of social pluralism within the context of egalitarian and identitarian federalism in the sense of a "no, but . . .".

The second option, which I called multicultural and bilingual federalism, aims to recognize social pluralism, or, more exactly, the linguistic and cultural diversity of the Canadian society. However, this recognition of diversity disregards political borders in which this pluralism can take hold, as is the case in Quebec. Although both the Charter and the Official Languages Act guarantee individual language rights, they do not give linguistic communities (more particularly, the French community) the means to ensure their own survival and development (Burelle 1995:72), as if individual linguistic rights can be uprooted or separated from the communities from which they arise. Trudeau's legacy, wrote André Burelle (1995:66–67), "does not recognize communities as necessary instruments for transmitting language and culture which are, for all human beings, a social legacy much more than an individual right."

Furthermore, individual bilingualism of an egalitarian nature that presently exists in Canada, within an obvious context of linguistic inequality, cannot increase to any great extent the use and prevalence of the French language throughout the entire federation. All the data support this conclusion, particularly when one looks at the linguistic assimilation of immigrants and francophones outside of Quebec and the unceasing decrease of the size of the francophone population in Canada (Pelletier 1991, 1999).

In Canada, multiculturalism has been raised to the level of a fundamental characteristic of the country. "The purpose of multiculturalism," according to Will Kymlicka (1998:58), "is not to prevent or impede integration, but to renegotiate the terms of integration . . . [that is,] what we can expect from immigrants in terms of their integration into mainstream society, and what immigrants can expect from us in terms of accommodation of their ethnocultural identities." However, such a vision has its limits. Multiculturalism as it is practised in Canada is at best the "folkloric" recognition of other cultures and at worst a euphemism for a kind of cultural apartheid or ghetto. "Multiculturalism," wrote Neil Bissoondath (1994:212), "is ethnicity as public policy: it is society's view of the individual's assigned place within its construct." This is a very good description of the notion of the Canadian cultural mosaic, as opposed to the American melting pot. The notion of a mosaic encompasses a notion of segregation—each piece of the mosaic must occupy its assigned place and none other to ensure overall harmony. Pushed to the limit, such a vision can only lead to the straight coexistence of individuals unable to share national objectives or common purposes.

In light of these developments, it is therefore necessary to qualify our first conclusion with regard to the recognition of social pluralism within a context of multicultural and bilingual federalism in terms of a "yes, but . . .".

The third option, which I called asymmetrical federalism, aims to recognize—within the constitution, or within particular arrangements—ethnocultural diversity as well as the political borders in which this diversity takes hold. This option allows a response to both social and territorial pluralism. But this raises an equally fundamental problem: how far can we go in accepting not only social, but also territorial diversity without creating special statuses that risk provoking sentiments of injustice or inequality among the other components of the federation? Equality of the provinces and equality of individuals can be considered today as the two great pillars of the Canadian identity. In the name of equality, the notion of asymmetry and that of "distinct society" in Quebec (that is, a society in which the language, the culture, the civil law system are different from what exists in the other provinces) were vigorously fought against outside Quebec as they appeared incompatible with these two essential values. In this context, could we replace asymmetry by decentralization of powers toward all the provinces, the result being that some provinces will take advantage of this decentralization and others will not? Quebec could therefore obtain de facto the sought-after asymmetry, while maintaining the fiction of equality between the provinces.

It is quite obvious that the notion of asymmetrical federalism does not appeal to all. It appears to some people to be incompatible with the idea of equality perceived as a fundamental and essential element of the Canadian identity and the unity of the country. This is why we have to once again qualify our first conclusion regarding the recognition of territorial pluralism within the context of asymmetrical federalism in terms of a "yes, but . . .".

Taking into account the preceding analysis, it would therefore be necessary to correct Table 2, which would now read as in Table 3. As we can see, none of these approaches used within the Canadian Federation is totally satisfactory. Either they do not entirely respond to the notion of diversity, within its social and territorial dimensions, or they emphasize unity instead of diversity, or they endanger the unity of the country. In reality, it is a delicate balance between the notions of unity and diversity to which we must arrive, this balance never being reached and having to be constantly restructured.

Table 3 Managing Diversity in the Canadian Federation—Reconsidered

	Social pluralism	Territorial pluralism
Obliged inclusion Egalitarian and identitarian federalism	No, but . . .	No
Consensual inclusion Multicultural federalism and bilingualism	Yes, but . . .	No
Differentiated inclusion Asymmetrical federalism	Yes	Yes, but . . .

END NOTES

1. Such a question, because of its scope and its importance, requires further study. It is however winthin the context of this chapter to the extent that I will examine territorial pluralism, territory being native peoples' most important claim. However, not all native peoples' claims are based on territorial issues, especially in the case of numerous native Canadians already living in urban centers.
2. As I have mentioned, I limit my study to this sole question, even though this analysis can also apply to other types of territorial cleavages, such as religious cleavages.
3. I have already addressed more fully this question of bipolarization, referring to the institutional arrangements of a Quebec–Canada partnership in "Institutional Arrangements of a New Canadian Partnership." In R. Gibbins and G. Laforest (eds.), *Beyond the Impasse*. Montreal: Institute for Research on Public Policy.
4. According to Robert Vandycke (1995:142), "Quantitative data have been collected concerning the Supreme Court's first one hundred Charter decisions (Morton et al., 1992:25–30). By 1989, the Court had struck down nineteen statutes in whole or in part and upheld thirty-one. Among the nullified statutes, eleven were provincial and eight federal. From a qualitative point of view, seven of the eight nullifications of federal legislation were based on procedural grounds; in contrast, nine of the eleven invalidations of provincial statutes were made on substantive grounds. Five provincial laws struck down were Québec statutes concerning important language or education issues, while the invalidations of other provincial statutes were considered less essential by their governments. These data tend to confirm an homogenizing trend of judicial review under the Charter, and Québec as its privileged targets."
5. This bilingual legislative regime had been imposed on the federal and Quebec governments only by Section 133 of the Constitution Act, 1867. New Brunswick has been added to this short list with the adoption of the Constitution Act, 1982 (Sections 16–22).
6. An amendment that derogates from the legislative powers, the proprietary rights or any other rights or privileges of the legislature or government of a province, "shall not have effect in a province the legislative assembly of which has expressed its dis-

sent thereto by resolution supported by a majority of its members prior to the issue of the proclamation to which the amendment relates'' (Section 38(3) of the amending formula).

7. Section 33(1) of the Charter reads as follows: "Parliament or the legislature of a province may expressly declare in an Act of Parliament or of the legislature, as the case may be, that the Act or a provision thereof shall operate notwithstanding a provision included in section 2 [fundamental freedoms] or sections 7 to 15 [legal rights and equality rights] of this Charter." Such a declaration shall cease to have effect five years after it comes into force unless it is re-enacted.

REFERENCES

Bissoondath, N. (1994). *Selling Illusions: The Cult of Multiculturalism in Canada*. Toronto: Penguin Books.

Burelle, A. (1995). *Le Mal Canadien: Essai de Diagnostic et Esquisse d'une Thérapie*. Montreal: Fides.

Burgess, M. (1993). Federalism and federation: A reappraisal. In M. Burgess and A.-G. Gagnon (eds.), *Comparative Federalism and Federation: Competing Traditions and Future Directions*. Toronto: University of Toronto Press.

Cairns, A. C. (1991). In D. E. Williams (ed.), *Disruptions: Constitutional Struggles, from the Charter to Meech Lake*. Toronto: McClelland & Stewart.

Cairns, A. C. (1992). *Charter Versus Federalism: The Dilemmas of Constitutional Reform*. Montreal and Kingston: McGill–Queen's University Press.

Eisenberg, A. (1994). The politics of individual and group difference in Canadian jurisprudence. *Canadian Journal of Political Science 27*(1), 3–21.

Elazar, D. J. (1987). *Exploring Federalism*. Tuscaloosa, AL: The University of Alabama Press.

Forsyth, M. (ed.) (1989). *Federalism and Nationalism*. New York: St. Martin's Press.

Knopff, R. and Morton, F. L. (1992). *Charter Politics*. Toronto: Nelson Canada.

Kymlicka, W. (1998). *Finding Our Way: Rethinking Ethnocultural Relations in Canada*. Toronto: Oxford University Press.

Lapierre, J.-W. (1988). *Le Pouvoir Politique et les Langues*. Paris: Presses Universitaires de France.

Laponce, J. (1984). *Langue et Territoire*. Ste-Foy, Quebec: Les Presses de l'Université Laval.

Milne, D. (1991). Equality or asymmetry: Why choose? In R. L. Watts and D. M. Brown (eds.), *Options for a New Canada*. Toronto: University of Toronto Press.

Morton, F. L. et al. (1992). The Supreme Court's first one hundred Charter decisions: A statistical analysis. *Osgoode Hall Law Journal 30*(1), 1–56.

McRoberts, K. (1993). Disagreeing on fundamentals: English Canada and Quebec. In K. McRoberts and P. Monahan (eds.), *The Charlottetown Accord, the Referendum, and the Future of Canada*. Toronto: University of Toronto Press.

McRoberts, K. (1997). *Misconceiving Canada: The Struggle for National Unity*. Toronto: Oxford University Press.

Norman, W. (1995). The ideology of shared values: A myopic vision of unity in the multi-nation state. In J. H. Carens (ed.), *Is Quebec Nationalism Just? Perspectives from Anglophone Canada*. Montreal and Kingston: McGill–Queen's University Press.

Pelletier, R. (1991). Fédéralisme et politiques linguistiques: De l'individualité à la territorialité. Le cas canadien. *Fédéralisme* (Bruxelles), No. (3), 197–219.

Pelletier, R. (1996). Le Québec et le Canada: Asymétrie des pouvoirs et logique d'égalité. In J.- P. Augustin (ed.), *L'institutionnalisation du Territoire au Canada*. Ste-Foy, Quebec, and Talence, France: Les Presses de l'Université Laval and Presses Universitaires de Bordeaux.

Pelletier, R. (1999). La fragmentation politique du territoire canadien. Paper presented at the Annual Conference of the French Association for Canadian Studies, Toulouse.

Russell, P. H. (1983). The political purposes of the Canadian Charter of Rights and Freedoms. *Canadian Bar Review 61*, 30–54.

Trudeau, P. E. (1990). Des valeurs d'une société juste. In T. S. Axworthy and P. E. Trudeau (eds.), *Les Années Trudeau: La Recherche d'une Société Juste*. Montreal: Le Jour.

Tully, J. (1995). *Strange Multiplicity: Constitutionalism in an Age of Diversity*. Cambridge: Cambridge University Press.

Vandycke, R. (1995). The 1982 Constitution and the Charter of Rights: A view from Québec. In F. Rocher and M. Smith (eds.), *New Trends in Canadian Federalism*. Peterborough, Ontario: Broadview Press.

Index